GUIDE
FOR IRELAND

John Gormley

The GREEN GUIDE

FOR IRELAND

An Information Resource
A Consumer Handbook
A Guide to Practical Action

WOLFHOUND PRESS

British Library Cataloguing in Publication Data
Gormley, John
The green guide for Ireland.
1. Ireland (Republic)—Visitor's guides
I. Title
914.170424

ISBN 0-86327-251-7

Cover design: Jan de Fouw
Cartoon Illustrations: Piet Sluis
Typesetting: Seton Music Graphics Ltd, Bantry, Co. Cork.
Printed by: The Guernsey Press Co. Ltd., Guernsey.

Contents

ACKNOWLEDGEMENTS
Special thanks to Mary Walsh and Fran McKeagney, Elizabeth Healy, Tina Adams and Ann Holliday.

Thanks also to Richard Douthwaite, Jack O'Sullivan, Jim Woolridge, Jeremy Wates, Bob Edwards, John Bowler, Orla Ní Eilí, Nuala Donlon, Mike Curtis, Cecilia Armelin, Clare Mooney, Gillies McBain, Frank McDonald, Yvonne Scannell, Karen Dubsky, David Hickie, Josephine Lynch, Catherine O'Connell, Ciaran Cuffe, Trevor Sargent, Margaret Caulfield, Eoin Dinan, Roger Garland, Steve Rawson, Rebecca Harris and Brenda McDonagh.

In the compilation of such a vast mass of data it is inevitable that some relevant and important matters have escaped our research nets. We hope that our endeavours to avoid any errors have been successful. For future editions, the author and publisher welcome suggestions, corrections etc. Write to: The Editor, The Green Guide, Wolfhound Press, 68 Mountjoy Square, Dublin 1.

For information on the leading green organisations such as Earthwatch (p.306), Greenpeace (p.308), Sonairte (p.319), An Taisce (p.303), etc., see the Directory on pages 303-332.

The publisher is grateful for the support of those who have advertised with us in this guide – see pages 90, 125, 131, 146, 166, 168, 170, 203, 204, 230, 302.

Introduction

As we head into the 90s GREEN is set to become the most abused word of the decade—especially now that the politicians and advertisers have got a hold of it. In their exploitative hands there's a real danger that the true meaning of the word will somehow become 'extinct'. So let's begin appropriately enough with an act of conservation. Let's save the word 'green' from all this degradation by trying to define it.

For people in the Green Movement 'green' does not just mean 'environmental'. It goes a step further. It means 'ecological'. Ecology is about the web of life, the 'whole' environment, an environment which we are but part of, not apart from. It's about the interconnectedness of all creation and it's about looking at the 'root causes' of our pollution problems, as opposed to dealing with the symptoms.

Perhaps all of that sounds complicated, but a common pollution problem in this country will serve to illustrate the point. Fish kills from agricultural effluent have become a far too regular occurrence here in the past number of years. Each time there's a fish kill, the familiar cry goes up that fines are not high enough, that farmers need grants for proper effluent storage, that the rivers need to be restocked etc. These are all valid points in themselves, but very few people look to the real cause of the problem—intensive agriculture.

Intensive agriculture means more water pollution, wider use of poisonous chemicals, terrible cruelty to animals and the destruction of wildlife habitats. It is also energy intensive (contributing to the Greenhouse Effect), results in fewer people being employed on the land and causes massive food mountains while millions starve in the Third World. Is this progress? Does it make sense? Of course not. And yet those profoundly rational people who advocate a return to more traditional farming methods are labelled 'cranks' and 'anti-progress'. Those in power, on the other hand—who now claim to be green—refuse utterly to look at the root causes of the world's problems. Instead, they tell us that a few minor adjustments to the present consumerist system are required—and everything will be all right. But this is a dangerous myth. For let us not be in any doubt about it—we are no longer facing an ecological crisis, we are in an ecological crisis, whose root cause is rampant consumerism. The new trend in green consumerism is to be welcomed, but really, we need to consume not just differently but less. Driving your car on unleaded is fine. Not driving your car is better and greener. And why make it the choice between plastic and a paper bag at the checkout, when you can always bring your own bag?

Does being green then mean a return to a harsh and spartan existence? Not at all. In fact, if governments implemented truly green policies and people adopted green lifestyles, the quality of life would improve for everyone. We are at a stage in human development where we can combine the technology of the new with the wisdom of the old to make for a better world. Energy conservation and renewable energy must become the norm, built-in obsolescence will itself have to become an obsolete concept, waste production will have to cease and recycling should become part of everyday life. And perhaps to help us on our way we human beings could take a crash course in humility. We're not the end-all and be-all of creation. The Planet survived for millions of years without us and it can continue to survive without us once we're gone. Paradoxically, it's only by realizing our own insignificance in terms of the planet that we see what an important role we play in determining our own survival. If only for the most selfish of reasons we need to become less materialistic, less greedy and –yes– less selfish. It's an enormous challenge and one in which each of us can play a small but decisive role.

In Ireland, the upsurge in green awareness in 1989 took everyone, including those in the Green Movement, by surprise. Suddenly, it seemed, the Greenhouse Effect and the depletion of the ozone layer were on people's minds. The Green Party emerged as a political force and the Government responded by setting up a new Ministry for the protection of the natural environment. There followed an absolute barrage of green advertising in the media. Green was suddenly in and in real danger of over exposure. To those genuine souls who had been green long before it was fashionable or indeed profitable all of this hype led to a certain resentment. A new phenomenon of the 'greener than thou' attitude manifested itself.

But the green bandwagon could not be stopped and rolled merrily along into the nineties with Government's announcement of the 'green' Presidency of the EC. Along the way environmental controversies such as the proposed siting of the Merrell Dow Chemical plant in East Cork and gold mining in Mayo and Galway showed that the Government was perhaps a lighter shade of green, than they would have us believe.

The debate of jobs versus the environment is an important one in Ireland. Often the simplistic view, the 'you can't eat the scenery' is put forward. It's a shortsighted attitude, which fails to address the real costs of environmental degradation. Those in the Green Movement have consistently argued that our environment is our greatest asset in terms of employment. Situated on the periphery of a highly industrialised and polluted Europe, our image as a clean and unspoilt land is vital for our tourist and food industry. Unfortunately, the image and the reality sometimes don't match, and if the gap between both widens too much we will have lost a unique opportunity. There is tremendous potential to develop this country into a truly 'green isle' and there are grounds for optimism if we act now. We have huge renewable, non-polluting energy sources such as wind; our soil has not yet been wrecked by fertilizers and pesticides and is ideal for organic agriculture; our rivers, lakes and seas are still relatively unpolluted. Our environment is certainly under threat, but if each of us as individuals acts and above all if the political will is there we can protect our heritage.

Many of the Government's environmental reforms have been simply a matter of fulfilling our EC obligations. But we need to go further than that. The polluter pays principle, the precautionary principle (if you're not sure of the consequences don't pump or dump) and the concept of ecologically sustainable growth should all be part of economic development. There needs to be far greater co-ordination between Departments to work out the environmental consequences of policies and planning. The basis of all environmental legislation has to be the elimination of pollution rather than its reduction. The US Environmental Protection Agency, on which our EPA is based, has shown, in Green Peace studies, that limiting pollution does not work in the long term.

More specifically, we need far more investment in renewable energy and energy conservation. CFCs will have to be banned and the importation of tropical hardwoods stopped. Farmers need incentives to go organic and environmental education has to become a priority in schools.

11

This book looks at the current state of the Irish environment and suggests ways in which you can make a positive contribution to safeguarding the future. You can do this by what you eat and buy and by recycling. You can also help by contacting and supporting the various groups listed in this book, who are working to make Ireland a greener and better place to live.

AIR

The Ozone Layer, Greenhouse Effect, Acid Rain and Dublin Smog

Air is essential for human life. Every day—without even having to make an effort or decision—we breathe in about 16 Kilos of this colourless, odourless and tasteless gas. This amounts to six times our daily intake of food and drink. The internal combustion of food and the oxygen in the air provide us with a source of power. A by-product of this reaction is carbon dioxide, which is then breathed in by the plants and trees.

A similar reaction is produced when we burn fossil fuels such as coal and oil for power generation. But our use of fossil fuels is now so excessive that the harmonious cycle between humans and nature has been broken, resulting in the Greenhouse Effect and other pollution such as acid rain.

And yet oxygen itself, now seen as a life-giving gas, was once perhaps the most serious pollutant on this planet. Two aeons ago most of the life forms on this planet were anaerobic, i.e. they lived without oxygen. The release of this gas could have meant the end of all life on this planet, but instead the planet adapted to the situation and other life-forms, dependent on oxygen, developed. Every time we breathe, therefore, we ought to be reminded of the adaptability and robustness of our planet. We ought to be reminded also of our own vulnerability. By polluting our air we do not place our planet in jeopardy. It is our own future which is endangered.

Air quality in Ireland

Generally speaking, air quality in Ireland is quite good but this is due to the prevailing winds, which blow most of the pollutants away, and not to any far sighted government action. Moneypoint, which contributes to acid rain, was built without scrubbers; in the 1970s grants were made available to people to burn coal; the lead emissions from cars have been way above EC limits in the 1970s; the coal we use to produce electricity has a very high carbon burden and contributes to the Greenhouse Effect.

Finally, the amount of state money invested in alternative, non-polluting, forms of energy has decreased annually for the past three years. In 1989 not one penny was invested in alternative energy. This, in a country which has vast potential in this area. (See Energy Chapter)

The Ozone Layer

The depletion of the ozone layer is one of the three most desperate environmental problems facing humankind. The other two are the destruction of the tropical rainforests and the greenhouse effect. All three are interrelated.

Since ozone loss is much more easily stopped than the others, it is a test case. How we handle it will give some indication of whether life, as we know it, on this planet will continue.

What Is Ozone?

Ozone (O_3) is an altered form of the oxygen molecule (O_2). This form of oxygen is present in the atmosphere some 10–30 Km above the Earth. Though only present in very small amounts, the ozone layer has been protecting us from damaging ultraviolet (UV) radiation for millions of years.

The Effects Of Ozone Loss

Ozone loss is far more serious than has been admitted until recently. Globally the Earth's ozone layer is getting thinner—by some 6% during winter over most of Ireland. A 1% drop in ozone cover allows a 2% increase in the level of UV radiation to get through from the sun. This in turn is estimated to cause an 8% increase in the incidence of skin cancers—which have actually doubled here since 1974. Increased UV also causes eye cataracts and reduces our resistance to disease. It breaks down molecules in plant cells, slowing photosynthesis and thus reducing crop yields.

At a high enough level, UV is capable of killing all terrestrial plant and animal life. But it is the marine food chain which is under the most immediate threat. UV radiation has already increased by about 10% over the southern oceans. This is close to the level at which the plant plankton living in them will be killed. Scientists say that the plankton is already

14

THE OZONE LAYER
Why do we need it?

Because without its protective screen around the earth, ultraviolet (UV) radiation from the sun would:

- reduce our resistance to disease
- cause increased skin cancer
- cause more eye cataracts
- reduce crop yields
- kill off the ocean's food chain

Every day we are thinning out the Ozone Layer by the use of Aerosols and in other ways.

---

under very severe stress and if it dies, the creatures which depend on it, from krill to penguins to whales, will die too. The loss of plankton would accelerate the Greenhouse Effect as plankton absorbs the main 'greenhouse gas', carbon dioxide, in order to grow.

Carbon dioxide is also absorbed by trees, and with the on-going destruction of the tropical rainforests it's certain that our Earth is facing a very serious problem.

What is destroying the ozone layer?

Two groups of gases are mainly responsible—chlorofluoro-carbons (CFCs) and, to a lesser degree, halons. Both these gases are very safe and stable at ground level but when they float up into the stratosphere, UV radiation from the sun breaks them down to release chlorine atoms from the CFCs and bromine atoms from the halons. These free atoms go blundering through space, breaking up the ozone, until they bump into one of their own kind and form a stable molecule which falls back to Earth. It is estimated that one chlorine atom will destroy 100,000 ozone molecules before finding a mate and settling down. Bromine atoms are even more destructive.

This process has been known for some time. However, what has alarmed the scientists and caused the recent flurry of international conferences is that the reaction is accelerated many times by the presence of ice particles, which is why it is

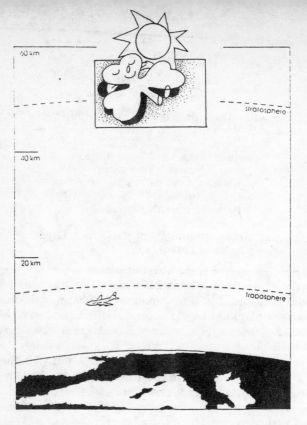

The Earth's atmosphere.   *Source:* UNEP

over the poles that the ozone holes have appeared, when the sun returns at the end of the polar winters.

Do CFCs do other damage?

Yes. They are also a greenhouse gas and have 10,000 times the heating effect of CO_2. Fiona Weir, Friends of the Earth's specialist in this area, reckons that this damage is at least as bad as their effects on the ozone layer.

What are CFCs used for?

CFCs are widely used:

• as cleansing agents in the electronics and dry cleaning industries

• as blowing agents in the production of polyurethane and polystyrene foams for furniture, building insulation and packaging

- as a refrigerant in the coil in your fridge.

Halons are used mainly as a smothering gas in fire extinguishers.

Can They Be Replaced?

Phasing out CFCs in aerosols—about a third of total consumption— is no problem. Neither is their elimination from cleansers and flexible foams. In other areas there is no 'drop-in' alternative, so manufacturing processes will have to be extensively modified or stopped altogether.

For example, rigid foam—the type used as insulation in fridges—might have to be abandoned but, since other insulating materials are not as effective at keeping heat out, fridges will need more of them. This will probably means a return to bigger fridges.

Some of the alternatives are CFCs themselves, but ones with much less destructive effects because they have less chlorine or none at all. However some of them may be flammable, poisonous or carcinogenic, and testing is still going on. Replacement refrigerants have been developed but will be more expensive when they get into volume production in 1991. There are no substitutes yet for halons except traditional fire extinguishers like water and CO_2.

OFFICE OZONE

Photocopiers and laser printers produce small quantities of ozone. When high-energy electrical discharges pass through the air the oxygen molecules are rearranged. The same phenomenon occurs in thunderstorms as a result of lightening bolts.

You'll know it's ozone if you get the whiff of the pungent-smelling fumes. While ozone is very welcome in the stratosphere, at nose level it can be poisonous. The smell of ozone is apparent in quantities as little as one part per 500,000. The threshold limit value for ozone is .3 parts per million.

Empathy Hairsprays	Johnson & Johnson
Empathy Styling Mousse	Johnson & Johnson
Finale	Bristol Myers
Gem Hairspray	Gillespie
Gillette Hair Care	Gillespie
Grafic Hairspray	Daelgate
Hardrock	L'Oreal
Harmony	Wella
Irish Sunrise	Elida Gibbs
Johnson's Baby Oil Mousse	Gillespie
L'Oreal Freestyle Hairspray	Johnson & Johnson
L'Oreal Freestyle Mousse	L'Oreal
News Fixing Spray	L'Oreal
News Mousse	Gillespie
Shockwaves Mousse	Gillespie
Silkience Hairspray	Wella
Silkience Mousse	Daelgate
Silvikrin Hairspray	Daelgate
Simple	Daelgate
Studioline Mousse	Beechams
Stylite Mousse	Simple
Sunsilk Hairspray	Smith & Nephew
Sunsilk Mousse	Wella
Supersoft Hairspray	Elida Gibbs
Take Shape Hairspray	Elida Gibbs
Vidal Sassoon Hairspray	Reckitt & Colman
Vidal Sassoon Mousse	Colet
VO5 Hairsprays	Johnson Bros
VO5 Styling Mousse	Johnson Bros
Wellaflex	Johnson Bros
	Wella

Shaving

Blue Stratos Smooth Shave	Shulton
Brut 33 Creme Shave	Fabergé
Cussons Super Shave	Johnson Bros
Denim	Elida Gibbs
Gillette	Daelgate
Old Spice Smooth Shave	Shulton
Palmolive	Colgate Palmolive
Rapid Shave Foam	Colgate Palmolive
Simple	Smith. & Nephew
Wilkinson Sword	Wilkinson

List of ozone friendly aerosols

Hard Surface Cleaner

White on White	Johnson Wax
Windolene Window Cleaner	Punch
	Reckitt & Colman

Household — Miscellaneous

Easy on Starch	Whitehall Labs
Robin Starch	Reckitt & Colman
Rustigard	Sterling Roncroft
Shoe Stretcher	Punch
Three In One Expert Oil	Whitehall Labs

Garden/plant/insect

Ant & Crawling Insect Killer	Rentokil
Autan Fly Spray	Bayer
Blackfly & Greenfly Killer	Rentokil
Carpet Beetle Killer & Moth Proofer	Rentokil
Flea Killer	Rentokil
Fioret Flykiller	Rentokil
Fly & Wasp Killer	Reckitt & Colman
Greenhouse & Garden Insect Killer	Rentokil
Houseplant Insect Killer	Rentokil
Insect Spray for House Plants	Rentokil
Kerishine	Fisons
Kerispray Insecticide	ICI
Lawn Spot Weeder	ICI
Malu Household Insecticide	Fisons
Path & Patio Weedkiller	Bayer
Raid Fly & Wasp Killer	Rentokil
Raid Triple Action Ant Killer	Johnson Wax
Rapid Greenfly Killer Insecticide	Johnson Wax
Sybol 2 Insecticide	ICI
Waspend Insecticide	ICI
Vapona Fly Killer	ICI
	Nicholas Labs

Cars

Cockpit Spray	Simoniz
Dri Clean	Simoniz
Dynaglaze Back to Black	Spectra
Glass Cleaner	Spectra
Spray Paints	Spectra
Steer Clear	Simoniz
Trim and Tyre Shine	Simoniz
Wheel Paints	Simoniz
Workmate	Spectra

Brand	Manufacturer or distributor
Antiperspirants, deodorants and body sprays	
Bodymist	Beechams
Brut 33 Body Spray	Fabergé
Brut 33 Deodorant	Fabergé
Charm Antiperspirant	British Products Sanmex
Charm Body Spray	British Products Sanmex
Cussons	Johnson Bros
Denim Antiperspirant	Elida Gibbs
Denim Body Spray	Elida Gibbs
Fresh 'n Dry	Bristol Myers
Gem Body Spray	Gillespie
Imperial Leather	Gillespie
Impulse Body Spray	Johnson Bros
Insignia Deodorant	Maguire & Paterson
Limara Deodorants	Smith & Nephew
Lynx Body Spray	Elida Gibbs
Natrel Deodorant	Daelgate
Nivea Body Mousse	Smith & Nephew
Old Spice Deodorant	T.P. Whelehan
Right Guard Deodorant	Daelgate
Simple	Smith & Nephew
Soft & Gentle	Colgate Palmolive
Sure	Elida Gibbs
Foot/leg	
Foot Anti-perspirant	Scholl
Foot Refresher	Scholl
Legs n Action	Gillespie
Louis Marcel Depilatory Shaving Foam	Nicholas Labs
Immac	Whitehall Labs
Reflex Antiperspirant	Scholl
Sneaker Treater	Scholl
Hair care products	
Brut 33 Hair Control	Fabergé
Charm Hair Sprays	British Products Sanmex
Charm Mousses	British Products Sanmex
Clairol Hairspray	Bristol Myers
Corfmist	Gillespie
Cossack Hairspray	Reckitt & Colman
Cussons Hair Control Spray	Johnson Bros
Cussons Styling Mousse	Johnson Bros

According to manufacturers, the following products are CFC free.

Brand	Manufacturer or distributor
Charm	British Products Sanmex
Glade	Johnson Wax
Haze	Reckitt & Colman
Klear	Johnson Wax
Wizard	Whitehall Labs
Household — polishes	
Big D Multipolish	J.V. McDaniel
Charm Furniture Polish	British Products Sanmex
Charm Spray & Shine	British Products Sanmex
Living Wood	Johnson Wax
Mansion	Reckitt & Colman
Mr Sheen	Reckitt & Colman
Pledge	Johnson Wax
Quinnsworth Yellow Pack Furniture Polish	Punch
Sparkle Polish	Johnson Wax
Spray 'n Klean Polish	Whitehall Labs
St Bernard Furniture Polish	Punch
Topps	Whitehall Labs
Household — cleaners	
Brillo Oven Grill	Johnson Wax
Charm Carpet Fresheners	British Products Sanmex
Colron Ring Cleaner	Sterling Roncroft
Dabitoff Stain Removing Spray	Nicholas Labs
Easy Off Oven Cleaner	Whitehall Labs
Easy Off Microwave Spray	Whitehall Labs
Fabric Protector	Punch
Leather Care	Punch
Lifeguard Cleaner	Johnson Wax
Matt Leather Dressing	Punch
Mr Muscle Carpet Stain Remover	Bristol Myers
Mr Muscle Oven Cleaner	Bristol Myers
Mr Muscle Tile Cleaner	Bristol Myers
Patent Glow	Punch
Saddle Soap Spray	Punch
Scotchguard	Punch
Shout Fabric Cleaner	Johnson Wax
Suede Renovator	Punch
Tops Bright & Clean	Whitehall Labs
Tops Teak Oil Spray	Whitehall Labs

Who Caused The Problem?

The developed nations. The OECD countries produce 80% of the world's CFCs and their consumption—about 900gm per head a year—is about ten times that of people in the poorer parts of the world. The EC makes about 33% of the 1m tonne world output, the US slightly less.

What Is Being Done To Correct The Situation?

The key agreement is the Montreal Protocol which came into effect only in January 1989. It commits its developed nation signatories to halve their consumption (not their production—they can make and export) of CFCs by 1999. Developing countries who signed were given a ten year deferment, so the result would be a 35% reduction in world use.

45 nations have signed (but not necessarily ratified) the Protocol and another 22 said they would do so at a meeting on the crisis in London in March 1989. However, it is agreed by everyone except the USSR, which wants more research, that the Protocol is much too weak and that 85% reduction is the least that would do any good. Many experts want a 100% ban. And, since the CFCs which have already been released will continue to do their damage for as long as a century, the cuts should be made as soon as possible.

Negotiations to stiffen the Protocol began in May 1989. The EC has already committed itself to a complete ban by 1999 and the US has said it will follow suit. There is a catch, however. Most developing nations feel they should not have to make sacrifices to help cure a crisis brought on by the greed of the West. The Chinese could soon become the world's biggest producers of CFCs as a result of their programme to put a fridge into every household. They have already announced plans for a ten-fold increase in CFC production. The key issue for the West is how to buy off this threat—and similar threats from the industrialising countries—by providing them with ICI and Dupont's technology for making the replacement chemicals and by giving them cash to help meet the higher costs involved. The UN Environment Programme, co-sponsor of the London meeting, has suggested a World Atmosphere Fund to pay for this.

Have We Gone Too Far?

Enough CFCs to sterilise the seas might already be on their way up to the ozone layer. Scientists are already suggesting restoring it by injecting 5,000 tonnes of ozone a day into the stratosphere for the next century. They think this could be done by attaching ozone generators to aircraft on ordinary commercial flights or shooting frozen ozone into the sky with special guns.

What Is The Situation In Ireland?

Ireland has agreed to phase out CFCs by the year 2000 in line with the rest of the EC. However some other countries in the EC have taken much stronger individual stances, with the elimination targets set for the mid-1990s and short-term measures in full swing. These include recycling CFCs from fridges and labelling aerosol cans. The Irish Government is now considering implementing such schemes (see Recycling).

The Greenhouse Effect

The Greenhouse Effect or global warming is at the heart of our present ecological crisis. It is now almost fully accepted in the scientific community that serious climatic changes will occur as a result of the build up of the greenhouse gases (ghg) in the atmosphere.

What Is The Greenhouse Effect?

When the sun's rays strike the Earth's atmosphere much of the heat is reflected back into space, but some of the heat is trapped by certain gases—such as carbon dioxide—in the

Based on illustration in *The Earth Report* (Mitchell Beazley)

Greenhouse Effect

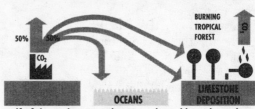

Half of the Carbon Dioxide (CO_2) released by industrial societies is absorbed by natural CO_2 "sinks" such as oceans, forests and the process of limestone deposition.
The rest collects in the atmosphere.

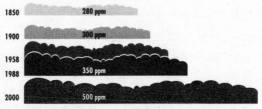

Since the beginning of the industrial revolution CO_2 levels have been on the increase. Today the rate of increase is itself increasing, which could lead to a doubling of the 1850 level by the end of the next century.

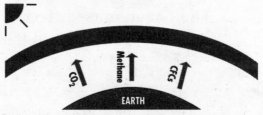

Apart from CO_2, atmospheric levels of methane and chloroflourocarbons (CFCs) are also on the increase.
All three are greenhouse gases, warming the atmosphere by trapping the heat radiated back into it from the Earth's surface.

atmosphere. This natural mechanism has been keeping the surface of the globe at a relatively steady temperature for thousands of years. It is known as the greenhouse effect.

Because of the greenhouse effect, the average temperature just above the Earth's surface is 15.5°C, making life as we know it possible. If it were not for this effect our planet would probably be an extremely cold and lifeless place.

However, the greenhouse effect is now being thrown out of balance by the rapid increase in many of the greenhouse gases, which leads to too much heat being trapped and thus to the phenomenon known as 'global warming'. It is this global warming which could have catastrophic consequences for the future of our planet.

WHAT HARM IS
THE GREENHOUSE EFFECT?

We don't really know!

The earth's temperature has never been more than 1° warmer since before the dawn of civilization.

BUT we do know that if goes on it must cause enormous flooding all around the world, wiping out many cities, and some countries entirely!

What Are The Greenhouse Gases?

The most common greenhouse gases are carbon dioxide, methane, water vapours and CFCs—which are also responsible for the depletion of the ozone layer. Carbon dioxide (CO_2) is a naturally occurring compound. It is part of the wonderful cycle of life, insofar as we humans and animals breathe out CO_2, which is then absorbed by the trees and oceans. They in turn convert it into oxygen, which we breathe in, to once more breathe out CO_2.

This cycle maintained its crucial balance until the arrival of the Industrial Revolution in the early 1800s when humankind began to burn large quantities of fossil fuels. Fossil fuels, particularly coal, release carbon dioxide during combustion. CO_2 levels have risen from an estimated 270 parts per million (ppm) in the 1850s to 375ppm today, an increase of around 39%.

GRASSLANDS

All plants absorb carbon dioxide, but until recently it was considered that trees topped the league at soaking up the gas. Grass, by comparison, rated hardly a mention. But a United Nations Environment Programme study begun in 1984 has challenged previous assessments. Grasslands are being burnt at the rate of 700 million acres a year. This clearance, scientists now believe, releases to the atmosphere three times the amount of carbon dioxide as would be produced by burning the rainforests. On this scale, the need to husband grasslands at a sustainable level of development is vital if the Greenhouse Effect is to be contained.

But carbon dioxide is not the only culprit. It only causes half the problem and there are other potentially more serious greenhouse gases, such as nitrous oxides from car exhausts, CFCs and methane.

Methane is twenty times more effective at absorbing heat than CO_2 and its concentration in the atmosphere is increasing by 1.2% annually. Methane is produced from the mud in rice paddies, the rotting rubbish in tipheads and in the stomachs of cattle.

The average cow eats about 4 kilos of food each day. Between 5 and 10 per cent of this is converted into methane, which is then released into the atmosphere—usually through the cow's rear end. Methane levels are set to increase as the cattle population of the world soars. In 1940 there were 700 million cows in the world. Today there are 1,300 million.

CFCs, better known for the damage they cause to the ozone layer, are also a very destructive greenhouse gas. One CFC

FOSSIL FUELS

Fossil Fuels are products stored deep in the earth until mined or otherwise released by man. *Oil*, *Coal* and *Natural Gas* are the fossil fuels most commonly used. Of these, Natural Gas (eg Kinsale) is the least polluting.

molecule is ten thousand times more destructive in terms of the heat it absorbs than a CO_2 molecule. Used as propellants in aerosols, as coolants in refrigerators and in the production of plastic foam, CFCs account for about 15% of the green-house effect.

Water vapour, usually harmless, just adds to the problem by thickening the cloud layer.

Where do Emissions Come From?

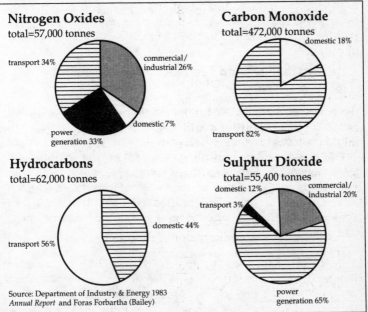

Nitrogen Oxides
total=57,000 tonnes
transport 34%
commercial/industrial 26%
power generation 33%
domestic 7%

Carbon Monoxide
total=472,000 tonnes
domestic 18%
transport 82%

Hydrocarbons
total=62,000 tonnes
domestic 44%
transport 56%

Sulphur Dioxide
total=55,400 tonnes
domestic 12%
commercial/industrial 20%
transport 3%
power generation 65%

Source: Department of Industry & Energy 1983 *Annual Report* and Foras Forbartha (Bailey)

25

What Will Global Warming Mean?

Scientific opinions on the exact consequences of global warming vary considerably. Some scientists—though they are a decreasing minority—dismiss the global warming theory as a load of bunkum. Others believe that increased temperatures and climate changes are inevitable in the long term, but humankind will cope as it always has.

The more pessimistic predictions are for quite sudden changes, perhaps within the next thirty years, which will have catastrophic consequences for our planet and humankind. Certainly the latest report from the UN Environment Programme makes for very unpleasant reading. Unless we reverse the trends of the greenhouse effect within the next ten years, it states, there will be rises in sea levels of up to 3m, resulting in widespread flooding. Low-lying countries such as Bangladesh will be wiped out, giving rise to a new phenomenon—the ecological refugee.

The whole thing is almost too hellish to contemplate. But we must think about it. As James Hansen, head of NASA's Goddard Institute for Space Studies, has said: 'It's time to stop waffling so much. The evidence is pretty strong that the greenhouse effect is here.'

Climate Changes and Feedback Mechanisms: The Worst Predictions

More and more evidence is now accumulating to suggest that the greenhouse warming will not be a gradual process but could be accelerated by what scientists call 'positive feedback mechanisms'. This basically means that the buildup of greenhouse gases, leading to an increase in temperatures, in turn leads to the release of more greenhouse gases—which means even higher temperatures etc. etc. It's a sort of ecological domino effect or vicious spiral. This vicious spiral can occur in at least four different ways:

1. SOIL: It has been estimated that a 2°C increase in temperature would release up to 383 billion tonnes of carbon from the soil. At present fossil fuel burning releases 5 billion tonnes of CO_2 into the atmosphere. Humus in particular is

very sensitive to changes in temperature and the largescale disruption of the soil surface through deforestation etc. can mean that up to a hundred times more CO_2 is emitted.

Emissions of carbon dioxide per unit energy content of various fuels. (*Source: Eolas*)

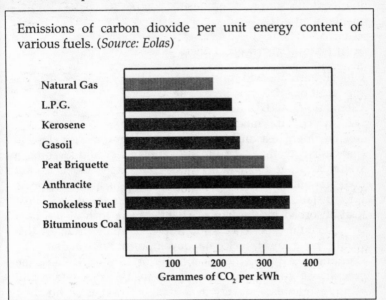

---

2. PLANKTON: The plankton in our seas absorbs nearly as much CO_2 as the disappearing rainforests. Because of the depletion of the ozone layer much of the plant plankton could be destroyed by the extra UV light. But the rate at which plankton is absorbing CO_2 is also slowing down because of global warming.

3. WATER: Carbon dioxide dissolves in water. But its solubility depends very much on the temperature of the water. During the ice age the freezing water could hold far more CO_2. With the rise in temperatures our oceans, which are gigantic CO_2 sinks, could soon be emitting more CO_2 than they absorb.

4. ICE: Again, as with water, ice absorbs vast quantities of CO_2 and there are indications that the polar

ice caps have already begun to melt. It is estimated that the ice in the North Pole has decreased by a third in the last ten years. A large decrease in the total area of ice also means that less sunlight will be reflected back into space, thus adding further to global warming.

Will Ireland's Climate Change?

Global warming will most certainly affect the weather patterns here. The General Circulation Models (GCMs) currently in use by climate modellers suggest that Ireland might reasonably expect a temperature rise close to the global average—1°C to 4°C. Ireland would become a wetter, warmer and windier place. But these models do not take account of the feedback mechanisms, as outlined above. If for instance the Gulf Stream, which carries about 30% of the heat absorbed by the North Atlantic, were to heat up, then Ireland could experience a sub-tropical climate. To many this would be a most welcome development and indeed the standing joke during the hot summer of '89 was: 'If this is the greenhouse effect—then I'm all for it'. But this rather glib attitude ignores the very real danger of coastal flooding posed by global warming and as an island we are particularly vulnerable. The cost alone of building sea defences would use up much of the Exchequer budget.

What Can Ireland Do?

As already mentioned, it is mostly a matter of our use of energy. See that chapter for proposals.

Acid Rain

Rain is naturally acidic—though only very mildly. When rainwater mixes with the carbon dioxide in the atmosphere it forms a weak carbonic acid. Since the last century, however, the rain in Europe and the industrial parts of North America has been getting gradually more acidic.

The effects on the environment have been catastrophic. 52% of Germany's trees are either dead or dying. Britain also suffers from 'forest death' with about 30% of the trees about

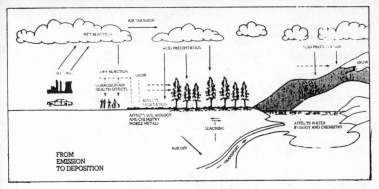

Illustration: Greenpeace

to die. Lakes in Scandinavia and North America are now so acidic that they can no longer support fish life. Ancient monuments which have survived through millennia are simply dissolving in the rain. Crops are suffering reduced growth rates and groundwater is being contaminated by heavy metals leached out by the increased acidity.

Like the greenhouse effect, the increased acidity is mainly due to the burning of fossil fuels, which produces sulphur dioxide and nitrogen oxides as well as the greenhouse gas, carbon dioxide. Worldwide, about half the sulphur in the atmosphere comes from natural sources such as volcanoes, plankton and rotting vegetation. The rest comes from human activities—powerplants, exhaust fumes. Vast quantities of sulphur which have been laid down in fossil fuels over enormous timespans are being released into the atmosphere in a few decades.

All of this is happening because certain Governments are refusing to fit the appropriate technology to reduce emissions on the grounds that it would cost too much. Because acid rain is a transboundary phenomenon countries who produce acid rain can actually 'export' their problem. Ireland is one of these countries. Government officials often put forward the excuse that Britain does not object to our emissions. But Britain does not object because it is the worst offender on this score in the EC.

29

This is scientists measure of acidity. Each additional pH unit means acidity is multiplied by ten, eg. pH5 is ten times more acidic than pH6. pH4 is one hundred times more acidic than pH6. Once acidity frees metals such as aluminium they can become toxic, and pass from the soil and water to plants, insects or fish, and so up the food chain to predators such as birds or mammals, or to grazing animals. The metals can then build up in the brain, bones, blood and liver, damaging animal and human health. When acid rain fall on buildings, it has the same corrosive effect that it has on natural soils and rocks. Sulphuric or nitric acids dissolve in rainfall, eat into stone, particularly limestone, causing statues and ancient buildings to crumble and flake away. New structures such as concrete bridges can also be seriously damaged.

The diagram shows the relationship of Acid Rain to familiar acidic products of the same pH value—in other words, if the pH level of rainfall goes to 2.8, it is like pouring raw vinegar on the earth!

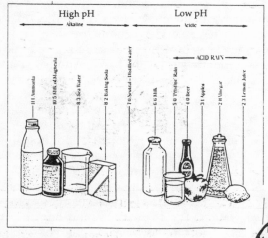

(*Courtesy Greenpeace*)

Acid Rain In Ireland

Despite Ireland's location on the western seaboard of Europe and despite our relatively low level of industrialisation, we are already being affected by acid rain. Approximately half of this derives from Irish emission sources, the other half being imported. Already signs of acidification are appearing all along the eastern seaboard. A Foras Forbartha study comparing two lakes in Connemara with two lakes in County Wickow found a reduced number of acid-sensitive species in the Wicklow lake.

Irish Emissions

For many years the Irish government failed to participate in the UN programme for a 30% reduction in sulphur emissions from 1980 levels despite the fac t that the scientific evidence suggests that across Europe a reduction of 80% is required. We obstructed progress within the EC on controlling large combustion plant emissions and sought a derogation from these proposals. But the government has now changed its tune, somewhat. Under the 1990 Environmental Action Programme it is proposed to use low-sulphur coal at Moneypoint to reduce emissions by 30%. The government has also agreed to fit scrubbers to the plant 'if necessary'. Earthwatch maintains that it is necessary.

AGREED SO$_2$ EMISSION REDUCTIONS AS OF MARCH 1987			
Sweden	65% by 1995	Denmark	30% by 1995
France	50% by 1990	Holland	40% by 1995
Belgium	50% by 1993	Austria	30% by 1993
West Germany	50% by 1993	Italy	30% by 1993
Norway	50% by 1994	Switzerland	30% by 1993

Transboundary fluxes from Bulgaria, Czechoslovakia, East Germany, Hungary and Russia will also be reduced by 30% by 1993. The UK has no written commitment to sulphur reductions. The aim of the policy is to achieve a 30% cut by the year 2000. Ireland has no agreement.

Courtesy Greenpeace.

Even before Moneypoint came on stream, annual SO_2 emissions from power plants in this country were in the order of 20kg per hectare, per year, according to ESB's own figures. Compare this with the critical level figures opposite.

Acid Rain—Critical Loads

Critical loads for acid depositions on forest soils, ground water and surface waters expressed as total annual deposition (kg S/ha/yr)

critical	
poor soils	2-7
medium soils	6-18
chalk soils	100

Critical load deposition of nitrogen
10-20 kg N/ha/yr
(actual 20-30kg N/ha/yr)

Moneypoint

The largest single contributor to acid rain in Ireland is Moneypoint. Moneypoint, in County Clare, is Ireland's largest power station. It has more than doubled the ESB's output and increased national SO_2 emissions by up to 50%. The ESB claims it has solved the problems of pollution by the 'environmental design' of the plant. Basically, this means that they have built two large chimney stacks. This method does not effectively reduce the quantities of acid deposition. It simply disperses it over a wider area. However, the government has now agreed to use low-sulphur coal at Moneypoint, which will go some way towards ameliorating the problem.

Can The Irish Environment Cope?

According to the ESB's own figures, the current levels of sulphur deposition are already in excess of the levels regarded as critical for both poor and medium soils. This does not mean that our forests and lakes will be critically affected in the short-term. Acid rain doesn't work like that. It has a slow cumulative effect, building up until the neutralising capacity of the soil becomes depleted, with disastrous conse-quences. According to Jeremy Wates of Earthwatch, the effects of acid rain will be visible within the thirty year life time of Moneypoint.

SPECIES AT RISK

The following indicate the range of species indirectly affected by acidification (the list is by no means complete.)

(Source: *The Observer*)

Butterflies	Apollo Butterfly severely endangered	Sweden
Birds	Ospreys 3,200 pairs at risk	Sweden
	Dippers. Declined from 9 pairs per 10km, to 2 pairs per 10km, 1970-85.	Wales
	Pied fly-catchers. Severe eggshell thinning and failure to hatch due to aluminium poisoning… population collapse.	Norway Sweden Finland
	Tits and other small insect-eating birds; due to collapse of spider population in acid forests.	Central Europe, UK, Scandinavia
Lichen	30 species of lichen, 12 severely endangered.	Sweden
Fungi	55 out of 130 mycorrhizal fungi (essential for tree development) severely decreased.	Netherlands
Amphibians	Common frog, smooth newt, natterjack toad; severe declines.	UK, Sweden
Flowers	Primroses, severe damage and decline in numbers.	UK
	Orchids: Fragrant and frog orchids, risk of extinction.	UK
	86 other species of wild-flower endangered.	Sweden
Mammals	Otters disappearing as fish stocks collapse.	Scotland Scandinavia
Trees	High incidence of ash disease related to magnesium deficiency.	England
	50% death rate among oaks.	Hungary

This list doesn't take into account Irish areas and species at risk, e.g. the Burren in Co. Clare.

Emission Controls

The ESB has turned its back on all this evidence, preferring instead to quote absurdly high estimates of the costs of emission controls. Initially they claimed that a programme of emission controls would raise electricity prices by 20%. Earthwatch believes that the actual figure would be in the region of 2-3% if proper scrubbers were fitted at Moneypoint. Either way, compared with average electricity price increases of the order of 13% each year between 1979-1984, a once-off price increase of say 2.5% is indeed a small price to pay for a cleaner environment.

Smog

Smog would appear to be a serious problem only in Dublin. There have been complaints from other cities such as Cork, Limerick and Galway, but the readings from the monitoring stations show that there have been very few breaches of the EC limits. It should be stated, however, that the accuracy of this monitoring equipment was called into question by the Irish Clean Air Group in the 1980s.

Dublin's Smog: A Brief History

The problem of urban smog is nothing new to Dublin. In 1729, in an essay entitled 'The Case of Many Poor Inhabitants of This City', Jonathan Swift noted that Dublin's polluted air was having a deleterious effect on the health of its citizens. The main problem then, as it is now, was the emissions from open fires. This was also the main cause of the famous 1952 London smog, when an estimated 4,000 people died. The public outcry which followed led directly to the introduction of the Clean Air Act some years later. Under this Act certain areas were designated to be smokeless zones and certain polluting fuels such as bituminous coal were banned.

In Ireland the deterioration of air quality was not seen as a major problem until the early 1980s. The oil crisis of the 1970s meant that most new houses constructed, particularly large estates in poorer areas, were fitted with open fireplaces. Besides the fact that this particular method of household heating is extremely inefficient, it ought to have been obvious to the planners that this decision could and would lead to a very serious smog problem. And alas the first signs that this would be so occurred in January 1982 when Dublin was shrouded in a thick pall of smog for about four days. Despite the fact that some monitoring stations had readings far in excess of EC limits, snow not smog was the main focus of all media attention.

Throughout the eighties smog has occurred without fail in Dublin in conditions of thermal inversion (see below). Unfortunately, it was not until November 1987 that smoke emission figures from five monitoring stations became available on a daily basis. This was a real boost for the campaign against smog. Smog now became the focus of much media attention and public pressure grew on the Government to do something about the problem.

Successive Governments had not responded to the problem. With added pressure from EC sources, Fianna Fail introduced the Air Pollution Act 1987. This legislation contained many loopholes which the coal lobby used to delay the introduction of smoke-control areas. Finally, in January 1990 the Government did the sensible thing and proposed the banning of bituminous coal from October of that year.

What Is Smog?

The word smog is derived from the combination of the words smoke and fog. However, smog often occurs without the presence of fog. On cold windless days smoke from house chimneys is not dispersed and gradually builds up. The worst smog occurs during a climatic condition known as thermal (temperature) inversion when the air in the upper atmosphere is warmer than that at ground level. This warm layer of air acts as a sort of lid, trapping the smoke below.

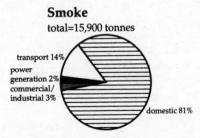

Smoke
total=15,900 tonnes

transport 14%
power generation 2%
commercial/ industrial 3%
domestic 81%

Domestic fires are the worst offenders. Source: Bailey.

THE BAN ON COAL—WILL IT WORK?

The first thing that must be remembered is that this is a ban on the sale of bituminous coal in the Dublin area. You are still permitted to burn smoky coal in most of Dublin with the exception of those areas which have already been designated as smoke-control zones under the Air Pollution Act 1987. These include Ballyfermot A and B. It would appear that plans for the creation of more smoke-control areas have come to a halt because it is felt that the ban on the sale of bituminous coal will provide the long term solution to the problem. A far wiser approach to the problem would have been to continue with the smoke-control orders, under which householders are given grants to convert to more energy efficient appliances, while at the same time banning the sale and burning of smoky coal. All of this could be achieved if the inadequate Air Pollution Act was amended. Of particular importance is the 'incidence and cause' clause in Section 39 of the Act—put in at the request of the coal lobby. This should be deleted as it means the local authority has to carry out a lengthy door to door survey, finding out what kind of fuel is used etc before an area can be designated a smoke-control area. There should be provision within the Act to make all of Dublin a smoke control area. As well as all this the automatic right to object to a smoke control area needs to be withdrawn. This has been abused by the coal industry.

Where Does Smog Come From?

The open household fire is the main source of Dublin's smog problem. 76% of the 16,000 tonnes of smoke emitted annually over Dublin is due directly to the burning of bituminous (smoky) coal in open grates. Bituminous coal  may emit 30–50kg smoke per tonne of fuel burnt. It has been estimated that over 300,000 tonnes of bituminous coal are burnt in 180,000 households in Dublin every year.

What is the Effect on Health?

Severe smog mainly affects the very young, the very old and those with respiratory or cardiovascular problems. Smoke and SO_2 are the main pollutants in Dublin. On their own, they are less harmful, but combined we get what is known as the 'synergistic effect'. This means that SO_2 molecules cling on to the smoke particulates and the combination is breathed in by people. The World Health Organisation has set limits for both smoke and SO_2, which have also been adopted by the EC. Smoke levels in excess of 250 micrograms per cubic metre of air per day mean an increase in morbidity (hospitalisation). Exceedances of 500 micrograms per cubic metre of air per day mean an increase in mortality (death). It should be stressed that these are the 'limits'; the WHO guidelines for health protection from air pollution— 100–150µg/m3/day—are in many ways more important and often conveniently ignored by our politicians. Their interest is to comply—even barely—with the 'limits' and not to bother too much about the guidelines.

Some case studies on the relationship between health and air quality have been carried out. Dr Denis Pringle from Maynooth has shown that the death rate from respiratory diseases in the Ballyfermot area—a pollution blackspot— was a staggering two and a half times the city average.

Two Dublin doctors, Ian Kelly and Luke Clancy, produced the most comprehensive and scientifically based report on this phenomenon to date in the Irish Medical Journal 1984. The Kelly/Clancy report (Mortality in a General Hospital and Urban Air Pollution) showed that increased levels of air pollution during a thermal inversion in January 1982 had led to a doubling of mortality among patients admitted to St James's

Expected Health effects of smoke and Sulphur dioxide and spectrum of biological response based on World Health Organisation criteria.

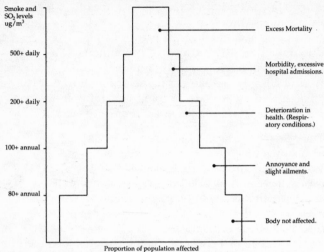

ug/m³ = micgograms per cubic metre.
Source: Dr G. Dean, "Air Pollution — Health Implications" (R.D.S. 1985)

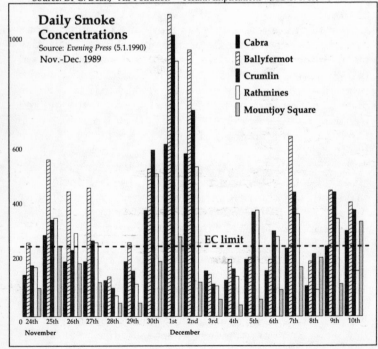

38

Hospital with cardiorespiratory disease. In January 1982 smoke levels reached as high as 1400µg/m3/day and Kelly and Clancy found that there was a peak in mortality of 120 deaths as compared to the monthly average of 54. When they later examined the figures for Dublin as a whole they found that precisely the same pattern appeared in the mortality rates throughout the Dublin area. This was done through computer analysis of Dublin hospital admission statistics.

SMOG ALERTS

One welcome development after many years of campaigning by environmental groups has been the inclusion of smog alerts in the weather forecasts. The Meteorological Office in conjunction with Dublin Corporation issue alerts of TV and radio whenever Dublin smog levels become dangerous.

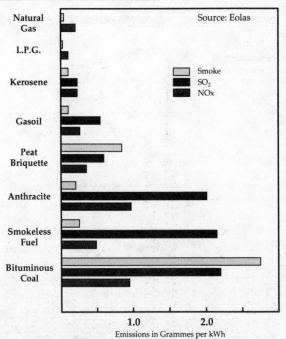

Typical emissions of smoke, sulphur dioxide, and oxides of nitrogen per unit energy content.

Which Fuels Can Best Reduce Smog?

You have a number of options for the open fire. *Coalite* is certainly the least polluting solid fuel. *Union nuggets* and *peat briquettes* are also relatively low in smoke. It should always be remembered however that using the open fire is a terribly inefficient way to heat your home—over 70% of the heat goes up the chimney. Using a closed appliance, which has up to 75% efficiency rates, will reduce smoke and your heating bills. *Anthracite* or *Rexco* can also be used in these stoves.

Natural gas is generally speaking the cleanest fuel and also very efficient. *Electricity* does not contribute to the smog problem, but if the source of electricity is a coal power plant it causes other environmental problems such as acid rain.

It should also be added that all burning of fossil fuels contributes to the greenhouse effect.

SOLID FUEL SMOKE EMMISSION CHART

Bituminous coal	36 grams/hour
Peat briquettes	14.8 grams/hour
Rheinbraun Union Nuggets	11.8 grams/hour
Coalite	1.8 grams/hour

These figures are from Eolas tests.

HOW TO LIGHT A COALITE FIRE

Coalite is a coal from which smog creating agents have been removed. It is much lighter than ordinary coal and gives out up to a third more heat.

When lighting the fire, make a base of sticks, paper and firelighters. Use medium sized pieces of coalite to build up a pyramid over the sticks. Pile on the coalite up to at least two thirds of the grate's capacity. Leave the air control open until the fire is burning well.

Although giving out intense glowing heat, coalite does not produce a flame. If you'd like a fire with flames you should add some Union nuggets or peat briquettes.

USEFUL ENERGY COSTS FOR DOMESTIC HEATING COMPARED (£)

The table comparing energy costs (published by Eolas, the Irish Science and Technology Agency) can help you decide which form of smokeless heating to opt for. Costs in the table are for *April 1989*, the most recent month for which the comparison was available.

In comparing the cost of one fuel-type with another (to decide which is the most efficient heat producer) it's necessary to convert the various units in which fuel is sold—gas in therms, electricity in kilowatt hours (kWh), coal in tonnes, and so on—into a common unit, that is pence per kilowatt hour (p/kWh) and to take into account the efficiency with which each fuel type is converted into heat.

Delivered costs

For purposes of comparison, see the column headed *Delivered cost*. This column gives you the price in pence per kilowatt hour (kWh) for each fuel type. For example, the cost of producing 1kWh of heat from machine turf is 1.28p. Loose briquettes cost 1.59p/kWh and are a cheaper fuel than baled briquettes at 1.79p/kWh. The general domestic rate for electricity is the most expensive, 7.50p/kWh.

But, different appliances have different efficiency ratings. So you should comjpare the columns headed *Useful costs (p/kWh) for different appliances*. The efficiency with which most fuels are used depends on the type, and in some cases, the model of heating appliance used. The exception to this is general domestic rate electricity because elecyric heaters work at 100% efficiency. The least heat efficient appliances are open fires. Here, 70%–80% of heat escapes up the chimney, therefore, the cost of producing a kWh of heat is high. For instance, in an open fire with an efficiency of 20%, heating by loose turf briquettes costs 7.95p/kWh. This is more expensive than heating by electricity at the General Domestic Rate.

Fuel/form	Delivered cost p/kWh	Roomheater, freestanding, boiler, cooker Efficiency 45%–55% (50%–60%) [2]		Open fire with high output back boiler Efficiency 35%–50% (40%–55%) [2]		Open fire Efficiency 20%–30%		Oil fired boiler/ burner Efficiency 55%–70% 60%–70% [3]		Gas fire boiler/ burner Efficiency 65%–75%		Electric fire Efficiency 100%	Fluessless[1] gas/storage heater Efficiency 90%
PEAT													
Machine turf	1.28	2.84	2.33	3.66	2.56	6.40	4.27						
Briquettes, loose	1.59	3.53	2.89	4.54	3.18	7.95	5.30						
Briquettes, baled	1.79	3.98	3.26	5.11	3.58	8.95	5.97						
COAL													
House coal	1.67	3.72	3.04	4.78	3.34	8.36	5.57						
Anthracite peas [2]	2.25	4.49	3.74										
Standard anthracite [2]	1.74	3.48	2.90										
Extracite[2]	2.36	4.71	3.93										
Grade A anthracite [2]	2.32	4.64	3.87										
Coalite[2]	2.02	4.05	3.37	5.06	3.68	10.12	6.74						
OIL													
Gas oil	2.02							3.68	2.89				
Kerosene	2.28							3.80	3.26				
GAS													
Bulk LPG	3.61									5.55	4.81		4.01
Bottled butane	5.76									8.86	7.68		6.40
0 – 20 therms	4.51									6.94	6.01		
21 – 40 therms	3.38									5.20	4.51		
41 + therms	2.39									3.68	3.19		
Minisaver	3.00									4.62	4.00		
Supersaver	2.25									3.46	3.00		
ELECTRICITY													
General domestic rate	7.50											7.50	
Night space heating	3.05												3.39

1 Adequate ventilation required for flueless gas heaters.   2 'Increased efficiency indicated for 'smokeless' fuels.   3 Increased efficiency indicated for kerosene burned in indoor boiler.

Courtesy: Consumer Choice (October 1989)

Fossil fuels consist mainly of the various compounds of the elements carbon and hydrogen. These are known as hydrocarbons. Air, which is a mixture of 79% nitrogen and 21% oxygen, combines with these hydrocarbons during combustion. If the temperature is high enough, then the hydrocarbons are changed almost entirely to Carbon dioxide, which is the major contributor to the Greenhouse Effect, and water vapour. Energy is given out in the form of heat.

Normally, however, combustion is incomplete and smoke and carbon monoxide, a very toxic gas, are produced. Any sulphur in the fuel produces sulphur dioxide, the main cause of acid rain. Small amounts of nitrogen oxides (NO_X) are produced from nitrogen in the combustion air and in the fuel; these contribute to acid rain and to the depletion of the ozone layer. NO_X and unburned hydrocarbons react together under ultraviolet radiation producing photochemical smog and ozone, which is poisonous in the lower atmosphere.

WHAT SHOULD BE DONE

Ozone

• There should be an immediate ban on CFCs. The Minister for the Environment can do this under the Air Pollution Act.

Greenhouse

• We need an energy policy which concentrates on alternative methods of energy production and emphasises energy conservation and efficiency. This is the only way to limit CO_2 emissions and counteract the Greenhouse Effect.

• We need a national tree planting programme with emphasis on broadleaves (see Trees chapter).

Acid Rain

• The ESB should be compelled to retrofit flue gas desulphurisation (FGD) at Moneypoint by 1991 at the latest.

• An independent review group should be established to explore possible strategies for limiting emissions to the required level and to examine the cost implications. Its findings should be made available to the public.

• We need a national programme for energy conservation, with full participation from the ESB. Far more money needs to be invested in the development of alternative energy.

Smog

• Smokeless fuels should be subsidised.
• A more comprehensive energy plan is needed.

WHAT CAN YOU DO?

Ozone

• If you insist on buying aerosols, make sure they're ozone friendly.

• Write to the Minister for the Environment, demanding that he or she ban CFCs.

• Try to make your own home or place of work into a CFC free zone.

Greenhouse

• You can start in your own home by being more energy efficient. See energy section.

Acid Rain

• Conserve electricity by using modern efficient lamps and appliances. Switch off unnecessary equipment.

• Change to lower sulphur fuel such as turf or kerosene, or to sulphur-free natural gas and L.P.G.

Smog

• Install closed appliances in your home.
• Burn smokeless fuels.
• Convert to natural gas.
• Insulate your home.

Organisations and Individual Campaigners

(For details see directory listing at back of book)

Smog:

Earthwatch, (Maeve O'Sullivan). Have produced a very helpful smog leaflet.

Eolas, can advise you about the types of fuel to use.

Greenpeace, Bob Edwards.

Dublin Corporation, Environment Section, 9 Aston Quay, Dublin 2. Ph. 01 712266. Can give you daily readings from five monitoring stations. This section also produces an annual report, which contains detailed information on air pollution in Dublin.

Ozone:

Earthwatch, Clare Heardman.

Greenpeace, Bob Edwards.

Greenhouse Effect:

Earthwatch, Jim Woolridge.

Greenpeace, Bob Edwards.

Acid rain:

Earthwatch, Jeremy Wates.

Greenpeace, John Bowler

Books and Publications

Ozone Layer: *Friends of the Earth: The Montreal Protocol 1989*, Fiona Weir (Friends of the Earth 1989); *Ozone Depletion 1988*, Fiona Weir (Friends of the Earth, 1988); *Alternatives to CFCs* (Friends of the Earth, 1989); United Nations Environment Programme, *The Ozone Layer* (UNEP 1987).

The Greenhouse Effect: *The Heat Trap* J. Karas and P. Kelly (Friends of the Earth, 1988); *The Greenhouse Effect*, Steward Boyle and John Ardill (New English Library, 1987); *GAIA*, James Lovelock (Oxford University Press, 1979).

Acid Rain: *Acid Waters*, Andrew Tickle (Greenpeace, 1988); *Acid Rain*, Jeremy Wates (Earthwatch, Bantry).

Smog: *Air Quality in Ireland*, Michael Bailey (Foras Forbartha 1983)

II
WATER

*'The number of water taps per 1000 persons is
a better indication of health than the number
of hospital beds'*
World Health Organisation

Clean water is vital for health, sanitation, industry, fisheries,
agriculture and tourism—and we take it very much for
granted.

The state of our waterways is very much a barometer for
the overall state of our environment, as most pollution,
whether it be from the air or soil, eventually finds its way into
our seas and rivers. Often too our seas and rivers are treated
quite deliberately as vast dumping grounds for our rubbish
and pollution.

The years 1981–1990 were designated 'The International
Drinking Water Supply and Sanitation Decade'. The WHO
calculated that if the programme were to be successful,
another 1.8 billion people in the Third World would need to
have access to clean water, with an additional 2.4 billion
needing access to sanitation.

While the overall picture regarding water quality in
Ireland would appear to be good, we have cause to worry
about the increasing amount of fish kills from agricultural
sources, the inadequate treatment of sewage and the
unsatisfactory monitoring of industrial effluents.

Ireland's Water Resources

With its fairly high rainfall, Ireland is assured of good fresh
water resources. The annual average rainfall is 1,150mm, with
a range of 700mm in the driest part of the country to 2,800mm
in the wettest part (in the western counties).

The latest available statistics on water resources and use were
compiled by An Foras Forbartha. For the purposes of data,
the country is divided up into seven regions (see chart).

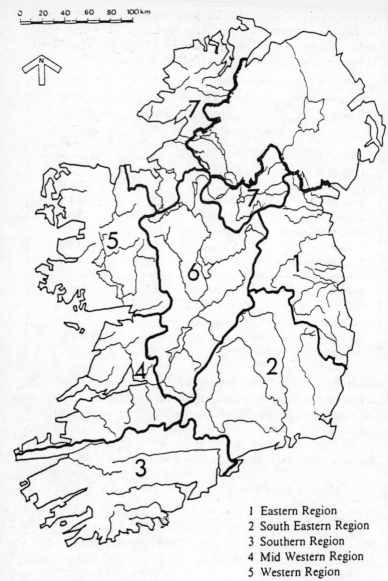

0 20 40 60 80 100 km

N

7

7

5

6

1

4

2

3

1 Eastern Region
2 South Eastern Region
3 Southern Region
4 Mid Western Region
5 Western Region
6 Shannon Region
7 North Western Region

Water Regions
Source: *An Foras Forbartha*

As the chart shows the Eastern region has the lowest availability of water per head of population (7174 litres from surface water per head per day or l/h/day). The North Western region has the highest (76117 l/h/day).

Water Resource Region	Population	Average Run-off m^3/s	Average Run-off per capita l/j/day
1. Eastern	1,373,000	114.0	7,174
2. South-Eastern	482,000	198.8	35,635
3. Southern	520,000	235.5	39,130
4. Shannon	294,000	178.5	52,457
5. Mid-Western	247,000	124.75	43,637
6. Western	261,000	186.2	61,639
7. North-Western	263,000	231.7	76,117
Ireland	3,440,000	1,269.5	31,885

Distribution of surface water resources
Source: An Foras Forbartha

According to the Foras Forbartha figures on water use, the volume of fresh water used daily in Ireland amounts to about 2.2 million m^3 (480 M gal) or about 650 l per person per day.

Abstractions	Surface Water m^3/day	Ground Water m^3/day	Total m^3/day
Public Bodies	830,000	168,000	998,00
Industry	510,000	174,000	684,000
Sub-Total	1,340,000	342,000	1,682,000
Additional			490,000
Total	—	—	2,172,000

Summary of water abstractions (water use)
Source: An Foran Forbartha

Power generation also requires huge volumes of water, and the total abstractions for it are three times that for all other purposes.

Source	Average Quantity Abstracted (m^3/day)
Fresh Water	759,000
Saline Water	5,952,000
Sea Water	33,000
Total	6,744,000

Abstractions for thermal power generation
Source: Electricity Supply Board

Inland Waters

Rivers

Officials from the Department of the Environment are fond of quoting the statistic that only 2% of our rivers are 'seriously polluted'. The figure is taken from the Foras Forbartha 1982–1986 survey of river pollution. Quoted out of context—as it often is—by Government ministers, it gives members of the public the false impression that only two out of every hundred rivers contain serious pollution. The 2% refers to the combined length of river (128km) surveyed which is seriously polluted and not to the amount of rivers containing seriously polluted stretches. **The 1988 survey carried out by the ERU revealed that 47 out of the 227 rivers surveyed contained seriously polluted stretches—about 20% of the total.**

According to a 1985 Foras Forbartha report, there has been 'little systematic investigation of the incidence of potentially toxic substances in Irish river waters'. There is a real need for more extensive monitoring of heavy metal concentrations and pesticides. Some monitoring has been carried out, but has not been sufficient to give an overall national picture. Clearly, this is an area in which the new EPA can play a leading role.

Lakes

Unlike rivers, most of the growth of organisms in lakes occurs in the water column, not in the substratum. Phytoplankton (algae) and zoo plankton (tiny animal organisms) are the main features of our lakes, and it is the density of these organisms which determines the quality of the lake water. The presence of nutrients such as phosphorous and nitrates encourages growth and these are more easily leached out of soft rock such as limestone. Lakes in limestone areas, therefore, tend to be productive. On the other hand, lakes in areas of hard rock such as granite are mostly unproductive. Unproductive lakes are referred to as oligotrophic. Productive lakes are known as eutrophic.

The most common form of lake pollution in this country is known as 'artificial eutrophication'. This occurs when additional nutrients from sewage or slurry are discharged into the water and the lake becomes over-productive. This excessive growth clouds the water and depletes the oxygen levels.

The government has tried to deal with the problem of artificial eutrophication at different times with varying degrees of success. The best known example is Lough Sheelin which has come back from the dead a few times only to be let die again. Back in the early eighties the government decided to transport the pig slurry away from the lake catchment area to outlying areas. But this scheme was then let lapse.

In the Environment Action Programme, the Government makes provision for remedial action at Loughs Sheelin, Derraveragh and the River Inny.

A pilot anaerobic digestor (see Waste and Recycling) has been set up by Eolas.

An additional £50,000 is being made available for slurry management plans. As well as this the sewage treatment works at Ballyjamesduff is going to be upgraded at a cost of £2m.

Sources of Pollution

Farm wastes

Far more waste is generated from farming activities in Ireland than that produced from industry and sewerage systems (see waste and sewage). It is often thought that organic or biodegradable products, such as farm wastes, are somehow non-polluting. But this is not so. Produced in excessive quantities, as is the case in Ireland, they are potentially far more polluting to our waterways than industrial chemicals.

The present excess in farm wastes is due directly to intensive methods of agriculture. Traditional mixed farming often recycled livestock excreta and vegetable residue, using them as valuable natural fertilizer. This change in farming practice, which has come about mainly since membership of the EC, has been quite dramatic. Take pig farming—the source of pig slurry—for example. Twenty years ago there were no large pig units. Now 80% of our pig units hold over 400 animals each. During the same time, the production of silage from grass has increased from less than 5 million tonnes to 20 million tonnes per annum.

50

SILAGE

During the first 7–10 days after ensiling silage produces an effluent that is 20 times more noxious than domestic sewage and can cause severe pollution of surface water and groundwater.

Silage pits should have an impermeable base, concrete or clay—so that effluent can't flow through the soil and rock beneath the silage into groundwater. Unlined limestone quarries and gravel pits are not suitable sites for silage pits. All the effluent should be collected by constructing a drainage channel around the pit and leading to a holding tank. The effluent should be sprayed on to adjoining land.

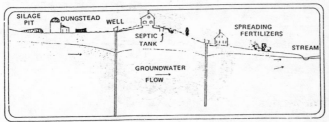

Geological Survey

Extent of the surveyed length of river and stream channel affected by three levels of pollution and the proportions of the polluted lengths attributed to agricultural activities. Based on surveys and observations in the period 1982–1986 (Toner et al. 1986)

Water Resource Region	Total Channel Length Surveyed [km]	Length in each category (% of polluted length attributed to agriculture)		
		Slightly Polluted	Moderately Polluted	Seriously Polluted
Eastern	902	186 (48)	160 (46)	35 (37)
South-eastern	1,564	333 (30)	131 (21)	29 (21)
Southern	692	78 (10)	37 (Nil)	2 (Nil)
Mid-western	406	134 (37)	50 (40)	14 (36)
Shannon	1,494	161 (35)	90 (14)	24 (Nil)
Western	900	85 (29)	66 (Nil)	10 (Nil)
North-western (Cavan-Monaghan)	353	73 (16)	70 (29)	8 (Nil)
North-western (Donegal-Sligo)	632	24 (17)	27 (52)	6 (17)
All Regions	**6,943**	**1,074 (32)**	**631 (27)**	**128 (21)**

Source: Farm Wastes and Water Pollution in Ireland, ERU

How Pollution Occurs: Farm wastes don't 'poison' the water, as is often thought. They pollute by removing the dissolved oxygen in the water, on which living creatures depend. An apparently wholesome product such as milk can therefore be far more polluting than say raw sewage, as it removes more oxygen from the waters. *The capacity to remove oxygen from the water is the real measurement of the polluting potential of a substance* and it is known in scientific terms as the Biochemical Oxygen Demand (BOD). The chart shows the BOD levels of the various farm wastes.

Estimated quantities of BOD and phosphorus generated in livestock manures and in silage compared to similar estimates for sewage and industrial wastes.		
Waste Source	*B.O.D.* *tonnes/a*	*Phosphorus* *tonnes/a*
Agricultural Wastes		
Livestock Manures		
Cattle	818,000	51,000
Sheep	64,000	600
Pigs	45,000	3,300
Poultry	9,000	1,500
Total, Livestock Manures	936	56,400
Silage Effluent	200,000	2,100
Total Agricultural Wastes	**1,136,000**	**58,500**
Domestic Sewage and **Industrial Wastes**		
Domestic Sewage	44,000	2,000
Industrial Wastes	70,000	3,200
Total, Sewage and Industry	**114,000**	**5,200**
Source: Farm Wastes and Water Pollution in Ireland ERU		

Oxygen is contained in natural water at a concentration of about 10 parts per million. If the oxygen level falls from ten to five most of the fish and other creatures which depend on oxygen will die. This is important to remember. You can restock a river with fish but it is difficult to replace some of the other valuable aquatic life which has been destroyed and can take up to 10 years to recover fully.

Natural water also contains two other key elements; phosphorous and nitrogen. If the concentration of either rises, 'eutrophication' occurs. The water becomes over-enriched with nutrients and the microscopic plants multiply too quickly, consuming the oxygen and making the water look murky. This is what happened to Lough Sheelin, once one of Ireland's best coarse angling lakes, now practically dead.

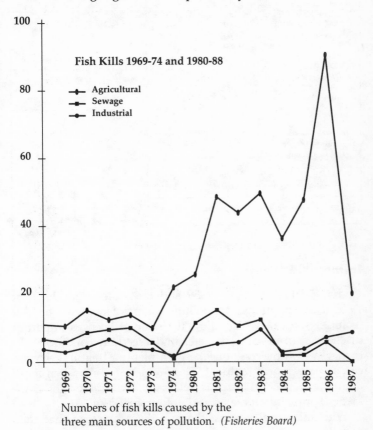

Numbers of fish kills caused by the three main sources of pollution. *(Fisheries Board)*

As the fishkill chart shows, agricultural effluent is by far and away the greatest cause of fishkills, with slurry and particularly silage 'liquor' being the worse offenders. Most fishkills occur during the summer when the rainfall and the water volume in rivers and steams is low. There is simply not enough water to dilute the high volume of farm wastes.

Typical sewage and phosphorus contents of farm wastes and of untreated domestic sewage and selected industrial wastes.
NA: not available

Wastes	BOD Content mg/l	Phosphorus Content mg/l
Farm Wastes		
Cattle Manure Slurry	17,000	630
Pig Manure Slurry	25,000	1,800
Poultry Manure Slurry	66,000	5,100
Dungstead Effluent	10,000	NA
Silage Effluent	65,000	560
Dirty Water	1,500	32
Whole Milk	105,000	NA
Skim Milk	70,000	NA
Whey	35,000	NA
Domestic Sewage	450	15
Industrial Wastes		
Milk processing	400	9
Slaughterhouse	850	8
Beet-sugar	1,200–4,600	3–13
Brewing	600	20
Pharmaceutical	4,600	NA

Source: Farm Wastes and Water Pollution in Ireland, ERU

Industrial Wastes

Under the Fisheries Act 1959 and the Water Pollution Act 1977 it is an offense to pollute waters. However the Act includes sections which allow the issue of licences to permit discharges from factories, etc. under certain conditions. In theory, a healthy river or lake with plenty of natural oxygen can actually purify effluent. The problem occurs when more than the permitted level is released. The waters get over-loaded, purification ceases and pollution occurs.

With industrial wastes, there is the advantage that they usually come from individual factories, or 'point sources' and are usually subject to monitoring and control. Many of the waste products from creameries, meatplants and other food based industries have high BOD levels and their control measures must be rigorously applied. Other waste products from the chemical and manufacturing industries usually pollute by poisoning the water.

Sewage (see also Costal Waters)

Raw sewage is still pumped into many of our lakes and rivers. A healthy river can cope with this if the amounts are limited. However, if the discharges are excessive—particularly in summer when there's a smaller volume of water—fish kills will occur because of lack of oxygen in the water. The culprits are usually the local authorities, who are themselves responsible for monitoring pollution a very unsatisfactory situation. The new EPA should have independent powers to monitor sewage discharges.

The Government has stated that it is committed to eliminating the practice of discharging raw sewage by the year 2000.

What should be done

- There should be extensive annual surveys of all our rivers and lakes, using both physico-chemical and biological analysis.
- Water quality management plans, which can be carried out under the present legislation, should become normal practice.
- We need far more information on the presence of pesticides and heavy metals in our waterways.
- We need much higher fines for companies or individuals who pollute our waterways. Our present legislation is wholly inadequate in this regard. (see law)

What you can do

- Take an interest in your nearest river or lake. Find out about the water quality. This information is available from the ERU in Dublin or from the local authority.
- If you know of anyone causing pollution get on immediately to the local authority.

Coastal Waters

The seas around our coast have long been seen as a cheap and convenient dump for the country's waste. Some of the waste reaches the sea through sewers and industrial outfalls. A great deal comes from the rivers or is dumped from ships. An increasing problem is the waste in the air, which is carried to the seas in the wind and the rain.

The latest information on the quality of our marine waters and shoreline comes mainly from the Coastwatch Survey 1989 and the monitoring of the Department of the Environment.

Coastwatch survey

The Coastwatch survey was organised by the Dublin Bay Environmental Group and carried out by volunteers north and south of the border. The in depth survey covered the entire coast and looked at a number of areas including the quality of the water at inflows, litter and oil. Some of the results are given here:

Inflows:

Inflows include small rivers, ditches, pipes and seepage (from overflowing septic tanks for example), all of which can cause localised pollution.

1,907 active inflows were surveyed, 21% contained discoloured water, some discolouration can be explained by bog drainage in the area, but 16% had an off smell which suggests pollution.

15% of the inflows had dumped debris around their banks and mouth.

10% of the inflows were affected by scum and froth from excessive sewage. (see also Sewage below)

3% of inflows showed traces of oil and petrol in the water.

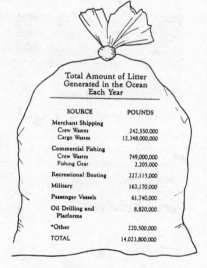

SOURCE	POUNDS
Merchant Shipping	
Crew Wastes	242,550,000
Cargo Wastes	12,348,000,000
Commercial Fishing	
Crew Wastes	749,000,000
Fishing Gear	2,205,000
Recreational Boating	227,115,000
Military	163,170,000
Passenger Vessels	61,740,000
Oil Drilling and Platforms	8,820,000
*Other	220,500,000
TOTAL	14,023,800,000

Total Amount of Litter Generated in the Ocean Each Year

Litter:

The worst problem with regard to litter in this country is the practice of illegal dumping of domestic rubbish. A lot of this ends up on our beaches and shoreline.

This includes debris from shipping accidents and from major storms in coastal areas. Centre for Marine Conservation, US.

Plastic:

7% of the areas surveyed were found to be grossly polluted by litter. By far the worst problem was plastic and this is in keeping with world trends, where plastic is now seen as one of the most dangerous pollutants of our seas.

~Plastics and polystyrene are the most common items on the whole shore, 59% of the areas surveyed had general plastics like carrier bags. Nylon fishing gear was found on a quarter of the areas surveyed, while a further 18% had plastic six pack holders and packing straps.

Items of plastic are particularly lethal for wildlife. Birds, seals, turtles and dolphins can become entangled in netting or mistake items of plastic for food and die as a consequence. Plastic pellets—the raw material for much plastic production and a major source of plastic pollution were not included in the survey. Cargoes of these pellets are often lost at sea and are then washed ashore and eaten by seabirds. Once enough are ingested they block the gut, causing the bird to starve to death.

Marpol Annex V is an international maritime agreement.

Marpol Annex V, Sticker Produced for Boaters. Centre for Marine Conservation, US. See details below.

Cans and Glass

51% of the areas surveyed had cans in the splash zone, as against 37% glass. These figures again emphasise the need for more recycling facilities.

DUMPING AT SEA,
Marpol Annex V. Protocol Table.

Plastic debris has until recently been free of dumping regulations. Annex V of the marpol protocol is designed to handle this problem. It came into effect on December 1988. Ireland has not yet become a signatory.

Garbage Type	All Vessels		Offshore Platforms & Assoc. Vessels ***
	Outside Special Areas	**In Special Areas	
Plastics—includes synthetic ropes fishing nets and plastic garbage bags	Disposal prohibited	Disposal prohibited	Disposal prohibited
Floating dunnage, lining, and packing materials	> 25 miles off shore	Disposal prohibited	Disposal prohibited
Paper rags, glass, metal bottles, crockery and similar refuse	> 12 miles	Disposal prohibited	Disposal prohibited
Paper, rags, glass, etc. communited	> 3 miles	> 12 miles	> 12 miles
Food waste communited or ground*	> 3 miles	> 12 miles	> 12 miles
Food waste not communited or ground	> 12 miles	> 12 miles	Disposal prohibited
Mixed refuse types	****	****	****

   * Communited or ground garbage must be able to pass through a screen with mesh size no larger than 1 inch.
  ** Special areas are the Mediterranean, Baltic, Red and Black seas areas, and the Gulf's areas.
 *** Offshore platforms and associated vessels include all fixed or floating platforms engaged in exploration or exploitation of seabed mineral resources, and all vessels alongside or within 500 m of such platforms.
**** When garbage is mixed with other harmful substances having different disposal or discharge requirements, the more stringent disposal requirements shall apply.

Sewage

It has been estimated that the population of Dublin produces about 60 million gallons of sewage daily. Enough sewage is pumped into the Irish Sea from Britain and Ireland to cover the Isle of Man to a depth of 6 feet. Ireland and the UK are the only countries in the North Sea region which discharge raw sewage into the sea.

Raw sewage is composed of municipal, industrial, agricultural and hospital waste. Included in this nasty cocktail are a range of bacteria and viruses, detergents, parasites, disinfectants, pesticides, toxic chemicals, radioactive isotopes and heavy metals. Of most concern to people are the infactions and disease that swimming in polluted water can cause. Those beaches which have been designated with the EC blue flag are sure to comply with the strictest regulations for water quality. 28 of our coastal towns discharge waste directly into tidal waters. 40 towns (urban populations of 1,500) pump raw sewage into our seas, lakes and rivers. There are many towns and villages which have no sewage facilities. Up to 20 of the existing secondary treatment plants have been shown to be inadequate, according to a 1989 Earthwatch Report.

SEWAGE TREATMENT METHODS

Preliminary treatment: Screening for large objects and removal of grit.

Primary treatment: Sedimentation; suspended solid material is separated out of the sludge. Typically removes about 60% of the raw sewage suspended solids and 30% of BOD (Biochemical Oxygen Demand).

Secondary (biological) treatment: Dissolved organic matter is aerated. This process utilises vast amounts of oxygen (aerobic treatment) producing sludge and a liquor (effluent) containing a range of chemicals. When the quality of the sludge is high you can use it as fertiliser on the land, but in many cases the sludge is polluted with heavy metals. Basic secondary treatment of raw sewage results in a ten-fold decrease in bacteria (faecal coliforms) thereby greatly reducing the risk of contamination/disease, and the solid fraction can be removed altogether. May remove more than 85% of the BOD.

Anaerobic treatment: The slurry produced in the biological treatment can be treated anaerobically (without oxygen), using methane digestors, and the resulting methane can be used as fuel.

Tertiary treatment: Specialised removal of nutrients (i.e. phosphates and nitrates), heavy metals and/or some dissolved chemicals, or further aeration to decrease the BOD of the effluent. Used when high quality effluent is required.

Source: Earthwatch Autumn 1989

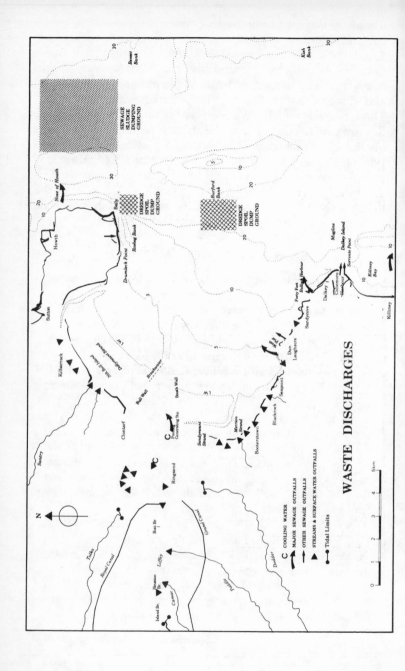

WASTE DISCHARGES

C COOLING WATER

→ MAJOR SEWAGE OUTFALLS

↑ OTHER SEWAGE OUTFALLS

▲ STREAMS & SURFACE WATER OUTFALLS

●— Tidal Limits

0 1 2 3 4 5km

SEWAGE SLUDGE DUMPING GROUND

DREDGE SPOIL DUMP GROUND

DREDGE SPOIL DUMP GROUND

Benet Bank

Kish Bank

Nose of Howth

Burford Bank

Howth

Sutton

Kilbarrack

Clontarf

Santry

Royal Canal

Tolka

Bull Br.

Island Br.

Camac

Liffey

Houston Ry.

Crystal Canal

Poddle

Dodder

Grand Canal

Ringsend

Poolbeg Generating Stn.

Sandymount Strand

Merrion Strand

Booterstown

Blackrock

Seapoint

Dun Laoghaire

Sandycove

Dalkey

Coliemore Harbour

Dalkey Island

Maglins

Sorrento Point

Killiney Bay

Killiney

Forty Foot

Bullock Harbour

Drumleck Point

Rowboy Bank

Bailly

Dredge Dumped Spoil

Nth Bull Wall

Bull Wall

Breakwater

South Wall

(M1)

(M1)

20

10

30

20

10

5

5

10

20

20

5

10

10

10

20

N

Technology

The 'Sewage Treatment Methods' section here gives some indication of the technology presently available to deal with the problem of sewage. It's often argued that proper treatment of sewage is a costly business and one which this country cannot afford. As usual this argument ignores the external costs such as health risks, fishkills and the damage done to our image abroad—all of which are less easy to quantify.

As a member of the Paris Commission (an inter-governmental conference on sea pollution from land-based sources) Ireland committed itself to a 50% reduction of sewage into our seas between 1985 and 1995. The EC is currently considering a directive for the regulation of sewage disposal for towns of over 10,000 inhabitants. In the long term the aim of EC directives will be to ban Long Sea Outfalls (LSOs). In Ireland there is no national plan for the development of our sanitary services—even though money is allocated through a National Development Plan.

**POLLUTION & HEALTH PROBLEMS
ASSOCIATED WITH RAW SEWAGE**

Sewage contains bacterial and viral pathogens. These cause mild infections resulting in vomiting, diarrhoea, headaches, fever and eye, ear, nose, throat and skin infections. Rarer and more virulent infections include cystitis, typhoid, polio, salmonella, hepatitis and meningitis to which unvaccinated swimmers, especially young children are most at risk. The intake of heavy metals can cause greater susceptibility to disease; higher animals in the food chain have been shown to concentrate such metals (eg. mercury, silver, zinc, copper, lead, chromium and nickel) in their tissues, leading to neurological disorders and fatalities in severe cases.

Earthwatch

Dublin Bay

Looking down on Dublin bay from the surrounding mountains on a fine summer's day one sees a coastline of rare beauty. Miles of golden beaches, the blue water dotted with boats and yachts—seldom has a city been so scenically situated. Our coastline is a fantastic resource and one which we are quickly destroying.

A close-up of Dublin bay reveals a different picture. Those who live in the city have seen the evidence—human excrement, toilet paper, tampons, condoms—all are part of the raw sewage washed up on our shores.

The largest sewage outfall at Ringsend serves the south and west of the city and has a contributing population of 600,000 persons. The discharges here receive primary treatment; those at Howth and Shanganagh receive screening; and those at West Pier (Dun Laoghaire) and Bullock Harbour are untreated.

Because sewage contains significant amount of nutrients such as phosphates and nitrates, eutrophication occurs and growths of unsightly green algae sometimes appear on beaches in the bay. This algae is not harmful in itself, but when decaying it does produce an offensive odour and it may make swimming an unpleasant experience. In the recent past the shorelines worst affected have been Dollymount and between Sandymount and Blackrock.

Most of the beaches in the bay conform to the limits set in the EC Bathing Water Directive. The monitoring stations at Blackrock and the Bull Wall have been exceptions and the readings at Dollymount have come close to the limit. On one occasion in May 1988 the presence of Salmonella bacteria was found in a sample at Dollymount.

Under the Environment Action Programme, Dublin Corporation will have to end the dumping of sewage sludge at sea be 1998 at the latest. By 1991 the discharges of raw sewage from Dun Laoghaire and Bullock Harbour will be diverted to Ringsend by pipeline, where they will receive secondary treatment. This will end the discharge of raw sewage into the bay. But the Dublin Bay Environmental Group and An Taisce have stated that this is not an adequate response to the pollution problems of the bay. Both groups have repeated their demands for tertiary treatment plant. Such a plant could be run on the methane gas produced from treatment and

provide fertilizer for flower beds. But besides all that we would have a much cleaner bay. Imagine it!
(See also Energy from Waste, Waste & Recycling chapter)

Cork Harbour

At present there are some 16 industrial premises consented to discharge in excess of 11 million tonnes of effluent into Cork harbour every year. The greatest concentration of factories is in the Little Island Industrial Estate where all companies discharge into a communal sewerage system. The effluent contains up to 11.9 tonnes of heavy metals and 29 tonnes of toxic organic chemicals every year. The total 'waste' content is poorly defined and the authorities have set limits for only 28 parameters. There is no reference to pharmaceuticals and their by-products. Since in general up to 10% of the product may be lost in the manufacturing effluent and discharged as waste, this lack of control is a matter of real concern.

The other industries discharging effluent into the estuary are located in the outer harbour at Ringaskiddy. The sewage from Cork city is also discharged into the river Lee in a largely untreated state.

Residents in the Cork harbour area have complained over a ten year period of foul odours from industry in the area. Dr. Mary Dunphy, who runs a medical practice in the area and who is herself an environmental campaigner, has said that she has noticed unusual tumours amongst some of her patients which she has attributed to industrial pollution. RICH (Responsible Industry for Cork Harbour) is a pressure group actively campaigning to have industry clean up its act in the area. In a preliminary report on water pollution in Cork Harbour, Greenpeace has stated when one looks at the lack of environmental controls in place 'concern becomes alarm'.

What Should be Done

- There should be independent monitoring of coastal waters.
- More vigorous testing for Heavy Metals in our seas
- A ban on all sea dumping
- Ireland should sign MARPOL Annex 5 (see above) and provide proper reception facilities (skips, etc.) for visiting ships.

What You Can Do

• Participate in the next Coastwatch Survey organised by Dublin Bay Environmental Group. (A similar project is run by a group called FAIRE in Galway (see Organisations).

• Recycle cans, bottles and plastics—a lot of which end up in our seas.

• Balloon launches at events are bad for the marine environment. Try to dissuade event organisers from this practice.

re *Sewage*

• Contact your local council and find out all you can about your local sewer system. How old is the system? Is there any evidence that the sewage system is being mismanaged in any way? There are a number of signs which indicate that this may be the case. In particular look for outfall pipes which discharge above the low tide mark on the shore and the state of repair of sewage pipes at discharge points. Is there much solid waste on the river bank/sea shore? Is there a lot of algae growth in the intertidal zone, especially in areas where it was not present before? Are there persistent odours in areas where there may be no visual evidence of sewage? Fishkills may also indicate that the sewage has been incorrectly treated.

• If things are not as they should be then send your findings to the engineering/sanitation section of your local council. Demand an explanation and ask what they intend to do about the situation. Send copies to the local TDs, the local press, the Sanitary Services Section of the Department of the Environment and/or the Pollution Section of the Department of the Marine if it is coastal pollution.

• Send some water samples to your local health board for analysis.

• Contact EARTHWATCH, who have a special raw sewage campaign.

• You can help in the home by using phosphate-free washing powder such as Ecover, Ark, or others (see List in Consumer Chapter).

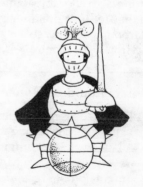

Radioactivity

It's almost a cliche at this stage to say that the Irish Sea is the most radioactive sea in the world. For over thirty years the Sellafield nuclear reprocessing plant (formerly Windscale) has been discharging radioactive effluent into the Irish Sea. Because of these 'low-level' discharges the Irish Sea now contains between ¼ and ½ tonne of plutonium.

One of the most important components of the effluent is the radionuclide Caesium 137. Caesium 134, which has a much shorter life, is also measurable.

The radioactive waste decays and forms Americium, a highly effective alpha emitter. This has been found in the froth on beaches in Britain and undoubtedly finds its way onto Irish beaches.

At the Environmental Emergency Conference held in Dublin in November 1987, Mr Jeffrey Preece of British Nuclear Fuels Ltd (BNFL) said that environmentalists eating their muesli containing hazelnuts would receive a higher radiation dose than from eating fish from the Irish Sea. He also said that BNFL had nothing to do with the nuclear subs in the Irish Sea (see Ongoing Campaigns), but if they had they would use them to torpedo the Greenpeace ships. This was intended as a joke, but it didn't go down well with the Greenpeace campaigners in the audience, who had lost one of their friends in the Rainbow Warrior explosion. Such appalling insensitivity is not unusual for the nuclear lobby, who basically see environmentalists as a damned nuisance and are prepared to go to extreme lengths to protect their interests. Money and 'science' take precedence over people. This is obvious from the sinister experiment that was carried out at the Sellafield plant. According to Mr John Dunster, then Chief Health Physicist at Sellafield and now head of the UK's National Radiological Protection Board, 'The intention has been to discharge fairly substantial amounts of radioactivity as part of an organised and deliberate scientific experiment . . . the aims of this experiment would have been defeated if the level of radioactivity had been kept to a minimum.'

As a direct result of this 'experiment' the Irish Sea is now the most radioactive sea in the world. Many green movement people, including the author, no longer eat fish from the Irish Sea.

What Should be Done

Greenpeace believes that Ireland should take the British Government to the European Court of Justice to force the closure of Sellafield. But successive Irish Governments have refused to do this.

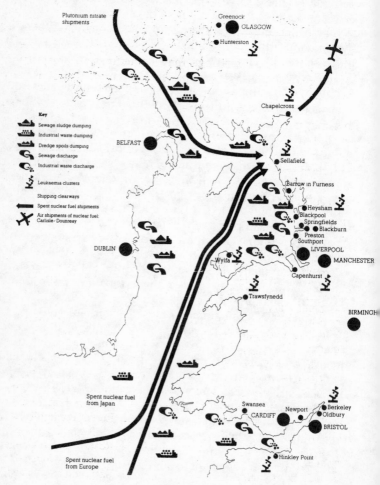

Key

Sewage sludge dumping
Industrial waste dumping
Dredge spoils dumping
Sewage discharge
Industrial waste discharge
Leukaemia clusters
Shipping clearways
Spent nuclear fuel shipments
Air shipments of nuclear fuel: Carlisle / Dounreay

Bathing Water

The map (p.69) shows the bathing areas in Ireland which are monitored by local authorities for water quality under the Bathing Water Directive (76/160/EEC). According to the 1988 results, the vast majority complied easily, but some failed to meet required standards. These included Donabate, Co. Dublin, Burrow Beach, Sutton, Co. Dublin, Bunmahon (Co. Waterford), Laytown/Bettystown (Co. Meath) and of course Blackrock and the Bull Wall in Dublin City.

A number of points need to be made about the monitoring of bathing waters. Firstly, monitoring is not carried out by an independent agency but by the local authorities, who are responsible for sewage discharges—the main source of pollution. Readings on any day depend on wind and tides in the area, so good readings may sometimes be misleading. Many environmentalist groups feel that an independent body would give a far more accurate picture.

Some of the standards are too vague. For example, there exists a parameter for 'Tarry residues and floating material, such as wood, plastic articles, bottles, containers of glass, plastic rubber and other substances, waste or splinters.' The standard states 'no offensive presence.' It has been known for a bathing area to have toilet waste floating on the surface and still comply with the standards.

The list of Ireland's Blue Flag beaches is as follows:

1 Skerries (Dublin)	19 Kilkee (Clare)
2 Portrane (Dublin)	20 Spanish Point (Clare)
3 Donabate (Dublin)	21 Silver Strand (Galway)
4 Malahide (Dublin)	22 Spiddel (Galway)
5 Portmarnock (Dublin)	23 Knock (Galway)
6 Killiney (Dun Laoighaire)	24 Old Head (Mayo)
7 Brittas Bay-North (Wicklow	25 Carrowmore (Mayo)
8 Brittas Bay-South (Wicklow)	26 Bertra (Mayo)
9 Courtown (Wexford)	27 Mulranny (Mayo)
10 Curascloe (Wexford)	28 Keel, Achill (Mayo)
11 Rosslare (Wexford)	29 Keem, Achill (Mayo)
12 Duncannon (Wexford)	30 Ross, Killala (Mayo)
13 Dunmore East (Waterford)	31 Enniscrone (Sligo)
14 Clonee (Waterford)	32 Rosses Point (Sligo)
15 Ardmore (Waterford)	33 Mullaghmore (Sligo)
16 Rossbeigh (Kerry)	34 Rosnowlagh (Donegal)
17 Banna (Kerry)	35 Portsalon (Donegal)
18 Ballyheige (Kerry)	36 Rathmullan (Donegal)

A beach is awarded a Blue Flag when it meets a series of Requirements. Not all of these requirements are obligatory (o) as indicated in the following summary:

Water and coastal quality

• Compliance with the binding micro-biological parameters of the EEC bathing water directive (or national values if stricter) (o). • No industrial or sewage discharges into the beach area (o). • Reliable and frequent monitoring of bathing water (o). • No visible oil pollution (o) • Emergency plans to cope with oil or other pollution incidents. • No algal materials growing or decaying in the beach area (except during or after storms, or on rocks).

Environmental education and information

• Prompt public warning of danger or major pollution (o). • Laws covering beach use put on public display (o). • Information on protected sites and/or rare or protected species publicly displayed and included in tourist information (o). • Information on water quality and sampling points publicly displayed on or close to the beach and/or published in the media with, at a minimum, monthly updates during the bathing season. • Education courses and activities or lectures for the public on the natural environment of the beach area or on health and safety. • Environmental Study Centres or Ecology Centres.

Beach area management and safety

• Beaches to be cleaned daily during the bathing season (o). • Litterbins in adequate numbers, regularly emptied (o). • Strict control of domestic animals in the beach area (o). • Driving or vehicle racing on the beach prohibited (o). • Adequate and clean toilet facilities with controlled sewage disposal (o). • Adequate and operational life-saving equipment (o). • First-aid post and life-guard (o). • Safe access. • Drinking water and telephones. • Facilities for handicapped persons.

The most important criteria for the award of the Blue Flag for Ports are:

Environmental quality of port and surrounding area

• The port to be ecologically integrated in the surrounding environment and not interfere with local fishing activities. • The water surface (and bed) inside the port should be free from visible waste or liquid pollutants and should be regularly inspected. • No untreated waste from residential areas to flow into the port or its surroundings.

Equipment

Ports should be equipped with: • waste bins at disembarcation points; • toilet facilities; • receptacles for used oil for recycling; • facilities for bilge pumping; • water agitation system (if inadequate natural circulation); • telephones, lighting.

Public information and education

• Information on the European Blue Flag to be displayed on the port authority office. • Advice to boat users on safety and on efforts made for the protection of the Environment.

The map shows the location of all the beaches now covered by the European Communities (Quality of Bathing Water) Regulations, 1988 and 1989. Results for individual beaches are available for inspection at the offices of the relevant local authorities.

BEACHES DESIGNATED UNDER E.C. DIRECTIVE

Source: Dept. of Environment

Drinking Water

The water in some Irish taps is far from pure. For example, Dublin Corporation uses a selection of chemicals to 'purify' our water. Water from the reservoir is first treated with aluminium sulphate, dosed at 5ppm (parts per million), which helps to clear particulates out of the water. Another chemical, a polyelectrolyte, is then added to clear even smaller particles; this material and the aluminium sulphate are then left behind. After filtration, the cleared water may be treated with lime to regulate acidity. Flouride is added at 1ppm to help prevent dental caries. Gaseous chlorine dissolved in water is then injected to the supply to disinfect it. The chlorine, at 2ppm and 7ppm, remains in the water to act as a bactericide, should later contamination of the supply occur.

In 1988 plans were drawn up to improve unsatisfactory plants, aimed at complying with the Regulations (Quality of Water Intended for Human Consumption, Statutory Instrument 81 1988). These provide for periodic sampling of over 50 parameters and set maximum admissable concentrations (MAC) for each.

The smaller the water network, the fewer samples are required. For example, for schemes serving 1000 persons, the authorities need only sample twice a year and for smaller units they have complete discretion.

A major problem is the fact that the local authorities are not obliged to give members of the public the results of their drinking water monitoring. Some have even refused this information to public representatives.

Again, this unsatisfactory situation shows that there is a real need for an independent body to carry out the monitoring of supplies.

Aluminium

The drinking water piped to 1.5 million people in the Dublin area, though generally good, contains excessively high levels of aluminium. This is due mainly to inadequate control measures at Dublin's treatment plants. This ought to be a cause for alarm as scientists and doctors have long since been convinced of a link between the dietary intake of aluminium and the incidence of Alzheimer's Disease. Alzheimer's Disease is the most common cause of senile dementia.

The most comprehensive study to date on the incidence of aluminium in water was carried out between October 1987 and March 1988 by Kathryn Young, who works for the Environmental Health Department of Dublin Corporation. Her report, 'Investigation of Aluminium Levels in Dublin's Drinking Water and possible implications for the incidence of Dementia', looked at the four water supplies for the Dublin area and found regular incidents where the aluminium content exceeded the EC mandatory limits.

The greatest problem exists in the Liffey/Poulaphouca supply where 72% of samples exceeded the EC limit, and 98% exceeded the guide value. The Liffey/Leixlip supply had an even higher concentration with 1.1 mgs of aluminium per litre of water. This is probably due to the dumping of aluminium sludge at the Ballymore Eustace plant.

In 1988 there was a slight improvement in aluminium levels in Dublin. However, 25% of samples still exceeded EC limits.

Outside of Dublin, the available data shows that aluminium levels in Donegal, Laois, Louth, Monaghan, Cavan and Athlone exceed EC limits. Sometimes the levels recorded were up to three times the maximum allowable concentration.

Chlorine

Using chlorine gas is the standard method of disinfecting treated water for almost a century. However, when chlorine reacts with peat or nutrient-rich waters the compounds created are suspected of causing cancer. Of particular concern is chloroform from the group of chemicals known as trihalomethanes. Chloroform has been connected to cancer of the bladder, colon and rectum. The US National Research Council has stated that the current limit of $100\mu g/l$ is too high.

Ground Water

Groundwater is the water that is stored in and moves through the pores and cracks in soil and rocks, feeding wells and springs. It is an important national resource. About a quarter of the total water supply in Ireland is groundwater taken by individual households from boreholes, wells and springs. In certain counties, particularly in the Midlands, the proportion is much greater, e.g. Roscommon 86%, Laois 54%, Kilkenny 52% and Wexford 40%. In rural areas where there is no public or group water scheme, ground water is often the only source of supply.

Water Resources	Area km2	Area of Aquifiers km^2	Estimated Abstrac- tions Mm^3/yr	Estimated Surplus Resources	
				Mm3/yr	Mm^3/year over region
Eastern	7,700	1,392	6.08	197.4	26
South-eastern	12,700	4,240	20.70	763.0	60
Southern	11,700	1,475.5	25.15	603.6	52
Mid-western	7,600	2,942.5	8.43	492.1	65
Shannon	10,520	3,124.9	16.69	471.7	45
Western	9,620	4,446	6.23	643.3	67
North-western	9,460	1,245.5	6.30	202.5	21
Total	69,370	18,865.4	89.58	3,373.6	48

Summary of groundwater resources by region Source: An Foras Forbartha

Pollution of Groundwater can be caused by something as simple as the inappropriate location of a septic tank. However, as with surface water, most groundwater pollution occurs through farming activities. The most common farming pollutants are nitrate, ammonia, chloride, sulphate, iron, bacteria and viruses. Groundwater pollution lasts much longer than surface water pollution because groundwater moves slowly. Once polluted it is often impossible to reclaim groundwater.

Half of the water in rivers is normally derived from groundwater sources. During dry periods the proportion of groundwater in rivers and streams can rise to more than 90%. If the groundwater becomes polluted, then the rivers are also affected.

Recent research has shown that it can take up to 40 years for nitrates to seep into the grounderwater. Once there, the damage is often irreversible.

Groundwater pollution is a very serious problem in Ireland. It has been estimated that up to 50% of the wells in Connaught are polluted.

GUARD YOUR DRINKING WATER

The Siting and Construction of Wells

Many wells are polluted because they are located too close to a source of pollution, or are not properly constructed.

As a general rule, wells should be located upslope from and as far away as possible from potential sources of pollution. The safe distance depends on the nature of the subsoil, the depth of the watertable, the slope of the land, the rate of pumping and the size of the pollution source. Suggested safe distances are shown on the table below.

Surface water should not be allowed to run down the well, inside or outside the casing. The ground should be built-up around the well so that there is a gradient of at least 1:4 away from the well. The overburden should be sealed by cement grout or puddled clay.

Oil, fertilizer, pesticides and other chemicals should not be stored or left in the pump-house or close to the well. Leaking tanks of diesel fuel have contaminated some wells in Ireland.

Suggested minimum distances of a well from septic tanks, silage pits, or farmyard slurry					
Depth of overburden or depth to water table	Type of Overburden	Distance from			
		Sceptic Tank		Farmyard and Silage	
Feet *(Metres)*		*Fee t* *(Metres)*		*Fee t* *(Metres)*	
Less than 5 (1.5)	Impermeable Clay	100	(30)	500	(150)
5-10 (1.5-3)	"	80	(24)	400	(120)
10-20 (3-6)	"	60	(18)	300	(90)
20-30 (6-9)	"	50	(15)	250	(75)
Over 30 (9)	"	40	(12)	200	(60)
Less than 5 (1.5)	Sand and Gravel	300	(90)	1,000	(300)
5-10 (1.5-3	"	200	(60)	1,000	(300)
10-20 (3-6)	"	100	(30)	800	(240)
20-30 (6-9)	"	70	(21)	700	(210)
Over 30 (9)	"	60	(18)	600	(180)

Nitrates are the main constituent in artificial or inorganic fertilizers, which help plants and crops to grow. However, up to half the nitrates applied to crops will leach out of the soil into our waterways through either irrigation or rainfall. This can have very serious consequences for water quality over a period of time. It can take as long as 40 years for nitrates to accumulate in the soil and seep into the groundwater. This is why the nitrate problem is often called the 'nitrate time bomb'.

Germany has a severe nitrate problem. Some towns and villages in the intensive agricultural areas import drinking water in large tankers. The nitrate levels in their own water makes it unsafe for human consumption.

Nitrate levels in drinking water in England have also been the subject of much controversy. Many water supplies were found to be in excess of the 50 mg per litre limit permitted under the EC directive. Britain then applied for a derogation and the limit was raised to 80 mg per litre. But many authorities cannot even reach this level.

The Position in Ireland: The nitrate time bomb has been planted in Ireland and, as its name implies, it's only a matter of time before it goes off. One need only look at the figures for nitrate application to know that we face a potentially huge problem. Already in June 1989 six local water supplies in Laois, Offaly and Tipperary had to be closed down because of high nitrate levels. According to the Geological Survey of Ireland (GSI), monitoring of nitrates in water is inadequate. The Department of the Environment are unable to give figures for nitrate levels in water supplies but they assure the public that there is 'no real problem'.

A survey of the wells in the stretch of the Barrow Valley between Athy and Carlow, carried out by Trinity College Environmental Sciences M.Sc. students in April 1987, has shown up a potential problem with nitrate levels. A total of 21 wells were sampled and subjected to a full chemical analysis. Nine of the wells exceeded the EC maximum admissible concentration.

What you can do

- You could invest in a water filtration system. This eliminates most pollutants and toxins. For information: Adrian Hamilton, Lake Park Ltd., 66 Temple Road, Blackrock, Co. Dublin. Tel. 01-892521

Fishfarming

From a green point of view, fishfarming could be described as merely turning one form of fish into another, more expensive one, with a great waste of energy and protein along the way.

Farmed fish are fed rations consisting almost entirely of fish meal made from other fish such as capelin, herring, blue whiting, scad and mackerel, all of which are perfectly edible directly themselves. Negligible amounts of fish offal are used. It takes about 7.5 tonnes of these 'industrial' fishes to make 1.5 tonnes of fishmeal which in turn produces one tonne of salmon. In other words, 87% of the food value of the original fishes is lost, a crime in a protein deficient world.

Fish farming can also be unhealthy for the fish. It is essentially a form of factory farming because the fish are kept in unnatural crowded conditions. The salmon is a territorial fish and it likes to keep its distance from its fellows. It is not surprising then that caged salmon are under considerable stress and very vulnerable to diseases, which on average will kill a third of them.

Another worrying feature of salmon farming is the threat it poses to wild salmon stocks. Most rivers in Ireland have at least one unique strain of salmon, which has evolved since the Ice Age to become ideally suited to the conditions there. Now geneticists are worried that when farmed salmon escape—as they do in large numbers—they will interbreed with native fish, weakening the strain and possibly causing it it to die out.

So far in Ireland, criticism of fish farming has concentrated on its polluting effects—the volume of droppings produced by the cages. In Finland water pollution by fish farms is greater than the combined pollution of the chemical and fertilizer industry. Let us hope that Irish fish farmers have learnt some valuable lessons from the Finnish experience.

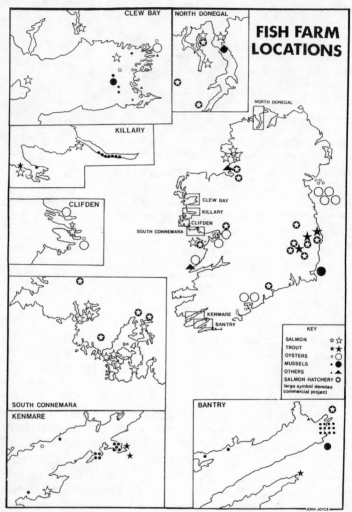

Map by permission of Bord Iascaigh Mhara.

Pollution

It is estimated that one ton of fish produces the same amount of sewage as 300 people; an average 25 tonne fish farm produces the same as over 7,000 people. This matter, along with uneaten food and detritus, sinks to the seabed and forms a black sludge. This sludge putrefies, producing toxic gases like ammonia and hydrogen sulphide which bubble up through the fish cages and which can cause high mortality rates. Four sites in the Outer Hebrides, Scotland, had to be abandoned as a result of this process.

Generally, the criticisms of seacages have been overdone. As fishfarmers point out, their stocks require pure water and will die if they don't get it. As a result, after a few mistakes in the early days, cages are now placed well offshore where there is sufficient water movement to carry the droppings away.

One major marine pollution worry is valid: the use of Nuvan, a potent organophosphorous pesticide which is used to rid the fish of skin parasites which would otherwise kill them. Although Nuvan breaks down in seawater, it many take three or four weeks to do so, depending on water temperature. In the meantime it can do considerable damage to other marine life such as crab and lobster larvae. It remains biologically active at extremely large dilutions. Nuvan is disliked by the fishfarmers as much as by the environmentalists—it is dangerous for their workers and is suspected of causing them to develop cancer—and the industry is frantically looking for a substitute.

Probably of far more serious concern are the antibiotics and the antifungal agents used when the young salmon are in their freshwater cages. These naturally get into the lake water which in most cases is used with minimal treatment as the water supply for nearby towns and cities. Dublin is no exception: the ESB kept young salmon in the Poulaphouca reservoir until recently. Many experts differ about the dangers of antibiotics in drinking water, but all of them are worried about the presence of Malachite green, an anti-fungal agent and suspected carcinogen used in all freshwater farms.

Another chemical used is the 'pinking agent' canthaxanthin. This is used to give the salmon their natural pink colour. Without it the farmed fish would be an unappetising grey colour. It is banned in the USA and thought to be carcinogenic; it is allowed in the EC only to colour salmon flesh and battery eggs.

Annual Consumption Chemical Figures (approx.)

Chemical	Annual consumption	Farm Type
Formalin	250 gallons	Hatchery/Smolt/Rainbow
Malachite Green	40 gallons	Hatchery/Smolt/Rainbow
Nuvan	42 gallons	Salmon

Antibiotics Commonly Added to Fish Feed

Drug	Recommended daily dose of active ingredient in mg/kg body weight	Recommended treatment period in days	Main disease indication
Di-n-butyl tin oxide	250	5	Tapeworms
Furazolidone	110	5–10	Heximita (Octomitus)
Nifurpirinol	0.8-3.5	5–10	Bacterial septicaemias
Oxoline acid	10	10	Bacterial septicaemias
Oxytetracycline	75	5–10	Bacterial septicaemias
Sulphamerazine	110-220	10	Bacterial septicaemias
Trimethoprim/ Sulphadiazine	30	10	Bacterial septicaemias

Concentrations of antibiotics in Fish Farm Effluent

Antibiotic	Concentration in P.P.M.
Chloramphenicol	1 : 6,666,666
Erythromycin	1 : 4,000,000
Oxolinic Acid	1 : 50,000,000
Oxytetracycline	1 : 6,666,666
Potentiated Sulphonamide	1 : 16,666,666

Courtesy: Roderick O'Sullivan

Economics

Aquaculture has grown very rapidly in Ireland from £1.9 million turnover in 1980 to an estimated £40 million in 1989. It accounted for 10% of the output of total seafish industry in 1986 and this will have grown to 40% by 1991.

There are over 200 fish farming units cultivating salmon, trout, mussels and oysters. Salmon accounted for 54% of total farmed fish export value in 1986, having risen from 4% in 1979. Since 1985, Ireland has increased its production of farmed salmon by a factor of eight, a growth rate exceeding that of Norway and Scotland. Irish production of 14,000 tonnes per annum by 1991 is predicted. According to the Irish Salmon Grower's Association, fishfarming currently employs 1,370 people.

WHAT SHOULD BE DONE

• Existing fish farms should have the strictest controls imposed on them. There should be frequent monitoring of water quality by the local authorities.
• There should be a switch to shell fish farming, which presents none of the above problems and dangers.
• There should be more research into and development of 'fish ranching'. In some parts of Norway and Sweden as well as Alaska, salmon are ranched. This is 'free range' fish farming and problem-free when compared with intensive methods.
• The Recommendations of the Task Force on Pollution (see below) should be fully implemented.

WHAT YOU CAN DO

• If there is a fish farm in your area, make sure that the local authorities are keeping a watchful eye on it. Ask that any drinking water in the area be monitored for antibiotics.

SLAUGHTER
The slaughter methods of farmed fish vary. They may be stunned or anaesthised by being hit on the head, eletrically shocked, or placed in a tank with CO_2 bubbling through, before being bled to death.

Special Recommendations by
The Task Force on Pollution and Conservation

(1) The use of Nuvan (Dichlorvos) be banned in the marine until an environmentally acceptable alternative be found.

(2) That an incinerator be set up adjacent to each fish farm site to dispose of dead and diseased fish.

(3) That an independent environmental impact study be carried out on all existing and potential fish farming sites, e.g. fresh water and salt water.

(4) That no further fin fish farming licences be granted until the above study be carried out.

(5) That farm smolts and trout fry be freeze branded, so as detailed records can be kept on each farm in respect of diseased fish, escapees, mortality rate etc., and that these records be monitored by the relevant government departments.

(6) That all farmed fin fish undergo an individual veterinary inspection similar to that carried out in the meat trade at the time of slaughter and processing.

(7) That legislation be introduced to cover the use of chemicals and therapeutics used in fish farming.

(8) That all chemicals and therapeutics be issued on veterinary prescription.

(9) That legislation be introduced setting out withdrawal periods for therapeutics and chemicals used in fish farming.

(10) That fish farming in the marine be subject to planning permission by the local planning authority.

(11) That no further fish farms or land based hatcheries be set up and/or in the catchment area of wild fisheries and/or sources of drinking water and that existing fish farms in any of the above be phased out immediately.

(12) That all farmed fish on sale commercially, should be branded as farmed fish.

(13) That a production limit be imposed on each fish farm company as is applicable in Norway.

(14) That no imports of live salmonoids spawn or eggs be allowed.

(15) That all fish farming industries indemnify the state and private fishery owners against possible losses due to these operations, e.g. disease transfer, genetic pollution, public health etc.

(16) That a national independent body be set up to monitor the operation of fish farming and the issuing of licences. The body shall consist of representatives of all interested parties.

(17) The representatives on the national body shall consist of members elected by their own national organisations.

(18) That all fish farms should produce their own brood stock and that any stripping of wild salmonoids and/or use of spawn, ova, smolts of wild salmon be made illegal for fish farming.

(19) That the source of supply of the raw material for the new fish feed factory in Westport, Co. Mayo, Ireland, be the subject of an environmental impact study as there are fears that if may endanger the food chain of other marine species.

(20) That an immediate special study be carried out on the possible link between the disappearance of sea trout in the Connemara and the South Mayo Region and the development of fin fish farming in the same regions.

(21) That all effluent discharged from fresh water fish farms be totally filtered and that only the filtered water be returned to the water course.

Organisations

(For details see Directory listing at back of book)

Inland water pollution:
An Taisce. Emer Colleran and Jack O'Sullivan. Both are very knowledgeable on sewage treatment and anaer-obic digestion.
Environmental Research Unit (ERU). Paul Toner
Earthwatch. Dom O'Brien.

Coastal pollution:
Dublin Bay Environmental Group. Karen Dubsky
Earthwatch. Dom O'Brien, Marine campaigner.

Nuclear pollution:
Greenpeace. Helen Kingham, Nuclear campaigner.
Earthwatch. Brian Wall, Nuclear campaigner.

Fishfarming: Earthwatch. Dom O'Brien.
Angler's Task Force on Pollution and Conservation. (ATFFC), John Gibbons.

Drinking water:Geological Survey of Ireland
(GSI). Donal Daly.

Books and Publications

Most of the publications on water pollution are quite technical. However, booklets worth getting are *Farm Wastes* and *Dublin Bay*, both available from the ERU. The ERU also has more detailed reports on water quality in Ireland. A lot of information on water quality is also contained in many of the Foras Forbartha reports. The AFF report *The State of the Environment*, is available from the Department of the Environment and has a very good section on water quality. For an interesting and humorous look at the problems of sewage read *The Toilet Papers* by Sim Van der Ryn (Capra Press 1978). Earthwatch have produced a very good report on *Fishfarming* by Dom O'Brien. Another study is available from The Task Force on Pollution and Conservation, written by Mr. Roderick O'Sullivan.

III
SOIL AND FOOD
Soil

Soil is the basis of all life—plant, animal and human. A minuscule quantity, and of the poorest quality, can be enough for some kinds of vegetation and various microorganisms; the higher the form of animal life, the more a healthy soil is needed to sustain it; and if human beings are at the apex, such soil is indispensable to existence.

Richard Body—*Red or Green for Farmers*

By mistreating the soil we are in a sense biting the hand that feeds us. Food production in the USA has decreased since the mid 1970s, when it peaked, and soil erosion is now reaching a crisis point. So much so that the Bush Administration is now advocating a move away from intensive farming toward more traditional methods. Worldwide, soil erosion results in the loss of 27.2 millions acres of farmland annually. With the impending climate changes caused by global warming and the exponential growth in population, soil loss is set to increase. Ecological damage could thus be the prelude to grave food shortages and even world starvation. Those famous lines spoken by an Indian chief and often quoted by Greens may yet come to pass:

'Only when you have felled the last tree, caught the last fish, and poisoned the last river, will you realise that you cannot eat money.'

Moving closer to home, Bedfordshire in England is losing its soil at an average rate of 1 tonne an acre every year. If this soil loss continues the county will be an agricultural wasteland by the next century. As of yet there are no exact figures available for soil loss in Ireland, but there is concern that intensive sheep farming is causing soil erosion in the west. The increased use of fertilizers and pesticides and the removal of hedgerows and trees has also damaged soil fertility. Artificial fertilizers may fertilize the soil, but they cannot replace soil which has been lost, unlike farmyard manure. John Seymour, in his book 'Blueprint for a Green Planet', says that using artificial fertilizer 'is like getting more warmth from a fire by emptying the coal scuttle on it; the fire blazes brightly before burning itself out.'

Certainly, there is a law of diminishing returns at work. Dutch farmers now apply three quarters of a tonne of fertilizer to each hectare of their land each year. Not only is the soil damaged, but pollution of groundwater is often irreparable.

The fact that the nitrate problem is not as acute here as elsewhere in the EC offers this country a unique opportunity to switch over to organic methods of farming with minimum difficulty. The soil is still relatively healthy and the transition period—the time it takes for the soil to regenerate and purify itself—is far shorter than say in Holland or Germany.

The demand for organic produce is now such that supply cannot meet it. This contrasts sharply with food produced through intensive farming, which has given rise to those famous food mountains and wine lakes.

We must recognise that organic farming is the farming of the future. We need to recognise that the basis for healthy food and a healthy environment is healthy soil.

AGRICULTURE

Visitors to this country are often surprised by the lack of crops. The agricultural landscape seems to consist of fields, on which cows and other livestock graze, and very little else. The fact that most farmland is devoted to dairying is certainly the result of government and EC policy. The aim of Irish agriculture policy since 1947 has been the development of an efficient and modern farming sector. Agriculture is now very much integrated into a more industrialised state and this has meant a trend toward intensive farming and bigger farms. The end result has been far more pollution from the agricultural sector, as the dramatic increase in fish kills shows.

Thirty years ago fertilizers, pesticides and insecticides were applied sparingly. Large concentrated units for housing stock hardly existed, and on-farm silage making was unknown. Fields and hedgerows remained almost unchanged and pollution incidents were minor and localised. But things have changed dramatically and often for the worst. The use of artificial fertilizers has increased fourteen fold. The runoff into our waterways can cause eutrophication of lakes (see Inland Water Pollution), intensive pig farming gives rise to severe problems with the disposal of the slurry—much of which ends up in our rivers. Silage making is now widely practised and the effluent is particularly polluting. Herbicides and pesticides, which can cause severe ecological damage, are used freely. In addition to all this, 2.8 million acres of land has been drained, causing damage to wildlife habitats, trees and hedgerows.

Farm Incomes

Yet despite some of the above 'drawbacks', we are often told that agriculture and the agribusiness form an industry which is becoming steadily more efficient. Profits for farmers are supposedly going up. But if you examine the figures, it becomes clear that the bigger farmers are benefiting, not those farmers on small holdings. Farm incomes rose by 20% in 1987, yet 75% of farmers are earning the equivalent of or less than the average industrial wage, while 25% of these are living below the poverty line. The trend in factory farming is concentrating more and more wealth in the hands of fewer farmers. At present there are approximately 100,000 farm units in this country compared with 185,000 in 1973 and it is estimated that in the year 2050 there will be no more than 10,000!

The EC Connection

It is estimated that the EC taxpayer pays an additional 13% on the purchase price of food to maintain the Common Agricultural Policy (CAP). Many people think that the money from the CAP goes directly to the farming community—yet only 20% of these funds remains in farmers' hands, most of it going toward the bigger farmers. The remainder of the EC agriculture budget is spent on artificial fertilizers, pesticides and farm machinery, or goes toward the cost of surplus production (food mountain, etc.).

Fertilizers

The agribusiness relies heavily on soluble nitrogen fertilizers which contain high amounts of nitrates and significantly increase crop yields. Plants need nitrogen to live, but too much nitrogen can pollute. Nitrates, particularly on arable land, accumulate and eventually find their way to the ground water. Water supplies in Holland and Germany have been very badly affected by the 'nitrate bomb' and there are increasing signs that we could be faced with a similar problem (see Inland Water Pollution).

Nitrogen has been shown to reduce the vitamin C content of some vegetables, notably lettuce, spinach and beetroot. Other research indicates that high nitrate intake is potentially carcinogenic. The WHO in its report 'Nitrates, Nitrites and N-nitroso Compounds', said 'N-nitroso compounds are carcinogenic in a wide range of animal species. . . it is highly probable that these compounds may also be carcinogenic in man.'

Because plants grown with heavy amounts of nitrogen fertilizers have a high water content, they are more likely to be attacked by insects and disease.

Pesticides

Because plants grown with heavy amounts of nitrogen fertilizers are more likely to be attacked by pests— those in the agribusiness use pesticides. Traces of pesticides
in food can cause various allergic reactions in many people. DDT, until recently one of the most widely used pesticides, was found to have damaging effects on the nervous system and was withdrawn from sale in 1984.

The WHO has estimated that 50,000 people die in the course of a year of acute pesticide poisoning (many as suicides, many through carelessness). Most of these casualties are the bread winners for Third World families. It has been shown that children whose parents work frequently with pesticides run six times the normal risk of contracting leukaemia.

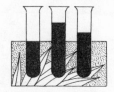

Hormones and Antibiotics

Growth hormones and antibiotics have long been used in stock farming to achieve an early maturity and weight gains in the animals. The use of hormones is now banned in the USA and the EC has also voted against the use of hormones as growth promoters. Despite this hormones are still widely used in this country.

Antibiotics are also used as growth promoters and to control parasitic and fungal diseases in animals. These diseases mainly occur in animals who have been kept in the confined, over-crowded conditions of the modern factory farm. The overuse of antibiotics can also build up resistance to the drugs which could become a problem.

Organic Farming

• Organic farming is environment friendly—no artificial fertilizers, pesticides or antibiotics are used.

• It is labour intensive, which means more jobs.

• The food produced from organic farming is extremely healthy and of the highest quality.

• Unlike factory farms, organic farming provides the animals with proper living conditions.

• Organic farms are very energy efficient. The use of fossil fuels such as oil is kept to a minimum. Also, the organic farm draws upon local resources as far as possible.

Basically organic farming is green philosophy put into practice.

A recent report from the National Academy of Sciences in the USA shows that chemical fertilizers and insecticides do not necessarily result in better crop yields than those of organic methods. The aim of the US Department of Agriculture is now to put 'US farming on an eco-sensitive basis within the life of the Bush Administration'. At present the subsidy structure for US farmers actively discourages them from rotating their crops, because this cuts the official acreage devoted to certain products on which the subsidies are based. But the agriculture department has already broken the link between crop yields and price support, which encouraged US farmers to grow crops for which there was no demand. This is very similar to CAP, which has produced the EC food mountains.

Organic farming is a simple word for what is often a very complex process, demanding discipline and diligence from the farmer. Crop rotation, careful soil analysis, and the planned interaction of crops are all part of organic farming. The vast majority of those presently engaged in organic farming in this country are not Irish. Why the Irish farmer is not attracted to these methods is not clear. It may have something to do with the fact that tillage is associated with lean times and poverty in the folk memory. Many of those with large dairy farms would not condescend to grow their own vegetables.

FEED THE SOIL NOT THE PLANT

What Should Be Done?

The solution to the problems associated with large scale intensive farming is to encourage the organic and biodynamic methods of farming.

Organic Produce

Because of the way organic produce is raised, you may notice slight differences from conventionally grown produce.
- There are sometimes blemishes on the produce due to the fact that pesticides are not used. These blemishes do not affect the nutritional quality or taste of the produce
- There may be insect residue, also because of the pesticide-free growing conditions. This should be washed off
- Organic produce may have a stronger natural aroma
- Produce has a longer shelf life because there is less water in the structure of the plant
- Some produce may be smaller

Organic Farms and Produce

The following Organic Farms, all members of IOFGA, have produce available for purchase.

Abbreviations:

V = Veg. including intensive veg.
F = fruit/soft fruit/apples.
C = Cereals/grain/wheat/rye/oats.
N = Nursery stock/bedding plants/shrubs
F = Flour/oat meal.
Fl = Flowers/dried flowers.
FB = Field Beans.
D = Dairy Products.
E = Eggs.
Ba = Bakery.
AJ = Apple Juice

H = Herbs
B = Beef
P = Pigs
L = Lamb
S = Sheep
Po = Poultry
W = Worm Compost
J = Juice
Dr = Deer
CV = Cider Vinegar
M = Mushrooms

Leinster Earthworm Technology, (G. Evans), Clontall, Drumconrath, Navan, Co. Meath. W.
Cormac Logue, Ballynamuddagh, Grange, Clonmel, Co. Tipperary. V.
Sean Love and Marion Clarke, Hilton Park, Scotshouse, Clones, Co. Monaghan. F.V.H.
Liz Lyons, The Cottages, Seabank, Bettystown, Co. Meath. V.F.Fl.N.
John Magee, Coolroe, Clonegal, Enniscorthy, Co. Wexford. V.
Kathy March, Toobersool, Balbriggan, Co. Dublin. F.V.H.
Hans Mass, The Kitchen Garden, 27 North Street, Skibbereen, Co. Cork. V.H.
Morris Megan, Lislevane, Bandon, Co. Cork. V.F.H.
Marc Michael, Tinna Park House, Kilpedder, Co. Wicklow. V.H.
Michael & Wendy Micklis, Raheen, Piltown, Co. Kilkenny. V.B.H.
Heiner Miller, Holyhill, Ballineen, Co. Cork. F.V.H.
Anthony Miller, Toreen, Dunmanway, Co. Cork. V.H.
Clare Mooney, Killegland, Ashbourne, Co. Meath. V.F.H.
Maggie Moran, Moneygoud Riding and Language Centre, Grange, Co. Sligo.V.F.H.
Patrick & Angela Mulrooney, Manganstown, Kilsheelan, Clonmel, Co. Tipperary. V.
Pat Murtagh, Glyndale, Maynooth, Celbridge, Co. Kildare. V.
G. McBain, Crannagh Castle, Templemore, Co. Tipperary. F.V.
Marcus McCabe, Training Workshop in Horticulture, All Hollows Garden, Dublin 9. F.H.N.V.
John McCormick & Kieran McFerran, Seaview Terrace, Hollywood, Co. Down. V.
Ian McGrigor, Ballintlea, Ventry, Tralee, Co. Kerry. V.F.H.
Ian & Sonia McLennan, Fairbrook, Kilmeaden, Co. Waterford. V.F.
Con McLoughlin, Lettercollum House, Timoleague, Co. Cork. V.F.
Maureen McNally, Kilclare P.O., Carrick-on-Shannon, Co. Leitrim. V.F.
Wendy Nairn, The Arches, Glanmore, Ashford, Co. Wicklow. V.F.H.
Michael O'Connor, Rathpierce, Gorey, Co. Wexford. C.V.
John O'Donovan, Castleview House, Ballincollig, Co. Cork. V.
Gearoid & Christine O'Morohu, Gra-Cre, Killeen, Claregalway, Co. Galway. V.H.F.
Rosette Paxman, Ballycormac House, Aglish, Near Borrisokane, Co. Tipperary. V.H.F.
Yvonne & Pakenham Pim, Furziestown House, Tacumshane, Rosslare, Co. Tipperary. V.F.H.

Dave Robinson, Sonairte National Ecology Centre, The Ninch, Laytown, Co. Meath. V.F.H.
Dave Robinson, Rathbeggan, Dunshaughlin, Co. Meath V.H.
Ulrich Roesler, Wells House, Gorey, Co. Wexford. C.B.V.
Wilhelm & Angelike Rost, Lough Atorick, Moyglass, Co. Galway AJ.CV.
Helga & Heinrich Schedwill, Rainbow, Evcikeens, Boyle, Co. Roscommon. V.F.
C. Smith, Clogher, Westport, Co. Mayo. V.H.F.
Pauline Stafford, Ballyhurst, Taghmon, Co. Wexford. V.
Ulrich Steffan, Meenagh, Kiltyclougher, Co. Leitrim. V.
David Storey, Bleachlands, Oylegate, Enniscorthy, Co. Wexford. V.F.
Philip Tirard, Clashganna Mills Trust, Ballykeenan, Borris, Co. Carlow. V.F.
Elmar Koomans van den Dries, Inisglas Trust Ltd., 'The Deeps', Crossabeg, Co. Wexford. V.
Desmond & Olive Thorpe, Knockroe House, New Ross, Co. Wexford. C.V.L.
Paul van Bree, Glounbrack, Reenascreena, Rosscarbery, Co. Cork. V.F.
George & Walburga Van Ow, Raheenbeg, Geashill, Co. Offaly. C.
Anne & Brian Watson, Ballinrea, Carrigaline, Co. Cork. F.V.H.
Manfred Wandel and Edite Rennings-Wandel, Trawlebawn, Bantry, Co. Cork. V.F.
Richard & Ivan Ward, Fortagusta, Arthurstown, New Ross, Wexford.   L.C.
Jennifer Whyte & Terry Cunningham, Grangebeg, Fethard, Co. Tipperary. V.
Billy Woolfe, Stuke, Ballydehob, Co. Cork. V.
Esther Zyderlaan, Kilebrack West, Loughrea, Co. Galway. F.V.H.

IN TRANSITION:
Paul Clenaghan, 4 Station Rd., Up. Ballinderry, Lisburn, Co. Antrim BT28 2ET C.V.
H. Crampton & P. Quinn, Castleruddery, Donnard, Co. Wicklow. V.
Herbert Kenny, Drumboory, Carrickmacross, Co. Monaghan. B.E.D.

W.W.O.O.F.
means
Willing Workers on Organic Farms

The aim of WWOOF is an ideal Green idea. It is an exchange, insofar as in return for a reasonable amount of help with the workload, Wwoofers expect to receive some practical working knowledge of organic methods and an insight into other aspects of organic holdings, as well as meals and accommodation.

For further information, and list of organic holdings which offer a WWOOF exchange, write to Annie Sampson, Crowhill, Newgrove, Tulla, Co. Clare.

Organic Gardening

There's no better place to begin eco-sensitive husbandry than in your back garden. But beware—organic gardening, while fulfilling and enjoyable, is hard work. It's much easier to use pesticides, weedkillers, and inorganic fertilizers, which is the approach of 'sterile gardening'. Organic gardening avoids these because they get us into a spiral of poison and eventually infertility. Pesticides kill caterpillars and slugs, but they also poison the creatures up along the food chain that feed on them. The same is true of weedkillers which often wipe out all life living on vegetation and also the life forms in the soil. This means that chemical fertilizers have to be used to get anything to grow on the sterile ground, and all of these poisons are then carried through the water system and food chain, polluting along the way.

So what do you do about pests?

You have a number of options, and organic gardeners are coming up with new innovative ideas the whole time. The simple rotation of crops, for instance, prevents the build-up of pests and diseases in the soil.

Organic gardeners also use barriers effectively against a whole range of pests. Discs of carpet under-laid around the stems of cabbages deter the cabbage root fly. You can recycle your plastic bottles by placing them over seedlings to protect them. Cloches when used at egg laying time can keep most airborne pests at bay. If possible, have a wild section in your garden so that birds, frogs and hedgehogs will take up residence. They're sure to look after many pests. Insect predators can be encouraged by planting their favourite host plant.

Soapy water is often used against aphids, or the poisonous plants derris and pretherum will also deal with many pests.

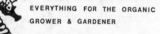

How do I deal with weeds?

Persistent weeds are a problem. Organic gardening is a labour intensive pursuit so be prepared to do a lot of pulling and hoeing. You can also keep weeds at bay by mulching. This basically means covering the ground between the plants with a layer of grass cuttings, compost, cardboard, leaf-mould, newspaper or plastic sheeting—anything that prevents light from getting through. Plastic can also be used beneath gravel paths. Often too weeds can be dealt with quickly by burning them with either a flame gun or a blow lamp.

Based on an article by Fergus Brogan.

BUILDING A COMPOST HEAP
So that your heap receives air from underneath, begin with a layer of branches and twigs several inches deep. If you have any unrotted organic matter on another heap, use this to cover your base layer. On top of this lay all your waste vegetation and all your other waste organic material which will rot down easily—such things as shredded newspapers, egg shells, fish heads and so on. When this layer is nine inches to a foot (23-30 cm) high, cover it with a thin layer of manure, or, if you don't have manure, sprinkle on some highly concentrated nitrogenous substance, such as fish meal or blood meal or urine or a layer of garden soil. On top of this build another layer of organic matter; then another layer of manure etc. Keep the sides fairly straight to begin with, then let them taper inwards to form a peak at the top. If there is no rain, sprinkle water on each layer to keep the heap moist. Tread the heap or thump it with a spade every evening. When the whole heap is built, cover it with a layer of earth.

COMPOST BINS
Compost bins are both convenient and effective. The very best thing is to have three bins, although for a small or medium-sized garden two will be quite adequate, and one is well worth having. Fill one bin at a time, so that you always have one containing mature compost. Bins should be about five feet (1.5m) square and five feet deep, made of seasoned wood, brick, stone or concrete, set in bare earth. The fronts should be removable, and there should be gaps in the sides for ventilation. When a bin is full, cover it with earth, carpet or black plastic.

COMPOST IN CONTAINERS
You can make compost in containers such as perforated oil drums or small wire cages. The ratio of surface area to volume is not ideal in small containers, but the compost is certainly worth having nonetheless.

from *The Essentials of Good Gardening* by John Seymour

What sort of replacements are there for inorganic fertilizers?

This presents you with no problem. Organic gardening is all about feeding the soil not the plant. This feeding is done by adding manure and compost to the soil and letting the worms, bacteria and other micro-organisms convert it into plant food. If you don't have any of your own compost there are many organic fertilizers on the market, made from sea-weed and animal waste. Plants can also be fed with organic compounds such as nettle juice during the growing season.

Foraging is another term which organic growers use. This simply means introducing soil food from outside. Again the most popolar choices for making compost are sea-weed and grass cuttings and hedge cuttings from other people's gardens. It's important to ensure that they haven't been sprayed with chemicals.

Much more information on organic techniques is available from IOFGA.

CITY FARMS

City Farms are as the name suggests—farms within the city—but they have a different emphasis than the ordinary country farm. These farms are usually situated on derelict land, on urban sites varying in size from a half an acre to five acres.

City farms are run for and by the local community with the purpose of rearing animals and growing crops for local benefit, thus providing a basis for understanding the local environment as well as an introduction to the countryside beyond. Such local enterprises or community projects are ones that enhance the recreational amenities of an area while at the same time offering city school children an educational outing to a productive and demonstrative city farm.

City farms create opportunities for local employment as well as providing education and training facilities in a large range of farm activities and in a variety of conservation projects.

From the British (up to 50 city farms) and European mainland experience—land has been restored and buildings renovated—the city has STARTED TO GROW in the real sense of the word.

Farms worthy of a visit are as follows: Reynoldstown House in Naul Co Dublin, Morrell Farm in Kildare, Farrset Community Farm in Belfast and Abington Farm near Limerick. City farms within urban Dublin are in starting stages in the Ballymun and Darndale districts.

For more details phone Eoin Dinan 01-336789

Food

We Are What We Eat

The rise in green consciousness has meant that the consumer now wants clean, pesticide-free, hormone-free food. Food processing means that much of the food we eat contains additives and is less nutritious. Much of the food we eat is responsible directly or indirectly for environmental pollution because modern methods of agriculture are energy intensive and also use a lot of pesticides and artificial fertilizers. Currently there are also fears that more and more food is being irradiated. If we want to live in harmony with nature, then one of the first steps is to choose carefully the type of foods we eat. By not polluting our own bodily systems we are in fact also contributing to a cleaner environment.

Once classed as a fad, health food is now an essential part of making people more aware of their environment. However, just how environment friendly some health food products are is very open to question. The IOFGA symbol is certainly a mark of quality.

'Organic' foods ought to become a daily part of our diets. The green approach to diet favours wholefoods which can be produced directly from the earth, without intensive farming and processing techniques. A lot of emphasis is also given to food locally grown and in season; root and dark green vegetables in winter, and lettuce and locally grown fruit in the summer.

Here Cecilia Armelin, one of Ireland's leading dieticians, outlines the various food groups of wholefoods.

How to introduce
Wholefoods
Into A Healthy Diet
by Cecilia Armelin B.Sc.,
Dietician, National Children's Hospital, Dublin

There is a growing awareness as to the value of 'organic' foods in our daily diet, and these are now more easily available throughout Ireland.

These wholefoods I am referring to are only those that can be produced directly from the earth, without intensive farming and processing techniques. I also emphasise foods that can grow in Ireland, or in other countries with similar weather conditions; that is foods that are locally grown and in season. The food groups of wholefoods are:

Wholegrains:

Oats, barley, wheat, rye, short grain brown rice, millet, buckwheat, quinoa, and long grain brown rice and corn.

All the grains, except the last two, grow either in Ireland or in countries with a similar temperate climate. All grains cook within one hour. It is best to use a heavy pot, such as cast-iron, or a pressure cooker, to allow the grains to cook well from the inside out. Longer cooking, from one and a half to two hours, is required for rice or millet pudding or if digestion is weak.

A pinch of salt, preferably sea salt, should be added at the beginning of cooking to all grains except millet and buckwheat.

Flour Products:

Breads and pastas—using freshly ground flour from a variety of organic grains. Breads are best leavened with yeast or sour dough starter, but even whole grain brown breads have been processed into flour from the whole-grain. They are not quite as good nutritionally, nor do they digest as easily and efficiently. It is best not to use bread or other flour products as often as whole grains.

Legumes or Dried Pulses:

Lentils—brown, green or red.
Peas—green or yellow split peas and marrowfat.
Beans—Aduki, mung, butter beans, haricot, black-eyed, pinto, field beans, kidney beans and chickpeas (garbanzo beans).

A few varieties of peas and beans can be bought cooked, in tins, but the weight of the product includes cooking water and sauce, plus sugar, in most brands. Raw, uncooked beans may be purchased at less than half the cost of the net weight of tinned beans (minus the weight of cooking water, sauce and salt). However, all these varieties of raw beans, except aduki and mung, need to be soaked overnight, drained, boiled rapidly for 10 minutes, froth removed with a large spoon, and then simmered for 1-2 hours or until soft. A pressure cooker reduces the time by half, otherwise heavy cast-iron pots are best. A small strip of kelp or kombu sea vegetable added at the start of cooking also shortens cooking time and adds flavour. Seasonings, such as sea salt and other spices, should not be added until the end of cooking, as they toughen the skins and delay cooking time.

Lentils and dried split peas cook in 20-40 minutes, with the lesser times if soaked overnight or boiled rapidly for 5 minutes and left to soak for one hour. Always drain the pre-soak water, or thoroughly wash lentils, peas and beans before cooking. Thoroughly remove froth that forms during soaking or cooking to prevent legumes being gas forming. All legumes and grains may be stored in a dry place for six months to a year, though cooking time may need to be increased if stored for a long time.

Always cook well—until soft.

Grains + Legumes = Complete Protein equal to that in meat, egg, or dairy products. Barley, Wheat or Rice + Lentils, Beans or Peas = Balance of 10 Amino Acids.

Vegetables

GREEN/LEAFY—cabbage, kale, brussel sprouts, broccoli, spinach, nettles, asparagus, cauliflower, leeks, scallions, dandelion, celery, green beans, artichokes, lettuce, carrot tops, chives, parsley, watercress and rhubarb. Most are good for calcium, vitamin C, and folate B vitamins.

ROOT VEGETABLES—carrots, turnips, parsnips, squash, onions, red radish, white daikon radish, burdock, salsify, mushrooms and potatoes.

SEA VEGETABLES—dillisk, carrageen, kelp, kombu and nori. Add kelp or kombu to beans during cooking for flavour and to shorten cooking time. They are good for calcium. Nori is good toasted over a flame or grill and added to foods as vegetables, rice, or 'flapjacks'. Carrageen is good for making jellied desserts. All are good added to soups.

Fruits

It would be particularly good to see Ireland grow more local varieties of fruit. Many of the imported varieties, such as citrus, are grown in hot countries, are more 'juicy', and have a cooling effect on the body which is not necessary with the already cool Irish weather. The Irish seasonal fruits are:

SUMMER—berries and currants such as strawberries, raspberries, red and blackcurrants.

AUTUMN—apples, pears, plums and damsons. Dried fruits are good for extra concentrated energy. Pickled fruits and vegetables store well and are especially good for winter meals.

Fruits cooked with sea salt are warming and easier to digest.

Nuts and Seed

Hazelnuts, walnuts, chestnuts, and sunflower seeds are particularly recommended for extra protein and fat (including essential fatty acids for the immune system).

In Ireland up to the early seventies there was a hope by many that the Irish people could produce much more local produce and potentially be able to survive on a diet of foods that were all grown from the Irish soil or sea.

The earth's soil and water are precious gifts, preserved for us from previous generations. They will continue to provide for our present young generation and their future generations of children if we respect their natural ability and don't abuse the soil and waterways with chemicals from intensive farming, industrial and domestic waste.

Beverages

Herbal Teas or Grain Coffee made from barley. Juices from locally grown fruits and vegetables, ideally organic. Spring water.

Balanced Meals

I include below examples of 3 meals that include primarily wholefoods:

Breakfast: Porridge of whole oats (groats), pinhead or jumbo flakes; or muesli of jumbo flakes of grains, nuts, seeds and dried fruit; and apple or pear juice, or milk.

Dinner: Brown rice, wholemeal pasta or millet with beans, peas, lentils or *fish or*free range egg occasionally, green and root vegetables. Fruit/yogurt, or pie or crumble dessert made with wholemeal flour or jumbo flakes.

Tea: Barley, lentil and vegetable soup with dillisk, flavoured with soya sauce, thyme and parsley or other herbs; or cold brown rice, millet salad, wholemeal brown bread or pasta and *Irish Farmhouse cheese, steamed vegetables, nuts and seeds. Pudding of short grain brown rice and/or millet with fruit, nuts, seeds and/or *live Bulgarian yogurt.

The recommended percentage portions of foods are:
50-60% wholegrains and their products
5-10% fruit, nuts, seeds and oil
25-30% vegetables
5-10% legumes, fish and sea vegetables

There is a wide variety of wholefood and vegetarian cookery books available in most bookstores and health food shops. Also a wide selection of wholefoods are now available in supermarkets around Ireland, and even local shops are carrying an increasing variety. However, health food shops carry the complete range of wholefoods, grains, legumes, fruits, nuts, seeds and sea vegetables at most reasonable prices. Many shops and supermarkets also carry a good selection of 'home-made' breads, crackers, rice cakes, biscuits, juices, jams and sweets that are free of sugar and 'E' additives.

Products from organically grown grains, fruits and vegetables and naturally preserved snack foods and sauces may cost more than the 'man-made' manufactured products, but overall meals will be cheaper than depending only on foods that are heavily processed, and the 'personal health bill' will be less.

As the world was created, food was made available locally for each population's ideal nutritional needs using sun, sea, soil to provide vitamin D (sun), fish and sea vegetables (sea), grains, legumes, vegetables and fruit (soil).

This will continue if we the consumers promote more Irish grown foods and do not lose contact with our Natural Resources.

First published in 'Common Ground'—the magazine for alternative living.

---

* foods good for vitamin B_{12}, and calcium including quality organic vegetables daily, oily type fish and oysters.

Additives

Nowadays consumers are more likely to scrutinise a packet or tin for the list of ingredients. The 'E' list of additives, which has received a lot of publicity lately, was devised for the EC in order to harmonise laws of importation within the Community.

Additives with an 'E' number are those generally recognised as safe by the EC. Yet, in practice, many of these are found to provoke a reaction sometimes, especially in young children and babies.

All foods for export in Ireland must now list additives by name or the appropriate 'E' number. Flavourings are an exception to the rule since they are considered to be 'trade secrets'.

Most of the common additives in the list given here are known to cause allergies or intolerant responses in some people, like asthma, eczema and other rashes, hayfever, blurred vision, hyperactivity and stomach upsets. Some are also irritant or corrosive and are known to cause problems like skin rashes.

According to the magazine *Environment Now*, the average person conusmes 12 lb of food additives and a half a gallon of pesticide evey year.

WHAT SHOULD BE DONE

• Labelling needs to include all additives, and suspect additives need to be highlighted.
• There are 25 additives for which there is evidence of toxicity (see list)—these should be banned.
• There should be severe restrictions on an additional 32 suspect additives.

WHAT CAN YOU DO?

• Read the list of additives below and take note of those which are particularly harmful.
• Always read the labels on packets and tins and avoid those which seem to consist of Es.
• Above all else try to eat as much fresh food as possible.

Additive	Common Foods	Comments
Colours		
E 101 Riboflavin (B2 Vitamin)	Processed Cheeses	No adverse effects known.
AZO/Synthetic Coal Tar Dyes	Used widely in food containing fats, foods such as: desserts, sweets, juices, soups, sauces, vegetables, fruits and shells of capsules.	People sensitive to aspirin and asthmatics are particularly susceptible. Adverse reactions include eczema, urticaria skin rash, wheezing, hyperactivity and wakefulness at night.
• E 102 Tartrazine Yellow		
• E 104 Quinoline Yellow		
• 107 Yellow 2G		
• E 110 Sunset Yellow		
• E 122 Carmoisine (Red)		
• E 123 Amaranth (Red)		
• E 124 Ponceau 4R (Red)		
• E 127 Erythrosine		
• 128 Red 2G		
• E 131 Patent Blue V		
• E 132 Indigo Carmine		
• 133 Brilliant Blue		
• E 142 Green S		
• E 151 Black PN		
• 154 Brown FK (Kipper Brown)		
• 155 Brown HT (Chocolate Brown)		
• E 180 Pigment Rubine		
• Contain AZO Chemicals		
Other Colours		
E 141 Chlorophyllins (Green)	Used in processed vegetables, oils and dairy products.	Average intake may exceed recommended levels.
E 150 (a) Caramels (Brown)		
E 160 (a) Alpha-Carotene		
E 160 (b) Annatto (Yellow/Orange)		
Preservatives		
Benzoic Acid & Benzoates E 210 - E 219	Used in jams, fruit juices, desserts, tinned fruit, salad cream, yoghurt and sauces.	The benzoates and sulphites may cause reactions in those who have asthma or recurrent urticaria (skin rash). Sulphites are banned in restaurants in U.S.A.

Sulphur Dioxide and Sulphites E 220 - E 227	Used in jam, fruit juice, beer, wine, sausage meat, dried vegetables and fruits.
Biphenyl (Diphenyl) E 230	Synthetic preservative — antifungal. Used onskins of citrus fruit.	Workers report nausea, vomiting and irritation to eyes and nose. Restricted in most European countries. Not permitted in baby foods. Potentially carcinogenic.
Nitrates and Nitrites E 249 - E 252	Used in smoked sausages, bacon, ham, cooked meats, tinned meats and cheese.
Propionic Acid & Propionates E 280 - E 283	Used in cakes, biscuits, breads and pizzas.	Banned in West Germany and Switzerland; the U.K. Bakers' Union has advised members not to use Calcium Proprionate (E 282).

Antioxidants

Ascorbic Acid (Vitamin C) E 300 - E 304	Used in fruit drinks, jams, butter, beer, powdered milk and dried potatoes and meat colour preservative in sausages and cooked meats.	E 301 and E 304 are prepared synthetically. No known toxicological problems in standard doses.
Tocopherols (Vitamin E) E 306 - E 309	Used in vegetable oils, packet dessert topping and sausages.	E 307 – E 309 are prepared synthetically.
Gallates E 310 - E 312	Used in breakfast cereals, margarine, oils, crisps, and dried potatoes.	All alkylgallates can cause gastric irritation and other problems for people sensitive to aspirin and asthmatics.
BHA and BHT E 320 - Butylated Hydroxyanisole E 321 - Butylated Hydroxytoluene	Used widely in foods containing fats, especially butter, margarine, oils and crisps.	Can increase the lipid and cholesterol levels, increase the breakdown of vitamin D in the liver and cause rashes.

Emulsifiers and Stabilizers

Lecithins E 322	Used widely in foods containing fats, soft margarine, cakes and confectionary.	Most commercial lecithin obtained from soya beans. No known toxicological effects.
Carrageenan E 407	Used in ice-cream, cakes, desserts, cheeses and frozen meals.	Reported to aggravate ulcerative colitis and may be carcenogenic, especially in liquid form.
Locust Bean Gum E 410	Used in packet salads, dessert mixes, sauces, soups and ice-cream.	No known adverse effects except in excessive quantities

Guar Gum E 412	Used in packet salads, dessert mixes, sauces, soups and ice-cream.	No known adverse effects except in excessive quantities.
Sorbitol & Mannitol E 420, E 421	Sweetening and texturizing agent for low sugar diabetic sweets and desserts.	Excessive amounts can cause flatulence, abdominal distension and diarrhoea.
Flavour Enhancers Glutamates 621 Monosodium Glutamate (M.S.G.) 622 Potassium Glutamate 623 Calcium Glutamate	Used in soups, snacks, sausages and frozen meals.	M.S.G. can cause Chinese restaurant syndrome with symptoms of heart palpitations, dizziness, nausea and migranes. Under consideration by the E.E.C. for a 'E' prefix.
Bleaching Agents Chlorine and Bromate 924 - 926	Bleaching and improving agents for flour, fats and oils, antibacterial and antifungal preservative.	Prepared synthetically. Destroys much of the Vitamin E.

In practical terms, the 'E' numbers I find most intolerant in patients with eczema, asthma, hyperactivity, urticaria or headaches, are among the first three groups of additives:
1) AZO + Coal Tar Dye (E 102 – E 155)
2) Preservatives (E 210 – E 230)
3) Antioxidants (E 310 – E321)

Also, when a child is admitted to hospital with asthma, bronchitis or other chest infections, the foods most requested by the patient to his parents are coloured sweets (dyes), juices and mineral drinks (preservatives) and crisps (antioxidants). It can be difficult for nurse, caterer, or dietitian to persuade the mother not to give the child's most requested foods unless strict hospital rules are established and agreed to by all hospital medical staff.

REFERENCES

1. E for Additives — The Complete E Number Guide by Maurice Hanssen, 1984
2. Good Enough to Eat —pamphlet by Thames Television, 1985.
3. 'Colourings and Preservatives in Food' by W.H.B. Denner. Human Nutrition: Applied Nutrition, 38A, No. 6, 1986.

Food Irradiation

Question: How do you dispose of nuclear waste—in particular caesium-137, a by product of nuclear reactors making plutonium for nuclear weapons?

Answer: Use it to irradiate foods for human consumption.

Irradiating food means exposing it to 'Ionising Radiation'. This process stops food decaying in the normal way without having to go through the other preservation techniques of freezing, canning or bottling. After irradiation potatoes won't grow eyes, even in direct sunlight. Onions don't sprout and mushrooms don't shrivel. It's no wonder then that there's an extremely strong pro-irradiation lobby within the food industry. This lobby has constantly tried to play down the sinister side of food irradiation. But see 'Food Irradiation Fact Sheet', produced by National Coalition to Stop Food Irradiation (CSFI), PO Box 59-0488, California, and repoduced here.

On 21 June 1989 Britain joined Belgium, Denmark, Spain, France, Italy and the Netherlands and lifted its ban on the irradiation of foodstuffs. This is in line with an EC directive which permits the irradiation of food. Ireland too would appear to be sympathetic to the EC position. A recent report from the Food Safety Advisory Committee approved of food irradiation. And yet, along with Greece and Portugal, we have no legislation on this issue. Food must be 'of nature, substance, and quality demanded by the consumer' according to our statute books.

In Ireland opposition to food irradiation has been led principally by Professor Paul McNulty of the Agricultural and Food Engineering Department in UCD. His arguments on the subject are extremely convincing. He believes that the high radiation levels permitted under the EC directive give cause for real concern. The directive forms part of the legislation related to the Single Market after 1992, allowing the free movement of goods and services. In its present form the directive permits a radiation exposure of up to 7 grays (Gy). The US Food and Drug Administration does not permit levels higher than 1 Gy.

Because of insufficient labelling, it's likely that many of us have eaten some irradiated food, which has been imported. Irradiation is difficult to detect and no legislative controls can be used to keep treated foodstuffs out of the country.

WHAT SHOULD BE DONE

- Food irradiation should be banned.
- Foods which are irradiated should be clearly labelled.
- Ireland should object to the EC directive.

WHAT CAN YOU DO?

- Avoid certain imported foods such as strawberries, which are most certainly irradiated.
- Ask your local shop or supermarket not to stock irradiated food.
- Ask your local TD what he/she is doing to stop the importation of irradiated food.

Food Irradiation Fact Sheet

Issued 1986 by the National Coalition to stop Food Irradiation (CSFI), PO Box 59-0488, San Francisco, CA 94159

1. Food irradiation is a technology designed to use radioactive WASTE PRODUCTS FROM WEAPONS MANUFACTURE to extend the shelf life of meats, grains, herbs and spices.

2. It is projected that by 1987 there will be 20,000 tons of high-level waste buried in temporary storage sites in the U.S., with a LIFE-SPAN OF 250,000 YEARS. Cesium-137 is the most radioactive of these waste materials, and the one promoted by the Department of Energy for food irradiation.

3. The process involves sending food on a conveyor belt into a concrete chamber where it is exposed to radiation for one or two minutes. The doses are 100,000 to 3,000,000 times that of a chest x-ray.

4. The food does not become radio-active, unless there is equipment or human error, but electrons are knocked out of orbit and massive molecular rearrangement takes place.

5. It is completely UNLIKE MICROWAVE, which does not possess sufficient energy to split apart molecules.

6. VITAMINS A, C, E, K, B1, B2, B3, B6 and folic acid are depleted or destroyed. The AMINO ACIDS tryptophan, cysteine, phenylalanine and methionine are broken down. FATS create very toxic chemicals. NUCLEIC ACIDS AND ENZYMES are adversely affected. Damaging FREE RADICALS are formed.

7. New chemicals called UNIQUE RADIOLYTIC PRODUCTS (URPS) are formed in the foods. Most URPS are unknown and untested.

8. AFLATOXIN, a highly carcinogenic substance produced by moulds, is produced in greater quantities in irradiated food.

9. BOTULISM is not killed by radiation, but its natural enemies are. Food may be contaminated without any warning smell.

10. STUDIES FROM AROUND THE WORLD have shown adverse effects when animals have been fed irradiated food. Some of of these are: tumours, cataracts, kidney damage, chromosome breakage, fewer offspring, and higher mortality.

11. Irradiation can cause MUTATIONS of disease-producing organisms.

12. Irradiated food can become RE-CONTAMINATED if not sealed properly, undermining its primary purpose.

13. Irradiation will NOT REDUCE THE USE OF CHEMICALS in food. It is applied after harvest, so all the chemicals used in growing the food will continue to be used. No one knows what will happen when the RESIDUES ARE IRRADIATED. In addition, other chemicals will be added to counteract the undesirable changes in texture, odour and flavour created by the irradiation process.

14. Hundreds or thousands of irradiation facilities will need to be built, many in highly populated areas. The permitted radioactive emissions are TWENTY TIMES HIGHER than nuclear power plants. The extremely high level of radiation involved will threaten workers and communities. Several serious accidents have already occurred. Emergency care and evacuation plans are seriously inadequate.

15. Cesium-137 is stored in a water-soluble form. A small leak into the ground water could IRREVERSIBLY CONTAMINATE the environment and work its way up the food chain.

16. There will be a great increase in the amount of RADIOACTIVITY MOVING ALONG THE NATION'S HIGHWAYS. The Department of Transportation has fewer than twenty inspectors of hazardous cargo for the entire country. Many transportation accidents have already occurred.

17. For irradiation to work, agriculture will become more CENTRA-LIZED to the detriment, once again, of the small farmer. Regional production will change. Plant species will be hybridized to facilitate radiation tolerance, increasing crop vulnerabilities.

18. Irradiated food will NOT FEED THE STARVING of the world. Hunger is an economic and political issue, not a technological one.

19. Taxpayers have financed almost the entire nuclear industry, including nearly $100 million for studies, research and development of food irradiation. Taxpayers will bear the cost of subsidizing the sale of cesium-137, transportation, regulation, and clean-up of accidents. They will also carry the economic burden of health problems caused by a diet of irradiated food. And, IRRADIATED FOOD WILL COST MORE—2¢ - 24¢ per pound, according to food processors.

20. There are SAFER, CHEAPER, VIABLE ALTERNATIVES for decontamination. Some of these are: Carbon dioxide fumigation, heat and cold treatments, and infra-red.

1. Only 'whole' irradiated foods such as fruits and vegetables are required to be labelled, not the irradiated ingredients of processed products which will comprise 80% of irradiated foods. There are NO PENALTIES in the Federal Drug Administration rule for failing to comply with labelling requirements. The FDA has no list of irradiators or irradiated foods. They have only twenty-two offices in the country.

2. There is NO WAY TO DETERMINE if a food has been irradiated, or at what dosage, or how many times.

Pesticides

Today's fruit and vegetables may be larger and look better, but they also contain more water, have less taste and have been sprayed with pesticides.

We are, of course, constantly assured that the chemicals sprayed on our food are harmless, but more and more evidence shows that some pesticides can cause cancer. The chemical daminozide, commonly known as Alar, is used in Ireland to improve colour, increase yield, and extend the shelf life of apples. In the USA the Environmental Protection Agency has moved to have Alar withdrawn as there is an 'inescapable and direct correlation' between the use of Alar and 'the development of life-threatening tumours'. In a UK study carried out by Parents for Safe Food, Alar was found in five out of six brands of apple juice tested, as well as in Heinz pure fruit baby food and Cow and Gate apple dessert. These products are also available in Ireland.

More recently the chemicals Maneb, Zineb and Mancozeb, all fungicides used against potato blight and several other plant diseases, have also been linked to cancer. Collectively these chemicals are known as the 'EBDC' group of fungicides and also include Dithane and others. According to the Central Statistics Office, over 1,600 tonnes of these sprays, worth nearly £6.5m, were used in Ireland in 1988. Dick Ahlstrom, the science correspondent with *The Irish Times*, has suggested that the continued use of the three fungicides could directly result in a significant rise of cancer cases here.

The pesticide regulations in Ireland are based on EC directives. The EC Pesticide Residues (Fruit and Vegetables) Regulations, enacted by the Minister for Agriculture and Food in May 1989, limits the residues of certain listed pesticides on various fruit and vegetables, but many consider the levels permitted to be far too high. Neither Alar nor the 'EBDC' group appear on this list. In other words, you can use as much of these chemicals as you like. Several pesticides such as Lindane, Malathion, Atrizine, Maleic Hydrazide and Paraquat, which are banned or severely restricted elsewhere, are freely available in this country.

Generally, the attitude at official level to pesticide control could be described as complacent. Unless a chemical is proven to be harmful it is assumed to be safe. But many are not safe and the assurances from Government sources that these residues do not appear in foodstuffs have been shown to be false. A recent study carried out by Friends of the Earth in Britain confirmed that residues were found in all foods tested.

The message would seem to be clear: safe food is organic food.

WHAT SHOULD BE DONE

• Food products should be clearly labelled if they contain pesticides in the same way that other health warnings are given.
• Commercial operators must be trained in the use of sprays and equipment and issued with permits only when they have passed a State test.
• A tax should be levied on pesticides and the revenue from it used to research the effects of these chemicals and the substitution of gentler alternatives.
• The use of any pesticide which is the subject of a safety review should be banned until it can be proved to be safe.
• Organic agriculture should be encouraged (see SOIL)

> 6,000 new chemicals have been introduced
> into food manufacturing in the last decade.

WHAT YOU CAN DO

• Ask your shop to stock organic produce.
• If you have a garden keep your use of chemicals to a minimum.

DIETARY THERAPY

What we eat obviously affects our health. Many health problems can be caused by an inappropriate diet. We may be allergic to certain foods without knowing it. A consultation with a dietary therapist will usually get to the root cause of the problem. For more information on dietary therapy contact:
Bernadette Connolly Martin, 'Slainte', Eaton Wood, Shankill, Co. Dublin. Tel. 822132

Health Food Outlets

ACKLOW (Co. Wicklow)
New Delhi, 11 Uper Main Street
ASHBOURNE (Co. Meath)
Pepperwood Traders Ltd.,
Coolfore, 01-354310
ATHLONE (Co. Westmeath)
The Honey Pot Health Food
Shop, Sean Costelloe Street,
902-72965
BLACKROCK (Co. Dublin)
Naturesway Naturecure
Centre, Unit 51, Superquinn
Shopping Centre, 01-886696
BLANCHARDSTOWN
see under Dublin 15
BLESSINGTON (Co. Wicklow)
The Natural Medicine Co.,
Broughton, Lacken, 045-65575
BRAY (Co. Wicklow)
Health is Wealth, 1c
Queensboro Road, 01-861773
The Nut Keg, Quinnsboro
Shopping Centre, Quinnsboro
Road, 01-861793
CARLINGFORD
Carlingford Pharmacy,
The Square, 042-73259
CARLOW (Co. Carlow)
The Honey Pot Health Food
Shop, Tullow Street House,
Tullow Street, 0503-32080
(Deirdre & Sean Hutchinson)
Country Table,
Hanover Shopping Centre,
Tumnery Trading Ltd,
Tullow Street House,
Tullow Street.
CASTLEBAR (Co. Mayo)
Heneghans Health Food Centre,
Ellison Street,
CAVAN (Co. Cavan)
Harvest Health Foods, 80,
Main Street, 049-32229
Back to Nature, Main Street,
049-61019
(Christine McGuinness)
CELBRIDGE (Co. Dublin)
Blake's Pharmacy, Main Street,
01-271141
CLAREMORRIS (Co. Mayo)
Hanleys Health Store,
Dalton Street
CLONAKILTY (Co. Cork)
Anne-Marie McCarthy, 19
Western Road, 023-33828
CLONDALKIN
see under Dublin 22
CLONMEL (Co. Tipperary)
The Honey Pot Health Food
Shop, Rainbow Warehouse,
Abbeygate Street, 052-21457
(Jim Sandvoss)
Abbey Restaurant, Abbey Street

CLONTARF
see under Dublin 3
CORK (Co. Cork)
Cork Health Studios, 6, Coach
Street, 021-273155
Natural Foods, Paul Street,
021-508244 (Wendy O'Byrne)
Natural Health Store,
13-14, Wilton Shopping Centre,
Naturesway Naturecure
Centre, Unit 5, City Car Park,
021-276553
The Health Food Centre,
66, Grand Parade Market,
021-272068
Andrew Ryan, 11 Castle Street,
021-271866
Brian Sullivan, Unit 25c,
Southside Industrial Estate,
021-968430
Uni-vite, 104 Oliver Plunket Str.
021-276968
DONEGAL (Co. Donegal)
Tirconaill Nature Products,
Main Street, 073-21025
DROGHEDA (Co. Louth)
Stockwell Delly,
Stockwell Street,
DRUMKEERIN (Co. Leitrim)
Drumduffy Wholefoods,
DUBLIN
1
The Secret Garden Restaurant,
10, Little Mary Street,
01-730117
Clery's Department Store,
(health section),
O'Connell Street, 01-786000
Country Harvest, 11,
Castleforbes Industrial Estate,
Upper Sherriff Street, 01-366406
Easons Health Department,
Easons, O'Connell Street,
01-733811
Fitzers at the Point Restaurant,
Point Depot,
The General Health Food
Store, 93, Marlborough Street,
01-743290 (Derek Kelly)
Independent Cambridge
Counsellor, 7, Bachelors Walk
Naturesway Naturecure
Centre, Unit 33, ILAC Centre,
Moore Street, 01-728391
Tony Quinn Health Centre,
Eccles Street 01-304998
2
FitzPatrick's, 40a, Camden
Street, 01-753290
Asia Markets,
30, Drury Street, 01-779764
Blazing Salads (Restaurant),
19b, Powerscourt Town House
Centre, 01-794292

Caspian Foods (Takeaway),
26, South Richmond Street,
'Ceres', 19b, Powerscourt Town
House Centre, 01-794292
Cornucopia, 19, Wicklow
Street, (has tea room) 01-777583
(Nigel & Deirdre McCafferty)
The Coffee Bean (Restaurant),
4, Nassau Street, 01-797140
Cranks Wholefoods, Bewleys,
11-12, Westmoreland Street,
Down to Earth, 73, South Great
Georges Street, 01-719702
Dublin Food Co-op, Saint
Andrews, Pearse Street,
FitzPatrick's restaurant,
National Art Gallery, Merrion
Square,
Green Acres Natural Foods, 9,
Fleet Street, 01-710880
(Helen Heapy)
Naturecure, Naturesway centre
St Stephen's Green Centre,
St Stephen Green
The Peoples Kitchen, Dublin
Resource Centre, Crow Street
3
Doyles Pharmacy, 3, Vernon
Avenue, Clontarf, 01-333269
Fairview Diet & Nutrician
Centre, 2, Saint Aidan's Park
(Roger) 01-338414
4
Lansa Importers Ltd., 68,
Merrion Road, 01-680416
5
Mrs. Adams, Pharmacy,
Watermill Road, 01-313831
6
Horizon Health, 11,
Sallymount Avenue, Ranelagh,
01-960331
John G. Bourke, 220, Lower
Rathmines Road, 01-971650
Good Bodies, 10, Orwell Street,
Rathgar
The Grape 'n Grain, 9, The
Triangle, Ranelagh, 01-962229
What on Earth, 255, Harold's
Cross Road, 01-968111 (Jim
Dempsey)
7
Newsleaf Wholefood Co., 35,
East Arran Street, 01-727587
Fibre Food Co. Ltd., 27, Manor
Street, 01-386350
Manor Health Store, Manor St.
8
Greenfields Fruit & Veg., 455,
South Circular Road, 01-537817
9
Bell Health Products, 156,
Botanic Avenue, Glasnevin,
01-304002

10
Wholefoods Wholesale Ltd.,
Unit 2D, Kylemore Industrial
Park, Killeen Road, 01-262315
11
Perrans Distributors Ltd.,
Saint Margaret's Road, Finglas,
01-341782
12
Uni-Vite, Unit 11B, Parkmore
Industrial Estate, 01-505131
The Health Food Hut, Unit 11
(upstairs), 78, Walkinstown
Road
13
R.N.J. Health Food Shop,
Donaghmede Shopping
Centre, 01-476181
14
Granny's Kitchen,
The Shopping Mews,
7, Main Street, Dundrum,
01-986319
15
Nature Store, Main Street,
Blanchardstown, 01-204266
22
Cadden, Vera, Unit 1, Tower
Shopping Centre, 01-573794
24
Kelkin, Whitestown Industrial
Estate, Tallaght, 01-520377
Granny's Kitchen, Town
Centre, Tallaght
Tony Fords, Tallaght Town
Centre, 01-512357
Herbalife, 17, Tyman Lawn,
Old Bawn, 01-511742
Herbalife, 11, Cois na hAbhann,
Old Bawn, 01-523896
DUNDALK (Co. Louth)
The Tony Quinn Health Centre,
18, Jocelyn Street, 042-38097
DUNDRUM
see under Dublin 14
DUN LAOGHAIRE
(Co. Dublin)
Perrans Distributors Ltd.,
29, Granitefield, 01-857081
Country Cellar, 8, Patrick Str.
Earth Works, 96, Lower
Georges Street, 01-809891
Food for Thought Restaurant,
56, Lower Georges Street
ENNIS (Co. Clare)
Open Sesame, 29, Parnell Str.
ENNISCORTHY (Co.Wexford)
Spice of Life,
054-33204 (Brenda Wall)
ENNISKILLEN
(Co. Fermanagh)
Health Wise, Imperial Arc,
Townhall Street, Enniskillen
080365-22022
FINGLAS
see under Dublin 11

GALWAY (Co. Galway)
Healthwise Ltd., 4, Lower
Abbeygate Street, 091-68761
Honeycombe Health Shop,
Abbeygate Street
GLASNEVIN
see under Dublin 9
GLENAGEARY (Co. Dublin)
Le Gourmet Wholefoods, Unit
1, Adelaide Court, Lower
Albert Road, 01-608608
GLENTIES (Co. Donegal)
Simple Simons, Mullantiboyle
GREYSTONES (Co. Wicklow)
Nature's Gold Wholefoods,
1, Killincarrig Road, 01-876301
KENMARE (Co. Kerry)
The Pantry
KILKENNY (Co. Kilkenny)
The Good Earth, 13, Kieran Str
056-65448 (Abbas Ghadimi)
KILLARNEY (Co. Kerry)
Munster Wholefoods,
Knockaderry, Farrenfore,
(Keily's Superstore)
LETTERKENNY (Co. Donegal)
Natural Way, 47A, Lower Main
Street, 074-21637
LIMERICK (Co. Limerick)
Cassidy's Family Pharmacy,
William Street, 061-46598
Eats of Eden, Lower Cecil Str,
061-49400 (Nancy Flaxman)
The Grove, Upper Cecil Street,
LOUGHLINSTOWN (Co. Dublin)
Unique Foods Ltd, Unit 4,
Loughlinstown Village Centre,
MONAGHAN
(Co. Monaghan)
Naturesway Naturescure
Centre, Church Street,
047-82882
MOYCULLEN (Co. Galway)
Feamainn Maghcuillinn Teo
(Seaweed) Ltd., Kylebroghlan,
091-851122
MULLINGAR (Co. Westmeath)
Nuts and Grains, Grove Street
NAVAN
Next to Nature, Brews Hill
NENAGH (Co. Tipperary)
Country Choice, 25, Kenyon St.
NEW ROSS (Co. Wexford)
Good Inside Harbour,
Shopping Centre, The Quay,
051-22506
PORTLAOISE (Co. Laois)
Dunne's, 83 Main Street,
0502-21965
The Fruit and Nut Place,
Tara Court, 0502-33313 (Home)
22239 (Shop) [Statia & Dick
Wellwood]
PORTMARNOCK (Co. Dublin)
Cleary's Pharmacy, Unit 2,
Strand Centre, Strand Road,
01-461466

RAHENY see under Dublin 1
RANELAGH
see under Dublin 6
RATHMINES
see under Dublin 6
SKERRIES (Co. Dublin)
Irish Health and Beauty
Products, Churchfield,
01-490305
SKIBEREEN (Co. Cork)
Grape and Grain,
SLIGO (Co. Sligo)
Tir na nOg, Grattan Street,
071-62752 (John and Mary
McDonnell)
Truffles Restaurant,
c/o The Old Coffe Bean,
The Mall
STILLORGAN (Co. Dublin)
Unit 41, Shopping Centre,
01-832221
SWORDS (Co. Dublin)
The Nut Meg, Castle Shopping
Centre, 01-404438 (Roger White)
TALLAGHT
See under Dublin 24
THURLES (Co. Tipperary)
Se do Bheatha Health Foods,
Liberty Square, 0504-23954
(Padraig O'Nuillain)
Jalary's Restaurant,
6, Liberty Square
TIPPERARY TOWN
(Co. Tipperary)
Vale of Health, 5, Abbey Street,
062-52075 (Anne Allen)
TRALEE (Co. Kerry)
Downtown Delly, Tralee
Shopping Centre,
Seanchara, Courthouse Lane,
Tralee Health Store, Tralee
Shopping Centre,
TULLAMORE (Co. Offaly)
Natural Stuff, 0506-41600
(Ann O'Malley)
WATERFORD (Co. Waterford)
Full of Beans, Georges Court,
051-84336 (Ian and Sonia
McLellan)
Natures Remedies,
Michael Street, 051-78350
(Therese Murphy)
WESTPORT (Co. Mayo)
West Coast Healthfood,
The North Mall, 098-26599
WEXFORD (Co. Wexford)
Only Natural, 56, North Main
Street, 053-22975 (Gerald Coffer)
Humble Natural Food Store,
Rowe Street, 053-24624
(Haike Wiehagan)
The Wild Rose Café,
Henrietta Street, 053-45231
WICKLOW (Co. Wicklow)
The Sunflower Health Food
Store, Main Street, 0404-6922.

WHAT SHOULD BE DONE?

- Shops should buy their fresh produce from local suppliers
- Supermarkets and grocery stores should increase their range of wholefoods
- Labelling ought to be clear so as to ascertain the place of origin and so that people can see which lines are wholefoods
- A shift towards organic agriculture is essential, with financial support
- Fresh salads and fruit must be made available in every canteen and restaurant, and where necessary should be subsidised to make them no more expensive than other foods
- There should be an intensive educational campaign on nutrition, on cutting back sugar consumption and salt consumption, and of the dangers of excessive fat intake.

WHAT YOU CAN DO

- Buy fresh food, daily if possible, using local suppliers—don't just use the supermarket because everyone else does—and avoid tins and packets.
- Learn to take an interest in where your food comes from; look at the place of origin, consider how the food has reached you and the effort involved in the process—ask the shopkeeper if the produce does not say where it was grown—and support local growers and food producers.
- Buy wholefoods rather than processed foods, choosing as much food and vegetables as can be afforded.
- Try organic vegetables and fruit.
- Cook everything for as little time as possible; but ensure that meat is cooked right through.
- Cut down on sugar—only put half the suggested amount in recipes, try drinks and fruit puddings without sugar for a while.
- Cook vegetables, fish and eggs without adding salt; use herbs and spices instead (e.g. caraway with cabbage and mint with peas and potatoes) and keep the salt off the dining table and away from children.
- If you have young children avoid giving them squash, sweets and biscuits—try giving them diluted fruit juice, sandwiches, fruit and raw vegetables.
- Grill, steam or bake food rather than fry it.
- Keep high fibre snacks, rather than sweets, biscuits and crisps in your food cupboard.
- Try herb tea or fruit juice, if you usually drink tea or coffee.

- Try eating less meat or buy smaller portions.
- Always insist on fresh milk rather than long-life or powdered milk.
- Eat no more than 2 or 3 eggs a week. (This will help keep your cholesterol intake to a safe level.)
- Join a food Co-op (See Organisations, Dublin Food Co-op. Carmichael House, Nth. Brunswick St Dublin 7—721199.)

Books and Publications

Blueprint for a Green Planet (Dorling Kindersley, 1987). *Chicken and Egg* (Green Print, 1989) Clare Druce. *Children's Food* (Unwin Hyman, 1988) Tim Lobstein. *Cook Yourself A Favour* (Thorsons, 1987). *F-Plan Diet* (Penguin, 1983) Audrey Eyton. *Feasting on Rawfoods* (Thorsons, 1987) Charles Gerras. *Food Additives* (Penguin, 1986) Erik Millstone. *Food Adulteration and How To Beat It* (Unwin Hyman, 1988). *Green Britain or Industrial Wasteland?* (Polity, 1986). *Guidelines for Humane Animal Farming* (Compassion in World Farming). *How to be Green* (Century, 1989) John Button. *Intensive Egg and Chicken Production* (Chickens Lib). *Laurel's Kitchen* (Routledge, 1979). *On Food and Cooking* (Allen and Unwin) Harold McGee. *Overcoming Food Allergies* (Ashgrove, 1985) Gwynne Davies. *Pure, White and Deadly* (Penguin, 1988) John Yudkin. *Stone Age Diet* (Optima, 1987) Leon Chaitow. *That's the Limit* (AlcoholicsAnonymous). *The Complete Book of Herbs* (Dorling Kindersley, 1988) Lesley Bremness. *The Food Scandal* (Century, 1985) Caroline Walker and Geoffrey Cannon. *The Great British Diet* (Century, 1985). *The Green Alternative* (Methuen, 1987). *The Holistic Cook* (Thorsons, 1986) Janet Hunt. *The Hunger Machine* (Polity, 1987) Jon Bennett. *The New E for Additives* (Thorsons, 1987) Maurice Hanssen. *The New Organic Food Guide* (Dent, 1987) Alan Gear. *The Politics of Food* (Century, 1987), Geoffrey Cannon. *The Real Cost* (Chatto and Windus, 1986) Richard North. *The Residue Report* (Thorsons, 1988) Stephanie Lashford. *The Vegetarian Magazine* (The Vegetarian Society). *The Wholefood Cookery Course* (Thorsons, 1986). *The Wholefood Express* (Food & Futures, 1986) Sue Mellis and Maggi Sikkings. *The World Human Rights Guide* (Pan, 1987). *This Poisoned Earth* (Piatkus, 1987) Nigel Dudley. *Why You Don't Need Meat* (Thorsons, 1986) Peter Cox. *Working The Land* (Temple Smith, 1984) Charles Pye and Richard North. *The Irish Food Guide*(Annalivia Press, Dublin) John & Sally McKenna.

IV
HEALTH

The green approach to our own and our Planet's ills could be summed up in the maxim, 'Prevention is better than cure'.

Like the conventional approach to the Planet's pollution problems—which looks for a quick technological fix or cure—conventional medicine is often symptom orientated. In fact, conventional medicine would appear to be more interested in illness than in health. But health is not merely a question of doctors, hospitals and expensive transplant operations. It should be about the integrated well-being of mind, body and spirit.

Lifestyle is a major factor in eight out of ten premature deaths. Diet, alcohol intake, whether or not you smoke, and how much exercise you get will all determine how and when you die. Most of these are a matter of personal choice. But there are other factors which can have a profound effect on your health—and are often  ignored. A monotonous, badly paying job or, more especially, no job at all can lead to ill health. Unemployment is now regarded as the single biggest factor influencing health and premature death in this country. Clearly, good health depends very much on what philosopher Schumacher called 'good work', i.e. doing work which is meaningful and fulfilling.

Environmental factors may also be outside the control of the individual. You may lead a green and healthy life style, but if you cycle in the city you inhale noxious fumes; the water you drink and use for cooking may contain traces of lead, aluminium, nitrates and other substances; the food you eat may contain pesticide residues and additives or may even be irradiated. All of these things can be changed in the long term but only by active campaigning on your part. By thinking globally and acting locally, you are also contributing to a healthier world.

Modern Medicine

Illness means big business for the drug companies. The market is now saturated with thousands of drugs for every kind of ailment. But sometimes these drugs can actually cause ill health. Every year millions of people throughout the world are hospitalised from the side effects of drugs, which result in the worsening of their condition.

The world actually needs to get rid of most of the drugs on the market. Over 205,000 drugs or combinations have been developed, most of which have been withdrawn. Moreover, 15,000 drugs are introduced each year while 12,000 are actually withdrawn annually. UNIDO (United Nations Industrial Development Organisation) in conjunction with the WHO (World Health Organisation) has trimmed the list of indispensable drugs down to 26.

New drug disasters are becoming more and more frequent. Thalidomide, Debendox, Opren are the best known examples, but there are many more. In 1986 we learned that Junior Aspirin, long trusted by the parents of young children, can cause liver and brain damage. Paracetemol is now recommended as a safe replacement for Junior Aspirin, despite the fact that in 1971, in Britain alone, 1,700 people were hospitalised due to its side effects.

The Health of The Irish

The Irish, regardless of class or background, tend to die of the diseases of Western affluence. Smoking, a high fat diet, high alcohol intake and lack of exercise are the main causes of premature death.

Northern Ireland now has the highest rate of heart disease in the world. The Republic is not far behind in fifth place. Our high fat diet is the main cause of heart disease but smoking is also a factor. In fact, the risks attached to smoking deserve to be spelled out.

SMOKING

• Smoking causes half of all cancers and is responsible for 30 to 40% of hospital admissions.

• The risk of lung cancer from smoking is 100 times greater than from working with asbestos 40 hours a week.

• Smoking kills 14 Irish people every day, 5,000 every year according to EC statistics.

• The children of smokers have an increased incidence of cancer of 30 to 50%.

- Sidestream smoke (the smoke inhaled by passive smokers) contains far higher concentrations of toxic chemicals than mainstream smoke.
- Smoking also causes three-quarters of the estimated 550 deaths from bronchitis, emphysema and asthma.
- Smoking causes one quarter of all coronary heart disease.

These horror statistics should be enough to persuade most people to break the habit. Yet, while Irish males have cut their smoking by half, smoking among Irish women is still high (32%), and Irish women now rank fifth in the world for lung cancer.

The Tobacco (Health Promotion and Protection) Act, 1988 will mean that smoking will be banned in most public places. However, restaurants, pubs and workplaces are excluded under the act. Under the new Health and Safety at Work Act, workers may be able to demand a smoke-free environment.

RADON—THE CANCER RISK

Radon is a naturally-occuring invisible gas that seeps from the ground. It is normally dispersed by the wind but can accumulate in spaces below buildings and come up through the floor boards. The gas then breaks down into other radioactive materials which, if breathed in, can lodge in the lungs, causing damage and, over time, increasing cancer risks.

The National Radiological Protection Board estimates that 2,500 people die of radon-related lung cancers in Britain each year and have reduced the action level for radon down from 400 to 200 becquerels (bq) per cubic metre of air. A completed survey of 1,300 homes in Ireland has shown that up to 3.5% of homes nationally could have radon levels in excess of the 200 bq action level. The survey showed that radon levels are particularly high in homes in the south and west of the country. Levels as high as 1,750 have been found.

Ireland is expected to adopt the EC's recommended action level, 400 bq in existing buildings and 200 bq in new buildings. In the US the action level is 150 bq and the US surgeon general has recently stated that radon is the second largest contribuor to lung cancer after smoking.

The Nuclear Energy Board is currently involved in a national monitoring programme. The high risk areas have been identified as Mayo, Galway and Clare.

Dealing with the problem of radon in your home is not that difficult. A 'Householders Guide to Radon' is available from the Northern Ireland Dept of the Environment. Information is also available from the Dept of Energy in Dublin.

Diet

More Irish people die prematurely of coronary heart disease (CHD) than of any other condition. One of the main reasons is the typical Irish diet, consisting of burgers, chips, eggs, butter etc which all contain saturated fat. The Irish have a high instance of CHD. People in Northern Ireland have the highest rate in the world. In the Republic, men now have the fifth highest rate of death from CHD in the developed countries and women have the third highest rate. A change of diet and more exercise are the best ways to combat heart disease. (See Food)

Work

In Ireland about one in 50 cancers is caused by exposure to a hazardous substance at work. Employers often fail to inform their workers about the dangers of certain chemicals—afraid that the workers would refuse to go near them if they knew. Employers simply want to know if the chemical works, not if it's dangerous or carcinogenic.

Dermatitis and asthma are two of the most common disabling diseases. Dermatitis is a painful skin rash and every year there are a hundred known cases caused by chemical exposure. Asthma is known to disable 24 workers annually, but the real toll may be far higher. As many as 20% of workers in the chemical, pharmaceutical, electronics and plastic industries may develop asthmatic symptoms.

In 1988, according to official figures, 3,500 workers were officially injured badly enough during the course of their work to require three days off. According to the Department of Labour, the true accident toll could be as high as 45,000 annually.

In 1988, 181 workers were permanently disabled by occupational diseases.

Depression

Around 200,000 Irish people are severely depressed at any one time. In 1986, 8,500 people were hospitalised for depression. Two thirds of them were women. Indeed, depression would appear to be an occupational hazard if you're a wife and mother trying to survive on a low income.

Holistic Medicine

In recent years there has been a tremendous increase in the interest in 'holistic' medicine. More and more people are becoming aware of the true benefits to be acquired from the traditional natural healing methods.

The holistic practitioner treats the whole person (the word holistic is derived from the Greek 'holos'—the whole or complete), taking into reckoning such details as environmental conditions, diet, heredity with the psychic and psychological make up of the person. This differs radically from the approach of conventional medicine, where the emphasis is placed on the diagnosis and treatment of the disease symptoms, and where sickness is regarded in terms of local disorders affecting specific parts of the body. On the other hand, the holistic therapist regards all spontaneous diseases as a general or overall imbalance of the person's vital energy flow, which may be corrected using natural healing methods with a prescription for the ideal conditions in which the body's own self-healing process can take place. According to the holistic view, sickness is not something you have, but something you are (e.g. an individual is not ill because he or she has an ulcer—but they have developed an ulcer because he or she is ill).

The first aim of a conventional practitioner is to diagnose the patient's illness by recording signs and symptoms such as pain, swelling, and rashes; whereas, the primary objective of a holistic practitioner is to find out as much as possible about the patient's background—not only the state of his or her health, but also lifestyle, mental outlook, ambitions, creative drive, diet et cetera. In holistic medicine the mind and body are regarded as one integral function, instead of separate mechanisms, and an emphasis is given to mental and emotional states and the effect they have on health.

A further feature of holistic medicine that distinguishes it from the allopathic approach is the emphasis given to preventive systems and, whereas most conventional doctors only see their patients when they are unwell, the natural therapist likes to see their clients regularly for a general check-up. Therefore conventional medicine is largely concerned with the suppression and control of the symptoms of a disease, whereas holistic medicine is aimed at preventing disease by eliminating its causes.

The various types of holistic treatments include:

ACUPUNCTURE: This ancient system, originally practised in China, is based on the principle that the body's energy travels along fixed channels (meridians), and by manipulating this energy through the insertion of needles into the skin at specific points along these channels, it is possible to eliminate pain, restore health et cetera. A disease is classified in terms of qualities of energy flow and body function, and diagnosis is made by close observation of the various physical signs such as the colour and texture of the skin, subtle body odours, the distribution of hot and cold patches, action of the joints and, most important, the reading of the twelve pulses. *The Acupuncture Foundation of Ireland, 87 North Circular Road, Dublin 7. Tel. 01-387699*

AROMATHERAPY: This system uses the essential oils of plants to treat illness. There are many oils, some of which can be safely used in the home, such as Lavendar, Rosemary, and Geranium, and others which are reserved for the use of skilled Aromatherapists. Most Wholefood shops now stock essential oils and information leaflets. Essential oils can be used for massage, in the bath and in oil burners, in poultices and steam baths.
The Natural Therapy and Yoga Centre, Mary Cavanagh, 12 Tivoli Terrace, Dun Laoghaire, Dublin. Tel. 01-809505.

BACH FLOWERS: The Bach Flower Remedies are herbal remedies which are used to treat moods and the emotions. They are available in many wholefood shops, along with leaflets and charts outlining their properties. They are generally used in conjunction with other systems when a state of mind or emotional pattern has become fixed and it is desirable to change. Guidelines to help identify a suitable remedy are given in a booklet by Dr. Edward Bach, who originated this system, and which is also widely available.

CHIROPRACTIC: This system emphasizes the importance of the correct alignment of the spinal vertebrae to relieve various symptoms, particularly back and neck problems. The system is based on four observations: (a), impulses are properly transmitted through the nerves and produce normal functions in a state of health; (b), any pressure applied on any part of the nervous system affects the efficiency of the system, diminishing or exaggerating its capacity for transmitting impulses; (c), pressures are caused by substances adjacent to the nerves, by irritation of the sensory nerves, by toxins which can irritate the sensory nerves, including muscular contractions with resultant pulling of the bone out of its correct position; and (d), slight pressure applied upon a nerve irritates, increase of irritation produces alteration of function which may develop, even to a large degree of paralysis. *The Chiropractic Association of Ireland, 6 Charlemont Terrace, Dun Laoghaire, Co. Dublin. Tel. 01-800488.*

HERBAL MEDICINE: This is the treatment of disease by use of the curative properties of plants, being the oldest system of healing ever recorded. It is said that traditionally a herbalist would go out walking in the countryside and instinctively pick the herbs to be administered to his patient. As time went by it became possible to identify specific herbs and their effects. Lists have been drawn up from which the whole system of herbal medicine has been developed. The herbs have been categorised into eleven groups: (1) Alteratives (particularly potent—used in the treatment of advanced diseases); (2) Astringents (used to tone the skin, increase the firmness of the mucous membranes and reduce secretions; (3) Calmatives (used to promote relaxation and sleep; (4) Carminatives (used to expel excess gas from the intestines and to produce a feeling of general well-being); (5) Cathartics (used as laxatives and to regulate bowel movements); (6) Demulcents (used to relieve sore throats, reduce inflammation of membranes, alleviate coughs and chest conditions); (7) Diaphoretics (used to promote the expulsion of toxins by sweating); (8) Diuretics (used to promote the expulsion of toxins through urination); (9) Expectorants (used to relieve catarrh, loosen phlegm, and clear airways; (10) Nervines (used to reduce tension and promote calm); and (11) Vulneraries (used as a direct application to minor wounds).

Sean Boylan, Edenmore, Dunboyne, Co. Meath. Tel 01-255250 Alan Chaytor-Grubb, Cork Clinic of Herbal Medicine, 5 Tuckey Street, Cork. Tel. 021-275638.

HOMEOPATHY: This natural therapy is based on the appreciation that the human body is a highly complex and vital entity; and being so complex it is highly misleading to suggest that there is any one cause for illness, but rather it is a result from a series of imbalances which allow the agents of the disease to take hold. It may sometimes be necessary to attack the disease directly (antibiotics) or to make mechanical adjustments (surgery), but the true role of therapy should be to restore the state of balance which constitutes health and this should be achieved whenever possible through strengthening the organism and by stimulating it to heal itself.

It is a system of natural drug therapeutics. It administers substances from the natural world to bring about healing. In this respect it is much akin to the traditional herbal medicine. Where homeopathy differs from herbal medicine is in the form the medicines take and in the understanding of how substances work to be healing.

The Irish Homeopathic Association, c/o Jonathan Griffith, Blessington, Co. Wicklow. Tel 045-65575.
The Irish School of Classical Homeopathy, 29/30 Dame Street, Dublin 2
The Northern Ireland Homeopathic Society, 32 Wauxhall Park, Belfast 9.

IRIDOLOGY: This system of diagnotistic technique is based on the premise that areas of the body are specifically reflected in the iris of the eye, and that the patterns, spots and colours of the iris can be interpreted to indicate the presence of disease.

Gloria Browne, Tel. 01-383459/522722.

NATUROPATHY: This system is based on the principle that the body's own self-healing powers can only be properly effective upon the removal of negative, artificial and unnatural conditions—including bad eating habits, faulty diet, destructive thoughts, irregular sleep, lack of fresh air and light, et cetera. Treatment may include a number of techniques, for instance, massage, herbal treatment, a diet programme and individual exercise. Symptoms of illness such as high temperature, shaking, rashes, etc. are seen as the body's natural mechanism of healing.

Information from Martin Forde, 316 Howth Road, Dublin 5. Tel 01-339902.

OSTEOPATHY: This system involves the manipulation of the joints and muscles to relieve tension and congestion around nerve routes. Particularly it is concerned with the condition of the spine, and diagnosis is made by 'palpating' (touching areas of the body to determine the quality of 'action' that is heat and speed or fluidity of blood beneath the area), which is largely an intuitive ability.

The Irish Register of Osteopaths, 3 Merrion Court, Ailesbury Road, Ballsbridge, Dublin 4. Tel. 01-695525.

REFLEXOLOGY: This system is based on the concept that different areas of the feet (zones) relate to various parts of the body, and that correctly applied pressure or massage of these zones will produce the remedial effect in the area of the body afflicted. Originally a Folk Medicine, it has been recorded in many civilisations, including the Egyptian, Chinese and Native American Indian.

The Irish Institute of Reflexology, 49 Rockville Crescent, Blackrock, Co. Dublin. Tel. 01-883093

The Society of Reflexologists of Ireland, 51 Parkfield, New Ross, Wexford. Tel. 051-22209.

SHIATSU: This system (pronounced 'Shee-atsu') is a form of healing massage based on similar principles to Acupuncture, save that a Shiatsu practitioner uses thumbs and fingertips in treatments. By working on the pressure points and along the meridians in general a great number of problems (physical, mental and emotional) can be relieved. The system works by helping body and mind (i.e. the whole person) to relax, and by stimulating the natural healing power of body and mind. *Further information from Anne Hyland, Lios Dana, Inch, Co. Kerry. Tel. 066-58189. or Josephine Lynch Dublin (01) 883378.*

VEGA TESTING: This is a diagnostic technique based on electronic readings, which may indicate the use of a specific homeopathic medicine as part of the information provided.

See Homeopathic Association, above

WHAT SHOULD BE DONE

• We need an environment which is not filled with health-threatening pollutants. Surgery and drugs should only be used when natural methods will not work.

• Natural healing techniques should be available through the Health Service.

• We must try to take responsibility for looking after our own bodies, rather than expect the experts to do it all for us.

• People should be educated to the fact that there is not 'a pill for every ill'.

• Allergy sufferers will need to be helped in identifying the particular substances to which they are allergic, so that it can be avoided, but more important, Ireland needs to ensure that all food, our air and our water, are free from harmful chemicals.

• The Government should ban tobacco advertising and sponsorship.

• Sources of stress must be reduced; air pollution, noise, glare and constant rapid movement. Restful environments must be created in all urban areas; quiet, pollution-free, open places where we can relax.

WHAT YOU CAN DO?

• When you feel under the weather feel what is really happening, and try and hear what your body is trying to tell you, rather than dwelling on the symptoms.

• Find out where the nearest herbal, homeopathic or alternative practitioner is situated.

• Avoid toxic chemicals and eat as healthily as you can; more fresh food and fewer additives.

• Stop smoking and cut down on alcohol.

• Rest when you need to, but also take some regular exercise.

• Inspect your medical shelf and take all the drugs no longer needed back to the chemist for disposal.

• Next time the family practitioner offers you a prescription, ask what the drug is designed to do, ask about side effects, and ask if there is a non-drug alternative.

• Only take dietary supplements if you need them for a specific reason, ensuring in such a case to take the advice of a qualified naturopath.

Books and Publications

A Manual on Nonviolence and Children (New Society, 1984). *A Smoker's Guide to Giving Up* (Health Education Authority). *Complete Guide to Vitamins and Minerals* (Thorsons, 1986) Leonard Mervyn. *Dieting makes you fat* (Century, 1983) Geoffrey Cannon and Helty Einzig. *Drugs for all* (Penguin, 1986) Jenny Bryan. *Executive Ease and Dis-Ease* (Gower, 1987) Beric Wright. *Exercise: Why Bother?* (Health Education Authority). *Fat is a Feminist Issue I* (Hamlyn, 1978) Susan Orbach. *Fat is a Feminist Issue II* (Hamlyn, 1984) Susan Orbach. *Guide to Stress Management* (Celestial Arts, 1985) John Mason. *Health with Humanity* (British Union for the Abolition of Vivisection). *Heart Politics* (New Society, 1986) Fran Peavey. *Holistic Living* (Dent, 1986) Patrick Pietroni. *How To Be Green* (Century, 1989) John Button. *Incest* (Stramullim, 1987) Sarah Nelson. *Kick It!* (Thorsons, 1987) Judy Perlmutter. *Learning to Live Without Violence* (Volcano, 1982) Daniel Sonkin and Michael Durphy. *Limits to Medicine* (Penguin, 1977) Ivan Illich. *Maximum Immunity* (Gateway, 1986) Michael Weiner. *Meditation* (Optina, 1988) Erica Smith and Nicholas Wilks. *New Approaches to Cancer* (Century, 1987) Shirley Harrison. *Overcoming Addictions* (Thorsons, 1989) Janet Pleshette. *Peace of Mind* (Prism, 1989) Ian Gawler. *Perhaps it's all an Allergy* (Foulsham, 1988) Ellen Rothera. *Sexual Violence* (Women's Press, 1984). *The Allergy Connection* (Thorsons, 1985) Barbara Paterson. *The Fate of the Earth* (Picador, 1982) Jonathan. *The Gaia Peace Atlas* (Pan, 1988). *The Handbook of Complementary Medicine* (Oxford, 1988) Stephen Fielder. *The Health Conspiracy* (Century, 1989) Joe Collier. *The Health Scandal* (Sidgwick and Jackson, 1988) Vernon Coleman. *The Practical Encyclopaedia of Natural Healing* (Rochdale, 1983) Mark Bricklin. *The Real Cost* (Chatto and Windus, 1986) Richard North. *You Can Conquer Cancer* (Thorsons, 1987) Ian Gawler.

Slainte: A Directory of Complementary and Alternative Medicine in Ireland, Sue Hassett (Wolfhound, June 1990).

V
TREES

History lessons at the Christian Brothers taught us that Ireland was once covered in trees—until the English came along and chopped them all down. While this account is perhaps slightly exaggerated, it is true that Ireland once had extensive broadleafed woodlands and their wholesale destruction can be likened to the present destruction of forests in the Amazon. It is estimated that in 1600 approximately 12% of the country was covered by broadleafed woodland. Sadly, this figure has now decreased to about 1.5%, according to Crann. (See Organisations)

The development of State forest plantations is the most significant land use change taking place in Ireland today.

Conifers

Nearly 80% of all the plantings in this country are of two evergreen coniferous species—Sitka spruce and lodgepole pine. The Sitka spruce is a native of western North America and favours high rainfall and humidity. The lodgepole pine is also a native of western North America and can grow on relatively poor peat soils.

Both species grow very quickly in this country. Ireland has the highest growth rate in Europe.

Coniferous forest plantations are unevenly distributed throughout Ireland with most being situated in the West. County Wicklow in the East also has extensive coniferous forests.

Broadleafs

Of all the forestry in Ireland, little over one per cent is of broadleaved or deciduous trees, and most of them are over 70 years old.

They are very beautiful. But apart altogether from aesthetic considerations, broadleaved trees are healthier for the environment. They keep the soil productive by bringing up essential minerals, returning them to the ground in the form of autumn leaves, which make the best organic compost.

THE KING AND THE HERMIT

'I have a hut in a wood, an ash tree closes it on one side, and a hazel, like a great tree by a rath, on the other. Will you go with me to see it?

Long branches of a green yew tree—the great greenery of oak—an apple tree with large apples— an excellent crop of green hazels.'

That is part of a 9th-century poem 'King and Hermit'. Can you imagine such a poem being written about a few Sitka Spruce or Lodgepole Pine?

The Tree Council of Ireland makes the point that: 'broadleaved woods make a contribution out of all proportion to their size to the character of Ireland's landscape and its facilities for public enjoyment. They are essential to the character of many of our areas of outstanding landscapes, such as Killarney, the Boyne Valley and the valleys of County Wicklow. They introduce a sense of scale and enclosure to the landscape, but their importance goes far beyond their visual appearance. They provide shelter to farmland and have potential for sustained timber and firewood production if properly managed. Broadleaved woods are also vital for sporting and wildlife interests. Over 20 per cent of our areas of scientific interest are broadleaved woodlands. The diversity of their structure—particularly old established woodland—gives them a greater value for nature conservation than any other type of woodland.'

As matters stand, woodlands cannot be protected by tree preservation orders as this leaves the local authorities open to compensation claims. The export of hardwood logs 'in the round' is still permitted, while we import hardwood from Third World Countries.

Under the recent Environment Programme, the Government has expressed the intention of providing more support for the planting and maintaining of hardwoods. Whilst this is to be welcomed, it remains to be seen how far the support goes in practice. It is still intended that up to 10 hectares of native woodland may be replaced with conifers at any time without reference to environmental factors.

WHAT SHOULD BE DONE

A more long-term view must be taken, both economically and environmentally, with regard to forestry and private plantations. Proposals by the Tree Council of Ireland include recommendations to:

• Conserve existing broadleaved high forest with a presumption against coniferisation or reclamation to agriculture.

• Promote the planting and sound management of broadleaved woods through incentives and advice on woodland management and timber marketing.

HOW TO PLANT A TREE

While awaiting planting, tree roots must be protected from drying winds and frost by covering them with soil or sacking.

The planting pit should be at least 18″ square and 18″ deep and the topsoil which is the darker upper layer should be retained and the lighter in colour subsoil should be removed and replaced with additional topsoil or peat moss.

Place tree in the pit and position a stake so that it doesn't interfere with the roots. Remove the tree and drive the stake into the ground leaving about 2ft above ground level.

Cut all dead or broken roots and place the tree in the pit to the same depth at which it was growing in the nursery. This is the part near the roots where the stem colour gets darker.

Roots should be first spread out before covering them with soil. Then shake the stem slightly to remove air pockets from around the roots. Cover with more soil, shake again and finally firm the soil to prevent the tree from moving in the wind. After planting, the soil should be slightly raised above ground level to allow for settlement. Secure the stake with a tree-tie approximately 1″ below the top of the stake. Then water the ground around the tree with approximately 1 bucketfull of water.

After-care of tree should include the following:

• Check the tree tie and adjust if necessary to allow for increased growth in stem thickness.

• Ensure that the stake is firm.

• Remove weeds from the base of the tree.

• Lightly fork in 3oz of general organic fertilizer in April/May.

• Water if necessary during the summer.

• Cut back broken branches and remove growth which arises from the base of the tree.

Source: Dublin Corporation Parks Department

• Plant increased numbers of broadleaved trees in both state and private forests. That should include as a long-term aim the goal of recreating broadleaved woodlands on its lowland holdings, such as former demesne lands, which are now under conifers, by progressive restocking with broad-leaves when the conifers are felled.

WHAT YOU CAN DO

• Join Crann, or the Irish Tree Council, or both.
• Visit our forests—particularly the broadleaved forests and forest parks regularly, and help your children to enjoy them.
• Plant a tree! Or several.
• Ask someone from the Tree Council, or your local forester, to give a talk at your school.
• Set up a School Project, e.g. encouraging youngsters to find and plant seeds, acorns, sycamore 'wings' etc.
• Try to stop children—adults too!—vandalising trees in your area.

ORGANISATIONS

Forestry has been tossed around between Government Departments for decades, from the Department of Agriculture to the Department of Lands, to the Forest & Wildlife Service, to the Department of Fisheries and Forestry, to the Department of Energy. At the last round of musical chairs it was split in two, the Department of Energy retaining its policy-making authority, and a completely new body, Coillte Teo, being set up. There are also several voluntary bodies with an interest in Forestry.

So now we have:

Coillte Teo, The Irish Forestry Board: established by the Government in 1988. It is responsible for the commercial management of State Forests, and also for the management of 12 forest parks, Killykeen Holiday Chalet Park and picnic and other amenity facilities. Leeson Lane, Dublin 2. Tel. 01-615666.

Department of Energy, Forestry Service: They retain the policy-making authority, along with such responsibilities as the giving of grants, tree-felling licences and so on. Leeson Lane, Dublin 2. Tel. 01-615666.

The Tree Council of Ireland: a voluntary group representing over 25 voluntary professional and public service bodies concerned with trees. Aims are to promote the propagation, planting, conservation and management of trees and to disseminate knowledge about their care. It organises National Tree Week and other events. 33 Botanic Road, Glasnevin, Dublin 9. Tel. 01-306996.

Crann/Woodland Trust: a non-profit organisation founded in 1986 with the aim of re-treeing Ireland with broadleaved trees. Four seasonal newsletters go to members, with information on tree growing: there are workshops and educational weekends. Write to Jan Alexander, Kilnamar, Kilbracken, Co. Cavan.

The Irish Timber Growers Association: a grouping of private growers. Knockranny, Kilmacanogue, Co. Wicklow. Tel: 01-863681.

Society of Irish Foresters: a professional and educational body. Organises the annual Forest Walks. c/o the Royal Dublin Society. Tel. the Secretary at 615666.

The Irish Timber Council: the representative body for the Irish timber industry. Members include timber companies, sawmills and timber processors. Is introducing a special quality symbol—an Irish Red Squirrel, to be stamped on all timber building materials reaching a required level of excellence.

BROADLEAVED WOODS TO VISIT

Avondale, Co. Wicklow
Donadee, Co. Kildare
Rossmore, Co. Monaghan
Ards Peninsula, Co. Donegal
Currahchase, Co. Limerick
Farran, Co. Cork
John F Kennedy Park, Co. Wexford
Doonaree, Co. Cavan
Lough Key Forest Part, Co. Roscommon
Portumna Forest Park, Co. Galway
Gougane Barra, Co. Cork
Killykeen, Co. Cavan

COILLTE TEORANTA
THE IRISH
FORESTRY BOARD

 Coillte

- Managing one million acres of State forests
- Planting 25,000 acres of trees every year
- Producing 1,500,000 M3 of timber annually
- Managing 12 forest parks
- Providing forest walks and picnic sites

LEESON LANE, DUBLIN 2.
Tel: 01-615666
Fax 01-789527

IRELAND IS AT PRESENT—

60% self-sufficient in structural timber.
100% self-sufficient for pallet wood, fencing and wood pulp.
20% self-sufficient for joinery.
The EC as a whole produces only 40% of its total wood requirements.

FORESTRY IN IRELAND

At the turn of this century Ireland had only one per cent of its land devoted to forestry. Even today we rate bottom of the EC league for forestry development, with just over six per cent of afforestation, as opposed to the EC average of 24%. Holland, which is far more densely populated, has over 8% tree cover. Ireland's poor performance with regard to forestry is now set to change. The setting up of Coillte Teo, the Irish Forestry Board, means that forestry will now become a much more attractive prospect for both the farmer and the private investor. Over the next three years, the EC will invest around £50 million in Irish forestry, while our Government is stepping up existing incentives and introducing sizeable tax concessions. As an inducement to farmers to convert to tree planting, the government now offers 85% grants towards the total establishment costs, up to a maximum of £800 per ha. The most attractive part of this package is undoubtedly the fact that all profits are tax-free. Coillte Teo, which has over £100 million to invest in State forestry, will be expected to achieve profitability in a relatively short period of time.

In the long term it is hoped that home-grown Irish products will replace the imported timber. In 1987 we imported some £400 million worth of foreign timber. At the moment some 450,000 ha of land are devoted to forestry in Ireland, but 60 per cent of that is less than 20 years old and not sufficiently mature to serve our present needs. The annual value of standing timber is put at £30 million and once this has been felled and processed its value increases dramatically to £100–£120.

Environmental Concerns

All of this sounds like good news, but many environmentalists, including David Bellamy, believe we should proceed with caution. Concentrating solely on conifers can bring its own environmental difficulties. Coniferisation can cause increased acidification of the soil which in turn pollutes waterways in the vicinity. Others object to the planting of conifers on bogs and other habitats. Unlike broadleaf woodlands they don't make particularly good habitats for birds and animals or plants. This is because such plantations do not allow much light to get through to the soil below.

Also, some experts suspect that the 150,000 hectares of forest which have been planted on peatlands do not act as a major carbon dioxide sink, as has been claimed by the Minister for the Environment in 1989. According to Dr Catherine O'Connell, spokeswoman for the Irish Peatland Conservation Council, peatlands are themselves major absorbers of CO_2 and planting conifers leads to oxidation of the peat and releases CO_2. It could in fact lead to a net increase in CO_2 emissions. Forests can certainly act as a CO_2 sink, but only when planted on mineral soils.

Crann and The Irish Tree Council believe that mixed forestry, concentrating on both broadleafs and conifers is by far the best approach.

TROPICAL RAINFORESTS

An area the size of twenty football pitches every minute—that's the size of the Phoenix Park every hour—which is the size of Wales every year which… We tend to make such comparisons when talking about the on-going destruction of the tropical rainforests in order to make the sheer scale of the destruction imaginable.

By destroying the rainforests we are in a sense committing ecological suicide. The rainforests are the lungs of the Planet, providing us with oxygen, absorbing Carbon dioxide and thus playing a vital role in the regulation of the Earth's climate. Though they only cover about 7% of the globe's surface, they are our richest source of life, containing more than half the world's species. Many other plant species which have not yet been discovered could be invaluable for medical research purposes.

What's Causing The Destruction?

Most of the damage is caused by logging companies, who cut down about 5 million hectares of rainforest every year. Logging practices take only 4-10% of trees but leave up to 1/3 of the land open to erosion, which means that many types of birds and insects die out. It is estimated that 1 ha of plantation is created for every 10 ha lost to logging every year. This surely is an unacceptable price to pay for your mahogany door or cabinet?

Last year Brazilian scientists studying satellite pictures reported that they had found up to 6,000 fires burning in the Amazon in one day. Most of these fires were due to what is known as 'slash and burn' cultivation carried out by poor landless farmers trying to make ends meet. Unfortunately, the soil only remains fertile for about a three year period and the farmers are then forced to destroy more trees. A similar technique is carried out by the big cattle ranchers in the area.

 Again the soil only supports cattle grazing for about seven years, after which time the ranchers will clear new areas. Most of the beef is exported to the USA, where it is used for the hamburger market. It takes approximately 55 sq ft of forest clearance to provide enough grazing for one burger. Think about that the next time you're wolfing down a Big Mac. You might also spare a thought for the dead animal you're eating. The hamburger chains in this country assure us that all our hamburgers are made from prime Irish beef.

Many so called development projects, often financed by the World Bank, have also led to terrible devastation of the rainforests. One of these latest building projects—the building of the Altamira hydroelectric dam system—would flood 7,200 sq km of rainforest and deprive many indigenous tribes of a homeland, if allowed to go ahead.

Ireland's Role

Some 50,000 tonnes of tropical timber are imported here every year. The bulk of this sawn timber, mostly mahogany and teak, is used for joinery and furniture. According to Earthwatch, we use the equivalent of 10 ha of tropical forest per working day.

These woods are by no means necessary for the production of furniture and be replaced by softwoods or native hardwoods such as oak—so we're back to the question of planting more broadleafs in this country.

GREEN TURNERS

The Green Turners are a group formed in 1989 by a dozen professional woodturners from the U.K. and Ireland. Their main intentions are to work either exclusively with native timbers or, if they do use some exotics, they endeavour to get their timber from a sustainable source. They wish the public to know that in fashioning their wood items they are bearing in mind questions of global ecology.

Noel Badrian	Brooklawn, Kilternan, Co.Dublin, 01-955556
James Foley	Ballina, Killaloe, Co. Clare, 061-76395
Bruce McDonald	Dunabrattin, Annestown, Co.Waterford, 051-96110
Liam O'Neill	Bay 19, Smithstown, Co.Clare, 061-363055 Fax 061-61309
Peter Sweetman	32, Ashgrove Park, Naas, Co.Kildare, 045-79385

Green Turners may be contacted through Liam O'Neill (address above)

VI
BOGS

Each year an area of Irish bogland almost twenty times the area of Monaco is destroyed by turf machines, tree planting, drainage, reclamation.

There are 2 kinds of acid peatlands: the thick dome shaped Raised Bogs and the thin, undulating Blanket Bogs. The raised bogs are usually found in the Midlands, while the blanket bogs are found in the high rainfall areas in the west and on our mountain ranges throughout the country.

Over 90% of the area of the raised bog type has been interfered with and peatland scientists predict that if the rates of exploitation continue, the last living examples of these bogs will have disappeared by 1994. Of the raised bog area remaining only 3.8% is sufficiently intact to merit conservation.

The blanket bogs, which are very much part of the renowned scenery of the west of Ireland, are also increasingly under threat. Approximately 35% of the original area of blanket bogs has either been afforested or cut away. Although this leaves almost 500,000 ha potentially suitable for conservation purposes, large areas of this are damaged by overgrazing and repeated burning. Forest plantations and other developments have also destroyed the integrity of these formerly extensive systems, making high quality, extensive tracts of blanket bog an increasing rarity in this country. At present only 11% of the original blanket bog area is listed as being of conservation interest in the Action Plan of the Irish Peatland Conservation Council (IPCC).

According to Catherine O'Connell of the IPCC, goldmining in the west poses a serious threat to the wetland eco-systems and blanket bogs in the area. The IPCC also view the proposed airport at Clifden in the area of the Derrywaking Loughs Bog as an unacceptable development.

In 1987 the Government committed itself to acquiring 10,000 ha of raised bogs and 40,000 ha of blanket bogs for conservation purposes. These figures represent only 4% of the original total area of peatland in Ireland. No target figure has yet been announced for the third peatland type occurring in Ireland, the type of lime-rich marsh called Fen, of which about 2,000 ha are regarded as important. The IPCC's current Action Plan recommends that an area of 2,000 ha should be conserved.

To date the area of raised bogs protected is 1090 ha (in 5 sites) or 11% of the official raised bog target. The area of blanket bog protected is 13,603 ha (in 18 sites) or 34% of the official blanket bog target. The conservation of fens has been extremely slow, with only 9.85% of the area recommended being protected. The peatland sites are either protected as National Nature Reserves (NNRs) under the Wildlife Act 1976 or they are included within National Parks. The majority of these sites have been protected within the last three years.

At present Ireland has the lowest percentage of land conserved in Europe, mainly because of its failure to establish an acquisition fund.

Why Save The Bogs?

Bogs have been traditionally denigrated in this country as worthless pieces of land. We associate them with a certain backwardness and the term 'bogman' is a derogatory one. This attitude probably helps to explain why we have neglected and abused this very important part of our heritage.

Ireland is among the last countries in Europe where a wide range of peatlands still exist in their natural state. At first, raised bogs may appear dull and lifeless, but a closer look reveals a variety of plants and animals which have specially adapted to life in this habitat. The dominant plant on the raised bog surface is the Sphagnum or bog moss, and different species of Sphagnum grow in the pools, and in the lawns and hummocks, forming a richly coloured mosaic. The plants of the hollows include bog asphodel, bog cotton, cross leaved heath, and white beaked sedge. The hummocks are dominated by ling heather, bog rosemary and a number of lichen species.

Insects and birds also occur on the bog. A number of moth species, including the green hairstreak, meadow brown, peacock, small white, orange tip, common blue, small copper and oak eggar, can all be found on the bog. The pheasant, curlew, snipe, meadow pipit, skylark and linnet often roost on bogs in winter, as does the Greenland white-fronted goose.

THE IPCC PEATLAND EDUCATION PACK PROJECT

The project aims to investigate the potential uses of peatlands to teachers, and to produce a series of interdisciplinary teaching modules within an education pack for use in secondary schools. The target audience will be teachers and students involved in junior cycle curricula, although some materials will be relevant in senior cycle studies. The project will be approached from the ecological, historical, sociological, economic/ political and the aesthetic/moral perspectives.

The Peatland Education Pack will be an interdisciplinary teaching package focusing on peatlands and meeting requirements of Junior Cycle curricula in Science, History/ Geography, English/Irish and Art/ Craft/Design.

It will contain teacher and pupil manuals, together with teaching materials such as field identification keys, fact sheets, wall chart and overhead projection teaching sheets. In addition, a limited number of audio-slide files and videos will be produced to supplement the teaching pack.

The teacher manual will be divided into the different subject areas outlined above. Within each discipline, the necessary information concerning peatlands will be provided to equip teachers to present the appropriate background information to students.

Further information from:
Dr. Catherine O'Connell, Education Officer,
Irish Peatland Conservation Council, 3 Lr. Mount Street,
Dublin 2. Tel. 01-616645.

Our bogs are also living history books. Because of the unique way in which bogs grow they preserve semi-fossilised plant remains, including wood and pollen as well as human artefacts. Taking small samples of peat and subjecting them to scientific analysis, it's possible to reconstruct the changing face of the Irish landscape and historical weather patterns. With the occurrence of global warming, this type of analysis will become very useful for predicting future climate changes.

In Holland where most of the bogs have disappeared, bogs are taken very seriously indeed and treated as a precious national treasure. The Dutch have even gone so far as to raise funds to buy four Irish bogs for the Irish nation. Our Government should learn from their example.

WHAT YOU CAN DO

1. Become a member of Conservation Organisations.

2. Make a donation to the IPCC towards the purchase of endangered bogs. They are currently running a 'friend of the bog' campaign.

3. Write to your TD's asking them to spend more money on conservation.

4. Visit bog sites and learn more about them.

5. If you live near a bog, be a watchdog. Always report illegal dumping or drainage etc.

How Can You Help?

To succeed—the IPCC needs your help. Bogs cost money—so why not make a donation to our Save the Bogs Campaign. By donating £5 you will automatically become a 'Friend of the Bog' and will receive a copy of Peatland News twice a year. This reports on campaign progress and the use to which your donation has been put. Alternatively, if you donate £25 you will receive a Symbolic Share Certificate in an endangered Irish peatland, specially designed by Eamon de Buitléar.

Bogs Of International Importance

We list here ONLY those bogs which are of international scientific importance, and which must be preserved at all costs. There are as many again, not listed, of national and regional importance, which demand our attention.

Raised Bogs

1. Addergoole Bog, Co. Galway (M310, 340) 310ha, Western, PM. This is one of the largest and most westerly raised bogs in the country, and features a 'soak' and a lichen-festooned Birch stand.
2. All Saints Bog, Co. Offaly (N010,110) 300ha, Midland, BM/P. This raised bog is noted for the large wet Birch wood which has developed on its central dome.
3. Ardgraigue Bog. Co. Galway (MB30,140) 80ha, Western, PM. The site is notable for the occurrence of *Sphagnum pulchrum*.
4. Ballyduff Bog, Co. Tipperary (NO10,030) 120ha, Midland, PM. The bog has a well developed pool and hummock system, showing active *Sphagnum* growth.
5. Barroughter, Co. Galway (M790,030) 136ha, Midland, PM. The site is notable for the occurrence of *Sphagnum pulchrum*.
6. Bellanagare, Co. Roscommon (M720, 870) 1100ha, Western, PM/BM. Raised bog with flushed areas containing *Sphagnum pulchrum*.
7. Brown Bog, Co. Longford (N095, 760) 60ha, Western, PM.A quaking 'soak', or surface drainage system occurs on this site.
8. Carrowbehy Bog, Co. Roscommon (M570, 935) 276ha, Western, BM/PM. This is a raised bog, with a wide range of morphological features.
9. Clara Bog, Co. Offaly NNR (N260,300) 665ha, Midland, WS/PM.This is the largest raised bog in Ireland that has a well developed 'soak' system.

The Irish Peatland Conservation Council (IPCC) was established in 1982 to campaign for the conservation of a representative sample of Irish bogs. It is a voluntary charitable organisation, and its aims include the raising of funds to purchase threatened bogs.
Head Office: 3 Lower Mount Street, Dublin 2.
Tel. 01-616645.

---

10. Cloonmoylan, Co. Galway (M790, 030) 530ha, Midland, PM/C. There is a well developed pool/hummock system on this bog, which supports *Sphagnum pulchrum*.
11. Clonfinane Bog, Co. Tipperary (M990, 030) 187ha, Midland, PM. This bog contains two wet wooded areas, a small stand of Birch and an actively spreading Pine Wood.
12. Curraghlehanagh, Co. Galway (M680, 540) 205ha, Western, BM/C. Quaking bog, partly burned with good *Sphagnum* growth pattern.
13. Firville, Co. Tipperary (M950,010) 240ha, Midland, PM. This bog supports a good pool/hummock system.
14. Garriskil Bog, Co. Westmeath (N360, 635) 165ha, Midland, PM/BM. A feature of this bog is an extensive and well developed system of concentrically aligned pools and hummocks, occupying about 25% of the dome.
15. Lough Lurgeen, Co. Galway (M660, 590) 1100ha, Western, PM/BM. A raised bog with flush, lake, river and turlough ecosystems. Greenland White-fronted Geese feed and roost in the turlough and are known to feed on the bog itself.
16. Mongan Bog, Co. Offaly NNR (N030, 306) 136ha, Midland, AT. Greenland White-fronted Geese use this bog as a winter roosting site. Mongan Bog is part of the Clonmacnoise Heritage Zone.
17. Shankill West, Co. Galway (M630, 520) 80ha, Western, PM/BM. Bog with excellent *Sphagnum* growth pattern and stream headwaters.

18. Shanville/Carricknabreena Bog, Co. Roscommon (M750, 910) 123ha, Midland, PM/F. Bog with wet flushes containing *Sphagnum pulchrum*, grading into fen at its margin beside a river.

Mountain Blanket Bogs

1. Cuilcagh Mountains/Lough Cratty, Cos Cavan/Ferma-nagh (H15, 27) 500ha, PM. A species rich, cross-border site. Breeding site for Dunlin.
2. Sally Gap, Co. Wicklow (014, 13) 1700ha, OPW/PM. This area of blanket bog is the least damaged in the eastern part of the country and contains lakes, pools and surface drains.
3. Slieve Blooms, Cos. Laois and Offaly NNR (N25, 10) 2100ha, WS. This area of blanket bog is part of the Slieve Blooms Environment Park.

Fens

1. Ballyeighter Lakes, Co. Clare (R34, 91) 1220ha, P. The largest fen system in the country, comprising a major network of calcareous, oligotrophic lakes surrounded by a complex of oligotrophic to mesotrophic floodplain fens.
2. Pollardstown Fen, Co. Kildare NNR (L77, 15) 225ha, WS/PM. Pollardstown Fen is the largest remaining calcareous, spring-fed fen in Ireland.
3. Scragh Bog, Co. Westmeath (N42, 59) 16ha, IPCC/PM. This is a small, extremely wet quaking fen, with incipient bog development taking place in the centre.

PEATLAND AREAS TO VISIT

Clonmacnoise Heritage Zone, Co. Offaly
Clara Bog, Co. Offaly
Sliabh Bloom Mountain Range, Co. Laois
Glenveagh National Park, Co. Donegal
Killarney National Park, Co. Kerry
Connemara National Park, Co. Galway
The Wicklow Way, Sli Cualann Nua

Lowland Blanket Bogs

1. Bealacooan Bog, Co. Galway (M090, 280) 1396ha, PM. This is the most extensive, intact lowland blanket bog in East Connemara. It features pool complexes, flushes and interconnecting pool/lawn systems. It is a feeding site for Greenland white-fronted goose.
2. Derryvickrone, Co. Galway (L740, 470) 468ha, P. This bog has extremely wet, quaking areas and is a Greenland White-fronted Geese feeding site.
3. Doobehy Bog, Co. Mayo (G050, 260) 1180ha, PM. This bog features extensive flush systems, some of which support small woodlands, extensive pool systems, hummock/ hollow areas, quaking mats with Sphagnum carpets and lush mineral soil drains.
4. Durlough, Co. Donegal (G66, 87) 20ha, WS. A wet valley bog with schwingmoor areas.
5. Formoyle Bog, Co. Mayo (G060, 220) 295ha, PM. This bog contains hummock/ hollow areas, pool systems, lakes, flushes and quaking areas rich in rare bryophytes.
6. Glenamoy, Co. Mayo (F89, 35) 4800ha, P. An extensive area of lowland blanket bog which includes the study site of the International Biological Programme.
7. Leam Bog, Co. Galway (M010, 430) 855ha, WS/PM. This is an intact and extensive area of highland and lowland blanket bog. Greenland white-fronted geese use this site for feeding and roosting.
8. Lettershinna Bog, Co. Galway (L850, 450) 995ha, WS/PM. This bog contains a lake-studded area, with intercon-necting pools and well developed hummocks, and is a feeding site for Greenland white-fronted geese.

9. Lough Barra, Co. Donegal NNR (B92, 10) 1000ha, WS/PM. A good example of lowland blanket bog, with several important feeding sites for Greenland white-fronted geese.

10. Maam Cross/Lettercraffroe/Screeb/Cashel/Glendollagh Lake, Co. Galway (L90, 40) 27000ha, PM/C. This blanket bog contains several rare plant species. Six Greenland white-fronted goose feeding sites are known within the area.

11. Owenduff, Co. Mayo NNR (F86, 07) 6000ha, WS/PM. The largest remaining undisturbed blanket bog catchment in the country. The site is a Greenland white-fronted goose feeding and roosting area.

12. Pettigo Plateau, Co. Donegal NNR (H02, 74) 900ha, WS. This bog contains pools, drainage features and is a wintering area for Greenland white-fronted goose.

13. Roundstone Bog, Co. Galway (L71, 45) 4250ha, OPW/PM. This area consists of a complex of oligotrophic lakes, streams, rivers, flushes and fens with well developed blanket bog. The site is a feeding and roosting area for Greenland white-fronted geese.

14. Shannavara Bog, Co. Galway (L920, 410) 1127ha, PM. This bog contains excellent pool/hummock and lawn complexes, with *Sphagnum pulchrum* and is a feeding site for Greenland white-fronted geese.

15. Sheskin/Knockmoyle, Co. Mayor NNR (F98, 25) 1200ha, WS. This bog contains diverse blanket bog features including drains, pool systems, hummock/hollow topography and flush systems with *Homalothecium nitens*.

16. Shralahy Bog, Co. Mayo (G000, 030) 990ha, PM. This bog has excellent pool systems, an extensive collapsed swallowhole system and some flushes.

Books and Publications

The information provided here may be supplemented by reading the IPCC *Guide to Irish Peatlands* available from the IPCC (Price £6), and from additional sources provided in the list below. A free brochure listing educational leaflets and charts stocked by the IPCC is available upon request (send s.a.e.).

Anonymous (1976) *Wetlands Discovered*. Forest and Wildlife Service, Dublin. Bellamy, D. (1986) *The Wild Boglands*— Bellamy's Ireland. Country House, Dublin. Caulfield, S. *Ceide Fields & Belderrig: A guide to two prehistoric farms in North Mayo*. Morrison Book Company, Killala, Mayo. Chinery, M. (1973) *A Field Guide to the Insects of Britain and Ireland*. Collins, London. Cross, J.R. (1989) *Peatlands, Wastelands or Heritage? An Introduction to Bogs and Fens*. Wildlife Service, Dublin. Doherty, C. *Early Christian Ireland*. Irish Environmental Library Series, Folens, Dublin. Ferguson-Lees, J., Willis, I., Sharrock, J.T.R. (1983) *The Shell Guide to the Birds of Britain and Ireland*. Michael Joseph Ltd., London. Goodhue, D. (1980) *Irish Bogs and Fens*. No. 63 of the Irish Environmental Library Series, Folens, Dublin. Herity, M. *Gold in Ancient Ireland*. Irish Environmental Library Series, Folens, Dublin. Hogan, D. (1986) *An Portach—The Bog*. Gasra Staideir an Chlochain agus Muintearas na hOilean, An Togra Oideachais, Gaillimh. Jones, N. *Bord na Mona*. No. 59 of the Irish Environmental Library Series, Folens, Dublin. O'Ceallachain, C.N. (1980) *Siar Tri na Portaigh*. Oifig an tSolathair, Baile Atha Cliath. O'Connell, C. (1986) *The Future of Irish Raised Bogs*. The Resource Source Environment Guide No. 7. Environment Awareness Bureau, Dublin. O'Connell, C. (1987) Ed. *The IPCC Guide to Irish Peatlands*. Irish Peatland Conservation Council, Dublin. Raftery, B. *Stone Age Ireland*. Irish Environmental Library Series, Folens, Dublin. Raftery, B. *Iron Age Ireland*. Irish Environmental Library Series, Folens, Dublin. Raftery, B. *Bronze Age Ireland*. Irish Environmental Library Series, Folens, Dublin. Raftery, N. *Irish Field Monuments*. Irish Environmental Library Series, Folens, Dublin. Webb, D.A. (1977) *An Irish Flora*. Dun Dealgan Press Ltd., Dundalk.

VII
WASTE AND RE-CYCLING

Waste

> **Your Waste is a Waste of the World's Resources**

We are a society of wasters. And if you're in any doubt about that just look at the worldwide figures for waste production. The USA—the worst offender of all—produces an estimated 560 million tons of hazardous waste each year. The EC produces 2.2 billion tons of waste annually, of which between 20 and 30 million tons are hazardous.

To illustrate the size of the problem, in 1985 the president of the Spanish chemical industry likened the quantity of EC waste to a train travelling at 100 hundred miles per hour, pulling wagons each containing 20 tons of waste. If you were standing looking at this train go past, it would take a year to go by—at which time a new train would be following behind.

Most of our waste is the inevitable result of the vast technological changes and the rise in consumerism since the second world war. The immediate solution in the 1950's and 60's to this explosion of production was indiscriminate landfill of both domestic and hazardous waste. The danger of these sites to ground water and public health was first highlighted in New York State in what became known as the 'Love Canal' saga in 1978 when the landfill of some of the most toxic substances known led to the evacuation of a whole community and in due course to the Resource Conservation and Recovery Act (RCRA). This legislation controlled landfill operations and established liability.

With increased research and environmental awareness of the dangers of landfill, plus increased restrictions on the available land, governments and industry began to advocate incineration as the *Technological Fix* to the waste problem. One of the main attractions of incineration for industrialists is the difficulty in establishing direct company liability for aerial emissions.

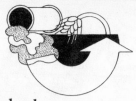

The Situation In Ireland

According to the Department of the Environment, 58,000 tonnes of toxic waste are produced here every year. More than half of this—31,140 tonnes—are organic solvents with chlorinated solvents, biocides, asbestos and lead wastes making up much of the rest. If not properly disposed of, these substances can poison groundwater and enter the foodchain.

The generation of toxic waste in this country has increased dramatically because Ireland is seen as an attractive location for the pharmaceutical and chemical industries. Lage Hansen, the managing director of Nordisk Gentoffe, a Danish pharmaceutical company, claimed that Ireland offered 'easier access to the necessary environmental approval'. Basically, this means that when it comes to environmental controls this country is seen as an 'easy touch'. And this is what attracts foreign chemical companies to this country in such large numbers. Ireland is now the twelfth largest producer of pharmaceuticals in the world and 10 of the world's top 15 chemical companies now operate here. By locating a plant here a company can make substantial savings, not just through cheaper labour costs and tax breaks but also through lax environmental control. For example, pollution controls amounted to 12% of the cost of building and operating factories in the U.S. by the mid 1970's. By moving to Ireland, where there is less vigorous control, this figure can be reduced to about 6%.

At present 66% of all toxic waste is disposed of by the producer on site. There are still no regulations to control or monitor waste once the producer has left the country. Records are often not kept. The Department of the Environment has admitted that it has little information about land contaminated by industrial toxic waste sites. This is certainly an area in which the EPA can play a decisive role.

It has been estimated that 3,000 tonnes of toxic waste are dumped annually into local authority landfill sites. The likely impact of such dumping on groundwater is very rarely assessed.

Problematic Wastes

21,000 tonnes of chemical, oil and other wastes, which are not defined as hazardous, are produced in Ireland every year. 80% of this is dumped in landfill sites. Another 54,000 tonnes of metal and chemical treatment plant sludge are generated annually. 87% of this is disposed of by landfill.

According to a 1985 study carried out by An Foras Forbartha, there is an additional 26,000 tonnes of lubricating oil dumped every year in Ireland.

Illegal Dumping

According to 1988 figures produced by Eolas, between 4,000 and 5,000 tonnes of toxic waste has disappeared since 1985. This would seem to be clear evidence that illegal dumping is taking place. Much of this waste probably found its way illegally to waste tipheads or was poured down drains. The maximum penalty for illegal dumping of toxic waste is a mere £1,000. There is also the problem of heavy metals entering the sea through the sewage system (see coastal water sewage, water chapter.)

Incineration

The chemical industry and its allies in the Department of the Environment insist that incineration is a safe and acceptable method of dealing with the global waste problem—providing the incinerator operator observes the three T's of: correct burn *temperature*, a minimum residence *time* in the burn chamber and sufficient *turbulence*.

Greenpeace research indicates that incineration is not a completely safe disposal method. Whatever the furnace temperature, dioxins are most commonly formed at lower temperatures in other parts of the incinerator, including the pollution control devices and smokestack. Thus, the temperature of the incinerator, no matter how high, does not reduce the potential for dioxin formation. Dioxins are, of course, extremely toxic and also carcinogenic.

Scientists in the US—those who work for the EPA and industry—have clearly shown that hazardous waste incinerators

LITTER

Litter is a serious and increasing environmental problem. Litter was described a 'national scandal' in the report *Litter and the Environment* prepared by the Environmental Council. The report goes on to state that 'the ugliness and squalor created by litter is now widespread throughout the country, not only in the streets of our cities and towns, but also deep in our countryside. It is affecting our tourist and industrial programmes, both of which are important to the future economic and social well-being of the country'. Tourist reaction to the problem has shown marked increase. In 1979 7.9% of visitors commented on litter. Now over half the letters received by the environment officer of Bord Failte concern the problem of litter.

About 46 tonnes of rubbish are removed from Dublin's streets every day. Dublin Corporation do their best to supply the city with litter bins, but an average of 600 have to be replaced every year because of vandalism.

Of far more concern to the authorities, however, is the now widespread practice of illegal dumping of domestic rubbish in rural areas. This is due primarily to people's reaction to the imposition of service charges, which vary considerably from county to county and even from district to district. For example, if you live in Galway city you pay a service charge of £40 for water and sewage disposal and refuse collection. In Ballinasloe you pay £83 for the same services. West of the Corrib, where they operate the 'tag a bag' system—at 50p a bag of rubbish—these services work out at £130 a year. East of the Corrib, you pay £82 for water and £70 for refuse collection, which is carried out by a private contractor.

This lack of uniformity has led to a certain resentment among people. It also means that poorer people simply can't afford to pay for refuse collection. Some counties operate a waiver system, whereby those who cannot afford it are given free tags and bags.

The Litter Act 1982 provides the local authorities with the powers for dealing with the problem of litter, fly-posting, graffiti and abandoned vehicles. The last of these is an increasing problem, with old cars being dumped often in the most scenic areas. The latest figures show that the Litter Act is now being enforced more vigorously than ever before, but the litter problem is getting worse.

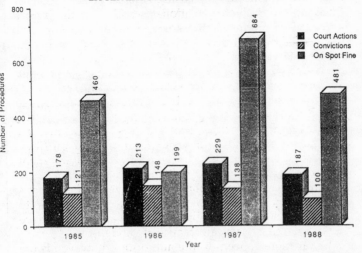

LITTER ENFORCEMENT PROCEDURES

emit toxic material into the air. The EPA science advisory board has stated that 'Land based hazardous waste incinerators are stationary point sources which emit pollutants into the air, land and water media. Emissions may occur as part of the incineration process, as part of the scrubber operations, or as fugitive emissions. Uptake of emissions by terrestrial life may occur through air, water, soil or via the food web'.

EPA operating standards for incinerators in the US specify destruction and removal efficiencies (DREs) of 99.99% and 99.9999% for critical items in the waste stream. This means that a proportion of the waste will always be emitted and given the complex mix of wastes in an incinerator, the chemicals formed in the incinerator plume are often more toxic and deadly than the original feedstock. Moreover, monitoring within the stack usually measures about 6 chemicals in the feedstock and cannot measure for the unknown range of compounds produced and emitted by the incineration process.

Greenpeace research also indicates that it is impossible to guarantee that incinerators will perform to stated standards. John Hanrahan, the Tipperary farmer, took eleven years to fight a court battle to establish that the Merck Sharpe and Dohme incinerator, functioning below recommended temperatures, caused wholesale fatalities in his dairy herd.

Having established that the functioning of incinerators is impossible to predict with assurance, there are other factors which make the technology a hazard to the environment and public health.

1. The formation and release of products of incomplete combustion (PICs) during incineration may pose a significant risk to the public, according to the EPA in the US. For example, when a chlorinated solvent is burned, most of it breaks down into carbon dioxide, water and chlorine. Of these, only the chlorine is toxic. However, the hot molecules also rearrange and recombine into many new, relatively complex chemicals. Among the more notoriously toxic PICs that were identified in the EPA's study of eight hazardous waste incinerators were benzene, chloroform, tetrachlor-ethylene, and napthalene as well as formaldehyde, phosgene, dioxins and furans...and these were only a fraction of the chemicals that are actually present in stack gases.

2. Toxic waste incinerators of the type proposed for Ireland are intended to burn all types of waste including the drums containing liquid waste and metals. Research shows that the metallic waste will not be burned. As much as 53% of the metal burned in an incinerator may be released in the stack gases.

3. Incinerators also generate waste: fly ash that goes up the stack, bottom ash that is left in the incinerator and residues from scrubbers.

When solid hazardous waste is burned, as much as 29% remains as ash. This incinerator ash carries toxic heavy metals and PICs which can cause serious water pollution if leached from landfilled sites.

Source Reduction And Clean Technology

So what are the solutions to the world's waste problems? Recycling, if possible, is one way out. It's far simpler, however, not to produce the waste in the first place. Greenpeace's toxic campaigns run on the slogan 'Reduce it, Don't Produce it' and this is the essence of clean technology and source reduction.

Clean Technology:

1. uses the minimum input of raw materials and energy to create a product
2. does not produce toxic waste during the manufacturing process
3. ensures that the final product itself does not create a waste problem after use

There are a variety of techniques used during a manufacturing process to avoid the generation of toxic waste:

Energy From Waste: Not only do human beings create a lot of waste, they also waste their waste. Waste is potential energy and it is a source of energy which we squander needlessly and use to pollute. Sewage and slurry could be used to produce biogas and fertilizer. Instead, they are dumped untreated into our seas and rivers causing disease and fishkills.

As the supply of fossil fuels decreases and pollution increases, energy from waste will become a more viable option.

Refuse: Generating energy from the combustion of refuse is becoming a more attractive prospect in large urban areas, where landfill sites are fast disappearing and the cost of refuse transportation is high.

There is a CHP (Combined Heat and Power—see ENERGY Chapter) district heating scheme based on waste incineration operating in Sheffield, England, and a refuse incinerator in North London produces £4 million worth of electricity annually.

As of yet there are no such schemes operating in Ireland. Dublin Corporation did propose such a scheme for Ballymun in Dublin but it was abandoned when locals objected on the grounds that the emissions from such an incinerator would be harmful to people's health. Indeed, if toxic waste is being burned it is very difficult to ensure that the emissions are not also toxic.

Dumps: Methane can be extracted from dumps. When certain micro-organisms are introduced the decomposition of the rubbish increases. Tapping dumps for methane gas is still not carried out in this country.

Straw: Ireland produces approximately 1.6 million tonnes of straw annually. In energy terms this is the equivalent of 0.86

million tonnes of coal. Much of this straw is wasted by burning it in the fields, when it could be burned in specialised burners for farm heating. There are over 8,800 such boilers operating in the UK.

Organic wastes: As we have seen, organic wastes, especially farm wastes, can have devastating effects on rivers because of their high BOD levels (see Water). But these wastes also contain chemical compounds such as sugars, amino acids and organic acids which are rich sources of energy.

These energy sources can be tapped through what is known as anaerobic digestion. This process occurs naturally in swamplands, producing marsh gas. In the absence of oxygen certain bacteria digest complex organic compounds giving out biogas. Biogas is similar in composition to natural gas. It contains between 60% and 80% methane, the remainder being made up of carbon dioxide.

Anaerobic digestion is a method which is particularly suited to dealing with dilute human, animal and vegetable wastes with a moisture content in excess of 45%.

Anaerobic digestors: Because of the high moisture content in organic waste such as animal slurry and sewage sludge they have been found not to be suitable for traditional methods of energy conversion such as combustion or gasification. Anaerobic digestion, however, is a method which has been found to be particularly well suited to dealing with dilute animal and vegetable wastes with a moisture content in excess of 45%. In the absence of oxygen certain bacteria digest complex organic compounds yielding a clean, energy-rich gaseous product—biogas, which retains 90% of the chemical energy available in the original waste. While this process occurs naturally under certain circumstances such as a swampland (producing swamp gas) or slurry lagoons, efficient energy extraction requires the optimisation of conditions, and this is achieved in a digestor.

Digestors are usually built of concrete and may be built on site—usually buried in the ground for strength and heat insulation—or from prefabricated insulated glass reinforced plastic (GRP) modules assembled to a specific situation. Anaerobic treatment of sewage sludge is now standard practice in many countries, whilst farm-based digestors are becoming increasingly popular in many countries. Cow manure is the basic feedstock being used by the Cistercian Monastic Community at Portglenone (Co. Antrim) in their digestor. The end products are methane, liquid fertiliser and organic compost.

Biogas: This is a high-grade source of energy, similar in composition to natural gas, it contains between 60-80% methane (CH_4), the remainder being mostly carbon dioxide with small traces of hydro sulphide. It can be burned cleanly in central heating boilers, or enclosed type ranges and gas cookers and can be piped over short distances to the point of use. Alternatively, it can be compressed into bottle liquid form (that is after scrubbing to remove the carbon dioxide) and used for vehicle propulsion.

However, there is a problem with biogas, namely its unsuitability for use in conventional engines as, on heating, carbonic and sulphuric acids are formed which cause damage to engine bearings. Les Gornall of Co. Derry has adapted the familiar 'nodding donkey' oilfields engine to overcome this problem. The single cylinder two-stroke cast iron engine has been given a sealed bulkhead behind its cylinder to block the acidic gases which are then expelled through a port. The engine, which has no mechanical valves and low velocity pistons, is also fitted with a heat recovery system and should have a 30 year lifetime. Heat and power are co-generated by the engine; the heat is used to warm the digestor whilst the electricity can be used to operate the installation and/or for grid export. The power is generated at 1p per unit as opposed to 7p conventionally.

Recycling

Did you know that we throw the equivalent of 4.5 million trees on the rubbish heap each year? It's true. It takes 17 trees to make one tonne of paper and every year we dump

Enviro Logic Consultancy

Contact: Donie or Mary Sheehy, 103 Balloonagh Estate, Tralee, Co. Kerry. Tel. 066-26260

We provide advice, data and materials regarding methods of recycling in a flexible service able to cater for the needs of UDCs, voluntary groups, etc. Past clients: Macra na Feirme, FÁS, Ógra Corcaí. We have personal experience in researching and running a recycling operation (KERRY RECYCLING) and will participate in workshops and lectures, info leaflets and audio visual materials provided. If related services other than mentioned are required, please enquire. Consultancy visits etc. all charged according to detail – concessionary fee available for voluntary groups.

approximately 270,000 tonnes of it. Paper makes up 25% of all Irish domestic and commercial waste, so clearly there ought to be a high potential for paper recycling in this country. Unfortunately, when it comes to the recycling business we come bottom of the EC league table (as is the case with most environmental matters). But, thankfully, things are changing in this area and a host of recycling units are springing up all over the country—so there can be no excuse anymore for simply discarding that heap of newspapers which has become a nuisance.

Why Recycle?

Well, for all sorts of good reasons. For a start, it's ecologically sound. Think of all the trees that can be saved.

• Recycling could save the country a lot of money by helping to eliminate the need for landfill sites, which are becoming more expensive as we run out of space. Every year we throw away approximately 1.1 million tonnes of refuse.

• Recycling means extra employment. It's a labour intensive industry which means more jobs, as the great success of the many Rehab bottle banks has shown.

• Recycling helps to cut down on our exploitation of the planet's finite resources. A lot of the energy required to mine and process these resources can also be saved. For example, the recycling of aluminium cans means a saving of up to 95% of the energy required to produce aluminium from bauxite ore.

All in all, the reasons for recycling can be summed up in the Victorian adage—Waste not, want not.

Paper

Newspapers actually make up the bulk of paper reclamation but almost any type of paper can be processed—magazines, cardboard, stationery, computer printout, even telephone directories. Generally speaking, paper of a similar type should be tied in bundles and all non-paper such as plastic and tin-foil removed.

If you wish to set up your own recycling scheme contact a waste paper merchant who will accept paper collected. Find out about the price to be paid, transport arrangements and the conditions which must be met as to the type of paper, quantities, amount of contamination (non-paper items) allowed, etc. Choose a site which is protected from the weather, highly visible and easily accessible.

Remember, also, that reusing or fully using paper is the first and best means of reducing our paper consumption. You can do this in the home or in the office by economical use of paper i.e. using paper on both sides and using the reverse sides of letters and reports for rough work. Envelopes can be reused using special labels available from Traidcraft Eireann.

By recycling paper and buying recycled products you are contributing to a healthier environment. *All those trees which you will save* provide the planet with life-giving oxygen and combat the Greenhouse Effect by absorbing carbon dioxide (one of the Greenhouse gases).

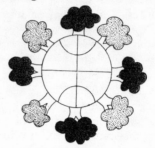

Glass

Glass containers can be reused or recycled many times. The glass milk bottle is a very eco-friendly product, having an average of 25 'lives'.

Returnable beer and soft drinks bottles have a return rate of about 12 trips unlike the 'six pack' type bottle which is 'disposable' (wasteful). 40% of the material used in the production of new glass may be in the form of cullet (crushed old glass) and it only takes 2,000-3,000 glass containers to make one tonne of this—a relatively small intake for a busy bottle bank.

In Germany, Belgium and Switzerland up to 40% of glass containers are recycled and the eco-conscious Swedes recycle nearly 90% of their glass containers. Again, Ireland lags well behind with only 10% of glass containers being recycled. On average, the Irish household discards 4-5 jars and bottles a week.

Rehab which has done trojan work in the area of glass reclamation is expanding its operation throughout the country, but most collection depots still tend to be concentrated in urban areas because of the high transport costs involved. Last year Rehab collected over six million bottles and jars.

All glass should be separated according to colour prior to delivery to the bottle bank. There are three colours, clear, brown (amber) and green (light green). Acceptable glass containers include jam jars, coffee jars, salad cream and sauce bottles. 'Non-returnable' bottles are suitable for recycling. Unacceptable items include crystal glass, plate glass, pyrex, opal glass, television tubes. Remember also to wash all bottles before delivery and to remove all steel and aluminium caps.

Plastic

Plastic is fast becoming the environmental scourge of this country. Supermarkets give out about 1000 million plastic bags every year. The average Irish household has 17 plastic carrier bags stuffed into bulging drawers and cupboards. Plastic is not bio-degradable. This means it does not decompose like natural products, but remains in the environment for hundreds, even thousands of years.

Two companies (see addresses below) specialise in plastic recycling in this country. Superwood Ltd. recycle bags, toys, trays, plastic packaging, bottles and containers, old crates and piping. From the recycled plastic they make a plastic 'lumber'. This is resistant to water, rot, fungus and insects and used primarily to make garden furniture. Wellman International Ltd. recycle large soft drink bottles, which are made from a substance called PET. These are shredded to make the lining for sleeping bags and parka jackets etc.

Superwood Ltd., Sandyford Industrial Estate, Dublin 18.
Tel: (01) 823913
Wellman International Ltd., Mullagh, Kells, Co. Meath.
Tel: (046) 40358

Superquinn & Quinsworth accept plastic bags. Superquinn Walkinstown and Recycle 2000, Donnelly Centre, Cork St (Tel. 531150) accept shampoo bottles, plastic mineral bottles and margarine tubs.

RECYCLING FROM FRIDGES

CFC's used as refrigerants are responsible for the depletion of the ozone layer as well as being one of the main greenhouse gases. Up until recently there was no facility in this country to recycle CFC's from old fridges. In 1990 the local authorities were asked to draw up plans for the recycling of coolants and the Government made £50,000 available for recycling facilities.

For more details contact the Department of the Environment.

Metals And Aluminium Cans

In this age of scarce resources metals are valuable and yet it is estimated that metals constitute 3% of domestic waste or approximately 33,000 tonnes. Aluminium is worth up to £300 per tonne, depending on the quality and the purchaser and 40,000–50,000 aluminium cans make one tonne. Every year over 57 million cans are sold in Ireland. So how can you recognise an aluminium can? It's quite simple, they're not magnetic so use the magnet test. If you can't find a magnet, use the magnetic catches on fridges and kitchen presses, etc. If it doesn't stick it's aluminium. We recycle only 4% at present.

There are other ways in which metals can be recycled.

• Ask your local authority to remove abandoned cars and trucks. They have powers to do so under the Litter Act, 1982.

• Make more use of scrap-metal merchants when you are finished with household goods such as washing machines, etc.
Address: Recoverable Resources, Tallaght, Dublin.Tel: (01) 503193

Oil

Waste oil can be a serious pollutant if it gets into drinking water supplies or natural habitats. A number of Irish companies reprocess waste oil into useful industrial by-products such as low-grade lubricant or boiler fuel.
Address: A&A Waste Oil, 58 Hadington Road, Dublin 4.
Tel: (01) 681355

WHAT YOU CAN DO

Recycling demands a certain amount of dedication and discipline—which perhaps explains why the Germans excel in all forms of recycling. There most households have three containers in their kitchen—one for bottles and jars, one for cans and one for food scraps which are bio-degradable and make excellent compost. Such dedication can't be expected immediately from the Irish householder, but you can make a start by forming a group and asking your local authority to facilitate and support you by the provision of equipment, removal of collected rubbish and the special opening of tip sites. You can also ask them to pay special attention to projects such as:

—clearance of areas of illegal dumping, removal of wrecked and abandoned cars and other debris;

—clean-up of amenity areas, including beaches, riversides, lay-byes, picnic sites, etc;

—clean up operations at public car-parks, public conveniences, and other public facilities;

—necessary redecoration work at public buildings and other public property;

—clearance and screening of derelict sites and other unsightly features;

—tidying of roadside verges and fences and other landscaping works;

—removal of unauthorised hoardings, etc. on public property and clearance of graffiti, posters, etc;

—removal or redundant traffic signs, poles and other street furniture.

RE-CYCLING INLETS:

Bottle Banks

ARTANE CASTLE (Dublin) Quinnsworth
BALBRIGGAN (Co. Dublin) Shopping Centre Entrance
BALLEALLY (Co. Dublin) Council Tip Head
BALLINCOLLIG (Co. Cork) L & N Shopping Centre
BALLINTEER (Co. Dublin) Superquinn
BALLYBRACK (Co. Dublin) Crazy Prices
BALLYOGAN (Co. Dublin) Council Tip Head
BALLYVOLANCE (Co. Cork) Dunnes Stores
BANDON (Co. Cork) Caulfields Supervalu
BANGOR (Co. Down) North Down Amenity Centre
BLACKROCK (Co. Dublin) Roches Stores
BLANCHARDSTOWN (Co. Dublin) Superquinn
BRAY (Co. Wicklow) Quinnsworth; Superquinn
CARRIGLANE (Co. Cork) Barry Collins Supermarket Car Park
CASTLEKNOCK (Co. Dublin) Village Shopping Centre
CHURCHTOWN (Co. Dublin) Supervalu
CLONDALKIN (Co. Dublin) Spar
CLONTARF (Co. Dublin) Nolan's Supermarket

COBH (Co. Cork) West View, Barrack Hill
CORNELSCOURT (Dublin) Dunnes Stores
CRUMLIN (Co. Dublin) Car Park
DALKEY (Co. Dublin) Supervalu
DONAGHMEDE (Co. Dublin) Shopping Centre
DOUGLAS (Co. Cork) Shopping Centre (beside Morris House)
DUBLIN 1 Dublin Simon Work Project at 9, Buckingham Street
4 Shelter Referral, Merrion Road
DUN LAOGHAIRE (Co. Dublin) Corporation Car Park
DUNSINK (Co. Dublin) Council Tip Head
FERMOY (Co. Cork) UDC Car Park (beside library)
FRIARSTOWN (Co. Dublin) Council Tip Head
GREYSTONES (Co. Wicklow) Quinnsworth
HOLLYHILL (Co. Cork) Quinnsworth
JANELLE shopping Centre Crazy Prices
KILLESTER (Co. Dublin) Supervalu
KINSALE (Co. Cork) Denis Key (beside candle factory)
KNOCKLYON (Dublin) Superquinn
LUCAN (Co. Dublin) Quinnsworth
MACROOM (Co. Cork) UDC Car Park (adjoining the Mart)
MALAHIDE (Co. Dublin) Supervalu

151

MALLOW (Co. Cork) UDC Car Park (adjoining Garda Station)
MAYNOOTH (Co. Kildare) Quinnsworth
MIDLETON (Co. Cork) Co-op Stores Car Park
NAAS (Co. Kildare) Main Street
NEWBRIDGE (Co. Dublin) Main Street
NUTGROVE Shopping Centre Quinnsworth
PORTLAOISE (Co. Laois) ring 0502-22301
RAHENY (Co. Dublin) Supervalu
RATHFARNHAM (Dublin) Quinnsworth
RATHMINES (Dublin) Quinnsworth
ROSELAWN Shopping Centre Quinnsworth

SANDYFORD (Dublin) Crazy Prices
SANDYMOUNT (Dublin) Quinnsworth
SHANKILL (Co. Dublin) Londis
SKERRIES (Co. Dublin) Holmpatrick Supermarket
SUTTON (Co. Dublin) Superquinn
SWORDS (Co. Dublin) Superquinn
TALLAGHT (Co. Dublin) Cuckoo's Nest Lounge
TERENURE (Co. Dublin) Corporation Car Park
TRABOLGAN (Co. Cork) Holiday Centre
WALKINSTOWN (Dublin) Superquinn
WILTON (Co. Cork) Shopping Centre
YOUGHAL (Co. Cork) UDC Car Park (beside Harbour Lights Bar)

Glass

BALBRIGGAN	Trevor Sargent (will collect) 01-412371
BALLYOGAN (Co. Dublin)	County Council Tip Head,
BANGOR (Co. Down)	North Down Amenity Centre, Rallyat Road, 08-0247-270371
CLONMEL (Co. Tipperary)	County Council Tip Head, Coole, 052-22100
DUBLIN 1	Dublin Simon Work Project, Old Fire Station, 9, Buckingham Street, 01-787138
	Shelter Referral, Merrion Road, 01-691686
FRIARSTOWN (Co. Dublin)	County Council Tip Head,
PORTLAOISE (Co. Laois)	Saint Mary's Workforce, 0502-22301
TULLAMORE (Co. Dublin)	County Council Tip Head, Derryclue, 0506-21419
WATERFORD (Co. Waterford)	Corporation Tip Head, 051-73501
WEXFORD (Co. Wexford)	County Council Tip Head, Carcur, 053-22211

Metals

ATHLONE (*Co. Roscommon*) O'Mearas Garage, Baylough, 0902-92325; ATHLONE (*Co. Westmeath*) Hammond Lane Metal Company, The Batteries, 0902-92965; BIRR (*Co. Offaly*) Arthur Bridge, Railway Road, 047-81596; BLACKPOOL (Co. Cork) Hammond Lane Metal Company, Spring Lane, 021-502271; BRAY (*Co. Wicklow*) Southside Waste Paper Ltd., (aluminium cans) 01-828467; Central Garage, Main Street, 01-862142; CASHEL (*Co. Tipperary*) O'Doherty and Dwyer,

Cork Road, 062-61544; CLONDRINAGH (*Limerick*) Thomond Metals Ltd.; CLONMEL (*Co. Tipperary*) Brian Murdart Motors, Davis Road Tipperary County Council, Tip Head, Coole, 052-22100; DUBLIN 2 Hammond Lane Metal Company, Sir John Rogerson's Quay, (Heavy and bulky scrap metals, household metal goods such as washing machines and cookers, car bodies, plated metal) 01-779414; DUBLIN 8 Camden Metals, 35, Pleasants Street, (cans, car batteries, and all types of non-ferrous metals) 01-786619; Cummins Metal Recycling Ltd., Old Naas Road, (any metal) 01-501049; P & D Metals Ltd., 63, Prussia Street, (all scrap metals except car bodies) 01-713517; DUBLIN 12 Recoverable Resources, 23A, Greenhills Industrial Estate, (aluminium cans) 01-503193; DUNGARVAN (*Co. Waterford*) C.A.B. Ltd., The Quay, 058-41900; EDENDERRY (*Co. Offaly*) Liam Hogan Motors, Dublin Road; ENNISCORTHY (*Co. Wexford*) J. Donaghue Ltd., Temple Shannon, 054-33214; KELLS (*Co. Meath*) P. Carney Ltd., Crossakiel, 046-43634; Pat Farrelly Motors, Mahonstown; LIMERICK (*Co. Limerick*) Long Pavement, 061-55188; MONAGHAN (*Co. Monaghan*) McElvaney Motors, Dublin Road, 047-81596; MULLINGAR (*Co. Westmeath*) C. Sleator & Sons, Lynn Industrial Estate, 044-40350; NAVAN (*Co. Meath*) Joe Norris Motors, Kells Road, 046-21312; NENAGH (*Co. Tipperary*) Cleary Garage, Limerick Road, 067-31310; NEW ROSS (Co. Wexford) James Ryan Haulage, Wexford Road, 051-21673; ROSCOMMON (*Co. Roscommon*) Connaught Motors, Lanes-boro Road, 0903-26443; TEMPLEMORE (*Co. Tipperary*) Templemore Motor Works, The Mall, 0504-31222; THURLES (*Co. Tipperary*) P.M.P.A. Garage, Stradaver, 054-21300; TIPPERARY (*Co. Tipperary*) Modern Motors, Golbally Road; Spooners Garage, Roscrea; Sean Ward Garage, Fethard, 052-31181; TRALEE (*Co. Kerry*) Kerry Recycling Cooperative, 119, Rock Street; TULLAMORE (*Co. Offaly*) R.F. Colton, Clara Road, 0506-21607; County Council Tip Head, Derryclue, 0506-21419; WALKINSTOWN *see under Dublin 12*; WATERFORD (*Co. Waterford*) Cove Motors, Dunmore Road, 051-75463; Saggart Garage, Cappoquin; Waterford Corporation, Tip Head, Kilbarry, 051-73501; WEXFORD (*Co. Wexford*) Ferrybank Motors, Dublin Road, 053-22544; Percival Motors, Newtown Road; Wexford County Council, Tip Head, Carcur, 053-22211; WICKLOW (*Co. Wicklow*) Porter Brothers, South Quay, 0404-67142

Oil

County	
Carlow	Byrnes Garage, Bunclody Road, Tullow.
	Sheedy Bros, Green Lane, Carlow.
Cavan	County Council Tip Head, Coranure, Cavan.
	Jackson Garage, Farnham Street, Cavan.
	O'Reilly Bros., The Diamond, Belturbet.
Clare	T. Shield Motors, Lifford Road, Ennis.
Cork	Barrys, Bantry; Tony Buckley, Quarterstown, Mallow;

	Corporation Tip Head, Kinsale Road, Cork; G. Galvin Garage, Dunmanway; Mike Hurley Motors, Skibbereen; Kanturk Motor Works, Kanturk; Tony Lowney Motors, Strand Road, Clonakilty; L.W.T. Motors, Clancy Street, Fermoy; Macroom Motor Services, Cork Road, Macroom; Middleton Car Care, The Green, Middleton; J.P. O'Hea & Co., Patrick's Quay, Cork; Smith's Garage, Bishoptown, Wilton, Cork; Star Garage, Bandon.
Donegal	James Gallagher, Drumkeen, Ballybofey.
	R.E. Johnson, Quay Street, Donegal.
	McDaid Bros., Ballybofey Road, Letterkenny.
Down	North Down Amenity Centre, Bangor.
Dublin	Cornelscourt Garage, Cornelscourt; Crawford's Garage, Beech Road, Sandymount, Dublin 4; County Council Tip Head, Balleally, Lusk; County Council Tip Head, Ballyogan, Sandyford; County Council Tip Head, Dunsink Lane, Finglas; County Council Tip Head, Friarstown, Tallaght; Gowan Motors, Parkgate Street, Dublin 8; Tom O'Neill Motors, 457, North Circular Road, Dublin 7; Sandycove Motors, Glasthule Road, Dun Laoghaire; Self Motoring Ltd., Newland's Cross, Clondalkin; Sweeney & Forte, Howth Road, Clontarf; A & A Waste Oil, 58 Haddington Rd., Dublin 4.
Galway	Bermingham & Doyle Garage, Loughrea, Galway.
	Castle Motors, Spanish Parade, Galway.
	Fred Kilmartin, Athlone Road, Ballinasloe.
	Tuam Motor Works, Galway Road, Tuam.
Kerry	Bowlers, Muckross Road, Killarney.
	S. Divane & Sons Ltd., Killarney Road, Castleisland.
	Listowel Motor Works, Listowel.
	Moran's Garage, Dingle.
	Brian Sheehey Car Sales, Boherbue, Tralee.
Kildare	Brennan Car Sales, Kildare Road, Newbridge.
	John Brown, Kilcock Service Station, Kilcock.
	FitzPatrick Garage, Dublin Road, Monasterevin.
	Joe Mallon Motors, Dublin Road, Naas.
	National Garage, Carlow Road, Athy.
Kilkenny	College Road Service Station, College Road, Kilkenny.
	Statham Kilkenny Ltd., 12, Patrick Street, Kilkenny.
Laois	Central Garage, Emmet Street, Mountmellick.
	Atlas Oil, Portlaoise.
	F. Cunningham & Sons, Abbeyleix Road, Portlaoise.
	County Council Tip Head, Kilateleesha, Portlaoise.
Leitrim	Motorland, Dublin Road, Carrick-on-Shannon.
Co. Limerick	B.P. Service Station, Dooradoyle, Limerick.
	Frank Bresnan Motors, Shanagolden, Limerick.
	Dooley Garage, Knocklong, Limerick.

	Ennis Road Motors, Ennis Road, Limerick.
	Council Machinery Yard, Limerick.
	M.A.G. Motors, Gerrynormyle, Newcastle West.
	Toy O'Connor, Main Street, Croom.
Longford	McNally Garage, Killaslee Street, Longford.
Louth	Mike Holecroft, Bridge View, Hand Street, Drogeda.
	Allied Waste Disposal, Dundalk.
	Rice & Roddy Ltd., Newry Road, Dundalk.
Mayo	J. Casey Motors, Turlough Road, Castlebar.
	Clarke Auto Service, Killala Road, Ballina.
	Tom Fahy Garage, Ballinrobe, Mayo.
	Hastings Garage, Westport.
	O'Brien's Garage, Westport.
	Rochford Motors, Ballyhaunis.

Paper

ATHLONE	(Co. Westmeath) Athlone Waste Paper, Cornamaddy Industrial Estate, 0902-78862
BANGOR	(Co. Down) North Down Amenity Centre, Rallyat Road, 08-0247-270371
BRAY	(Co. Wicklow) Southside Waste Paper, Dublin Road, 01-828467
CARLOW	(Co. Carlow) Frank Holden, 0503-21065
CLARA	(Co. Offaly) Flanagan & Fleming, 0506-31421
CLONMEL	(Co. Tipperary) 0'Meara Waste Disposal, 051-43144 Tipperary County Council Tip Head, Coole, 052-22100
DROGHEDA	(Co. Louth) Drogeda Waste Paper, 041-35748
DUBLIN 1	Leech Paper Ltd., Shamrock Place, North Strand, 01-740942
DUBLIN 7	Baily Waste Paper Ltd., 31, Manor Street, 01-386009
DUBLIN 8	Floods Waste Paper Merchants, 122, Cork Street, 01-535031
DUBLIN 12	Central Waste Paper Ltd., Ballymount Road, 01-552821
DUBLIN 14	Mrs. Boland, (Animal Welfare) 22, Balally Drive, 01-951770
DULEEK	(Co. Meath) James McKenna, Drogheda Road, 041-35748
DUNDALK	(Co. Louth) Matt Dullaghan, 042-38805
DUNDRUM	see Dublin 14
GALWAY	(Co. Galway) John Lynch, Palkeen Industrial Estate, Tuam Road, 091-92011
KILKENNY	(Co. Kilkenny) Kilkenny Waste Paper, 056-33457
LIMERICK City	(Co. Limerick) Limerick Waste Paper Enterprises, Blackboy Pike, Fairgreen, Ballysimon Road, 061-45908
LONGFORD	(Co. Longford) Alan O'Toole, 043-45170
MALLOW	(Co. Cork) Glenamore Waste Paper Ltd., 022-26250
MERLYN PARK GALWAY	(Co. Galway) Galway Waste Paper Recycling Ltd., Doughuisce, 091-53390

NAVAN	(Co. Meath) Duleek Co-operative, 041-23284
PEMBROKESTOWN	(Co. Wexford) Wexford Plant Hire, Carrigbawn, 053-22295
PORTLAOISE	(Co. Laois) Saint Mary's Workforce, 0502-22301
SKERRIES	(Co. Dublin) Community Centre Car Park, (first Saturday of the month) 01-491050
SLIGO	(Co. Sligo) Sligo Waste Paper, 071-85066
STILLORGAN	(Co. Dublin) Co-Workers of Mother Teresa, rear of Oaklands College, (Monday-Friday after 4pm, Weekends all day) 01-880784
TOGHER	(Co. Cork) Cork Recycling Ltd., Legenmore Industrial Estate, 021-871808
TRALEE	(Co. Kerry) Kerry Recycling Co-operative, 119, Rock Street, 066-26260
TULLAMORE	(Co. Offaly) Offaly County Council Tip Head, Derryclue, 0506-21419
WALKINSTOWN	see Dublin 12
WATERFORD	(Co. Waterford) David Phelem Waste Paper Merchant, 051-70722
	Corporation Tip Head, Kilbarry, 051-73501
WEXFORD	(Co. Wexford) County Council Tip Head, Carcur, 053-22211

Plastics

Superwood Ltd., Corke Abbey, Bray, Co. Wicklow, (recycles bags, toys, trays, plastic packaging, bottles, containers, old crates and piping). **Wellman International Ltd.**, Mullagh, Kells, Co. Meath, 046-40358 (recycles large soft drinks bottles). Both the above companies take plastics from industries only, not from the public. **The East Clare Waste Recycling Ltd.**

Vegetable Oil & Grease

LIMERICK	(Co. Limerick) B & N Foods, 1 Mulgrave Street

Your Waste Costs the Earth

The Average Family
throws away in one year —
- 624 family-size plastic drinks bottles
- 6 trees worth of paper
- 600 cans
80% of household waste is reusable

VIII
THE HOUSEHOLD CONSUMER

'If you pause to think about the environmental movement, it bears all the hallmarks of a carefully orchestrated and carefully thought through marketing onslaught: the fact, the emotion, the play on insecurity and need for reassurance, the promise'

The above quotation is taken from a paper entitled 'The Greening of Advertising' by an Irish Ad agency. Advertisers have been quick to realise that they cannot beat the Green revolution so they're intent on joining and, if possible, taking it over. They have taken the basic green message of 'consume less' and distorted it. Consume as much as you like, they tell us, as long as it's 'environment friendly'. Green and greed can live in perfect harmony. You can have your cake and eat it too.

'Green' is now such a big selling point that some of the claims made by advertisers are to say the least spurious. Products which never contained CFCs are suddenly 'ozone friendly'. Roll on deodorants are 'CFC free', washing up liquids which never contained phosphates are 'phosphate free'. A recent survey has shown that half of Irish shoppers believe the environment claims on packaging. 56% of our shoppers have difficulty identifying what is a green product and what is not and they are very much at the mercy of unscrupulous advertisers.

LABELLING

The shopper's confusion in the face of all these 'environment friendly' claims shows that there is a real need for a proper labelling system. The Consumer Association of Ireland has called for the introduction of a recognised and official symbol. It also believes that there should be prohibition on 'unofficial' labels 'passing off' as the official label. Their submissions are currently being considered by the Department of the Environment.

The Blue Angel symbol in Germany was set up in 1978. It now has over 3,000 products which have met specific environmental standards. The scheme is a voluntary one with the manufacturer paying an annual fee once the product has been approved. Canada has a similar scheme, but it places more emphasis on the environmental impact of the product from its production to its disposal.

This is how it should be when we're assessing just how environment friendly a product is, according to Dr David Jeffrey of Trinity College.

Ground Rules

Dr Jeffrey believes that the environmental impact can be simplified to comprise three key elements: *energy use*, *materials resource use* and *pollution*. There are other green criteria too such as animal welfare, effects on human health and safety, but if we're talking strictly about impact on the planet then the first three are the most important. When analysed in this way it implies that there are no 'environment friendly' products. Every human action leaves an environmental trace. The point is to minimise that impact.

When it comes then to green consumerism, there are some obvious 'don'ts'. The very first is don't buy 'disposable' goods. These use up a lot of precious energy in production and are then simply dumped. And if possible don't go for goods which don't last. Built-in obsolescence is simply an extended form of disposability.

Always go for durability. The fridge which lasts five years and the one which lasts thirty may have required the same amount of energy in their manufacture, but the five year fridge has six times the environmental impact because it has to be replaced so many times.

One more tip for green shoppers: Health food stores have been stocking green products – washing-up liquids etc. – for years before it became fashionable. People who work there will also be able to advise you. So try them before going to the bigger supermarket chains

AROUND THE HOUSE

Let's take a trip around the average house to see how we can improve our environment and health by the way we use our money.

Readers should note, however, that many of the areas such as recycling, ozone friendly products, timber products, energy use, etc are covered in detail in the relevant chapter in this book (– eg Chapters on AIR, WASTE, TREES, etc. see Contents List).

The Bathroom

We're told by advertisers that all germs need to be exterminated, especially those which lurk in the bathroom. We've become so obsessed with germs that the average household uses enough cleaners to fill a bath every year. There is no need for the excessive use of bleaches, which can cause the formation of poisonous chlorine gas if mixed with other cleaners. A solution of vinegar is a much cleaner and safer way to disinfect your toilet.

Bleaches create difficulty for the natural bacteria which are necessary to break down sewage. Some are based on the acidic material, sodium hydrogen sulphate, which can irritate the eyes, skin and lungs. Choose a toilet cleaner from the ECover range.

Some bathroom fresheners contain paradichlorbenzene, which causes cancer in animals: they are best avoided. Instead choose natural fragrances (see Health-aromatherapy). Essential oils such as lavender or can bergamot be used with a burner. They are stimulating and very refreshing.

Cosmetics and Toiletries: Most deodorants and sprays are now CFC-free and the Supermarkets carry a wide range. Some of the 'cruelty-free' cosmetics have already been listed under the Animals section. The Body Shop, which is expanding its chain throughout Ireland, stocks only cruelty free products.

If you're looking for cosmetics and toiletries which are not tested on animals and which are 100% natural, then look for the Weleda and Dr Hauschka ranges. Weleda products, which also include toothpaste, are available in many of the health-food stores. Dr Hauschka products are of a very high quality and more expensive and are being stocked by more health food stores.

More information on Dr. Hauschka products, is available at Dublin (01) 843153.

Loo paper, Sanitary Towels: Earthwatch have highlighted the fact that the claims by some manufacturers that their toilet paper is made from recycled paper are misleading. According to

Earthwatch, toilet paper has always been made from 90% recycled fibre. Many fancy toilet papers are also chlorine bleached, which results in the production of dioxins. Unbleached, recycled paper is still not widely available in this country.

Chlorine bleach is also used in some sanitary towel production, but this practice is now on the decrease. The plastic backing and strips on towels are not biodegradable and cause pollution of our seas (see Water) when they enter through sewers. Try to avoid flushing them down the toilet.

A few final tips for the bathroom:

Avoid buying the new fashionable mahogany toilet seats. Remember where they come from (see Trees)

Take a shower instead of a bath. Furthermore, a temperature control on the shower saves even more energy—and money too!

The flush toilet uses the greatest quantity of water in the home. Each flush consumes about ten litres of water. A dual flush system can be fitted by a plumber. The system allows you to give a full flush or half flush, and this saves water and energy.

The Kitchen

The Energy Chapter gives some hints on how to make your home more energy efficient and this applies very much in the kitchen. Perhaps we should recap briefly on the advice:

- use a gas cooker
- use the washing machine for full loads only
- use a pressure cooker and a kettle which switches itself off automatically
- a well stocked freezer or fridge uses less energy than one that is half-full.

Detergents and washing up liquids: The phosphates contained in washing up powders can cause eutrophication in lakes, rivers and seas. This build up of green algae uses up oxygen and can lead to fish kills (see Water). Most washing powders and liquids also contain enzymes, bleaches, optical brighteners, colourings and perfumes. (see Chart) These add to the toxic chemicals in our rivers and can cause allergies and skin irritations.

Choose your washing powder or washing up liquid from the Ecover or Ark range. These use substances derived from vegetables and break down naturally in the environment. They also do not involve animal testing.

Like the bathroom cleaning products, kitchen cleaners are often unnecessary and bad for the environment. For good kitchen management all that is required are three basic products – a washing up liquid, a washing powder or liquid and an all-purpose household cleaner such as baking soda. Add to these a little elbow grease and you're doing your bit for the environment.

Food: More and more stores are now claiming to stock organic food. Unless it carries the IOFGA symbol, don't believe them. (see Food and Soil) If there is a 'Country Market' in your area, support it.

Remember to avoid food which is over-packaged. Cling film and other forms of plastic wrapping are known to release plasticisers, potential carcinogens, into the contents. Fatty foods such as cheese and meat are particularly vulnerable and anyway, they are better left to breathe.

Over packaging also causes the build-up of rubbish, which is to be avoided if we're to get into a recycling frame of mind. (See the Waste and Recycling Chapter)

The Nursery

Many baby products are not environment friendly. The disposable nappy, a godsend for busy mums, is one such item. It takes one fully grown tree to make 500 nappies. If the nappies are bleached with poisonous chlorine – that's all the worse. Nappies using non-chlorine bleached pulp are now available in Quinns-worth and Superquinn, but they are disposable.

Green Baby Products: 100% cotton nappies from Eric and Amy Mitchell, Minard, Lispoll, Co Kerry.

The Marketplace

The major supermarkets are now becoming very Green-conscious. *Quinnsworth* have devised a completely new range of GREEN products, which are clearly identified.

Superquinn have in many ways led the field in this direction. A list of some of the Eco-friendly 'GREENWATCH' products stocked by them is given here.

Other recommended ranges include: Body Shop; Waleda; Simple; Dr. Hauschka.

CFC-free Sprays: See list under Ozone, AIR chapter.

Timber: See TREES Chapter

Food: See List of Organic Farmers, SOIL & FOOD Chapter.

Also list of Health-food Shops, HEALTH Chapter.

GIFTS

When you're buying gifts, consider looking for hand-crafted items. These small enterprises are more energy-efficient, and the goods are likely to be made of organic materials. The craftsman is preserving old skills and perhaps developing new ones, and each item is unique, unlike manufactured items, which come off a conveyor-belt of sameness.

BUILDING BIOLOGY

HOW alive is your living room? How healthy is your house? Is it breathing and living in harmony with the natural environment? The combination of low grade poisons emitted by certain paints and drying agents and electro stress caused by continuous exposure to fields of alternating current in our homes and places of work has caused a variety of symptoms for some people. The phenomenon has given rise to the phrases 'sick home' and 'sick building'.

A new scientific discipline has developed and has become well established on the continent: 'Building Biology'. This discipline is becoming increasingly recognised in the UK and Ireland as a solution to these kinds of problems.

A health hazard is posed by modern surface treatment, such as paint, adhesives, polishes, preservatives. These can cause asthma and allergies, according to William Bodewigs of Auro Paints, an organic paint company here in Ireland. He is himself a 'building biologist' and runs a counselling and testing service.

The petrochemicals in paints can cause serious pollution as the Alaskan oil spillage showed. Emulsion contains a fungicide – often pentachlorphenyl. This remains volatile after the paint has dried. Lead is still permitted in thinners, and undercoat and cadmium is often put in paint as a drying agent.

Auro's paints are made from plants and tree oils, minerals and resins. These allow air and moisture through, whereas vinyl paints seal walls.

Formaldehyde is perhaps the worst poison to be found in homes. It can cause cancer and allergies as well as headaches and depression. It is found in laminated plywood, chipboard, synthetic varnishes and as glue in house furnishings.

The 'Building Biologist' will also look at things that might affect the electrical stresses in our bodies. Traditional beds have metal springs and frames. Metal is a very energy intensive material to produce. It can also become charged with electro magnetic stresses from household electricity that can slightly alter the electrical impulses within our bodies. So it's better to choose a wooden frame, making sure that the wood is from a sustainable source (see Trees). If possible change to a mattress filled with cotton or latex. Futons are very comfortable and now widely available in Ireland.

For more details on organic house materials—which include varnishes and oilpaints (undercoat and gloss), wall paints and adhesives, household cleaners and polishes, artists' and children's paints, ring AURO IRELAND; W. Bodewigs, Doon Lough, Fivemilebourne, Co Leitrim. Tel. (071) 43452 Fax 44200. Another natural paint company is BIOFA (0619) 23014 OR (065) 25559; Garry Gleeson, Carrigmore, Clogheen, Co Tipperary. Tel. (052) 65235. It offers advice on home insulation and maintenance to ecological principals.

BAKING SODA

is the most useful General Cleaner for your household. Use it for silver, oven, loo, drains, stains.
It will save you using corrosive and toxic proprietary brands – and it's cheaper too!

GREENING YOUR HOME

It is essential first to understand the principles of a green approach, and then to begin gradually, perhaps room by room, to make yours a green, planet friendly household.

SUPERQUINN Selected list of GREENWATCH Products

Phosphate Free Detergents

Daz Auto Liquid	1	Albright & Wilson
Fairy Auto Liquid	1	Albright & Wilson
Ariel Auto Liquid	1	Albright & Wilson
Frend Auto Liquid	1	Reckitt & Colman
Bright White Auto Powder	1	Roma
Ecover Washing Powder	1	Gillespie
Ecover Washing Up Liquid	1	Gillespie
Ecover Fabric Conditioner	1	Gillespie
Ecover Cream Cleaner	1	Gillespie
Ecover Toilet Cleaner	1	Gillespie
Ecover Wool Wash Liquid	1	Gillespie
Ecover Floor soap	1	Gillespie
Green Force Bio Auto Powder	1	F A Wyatt
Green Force Bio Auto HDLD	1	F A Wyatt
Green Force Toilet Cleaner	1	F A Wyatt
Green Force Cream Cleaner	1	F A Wyatt
Green Force Liquid Cleaner	1	F A Wyatt
Green Force Fabric Conditioner	1	F A Wyatt
Green Force Washing Up Liquid	1	F A Wyatt

Chlorine Free Paper Products

Comfies Nappies	4	Nokia
Thrift Nappies	1	Nokia
Cuddlies	2	F A Wyatt
Southalls	2	Smith & Nephew
Lilets	3	Smith & Nephew
Meliltta Coffee Filters	2	Stafford Lynch

Recycled Paper Products

Thrift Luxury Toilet Rolls 2's	1	Nokia
Thrift toilet Rolls 6's	1	Nokia

Mercury Free Batteries

Phillips Green Line Batteries	3	Phillips

Environmental Friendly Cosmetics

Vegetable Soap	5	D Mayrs
Almond Scrub	1	D Mayrs
Cleansing Lotion	1	D Mayrs
Toning Lotion	1	D Mayrs
Moisturiser	4	D Mayrs
Body Oil	1	D Mayrs
Skin Care Travel Pack	1	D Mayrs
Shampoo	4	D Mayrs
Conditioner	3	D Mayrs
Only Natural Shampoo	5	Only Natural
Only Natural Foam Bath	3	Only Natural

Washday Options, Courtesy *Green*

Magazine 1989. The chart does not include liquid detergents which are often phosphate free

BRAND	USES	PETRO CHEMICAL BASE	TRAD. SOAP BASE	PLANT OIL BASE	PHOSPHATES	OXYGEN BLEACH	CHLORINE BLEACH	OPTICAL BRIGHTENING AGENT	ENZYMES	PERFUMES	COLOUR
ARIEL	Fabric (Not FLA) washing	Yes	No	No	Yes	Yes	No	Yes	Yes	Yes	Yes
ARIEL AUTO	Fabric (Inc. FLA)	Yes	No	No	Yes	Yes	No	Yes	Yes	Yes	Yes
BOLD 3	Fabric (Inc. FLA's)	Yes	No	No	Yes	Yes	No	Yes	Yes	Yes	Yes
DAZ	Fabrics (Not FLA's)	Yes	No	No	Yes	Yes	No	Yes	Yes	Yes	No
DAZ AUTO	Fabric (Inc. FLA's)	Yes	No	No	Yes	Yes	No	Yes	Yes	Yes	Yes
FAIRY SNOW	Fabrics (Not FLA's)	Yes	No	No	Yes	Yes	No	Yes	No	Yes	Yes
LUX	Hand wash Wool & delicates	No	Yes	No	No	No	No	No	No	Yes	No
PERSIL	Fabrics Top loaders & hand	No	Yes	No	Yes	No	No	Yes	No	Yes	No
NEW SYSTEM PERSIL AUTO	Fabric (Inc FLA's)	Yes	No	No	Yes	Yes	No	Yes	Yes	Yes	No
TIDE	Fabrics (Not FLA's)	Yes	No	No	Yes	Yes	No	No	No	Yes	No
SURF	Fabrics (Not FLA's)	Yes	No	No	Yes	Yes	No	Yes	Yes	Yes	Yes
SURF AUTO	Fabrics (Inc FLA's)	Yes	No	No	Yes	Yes	No	Yes	Yes	Yes	Yes
GREEN FORCE	Fabrics (Inc FLA's)	Yes	No	No	No	Yes	No	Yes	Yes	Yes	No
BOOTS AUTO	Fabrics (Inc FLA's)	Yes	No	No	Yes	Yes	No	Yes	Yes	No	No
ASDA NON BIO AUTO	Fabrics (Inc FLA's)	Yes	No	No	No	Yes	No	No	No	No	No
TESCO PHOS-FREE AUTO	Fabrics (Inc FLA's)	Yes	No	No	No	Yes	No	Yes	Yes	Yes	No
ARK CONCEN-TRATED	Fabrics (Inc FLA's)	Yes	Yes	Yes	No	Yes	No	No	No	Fragrance fruit-based	No
ECOVER	Fabrics (Inc FLA's)	No	No	Yes	No	No	No	No	No	No	No
M&S SENSITIVE SKIN	Fabrics (Inc FLA's)	Yes	No	No	30% less	Yes	No	Yes	No	No	No

TAKE A LEAF FROM OUR ROLL

We all want to do our bit for the environment. That's why Jumbos are now made from 100% recycled paper.

And they're now even better value than ever - with 300 large sheets in every roll.

Jumbos are softer, stronger and longer.

Sure you'd be out of your tree to use anything else!

Basic Ingredients

Five basic ingredients serve as the building blocks for many
safe home-cleaning needs:

Baking soda — cleans and deodorizes. Softens water to increase
sudsing and cleaning power of soap. Good scouring powder.

Borax — cleans and deodorizes. Excellent disinfectant.
Softens water. Available in laundry section of grocery store.

Soap — biodegrades safely and completely and is nontoxic.
Available in grocery stores and health food stores. Sold as
liquid, flakes, powder or in bars. Bars can be grated to dissolve
more easily in hot water. Insist on soap without synthetic scents,
colors or other additives. Synthetic detergents cause more poi-
sonings than any other household product. Even phosphate-free,
biodegradable laundry detergent contributes to water pollution.

Washing soda — cuts grease and removes stains. Disinfects.
Softens water. Available in laundry section of grocery store or
in pure form from chemical supply houses as "sodium carbonate."

White vinegar — cuts grease and freshens.

General Cleansers

Use the simplest, mildest formula to get the job done. First try
warm water mixed with soap (or vinegar if the surface will show
spots), adding borax, washing soda or baking soda if needed.

All purpose cleaner — mix 2 teaspoons borax and 1 tsp. soap
in 1 quart water for a cleaner you can store in a spray bottle.

Disinfectant — for hospital-quality disinfectant, use $1/4$ cup borax
dissolved in $1/2$ gallon hot water. Keeping surfaces clean and dry
reduces the need for disinfectants.

Scouring powder — if available, buy a powder without chlorine,
colors, detergents or talc; or scrub with a sponge or firm-bristle
brush, soap and either: borax, baking soda or table salt.

For a better environment
(in more ways than one.)

Air freshener — commercial fresheners work by masking smells, coating nasal passages and deadening nerves to diminish sense of smell. Instead:

- find sources of odors and eliminate them;
- keep house and closets clean and well-ventilated;
- grow lots of houseplants;
- to absorb odors, place 2 to 4 tablespoons baking soda or vinegar in small bowls in the refrigerator and around the house, and pour 1/2 cup baking soda in the bottom of trash cans;
- for natural fragrance, boil sweet herbs and spices.

Cleaning Methods

Carpets. Remove stains promptly by scraping up solids and blotting liquids; follow by dabbing with a solution of water and vinegar. Sponge with clean water and blot dry. To get rid of odors and greasy soil, mix 2 parts corn meal with 1 part borax, sprinkle liberally, leave one hour and vacuum. (As a last resort, a solution of water and ammonia can be used. First, neutralize spot with weak vinegar solution.)

Dishes. Use liquid or powdered soap. For tougher jobs, add 2 to 3 tsp. vinegar. In automatic dishwashers, use equal parts borax and washing soda. Commercial dishwashing liquids are detergents designed to create unnecessary suds.

Drains. Some rules-of-thumb: never pour grease down a drain, always use a drain sieve or hair trap and clean the metal screen or stopper mechanism regularly. Remove hair with a 1/4-inch bend in the end of a coat hanger. Once a week, as routine maintenance, plug the overflow drain with a wet rag, pour 1/4 cup baking soda down the drain, follow with 1/2 c. vinegar and close the drain tightly until fizzing stops. Flush with 1 gallon boiling water. If the flow slows or stops, plug the overflow drain, dissolve 1 lb. washing soda in 3 gal. boiling water, pour down the drain and use a plunger with petroleum jelly on its rim for a good seal. If the clog persists, flush the drain with same formula and use a plumber's snake instead of a plunger.

Ovens. Avoid over-filling pans, scrape up spills as soon as food is cool enough to handle, and put a cookie sheet on bottom rack when baking. When cleanup is needed, use steel wool and washing soda with a small amount of water. (As a last resort for particularly bad grime, use 1/2 cup ammonia dissolved in 1 gal. hot water for scrubbing; provide plenty of ventilation.)

Tub, Tile and Toilet. Scrub with sponge or firm-bristled brush, using powdered soap and a scouring powder of baking soda, borax or table salt. Use undiluted vinegar to loosen lime deposits.

Windows and Mirrors. For routine cleaning, use 3 tablespoons vinegar with 1 quart warm water. If the glass is particularly dirty, first wash with warm soapy water.

Laundry

When making the initial switch from a detergent to a soap laundry cleaner, wash items once with washing soda only. This will eliminate detergent residues that might otherwise react with soap to cause a yellowing of fabrics.

Bleach. Substitute 1/2 cup borax per washload to whiten whites and brighten colors. If needed, occasionally use powdered, non-chlorine bleach.

Dry cleaning. Buy items you can wash or clean on your own. Most dry cleaning solvents, such as perchloroethylene, are toxic. If you must dry clean, air clothing out thoroughly before bringing indoors. Many garments whose labels specify "dry clean only" can be safely handwashed using mild soap.

171

IX
URBAN AND RURAL LANDSCAPES

'Dublin is being savaged, with an almost methodical municipal vandalism. With distance perhaps one sees it more clearly, for it is a terrible savagery perpetrated by the greedy, the corrupt, the stupid, the uninspired, the mediocre, the cheap, the tawdry, the vulgar—but mainly the indifferent. Its tool is greed, its logic progress. But progress towards what?'
From Introduction by Bob Geldof to *Save our City* by Frank McDonald (Tomar, 1989)

Geldof's statement, quoted above, might be thought to be excessive, but it is a real cry from the heart of a concerned Dubliner. Dublin is fast becoming an ugly city and to have it designated as the cultural capital of the world in its present state in 1993 is an outrageous joke.

Defining beauty or good taste is often difficult. One person's eyesore is another's pride and joy, and there are people—mostly in the Corporation—who actually like the Civic Offices on Wood Quay. When defining beauty, Aristotle included the word 'wholeness' as one of his criteria. Wholeness or holistic is a word which crops up a lot in green philosophy. Applying it in the context of urban conservation means simply asking does a new building blend in with existing buildings and the general background or does it—as is so often the case—grate on the senses? If the Central Bank or even the Civic Offices were differently situated, they might even be pleasing to the eye.

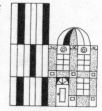

The picture is not so bleak in other towns and cities. Galway, Cork and most notably Kilkenny have retained their essential character. Limerick and Waterford also have promising urban renewal schemes.

Our rural landscape is under severe threat from the most unlikely quarters. It is being condemned to coniferisation and blitzed by bungalows. The situation is now so serious that many environmental groups believe that radical action must be taken if we are to stop the destruction of the countryside.

Urban Landscape

by Ciarán Cuffe, of SADD
(Students Against the
Destruction of Dublin)

Urban Conservation In Dublin

If you've any doubts about the need for Urban Conservation in Dublin, just take a walk along Parnell Street, behind the I.L.A.C. Centre. The no-man's land of multi-storey car parks, access ramps and red-brick pavements only came into being in the last fifteen years. Before that, the street was largely intact, a thriving community consisting of shops, pubs and businesses on the ground floors of buildings, with offices and flats above. It was this variety of life that gave the city its character in the first place. An entire neighbourhood was destroyed in order to build a few hundred yards of road.

The City is dying. The City that we grew up with, composed of street squares and public buildings, is being replaced by dual carriageways, offices and car parks. If this is allowed to continue, the Capital will soon become a 'dough-nut' city—a nine-to-five downtown zone that is deserted after dark, surrounded by miles of sprawling suburbs. It would be all too easy to chronicle the failures and set-backs of the Urban Conservation Movement over the last fifteen years, but perhaps it would be more refreshing to examine some root causes for the decline of the City, suggest possible changes, and end with a look at a few optimistic examples for the future.

Transportation

Dublin's current transportation problems are continuing to destroy the urban core. Although the draft Development Plan gives priority to public transportation, the Department of the Environment is concentrating its financing on more road plans, clearly at the expense of public transport. These road plans involve the demolition of large parts of the Inner City. As a result of this, areas such as Smithfield and Charlemont Street are being left to decay. The battle over Clanbrassil Street resulted in only a slight reduction in the width of the Inner Tangent Route over that particular section. The plans for the northern part of this road 'improvement' scheme are even more horrendous. They include a flyover at the junction of North King Street and Church Street. The bleakness and decay of Parnell Street is only a small portion of a scheme that intends to annihilate large areas of the city. Clearly the future, unless action is taken, looks bleak.

Even C.I.E. seems equally hell-bent on destruction. Up until recently their plans proposed demolishing half of the Temple Bar area in order to build a central bus station. Now their attention is focussed on the 18th century fabric of Bachelors Walk, with a proposal to build a bus station for double-decker buses, three floors up, on top of a shopping mall! In fact the need for this central depot was seriously called into question by the Government-appointed consultants, Davy, Kelleher & McCarthy.

By way of contrast, cities all over Europe are introducing innovative new approaches to the problems of transportation. Better public transport systems are seen as the key to traffic problems.

A new public transportation policy, in conjunction with a comprehensive traffic management plan, could radically improve the inner city. Traffic management could involve road pricing, better signposting, off-peak deliveries, lane reversal, and traffic signal software more favourable to public transport. Also, if we did seriously consider a tram option, an investment of £500 million over ten years could give the city, and especially the western suburbs, an efficient transport system that would be accessible by all, and that would dramatically improve our image of the city.

Housing

The numbers living within the canal ring have shown a steady decline over the last 50 years. The current population of the inner city is 75,000, one-third of what it was in the nineteen-thirties.

Although for many the move to suburbia was the first opportunity to own a house and garden, for others the benefits

174

were far less tangible. People became increasingly dependent on the motor-car. In one-car households the car is often needed by the wage earner to travel to work, leaving the spouse at home, minding the children, often isolated from shops, telephone and other basic facilities.

Suburban housing estates have separated people into public or private sector domains, stratified virtually exclusively by income level, increasing the gap between rich and poor. The mixture of ages, incomes and occupations characteristic of city life has disappeared, replaced by the numbness of suburbia. It's no accident that people still return to the markets of Camden Street, Thomas Street and Moore Street to try and recapture the community life that was left behind in the flight to the suburbs. The city still contains the churches, pubs, shops, parks, cinemas, street markets and activity that adds to life, and all within walking distance. It may not be the ideal location in which to raise a large family, but for young people, for students, for those who have retired, and for many others, the wealth of social facilities and community resources, and of sound existing buildings, will ensure its survival.

It would be refreshing if Central Government took the lead in priming the pump for the revitalisation of Dublin. A few well-placed housing initiatives, perhaps in the form of joint public and private financing through housing cooperatives, could do much to reverse the city's decline.

Legal Obstacles

Article 40 of the constitution ensures that the state protects the right of the individual to own property. A variety of problems have arisen because of the power of this statute. Surface car parks are allowed to spread over vacant sites, upper stories of buildings are left to deteriorate, and speculative developers are allowed to collect high compensation sums due to land re-zoning. Clearly it has proved difficult to apply either the Derelict Sites Act 1961 or the Sanitary Services Act 1963 due to these constitutional difficulties. Both of these acts allow for wide powers of redevelopment or renovation on behalf of the Corporation, in default of action by the owner. Whether the current review of the Derelict Sites

Act will transform it into a useful tool for urban renewal remains to be seen.

From the opposite hue of the political spectrum, the right of tenants to a 35 year tenancy after 3 years occupancy is a major disincentive to property owners allowing residency. Perhaps a review of the law is also called for here.

A Reform of Local Government

Perhaps the single most important change that would aid conservation would be decentralisation of local government. The current division of City and County Council is too large for the people to develop a sense of interest in community affairs. It also does not allow people to have any real say in the decisions being made for them by their elected representatives.

If population areas of around 50,000 inhabitants had their own Town Hall, Council and administrative Office, there could be far more participation in the decision making process. This group of communities could be overseen by a municipal Council for the Greater Dublin area, operating from City Hall with overall co-ordinating responsibility. It is perhaps refreshing to consider the Italian 'commune' system, whereby citizens are actually invited along to participate at council meetings by way of posters displayed in prominent locations. If people felt that THEY could make decisions affecting derelict sites, bus services, rubbish collections or planning matters, these things would surely change for the better.

Hopeful Signs of Conservation From The Last Few Years

One of the most inspiring examples of recent urban conservation is the rehabilitation of the Iveagh Trust housing on Patrick Street. These buildings, three quarters of a century old, have been refurbished and adapted to the housing needs of the 1990's and beyond. Modern bathrooms have been installed, new electrical and heating systems, and the buildings have been made ready for another century of useful life. On a smaller scale the owners of Cathair Books have recently renovated their premises at Essex Gate, just up the road from the Project Acts Centre. The building now has a bookshop opening out onto the street with an upstairs office, and above that again, a flat for the owners. It's interesting to note that 300 years ago there used to be a bookshop on the site, a nice note of continuity and tradition.

The Riverrun Buildings on Dame Street is another careful example of refurbishment. What was once offices now houses a variety of functions. The basement and part of the ground floor now form an art gallery. There is also a ground floor cafe, an upstairs restaurant, and above that a six bedroom flat for the owners and their children, complete with winter garden.

At Trinity College, the interventions in the dining hall complex show the careful restoration and adaptation of an older building to changing uses. The Eighteenth Century building was sadly damaged in a fire a few years ago. However the hall was painstakingly restored, and the surrounding cluster of rooms has had the addition of a four storey atrium while retaining the original structure. A large glass rooflight brings life into a central space that can be adapted to many functions. In its first few years of use it has served as a debating hall, gallery, theatre and conference room. It is also encouraging as Trinity approaches its 300th Anniversary that the college authorities have decided to retain all the Georgian buildings along Pearse Street and refurbish them as student residences.

The conversion of Powerscourt Townhouse into a covered shopping gallery marked a new role for the 200 year old building. What was previously an open air courtyard, was glazed over and now houses shops, restaurants, and the headquarters of the Crafts Council of Ireland. The Guinness Hop Store off Thomas Street has given new life to an old warehouse, as an exhibition centre.

The artisans' cottages of the Liberties, the simple terraces of Stonybatter, the Nineteenth Century houses off Clanbrassil Street; all of these can continue to be lived in and adapted to the needs of the Twenty-first Century without destroying their character.

Neglected areas such as Temple Bar and Bachelors Walk need the careful addition of modern buildings that respect the plot ratio, but yet do not succumb to the superficial allure of pastiche. We have been fortunate enough to inherit a beautiful city, we now need the courage to preserve it for future generations, without neglecting the traditions and continuity of the past.

Crisis Action

If you see a building being demolished that you believe shouldn't be, there are two broad approaches to halting its demolition. One way is to try and use the proper legal channels, the other is direct intervention. Time is of the essence, as a building can be demolished in a minute. From a legal point of view, buildings that are listed for either preservation or protection under the 1963 and 1976 Planning Acts need planning permission in order to be demolished. Listed buildings should appear in the appendix to the development plan, on display in your local authority planning office or your local library. Also, if a building is deemed to be 'habitable', planning permission is again required for demolition. This is difficult to define but try checking the voting register in the nearest Post Office, to give you a rough check.

The Rural Landscape

We tend to think of the countryside in terms of vistas of unchanging tranquility—unchanging, that is, until now, when suddenly our favourite view or strip of coast sprouts an intrusive factory, house or petrol station.

It is easy to forget that the rural landscape has largely been created by man, over thousands of years, and that it is a continuous process, just as it is in urban situations.

Down through the ages the changes have been gentle and gradual and, because the lives of the people of the countryside were intimately bound up with the elements, their activities were almost automatically 'environment-friendly'—if we except the large-scale felling of forests and sometimes over-grazing of uplands.

However, great changes are coming, and have come, through the growing efficiency and changed methods of farming, encouraged by State finance. Hedges and boundaries are being removed to expand fields, rough lands are being reclaimed, wetlands drained. Natural and semi-natural wildlife habitats are affected. New and often obtrusive farm buildings are appearing, as well as new houses, often at the cost of abandoning fine old houses to decay. Afforestation and commercial exploitation of the peat bogs, as well as recreational and tourism developments, all have effects on our rural heritage. Most of these developments are to be welcomed—up to a point. But they are mostly exempt from planning controls and, with increasing pressures, this situation should not be allowed to continue.

Planning is supposed to be concerned with reconciliation between opposing interests, and the adjudication of conflict situations. In Ireland, even where planning controls do exist, there is a serious failure in the implementation of policies.

A coherent landscape policy is badly needed, over a wide range of issues concerning land use, environmental and economic priorities, community values and competing sectional interests. Two important issues are being fought out as we go to press (March 1990), that of Clifden Airport and gold-mining in Co. Mayo. In the year of Ireland's EC 'Green Presidency', it is to be hoped that the environment will emerge the winner.

Of all the many complex issues which the Government is failing to address decisively, the most obvious and in many ways the most damaging, is what has come to be known as the 'Bungalow Blight'.

'Bungalows'

When the Gorbachevs visited Ireland briefly in 1989, Raisa was brought to Bunratty Folk Park to see what official sources described as 'a bit of the real Ireland'. What traditional thatched cottages have to do with the real Ireland is anyone's guess. The thatched roof is now such a rarity in our rural landscape that tourists make a point of photographing the few remaining ones. Most have been abandoned or fallen into disuse. Others are used as outhouses and stand forlornly beside a new bungalow. The Government is now offering grants to help preserve the handful that are left.

The ubiquitous bungalow is now ravaging our countryside and is recognised by environmental groups as a real threat to our rural landscape.

What's Wrong with Bungalows?

Basically, there are too many of them and many of them are badly sited and clash with the landscape. The traditional cottages were made from indigenous building materials—stone for the walls and reeds for the roof—and suited the rugged landscape. Unfortunately, this traditional architecture is associated in the minds of many with an era of poverty.

Architects are not usually responsible. An in-depth report commissioned by An Taisce and Bord Failte shows that only one house of the 40 houses studied (especially bad cases were chosen) had been designed by a fully qualified architect. Nearly half of the house designs were simply borrowed from design catalogues, 'Bungalow Bliss' being the best known.

These new houses are by no means all single-storey dwellings. Many of the larger ones have up to three storeys, but we will use the term 'Bungalow' here for convenience, to refer to unsuitably designed houses, insensitively sited.

How Bad is the Problem?

Bungalow blight is spreading at a frightening rate. Figures compiled by An Foras Forbartha show that the output of 'one-off' houses in rural areas increased from 5,530 to 11,050 between 1976 and 1983, and they now account for over half the houses built. Most of those living in these houses are not engaged in any form of agricultural activity. In fact, rural Ireland is fast becoming a type of sprawling suburbia, with the distinction between countryside and city becoming blurred. Many of those living in bungalows commute daily to their place of work in the nearest town or city.

Bungalows also mean the loss of agricultural land. It has been calculated that at present rates of expansion, 55,000 acres would be lost in ten years.

What Areas Are Worst Affected?

The west coast suffers most, particularly the Gaelteacht areas of Galway and Donegal; parts of Gweedore have the highest rural population density in Europe because of the close proximity of new houses.

In Galway, the population of the rural districts within a ten mile radius of the city doubled between 1961 and 1981. Over half of the city's working population live more than four miles away from their place of employment and the car is the main mode of transport. Figures from the Census show that a total of 2,400 were commuting between 5 and 14 miles to work, 2,000 others travelled 15 miles or more.

All of this has resulted in parts of Galway county and especially Connemara becoming a suburb of Galway city. The Galway-Moycullen road is a very good example of ribbon development. In the past 20 years, over 60 new houses have been built in the countryside along this five mile stretch of road. It works out at an average of a new house every tenth of a mile or less.

Economics

Not only do bungalows disfigure the scenic landscape, the vast sprawl of housing is also a very inefficient use of energy. The distances to be travelled by car have already been mentioned, rural roads have to be maintained, water supplies have to be extended, electricity and telephone services supplied. It costs twice as much—at public expense—to do all this for outlying areas than for an ordinary housing estate. Refuse collection, post delivery and school transport costs are almost five times higher.

Why Was This Allowed To Happen?

Ribbon development was identified as a potentially serious problem in a 1972 'National Coastline Study', commissioned by Bord Failte and An Foras Forbartha. The report stated bluntly that there was a need for 'urgent and deliberate' action by the planning authorities to conserve the unspoilt areas of the coastline.

The politicians did not listen. Political clientelism ensured that local politicians granted permission for unsuitable bun-

181

galows as political favours for constituents. They can do this through what is known as a Section 4 motion. 'Section 4' is the clause in the 1955 City and County Management Act, under which councillors may override the decisions of their own planning officials and direct the county manager to grant permission for inappropriate developments. This is a very common practice in Galway, with Section 4 permissions running at about 50 a year.

Farmers can hardly be blamed for wishing to make a quick financial killing by selling a site for development. Most sites for bungalows cost less than £15,000, exempting them from capital gains tax.

It should be said that often local people simply can't afford to buy old farmhouses in scenic coastal areas. Foreigners can outbid them everytime and so they're sometimes forced to look for a cheaper and less suitable site.

WHAT YOU CAN DO

- Join your local branch of An Taisce.
- Keep an eye on Planning Applications in newspapers.
- Make sure you see your Local Authority, Corporation or County Council plans for Development, Roads, Parks or whatever, in your own and even other areas.
- Find out whether any developments, by individuals, private enterprises or public bodies, are likely to affect you or your environment adversely. If so—OBJECT! You have a legal right to do so.

Guidelines for siting and design if you are thinking of building a house in the countryside

(*Courtesy: An Taisce and Bord Failte*)

Build Sensitively

If you are thinking of building a house in a country location you will want the very best designs at a price you can afford. In the last twenty years a large proportion of houses built in the countryside look out of place because they are designed as though their appearance in the landscape didn't matter.

Good design and siting of houses in the landscape is essential. Otherwise Ireland will end up with more irreparably damaged coastlines or landscapes destroyed by unsympathetic development. One house in the wrong place or built out of inappropriate materials can do untold harm to the landscape. On the other hand, thought and care about what may be appropriate need not cost money and should result in a house which will contribute to the landscape. All houses have to be submitted for planning approval. The local planning authority will wish to ensure that the building is located in the best place possible and its form, materials and landscape treatment all help to give it a place and setting in the landscape.

The guidelines for siting and design which follow are meant to give a positive approach and to help you make good decisions from the earlier stage of a project. They are not absolute as every site will pose particular questions. It is important therefore to work closely with a qualified architect or designer and to consult with the planning staff of your local authority from the earlier stages, to make sure that you get the house you want and that it fits well into the landscape.

In doing this you can play your part in ensuring that Ireland's landscapes continue to be a source of delight not only for those who live and work in them but also for the visitors for whom the unspoilt landscapes of Ireland are a major attraction.

Locate Your House Sensitively in the Landscape
• Set buildings into their landscape. • Use simple forms. • Face the house towards the sun. • Shelter it from the wind. • Keep building below horizon.

Use Planting and the Form of the Landscape
• Conserve and use the existing landscape to settle and shelter the building.
• Cut into the hill in preference to building up and grade the fill carefully.
• Observe and use local plant-types to complete landscaping.

Observe and Use Patterns of Houses in Your Area
• Cluster the house and its ancillary buildings. • Recognise and use local house forms and materials. • Keep houses in existing landscape development zones. • Dense development should be grouped.

Follow Simple Guidelines for Your House Design
• The overriding message is keep it simple and observe the timeless ways of building which are used because they work best. • Use a single-storey form if possible in areas where single-storey houses are prevalent. It is less conspicuous in sensitive landscapes. • If you use a two-storey form explore ways of reducing the exterior volume by using the roof space for bedrooms. • Make the plan longer than it is deep to avoid making a squat bulky form on the landscape. • Keep the plan form simple to maintain a clean roof shape.

- Extend the house at the rear and side in preference to the front, apart from the entrance porch. • Maintain the roof pitch at 45° if possible, and not below 30°.

Walls, Gables, Roofs
- Use materials prevalent in the area; do not mix materials such as stone and brickwork. • Avoid feature elements in different materials. • Observe and use colours used locally on painted house: if in doubt stick to white or light colours. • Use stone if affordable in areas where stone is prevalent. • Stick to small openings in the gable, away from the corner. • Avoid very large windows. • Use proportions which make the window higher than it is wide.
- Use slate if possible, or slate-substitute, or darker coloured concrete tiles.
- Dormers should look like an extension to the roof, using the same materials.

Where To Get More Information

The Guidelines are published jointly by Bord Failte and An Taisce, prepared by the Housing and Urban Design Research Unit of the School of Architecture, University of Dublin. Drawings were made during a 1985 survey of Connemara.

Detailed information on these guidelines is available in a booklet entitled 'Building Sensitively in Ireland's Landscapes'. Copies may be obtained from your local planning office and most good bookshops or send IR£1 and an A5 (approx. 6" x 8 1/2") stamped addressed envelope to your local tourist information office for a copy of this comprehensive 100 page booklet.

Organisations

The best organisation to contact on planning matters is An Taisce. Other organisations with a specific interest in the rural landscape include the IWC and IWF (see Directory).

Books and Publications

The Destruction of Dublin, Frank McDonald (Gill & Macmillan 1985). *Saving the City*, Frank McDonald (Tomar 1989). *Planning: The Irish Experience*, Edited by Michael J. Bannon (Wolfhound Press, 1989).

Statutory Nature Reserves

Nature reserves and National Parks are a very important part of rural landscape. Ireland has thousands of Areas of scientific interest (ASI), but only some are protected under the Wildlife Act and have been made Nature Reserves.

Derryclare: NW shore of Derryclare Lough, Ballinahinch, Co. Galway is an excellent example of native semi-natural woodland of the hyper-oceanic type. Its total area is 19 ha of which about 8ha are woodland, the balance comprising pond, wet moorland and lake-shore ecosystems.

Glen of the Downs: about 8km south of Bray, Co. Wicklow is an area of sessile oak and is 59ha in extent. It is a very good example of the drier type of oak woodland characteristic of acid soils in Wicklow.

Ballykeefe: 6km north of Callan town, Co. Kilkenny, 55.4ha, and

Garryricken: 5km S S W of Callan, 27.9ha, and

Kyleadohir: 5km WSW. of Callan, 58.7 ha These three nature reserves are good examples of young quasi-natural elm/ash/oak woods on fertile soil and constitute some of the largest woods of their kind left in Ireland.

Caher (Murphy): In the Slieveaughty Mountain Range, Co. Clare, is an area of oak wood on moist fertile soil and contains a rich ground flora. It is about 9ha in extent.

The Wexford Wildfowl Reserve: 110ha situated on the sloblands north of Wexford Harbour. It is owned jointly by the Wildlife Service and the Irish Wildbird Conservancy and it forms a wintering ground of international importance for a number of migratory waterfowl species including in particular the Greenland White-fronted Goose.

Lough Hyne Nature Reserve: This is a sea lough with a very wide range of important habitats within the lough and its seaward approaches, a range seldom found in more extensive areas elsewhere. These varied habitats support an exceptionally wide range of animal and plant species. About 6km south-west of Skibbereen, Co. Cork. 65ha in size.

Uragh Wood: comprising 87ha on the south-west shore of Lough Inchiquin, west of Kenmare, Co. Kerry, is an excellent example of hyperoceanic, semi-natural woodland with sessile oak the dominant species.

)) **Deputy's Pass**: near Glenealy, Co. Wicklow comprising 47ha although coppice in origin this woodland is a good example of its type.

) **Grantstown Wood** and **Granstown Lough**: 48.6ha.

:) **Coolacurragh Wood**: 8.5ha These two reserves are situated about 8 km west-north-west of Durrow, Co. Laois. They are rare examples of wet woodland on base-rich soils while Granstown Lough is a classic example of a lake which has gradually infilled through fen to alder carr.

;) **The Raven**: comprising 589ha situated 8km north-east of Wexford town is a large, well developed sand dune ecosystem, foreshore and seabed. The area supports a full range of duneland animals, several of which are of particular interest and has a rich flora including some rare species. It is one of the best developed sand dune systems on the east coast. Important also as a roosting area for geese and waders.

(14) **Vale of Clara**: comprising 220.57ha is a large area of fragmented oakwood mostly on the eastern side of the Avonmore River. It contains the largest area of semi-natural woodland in Co. Wicklow and is potentially one of the largest stands of native hardwoods in the country. The area has been at least partially under woodland since the Ice Age. The oakwoods are also of high scenic value.

(15) **Rosturra Wood**: 3km east-north-east of Woodford (17.68ha), and

(16) **Derrycrag Wood**: 1km south-east of Woodford (110.477ha). These two reserves comprise fragments of a once extensive forest and now contain stands of oak and ash with an understorey of holly and hazel and a rich ground flora.

(17) **Ballynastaig Wood**: (9,758 ha), and

(18) **Coole-Garryland**: (363.583ha) These two reserves near Gort, Co. Galway, through their combination of deciduous woods, limestone reefs, lakes and turloughs, constitute one of the most interesting Irish vegetation and faunal complexes still in existence. The Coole-Garryland reserve contains a variety of floral habitats including well-formed high forest on deep pockets of soil, dwarf woodland on limestone pavement, a turlough complex in the Callows and Coole Lake. A large portion of this reserve was formerly owned by Lady Gregory, co-founder with W.B. Yeats and Edward Martyn of the Abbey Theatre.

(19) **Pollnaknockaun Wood**: comprising 38.85ha 1km north-east of Woodford village, Co. Galway, is a semi-natural woodland which once formed part of the extensive forest referred to under (15) and (16) above.

(20) **Oldhead Wood**: 3km north-east of Louisburg, Co. Mayo, (17ha). This small reserve lies on the east side of two knolls which form a promontory on the southern shore of Clew Bay. It is an example of semi-natural woodland, oak being the dominant species, with birch, rowan, willow and some introduced beech and sycamore.

(21) **Pettigo Plateau**: 11km north-west of Pettigo, Co. Donegal (900ha). This large reserve is an excellent example of a Donegal blanket bog, wet heath complete with a head water lake complex.

(22) **Dromore**: 10km north of Ennis, Co. Clare (370 ha). This reserve comprises semi-natural woodland and four major wetland types.

(23) **Richmond Esker**: 4km north-west of Moylough, Co. Galway (15.7ha), and

(24) **Timahoe Esker**: 1 km north east of Timahoe, Co. Laois (13.5ha). These are two of the few esker ridges left in the country which still carry native woodland. Although extensively planted with conifers and other exotic species it is planned to expand the native woodland by using appropriate management techniques.

(25) **Slieve Bloom Mountains**: situated on the border of Cos. Laois and Offaly (2,230ha) is an excellent example of mountain blanket bog.

(26) **Capel Island** and **Knockadoon Head**: (126.9ha). State owned, and

(27) **Capel Island** and **Knockadoon Head**: (161ha). Privately owned. These reserves comprise all of Capel Island off the south coast near Youghal, Co. Cork, part of Knockadoon headland opposite the island and the intervening sea area. This the first privately owned statutory nature reserve established in the State.

(28) **Keelhilla, Slieve Carron**: (145.5ha) situated at the north-east edge of the Burren plateau is a good example of Karst topography containing three distinct vegetation communities i.e. woodland, scrub grassland and pavement.

(29) **Duntally Wood**: (15.3ha) situated in a deep valley 0.5km.south-east of Cresslough is rich in plant species with alder woodland on the valley floor and hazel/ash woodland on the valley sides.

(30) **Rathmullan Wood**: (32.73ha) situated on the western shore of Lough Swilly, 20 km north east of Letterkenny. This oakwood has a well developed structure and is rich in plant species.

31) **Ballyarr Wood**: (30ha) situated 11km. north of Letterkenny and 5km west of Ramelton on the eastern bank of a low ridge of hills is an oak wood growing on a range of soil types and with a rich flora. It contains areas of old coppice and old field systems reverting to woodland.

32) **Knockmoyle Sheskin**: (732.4ha) situated north of Bord na Mona works at Bellacorick between Oweniny River on the eastern side and Sheskin Lodge and the ruined settlement of Sheskin on the western side. An extensive area of lowland blanket bog densely pool-studded and containing interesting flushes.

33) **Mount Brandon**: (461.75ha) situated on the north-east side of the Dingle Peninsula consists of part of the Mount Brandon range of mountains and the foothills. It was acquired to conserve the mountain blanket bog/heath complex there and its famed alpine flora.

34) **Pollardstown Fen**: (130ha) situated on the northern margin of the Curragh approximately 3km west-north-west of Newbridge is the largest remaining spring fed fen in Ireland possessing a large number of characteristic fenland species and communities.

35) **Eirk Bog**: (16ha) situated in the Owenreagh valley, Killarney, 1km north of Moll's Gap is part of a very well developed and little disturbed example of an inter-mediate bog with associated poor fen and blanked bog/wet heath communities.

36) **Ballygilgan, Lissadell**: (29.5ha) is a large grass field sloping south-westwards from a public road from Carney to Lissadell. It is a site of international importance for Barnacle Geese due to the number it supports (c1,000 birds)

37) **Owenboy**: (397.1ha) situated 10km west of Crossmolina and 10 km east of Bellacorrick on the south side of the Ballina/Belmullet Road at Eskeragh Bridge. An extensive bog of intermediate type utilised by Greenland White-fronted Geese and lying in a broad basin. It contains a number of low domes resembling raised bogs and numerous flushes with a rare species of moss.

38) **Ballyteige**: (6.4ha) situated 2 km west of Lisdoonvarna, Co. Clare. It consists of 5 parcels of wet meadow heath. These are being managed in the traditional way for hay making with the objective of maintaining them as examples of the wet meadows found over the shale soils of the region.

39) **Clara Bog**: (460ha) situated in Co. Offaly is among the few large raised mid-land bogs remaining substantially intact. It contains a wide variety of vegetation types and habitats and a well developed drainage (or soak) system.

40) **Lough Barra Bog**: (176.4ha) situated in the upper part of the Gweebarra River Valley, Co. Donegal. It is a lowland blanket bog with a characteristic assem-blage of plant species. It is also the habitat of three species of birds given special protection under the EC Bird Directive i.e. Greenland White-fronted Goose, Merlin, Golden Plover.

41) **Puffin Island**: State owned (32.73ha), and

42) **Puffin Island**: Privately owned (53.77ha). Puffin Island is situated off the Iveragh Peninsula, Co. Kerry, and is well known for its large colonies of breeding seabirds. It is owned by the State and the Irish Wildbird Conservancy. A marine reserve has been established on the surrounding area of sea and sea shore to ensure the protection of the birds and control activities which might cause disturbance.

43) **Mongan Bog**: (119ha) is situated near Clonmacnoise, Co. Offaly and is an excellent example of a midland raised bog with a well developed system of pools. It is a valuable addition to the growing network of peatland reserves and is owned by An Taisce.

44) **The Gearagh**: (300ha) is situated in the middle reaches of the Lee River, Co. Cork and is the property of the E.S.B. It is the only extensive alluvial soil forest in Europe west of the Rhine and is therefore unique to the network of wood

land nature reserves. It consists of a network of narrow channels separating islands which are covered in oak, ash and birch.

(45) **Raheenmore Bog**: (162 ha) is situated 6 km north west of Daingean, Co. Offaly. It is a well developed and exceptional example of deep midland raised bog which is regarded as being of national importance.

(46) **Ballyteige Burrow**: (227ha) is a 9km long shingle spit running north west from the coastal village of Kilmore Quay in south Co. Wexford and adjoining foreshore. The flora of Ballyteige Burrow includes a number of rare plants such as *asparagus officinalis* and is especially rich in dune plants and those which prosper in coastal habitats.

(47) **Glendalough**: (157ha) comprises a series of oak woods extending from the Upper lake to the lower slopes of Derrybawn mountain and including some conifer plantations.

(48) **Glenealo Valley**: (1958ha) lies above and to the west of Glendalough. It is a broad open valley surrounded by mountains and generally consists of a large plateau of mixed heathland and peatland.

(49) **Lough Yganavan**: (25.3ha), and

(50) **Lough Nambrackdarrig**: (3.9ha). These two reserves are situated in Co. Kerry in the vicinity of Castlemaine Harbour. They consist of freshwater lakes and are important breeding sites for the Natterjack Toad.

(51) **Derkmore Wood**: (7.0ha) situated in Gweebarra Forest, Co. Donegal on exposed undulating ground on the southern flank of Cleangort Hill. An area of oak scrub with well developed bryophyte and lichen flora.

(52) **Rogertown Estuary**: (195.5ha) a small tidal bay in north Co. Dublin which is an estuary of several small river/streams which flow in at the western and north western sides. It is a site of international importance for Brent Geese.

(53) **North Bull Island**: (118ha). Privately owned, and

(54) **North Bull Island**: (1318 ha). State owned.
These two reserves are situated in the northern part of Dublin Bay within the boundaries of Dublin city and only 8km. from the city centre. The island is covered with dune grassland. An extensive salt marsh lies to the north west and at extreme low tides there are extensive mud flats between the island and the mainland. The reserves are of international scientific importance for Brent Geese and also on botanical, ornithological, zoological and geomorphological grounds.

(55) **Baldoyle Estuary**: Co. Dublin (203ha) a tidal bay situated north east of Dublin city. The reserve is rated as of international importance for Brent Geese.

(56) **Fiddown Island**: (62.6ha) a long narrow island of marsh/woodland on the River Suir. It is covered in willow scrub and bordered by reed swamps—the only known site of its type in Ireland.

(57) **Great Skellig**: (22.6ha) also known as Sceilig Michil, is a small precipitous rocky pinnacle rising from the Atlantic Ocean off the Iveragh Peninsula. It is rated as of international importance for certain seabird species— Manx Shearwaters, Storm Petrels and Puffins. It also provides a good example of typical plant communities of a small and remote marine island.

(58) **Little Skellig**: (7.8ha) is a small precipitous rocky pinnacle rising from the Atlantic Ocean off the Iveragh Peninsula. It is rated as of international importance because of the colonies of Gannets that inhabit the island.

National Parks

Glenveagh NP, Co. Donegal (10,000ha)
Killarney NP, Co. Kerry (10,000ha)
Connemara NP, Co. Galway (2000ha)
For information: Wildlife Service, Leeson Lane, Dublin 2 (615666)

X
ENERGY

Despite what certain advertisements may try to tell you, lost energy cannot be replaced. Energy is never really lost in the first place, merely transformed from a usable form to a non-useable form. Unfortunately, the non-usable form of energy is often a form of pollution.

The laws of physics tell us that energy cannot be created or destroyed but only transformed from one state to another. This means that the amount of energy in the universe today is exactly the same as the amount of energy present when the universe was first created. It is the constant which connects us to the billions of years of evolution of this planet. How long human beings continue to live in this universe depends very much on our future use of energy resources.

The more conventional view of energy is energy which can be harnessed to perform 'work'. Seen in this sense, the energy on Planet Earth is derived from the sun and can be divided into two categories renewable and non-renewable.

Renewable energy sources—those most favoured by the Green Movement—include solar-, wind-, tidal-, and wave-energy. As long as the sun exists these energy resources will be with us. According to reliable scientific predictions, the sun will continue to produce heat for many billions of years.

On the other hand, non-renewable resources such as coal, oil and gas, which are in effect forms of stored solar energy, will run out much sooner. Recoverable oil deposits are expected to last another 60 years. The world is still rich in coal and the resources may last as long as two hundred years.

It is, however, our overuse of these fuels which has led to some of the worst environmental problems, among them acid rain and urban smog. But the problem which is of most concern to governments, scientists and environmentalists is the 'Greenhouse Effect' (see AIR chapter). Carbon dioxide released when fossil fuels are burnt is one of the main greenhouse gases. What is perhaps even more alarming is the way in which the nuclear industry is using the 'Greenhouse

Effect' as a way of promoting nuclear power as an environmentally safe energy source!

Energy Policy in Ireland

Almost 20% of the national income is spent on energy. In 1987 Ireland's Primary Energy Requirement was approximately 8,652.5 tonnes of oil equivalent (MTOE). With a population of 3.44 million this works out at an equivalent of 2.5 tonnes of oil per person for the provision of food, warmth, goods, transport, etc.

Approximately 98% of energy used in Ireland in 1987 came from non-renewable sources, the only renewable resource being provided by hydropower. Compare this to fifty years ago when 87% of our electricity demand came from the Ardnacrusha scheme on the Shannon. 40% of energy in Ireland goes on space and water heating, 33% on industrial processes, 27% on transport.

Ireland relies heavily on imports of oil and other fuels, which in 1987 accounted for 71% of primary energy supply. This over-dependence on fossil fuels carries with it a heavy environmental penalty, as the examples of Moneypoint (see

Acid rain) and Dublin's smog show. Currently the domestic market for coal p.a. is 1.1-1.2m. tonnes of coal for the consumer the importation of fossil fuels also means that Irish energy prices are uncompetitive within the EC. In 1988 our prices showed a handicap of about £145.3 million compared to the EC as a whole. Energy prices in this country could soar if fuels are taxed on their carbon burden (the amount of CO_2 they emit) as part of an international climate treaty. The ESB has increased its reliance on coal which emits the highest amount of CO_2.

The most depressing feature of the Government's energy strategy is the paltry amount invested in Research and Development and Demonstration (RD and D). We are currently at the bottom of a 'league table' for investment in alternative energy. We have the scientists, we have the skills. Above all else, we have the renewable energy resources. Now all we need is the political will and the investment. The table below shows the declining Government investment in alternative energy.

In '000 IR Punts

Energy Form	1980	1981	1982	1983	1984	1985	1986	1987
Wind Energy	122	990	296	235	220	189	114	52
Ocean, Tidal and Small Hydro	254	237	649	133	150	70	73	13

Source: Nat. Board for Science and Technology report.

The Alternatives

Wind

'Ireland should be able to export wind power'. This is the conclusion of a report from the Commission of European Communities (CEC) entitled 'Assessment of the Technical and Economic Prospects for Wind Energy in the European Communities.' According to the CEC report, Ireland could produce more than five times our present energy needs by wind alone. This is confirmed in the more recent Hurley-Staudt report

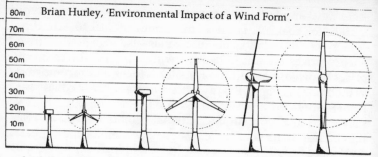

80m   Brian Hurley, 'Environmental Impact of a Wind Form'.
70m
60m
50m
40m
30m
20m
10m

which looked at the potential wind farm sites in the west of Ireland. They found that if these sites were developed, they could produce the equivalent in electricity of the Moneypoint plant, without the equivalent in pollution, of course.

Economics: The ESB argues that conventional electricity generation is still cheaper than windpower. In purely monetary terms this may be so, but the argument fails to address the external costs such as pollution (the cost of erecting sea barriers against the rising seas, destruction of soil through acid rain etc.) At present the generation of electricity of electricity through gas and coal costs around 2p per Kilowatt hour (KWh). The present average cost of wind generated electricity is under 10 pence per KWh. In a 1987 position paper the British Wind Energy Association states that it is possible for present wind technology to produce electricity for less than 3p per KWh. Currently the ESB charges about 7.5p per KWh.

As wind generation technology becomes more advanced it is certain that the cost per KWh will decrease. With this in mind, countries such as Denmark—which has less wind than Ireland—have embarked on ambitious wind energy programmes. The Danes hope to install 1000 megawatts of wind turbines by the year 2000. That's 100 megawatts more than the Moneypoint plant. The State of California has encouraged 'alternative' energy projects through tax allowances and long term power contracts since the late '70s. This far reaching decision meant that by 1988 their wind electricity production was about 15% of the total electricity demand for the Republic of Ireland. The savings for the environment are enormous. It's been calculated that in 1986 alone 4,500 tonnes of pollutants and 3.6 billion KWh of waste heat did not enter the Californian atmosphere because of the oil saved.

Wind Turbines and Wind Farms: The modern wind turbine is far removed from the windmill of old. Some of them are gigantic creations, having a rotor diameter of up to 30 meters. Most turbines have two or three blades (rotors) spinning about a horizontal axis. This is mounted on a tower which contains a generator and the current is carried down the tower by electrical cable.

The horizontal axis machines may be superseded by a turbine whose blades rotate on a vertical axis. The blades rotate then regardless of wind direction, giving it a distinct advantage.

Windpower is proportional to the cube of the windspeed—so doubling the speed increases the power eight times. Modern wind turbines also have an availability of around 90%, i.e. they rarely break down, compared to an availability of 75% for a fossil fuel plant.

The largest windfarm in the world is at the Altamont Pass in California which has about 5,600 machines. Some environmentalists are concerned—with some justification— about the visual impact of so many wind turbines on the natural landscape. But windfarms, it could be argued, are as much a blot on the landscape as miles and miles of coniferous forest.

This problem and the additional problem of noise may not arise if we concentrate on off-shore windfarms, which capitalise on much higher wind speeds.

Employment:

Wind energy provides more jobs per unit of electricity than other technologies. Whereas much conventional generating plant cannot be manufactured in this country, wind turbines could be.

Solar

Passive: It's difficult to believe, but in 1981 Ireland received enough energy from sunlight to fill that year's energy needs

700 times over. The difficulty lies in trying to harness that energy. Solar energy can be harnessed by both active and passive means.

The design, situation and shape of a building is used to store solar energy. Glazing materials used in the building act as one way valves, letting heat in and preventing it from getting out. Generally about half of annual space heating requirements can be achieved in passive solar buildings.

Active: Solar collectors can be mounted on a house roof and deliver hot water into a conventional plumbing system. Over a year, an efficient solar water heating system can save 68% of costs with a contribution of 21% even in December!

Sunlight can also produce electricity through what is known as the 'photovoltaic effect' in a solar cell. In bright sunlight a solar cell will give a current of 2 Amps, which is about 1 watt of power. If light intensity drops then the current drops proportionately.

The cost of solar electricity in the US is now quoted at $6.5 per Wp, which is significantly down from $10 per Wp in 1983. At this price solar power still cannot compete with conventional energy sources.

Solar cells are now used increasingly in watches and calculators and wider use is expected for boats.

Solar Cells in Ireland: A 50 KW photovoltaic array has been installed in a dairy farm on Fota island, Co Cork by the Microelectronics Research Centre in 1984. It is Ireland's first solar power station.

Hydro power

At the beginning of this century there were over 1,800 mill sites producing mechanical and electrical power in Ireland. With the development of the national electricity grid most of these sites have fallen into disuse.

Ardnacrusha, which was commissioned first in 1929, is the country's largest hydro power station with a capacity of 87 MW. During the year 1936/37 it supplied 87%

of Ireland's energy demand, but this has since decreased to a 2% level.

The obvious advantage of hydro power is that it is non-polluting, but it also generates at 85% efficiency and small units can achieve 60% efficiency.

The ESB now operates 9 hydro power stations with an overall capacity of 220 MW. There is also a 292MW pumped storage facility at Turlough Hill, where off peak electricity is used to pump water into the reservoir. This water is then released during periods of high demand to generate electricity.

Small Scale: The Department of Energy has identified 483 sites in Ireland suitable for small scale hydro power. 85 sites are already oper-ating and the combined capacity of all these sites would be in the region 38MW, which is about 20% of the ESB's existing hydro capacity. If these sites were exploited it would mean a saving of over £9 million in imported oil.

In 1987, the Department of Energy received between £3 and £4 million of European aid for the Valoren programme, under which 10 small-scale hydro generating stations will be built by the ESB, mostly in counties Cork and Kerry.

Wave Power

The seas about our shores offer huge potential for the development of wave power. The NBST estimates the exploitable resource off the west and south coasts to be around 11 Gigawatts, which is around four times the current Irish electricity demand. The most efficient wave converters 'land' nearly 50% of the available power—approximately 20 KW/m from a prime site. It's possible, therefore, for a 10 Km line of wave power devices to produce 20% of current Irish demand. In Ireland the best sites are on the Atlantic coasts, between Belmullet and Slyne Head or between Innislearaigh and Cape Clear.

At present wave energy technology is still not at an advanced stage and much work needs to be done to improve the efficiency of existing wave converters such as the Slater Duck, the Clam and the Oscillating Water Column (OWC).

The Oscillating Water Column: A prototype OWC has been built and installed in Norway. It has a peak rated output of about 500kW and cost £500,000 to build. So far it is working extremely well and produces electricity for less than 4p per unit. The turbine for this OWC was actually developed by Professor Alan Wells of Queen's University, Belfast. Dr Tony Lewis of UCC has carried out a survey of sites on the west coast which would be suitable for the construction of OWCs. Because the wave power on these sites is 3 to 4 times greater than in Norway, a similar sized OWC would produce up to 2 MW of electricity. It has been calculated that 1 Km length of breakwater containing OWCs could produce an average of 75 MW of electricity. On this basis, Ireland could easily be self sufficient in wave energy.

The OWC consists of a hollow concrete tower built at the foot of a cliff. The bottom is open to the sea and waves pounding the device cause the water inside the tower to oscillate. This acts like a piston, forcing air through an over-head turbine, generating power continuously.

Many of our offshore islands have 'blow-holes' on their rocky coastline and these are in effect natural oscillating water columns. Research has shown that the energy from these 'blow-holes' could be used to provide electricity.

Tidal power

A barrage across an estuary is used to store water when the tide is in. When the tidal level changes the water is then released through turbines, generating electricity in the process. Tidal barrages can result in some environmental damage and would need a rigorous Environmental Impact Assessment. A lot of these problems could be avoided by building open sea tidal barrages.

The largest tidal power station is on the Rance Estuary near St Malo in France and produces 240 MW of electricity.

In Ireland research has shown that a barrage with 30 turbines at Coalhill point in the Shannon Estuary could produce 318MW of electricity.

Geothermal Energy

While geothermal energy is not strictly a renewable energy source, it is generally considered as such because of the vast scale of the total resource.

The earth's temperature increases with depth at a rate of 25–80°C per km. Two kinds of drilling are being done to exploit this heat source: the first, at depths of 1–2 km is well tested; the second, down to 5–7 km, known as 'hot dry rock' technology, involves new techniques and is still very much at the experimental stage.

Shallow drilling: The shallow drillings exploit so called 'hot aquifers'—water that has been trapped in permeable rocks at temperatures that can go as high as 110°C. This hot water can be pumped to the surface, a standard well providing heat for up to 30 years in sufficient amounts for the space and water heating needs of 2,000 dwellings. When the well is exhausted, a new one can be drilled nearby or even at an angle to the original well head.

Since 1979 the Irish government, in conjunction with the EC, has engaged in a number of geothermal research and development projects. This work has led to an EC demonstration project at the famous hot springs of Mallow where water at 220°C has been found 80 meters down. The heat recovered will be used to heat the local swimming pool.

A number of other projects are in hand, at Carberry, Co. Kildare, Leixlip, Co. Kildare and Ballynagoul near Charleville, Co. Cork among others, and are showing promising results.

Hot Dry Rock: In the longer term the natural heat potential of Irish granites may be utilised by hot dry rock technology, but this is still an area for further research rather than immediate application.

Heat Pumps

When a gas is compressed, its temperature rises, when a gas expands, its temperature falls. These simple principles give rise to the heat pump, a device which, as its name implies, pumps heat from one location to another. More energy is recovered as heat than is used as electricity to drive the mechanism.

The most familiar application of the heat pump principle is in fridges and freezers where heat is taken from the storage compartment and expelled as waste heat. Heat pumps can provide a very cheap and efficient form of domestic heating.

In recent years research has been done at UCG on the use of wind convectors as heat collectors, these having the advantage of not requiring the use of an air pump or a defrost cycle.

Heat pumps are an increasingly widely used means of saving money and energy in industry and commerce as well as domestically. Unfortunately they tend to use CFCs as refrigerants but research is under way to find an acceptable alternative.

The Fuel Cell

A fuel cell generates electricity out of the chemical reaction of hydrogen and oxygen in the presence of a nickel or platinum catalyst. As bulk bio-production of hydrogen and methane is now in sight to complement the use of naphtha and other hydrocarbons, a new range of prototypes in the 50 megawatt range is being developed. At present, in USA and Japan utilities are placing a greater emphasis on fuel cell development than upon nuclear power.

Combined Heat and Power (CHP) Cogeneration

Conventional electricity generating plant wastes about 65% of the energy consumed, much of it as heat which is lost up the chimney. Meanwhile about one-third of the electricity generated goes to provide heat, either for industrial processes or for domestic and commercial space and water heating. Furthermore, much of this heat is used at temperatures below the boiling point of water.

Plants utilise primary energy at an efficiency of 80%, 30% as electricity generated and 50% as heat. District heating schemes in which hot water is supplied direct to houses in residential areas have already proven themselves viable in countries such as Denmark and Germany. For Europe as a whole, 36% of installed heat capacity is chp generated.

In Ireland, the share of total electricity generated by chp fell from 2% in 1973 to 1.5% in 1981.

Conserving Energy

If energy is such a precious commodity and if its production can have serious environmental effects—then it makes sense to use it sparingly. It should strike the relatively sane person, therefore, as absolutely bizarre that a state body like the ESB actively encourages people to use more electricity. The energy demand is increasing by about 4% annually. During the lean years of the oil crisis there was an attempt made to encourage energy conservation in households, but this led to a typical bureaucratic schizophrenia with two Departments competing with one another within the ESB—one urging people to switch off, the other telling them to use more electricity.

With the advances in technology, there is tremendous scope for energy conservation. For example, it is now possible to save twice as much electricity as we could in 1985 for only one third of the real cost. In the UK it has been estimated that electricity demand could be reduced by 70% by using the latest available technologies to provide the electricity at the least cost. Earthwatch claim that the same sort of savings could be made in Ireland.

According to Jim Woolridge, Earthwatch's Energy campaigner, bad energy conservation levels cost the Irish economy more that IR£200 million per year. While the link between economic growth and energy demand continues to be strong in Ireland, in the EC generally there is not such a close correspondence. Between 1973 and 1986 EC gross domestic product rose by 30% while energy demand grew by only 4%; this is due to the efficiency and conservation methods introduced because of the oil crisis.

Typical Domestic Heating Systems—Which are most efficient?	
Decorative gas fire without heat exchanger	10%-20%
Open fire	20%-30%
Open fire and high output back boiler burning bituminous coal	35%-50%
Open fire and high output back boiler burning smokeless fuel or anthracite	40%-55%
Closed heater/cooker burning smokeless fuel	50%-60%
Oil fired burner	60%-70%
Low heat capacity gas fired boiler	65%-75%
Flued gas fire with heat exchanger	65%-75%
Flueless or portable gas fire	90%

Courtesy: *Eolas*

To its credit Irish industry did achieve a 25% drop in energy per unit of output and this is line with industry in the rest of the EC. However, the commercial and domestic sectors still lag far behind most EC countries.

Energy conservation makes sense for so many good reasons. The consumer also benefits enormously through the huge savings that can be made. Insulation in floors, walls, ceilings and roof, plus draughtproofing and solar features can reduce space and water heating bills for a three bedroom house from £400 to £80 per annum, according to Earthwatch.

Lights: Even in our own homes there are many examples of gross energy inefficiency. The small and humble light bulb converts coal energy to light at around 3% efficiency. Low energy light fittings are five to seven times more efficient, as they are designed for a 5,000 hour life, which is five times the design life for most ordinary light bulbs.

One of the best available is the 2D lamp from Thorn, which requires a special fitting and consumes only 21 watts. Yet it has a light output approaching that of a 100 watt bulb. It saves around 75% of the energy, and it's calculated that by using the low energy lamp you will reduce carbon dioxide emissions to the atmosphere by almost a ton.

The reduced running costs and the longer life more than pay for the new fittings.

Insulation: About 40% of our total energy consumption goes on heating our buildings and water. In Ireland, most houses built to current building regulations are badly under-insulated. It's possible to build houses which use a third less energy and cost only 11% more than ordinary houses.

Draught proofing: Otherwise known as weatherstripping, can reduce heating bills by saving 11% of wasted energy.

Windows: If you cannot afford double glazing then heavy curtains will conserve a lot of heat. It's estimated that up to 25% of domestic heat loss can be through the window glass,

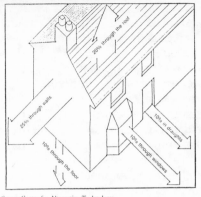

Source: Centre for Alternative Technology

which is not surprising when you consider that glass makes up 16% of the wall area of the average house.

Conservatories: A conservatory, if properly designed, can cut the space heating needs of a house by up to 22%.

Comparative Costs Of Domestic Space and Water Heating Systems				
System	Oil	Bulk LPG	Electric Storage	Solterra
Capital Cost (£s)	1,600	1,600	800	4,800
10 year Fuel (£s)	11,000	15,000	12,000	5,000
Total Cost	12,600	16,600	12,800	9,800

The above table (supplied by Solterra—a division of HRG Ltd, Co. Cork) shows that solar heating for a typical family house compares favourably in cost over a TEN YEAR PERIOD with other methods of heating. The system uses a 'greenhouse effect' collector and a specially designed heat pump; the system can be adapted to suit different types of building.

Energy

WHAT SHOULD BE DONE

* We need an integrated energy policy which supports energy efficiency and conservation.
* There should be more financial help for home insulation.
* House-buyers should demand high insulation standards.
* Free Heating Advice should be offered by local Councils.

WHAT YOU CAN DO

* Draughtproof your windows and doors. Windows should be double-glazed. Reduce heat loss through the floor by use of carpeting.
* Insulate pipes and tanks. Fitting a 10 centimetre jacket around a hot water cylinder is the most effective way of preventing heatloss from your house
* An open fire is one of the most inefficient means of heating your house. About 70% of the heat is lost up the chimney. Bituminous (smoky) coal is also the cause of Dublin's appalling smog. Closed appliances, which use anthracite and extracite, are far more efficient and environment friendly. You could consider switching over to natural gas which is an extremely clean fuel.
* Use a pressure cooker to cut cooking time.
* Chest freezers are more energy efficient than upright models. Defrost your freezer regularly and try to keep it full.
* When doing your laundry, wash full loads. A spin dryer can halve the time and energy needed to tumble dry wet clothes, (use it even after they have been spun in a washing machine).
* Switch off lights when you don't need them. Use low wattage and long life bulbs.

All common sense really, but then so are all green ideas.

Books and Publications

Energy Savings with Home Improvements (Hodder and Stoughton, 1987); *How to be Green* (Century, 1989) John Button; *Network Energy Directory* (Government Energy Efficiency Office); *The Green Consumer Guide* (Gollancz, 1988); *The Heating Advice Handbook* (London Energy and Employment Network); *The Safe Energy Journal* (SCRAM).

Most of the information in this Chapter was supplied by Earthwatch, and is covered in more detail in Earthwatch's highly recommended 'Alternative Energy Options for Ireland' by Jim Woolridge. Available from Earthwatch, Harbour View, Bantry.

Organisations

Earthwatch, Energy campaigner, Jim Woolridge; Solar Energy Society; Energy Conservation Society; E.S.B.; Eolas. (See Directory)
Energy Action, St Andrew's Centre, 114-116 Pearse St., Dublin 2 (01-771930). Sponsored by Depts of Energy and Labour, this body provides *free* housing insulation for: old age pensioners; invalidity pensioners; blind pensioners; disabled persons M.A.

XI
TRANSPORT

The sections dealing with air pollution, planning, and energy show the fundamental effects of transport policies on our environment. The internal combustion engine and the jet engine have changed our lives irrevocably, but like many good and necessary inventions, their unrestricted and excessive use is having appalling environmental consequences worldwide. The skies over Europe are choc a bloc with air traffic, and many airports are now dangerously overcrowded. Every day we see evidence of traffic chaos in our major cities.

In Dublin the situation is so bad that a helicopter monitors the traffic from above for the 2FM radio station, Motorists are then advised to avoid certain areas, because 'roadworks' are causing delays. But even without the inevitable 'roadworks' there would be delays and traffic congestion. The real problem needs to be addressed. There are far too many cars on the road. Too many cars? Then build more roads. Again, this is not the solution to the problem. Extra roads mean more traffic, which means more roads . . . and on and on into a spiral of environmental chaos. Studies from other countries have shown this to be the case and we ought to learn from this.

When first introduced, the automobile was seen as a symbol of democracy, offering the individual a much wider freedom of movement. Of course, the irony is that if everyone were to possess this symbol of freedom our roads would be terminally blocked, allowing very little freedom of movement for anyone. There is an added irony in that the car is also seen as a means of escape from the polluted, crowded and noisy city into the clean countryside. But wouldn't our cities be less polluted, less crowded and noisy without the car? If car use was restricted, people might actually enjoy living in cities. Urban areas would be built for people, not cars. Sprawling suburbia would cease to spread any further and the countryside would be far more accessible.

Some cities in the world plan to tackle the car problem head on. The authorities in Los Angeles are planning a phased reduction in the car fleet. Larger firms are now obliged under law to arrange car pools for their staff, and there are plans for the construction of an underground and tramways.

The Dutch government has adopted similar far-sighted policies. In a document entitled 'To Choose or to Lose', there are proposals to charge motorists for the use of the roads. It is recommended that tax reductions for car commuters should be phased out and the money saved used to improve the public transport system. It is also recommended that there be a price increase in petrol.

Perhaps the most encouraging aspect of the document is the recognition of the root cause of the problem. 'The locations where people live, work and spend their leisure time will be co-ordinated in such a way that the need to travel is minimal,' it says bluntly. This is, in essence, a proposal for decentralisation and it is a fundamentally green approach to the problem.

Transport Policy In Ireland

The Irish Government has clearly not learned from the mistakes of other countries. Most discussions on transport in this country seem to centre on the national obsession with potholes. People may have valid reasons for complaint—many of our existing roads are in a terrible state of disrepair—but a national transport policy should have a much broader focus than the building and repair of roads.

The allocation of monies to the National Development Plan gives some idea of the strength of the roads lobby. Public transport receives £45 million. Road construction, on the other hand, receives a massive £1,000 million. Even in Dublin, where there is an acute need for an improved public transport system, £212 million is to be spent on the roads, while a mere £36 million goes on rail and bus services. The much maligned CIE, now known as Iarnrod Eireann and Bus Eireann, can do little in the face of such obvious Government bias to improve our public transport system. As car numbers increase, bus speeds are reduced in urban areas, making the bus a less attractive option. Dublin once had an excellent tram system—one of the best in Europe—but this was abandoned in favour of the bus. Trams are not only clean, operating as they do on electric power—they are also efficient. Studies on the continent show that rail—either tramways or train—is by far the best option for transporting large numbers of commuters into cities. This is borne out by the notable success of the DART (Dublin Area Rapid Transport). The success of DART shows beyond doubt that people will use public transport if it is efficient.

Yet despite the obvious advantages of public transport, our Government persists with its roadbuilding plans. Much of Dublin has already been decimated by road schemes and now there are plans to build the Eastern ByPass motorway, which will cut through the bird sanctuary at Booterstown marsh.

The Car

 There are now more than 400 million motorised vehicles in the world, and every working day 126,000 new cars roll off the assembly lines.

These new cars will no doubt add significantly to the already high pollution levels from car emissions (see Air Pollution). In the OECD countries cars contribute 75% of carbon monoxide emissions, 40% of hydrocarbons, 48% of nitrogen oxides, 13% of smoke and 3% of sulphur dioxide. These pollutants make up some of the constituents of smog and acid rain. The production and use of petrol also causes about 17% of the world's carbon dioxide emissions, which contribute to the Greenhouse Effect.

In the Republic there seems to be a real problem measuring some of these pollutants, with only very scant data available on carbon monoxide and nitrogen oxide emissions. Measurements for carbon dioxide are not available.

In 1988—after what was seen as the stagnant years—the purchase of new cars increased significantly in the Republic. 80,000 new vehicles were registered, which was a 12% increase on 1987. The total number of vehicles on the road reached 98,000—the highest ever recorded—and 74,950 of these were private cars.

Road Deaths

If the year's road deaths were to happen in one day a national day of mourning would be declared. Instead annual road deaths are accepted as the inevitable price of progress. In 1988 there were 433 fatal accidents in the Republic, in which 463 people were killed.

Far more people have been killed on the roads since 1969 than in the violence in Northern Ireland. And yet the problem of road deaths—which could easily be solved—does not merit the same amount of media coverage.

Often forgotten are the 8,000 or so who suffer injuries from car accidents every year. The suffering that many lifelong injuries such as brain damage or paralysis bring to the victim—and family and friends—is incalculable.

Car Emissions

So. You have changed over to lead-free petrol. Good! BUT… statements such as 'leadfree petrol is good for the environment' are misleading. Many motorists are now under the illusion that driving their cars on unleaded petrol somehow makes their vehicle pollution-free. This is not so.

ELECTRICALLY PROPELLED VEHICLES

The wider use of electric vehicles would pay off in terms of fuel savings, use of off-peak electricity and decrease in noise and pollution.

In the early '80s there were 600 electric vehicles operating in Ireland, mainly in urban delivery work. In spite of their characteristically poor acceleration and low top speed, they had certain advantages:—

(a) Low maintenance costs (fewer moving parts and less vibration).

(b) Longer vehicle life—fifteen years as opposed to five to seven years.

(c) Fuel economy (in particular, no engine idling).

(d) Low fuel costs, as unlike petrol there is no tax on electricity.

There has been an increased interest in the electric vehicle since the improvement of speed controls and the use of braking energy to recharge the battery (giving a range increase of up to 15%). Further costs should fall dramatically with the start-up of production lines for specifically electrical vehicles—rather than adapted conventional cars.

While the introduction of unleaded petrol is to be welcomed, it must be stressed that petrol contains other substances which are far more hazardous for the environment.

In terms of volume, most of what comes out as exhaust fumes could be considered harmless, 95% consisting of carbon dioxide, nitrogen and vapours. But the remaining 5% contains several thousand substances and compounds which together can cause harm.

That 5% means that a medium-sized petrol driven car with moderate mileage (approx. 1000 litres per year) will spew out some 350 kilograms of carbon monoxide, 50 kilograms of hydrocarbons, 20 kilograms of nitrogen oxides, .6 kilograms of sulphur dioxide and .3 kilograms of lead per year. With the introduction of unleaded petrol these ratios are now set to diminish but at the same time the car fleet is getting bigger.

ETHANOL

In many countries cars run on a petro-ethanol mix; the mix has 10% ethanol (ethyl alcohol), the most that can be taken by unmodified engines. Ethanol can be produced from a wide range of plant sources. At the present time, the European Community is seeking alternative uses for surplus farm produce and ethanol production is a very sensible possibility. The search is a fairly urgent as it is estimated that EC surplus cereal stocks may reach 80 million tonnes in 1991.

In Ireland ethanol could be produced by using the surplus sugarbeet.

Several constituents of exhaust fumes affect our respiratory tracts and impair pulmonary functions, the most harmful being the sulphur dioxide, carbon monoxide and nitrogen oxide. Some of these sub-  stances also contribute to acid rain and to the deterioration of historical buildings.

Petrol also contains at least 30 substances which are believed to be mutagenic or carcinogenic.

The Government ought to consider switching cars over to natural gas— a very clean fuel. This has been done with great success in New Zealand and in the USA.

Lead

Lead was originally added to petrol to raise the octane number of the fuel and to produce higher compression. This makes the engine more efficient with greater fuel economy and prevents 'knocking' (the explosion combustion of fuel in the cylinder, which can cause noise, damage to the spark plugs and overheating).

Unleaded petrol contains no 'tetraethyl lead', although there are still background levels of lead compounds in petrol sold in this country. These lead compounds are limited to 0.013 grammes per litre.

However, while preferable to the leaded variety, unleaded petrol still contains up to 5% benzene, which has been shown to be carcinogenic and toxic. While a non-toxic additive called MRBE is widely used in Europe and USA, our oil companies are taking the cheapest unleaded option.

Health

Studies carried out by the World Health Organisation show that certain concentrations of lead can cause brain damage to developing children. Lead is absorbed by the human body not only from the air we breathe but also from the food chain. Lead enters the environment from a variety of sources including lead water pipes, paints, canned foods and from the smelting and mining industries. However, vehicle exhaust emissions are responsible for up to 90% of airborne lead in areas where there is heavy traffic congestion.

Monitoring

Until the late 1970's lead levels of up to .84 grammes per litre occurred, and there was no legal limit on the content of petrol. During the late 70's and early 80's lead levels of many

210

times the EC limits were recorded in Dublin's city centre. Since that time there has been a phased reduction in the lead levels of petrol. By January 1981 the limit was 0.64 grammes per litre. The limit in Ireland is now 0.15 grammes per litre.

The monitoring of atmospheric lead is carried out by the local authorities. According to the Department of the Environment the latest results from the monitoring stations show a marked decline in the levels of lead since the early 1980's. We now comply with the EC Directive on Air Quality standards for lead.

Outlets

Unleaded petrol was first introduced into Ireland in October 1986. At present there are well over a thousand petrol stations out of about 3,100 which sell unleaded, but sales still only account for 12% of the market, according to 1989 figures. Further expansion of the unleaded petrol market depends very much on demand and this unfortunately, has been disappointing, despite the incentive of a 5p–7p price difference. Perhaps the price difference ought to be increased to around 12p as it is in England, where the 'unleaded' campaign has been far more successful.

Can My Car Take Unleaded?

If your car is fitted with a catalytic converter then under no circumstances should leaded petrol be used.

In general, however, there shouldn't be a problem switching from leaded to unleaded. On the basis of the Society of Irish Motor Industry (SIMI) list up to 85% of new petrol driven cars can use unleaded petrol without any adjustment. Other vehicles may need minor adjustment—so check.

From 1990 onwards all new cars must be able to run on unleaded petrol.

Catalytic Converters

Catalytic Converters (cats) can reduce harmful car emissions by eighty per cent. They convert Carbon monoxide (CO), hydrocarbons (HC) and nitrogen oxide

(NOx) into carbon dioxide (CO_2), water vapour and nitrogen (N). These are not harmful to your health, but CO_2 still contributes to the greenhouse effect.

'Cats' are about the size of small silencers and fit inside the exhaust system of a car. They are usually made from ceramic or metal which has been coated with platinum, rhodium and palladium. There are two types of catalysts. The oxidisation catalyst which is commonly used with 'lean burn' engines controls CO and HC emissions. The more sophisticated three way catalyst controls NOx emissions as well as CO and HC.

By 1993 all new cars must, under EC law be fitted with 'Cats'.

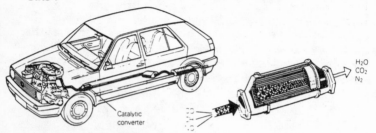

The Catalytic Converter converts poisonous gases from the engine into relatively harmless emissions. The precious metal platinum acts as a catalyst to the chemical reaction.

The Bike

Cycling is by far the most energy efficient mode of transport. It is also non-polluting, very safe, and does not cause congestion.

According to Friends of the Earth in England, 75% of all journeys made are less than 8km long, and yet a mere 4% of all journeys travelled in Britain are by bike. In Denmark, cycling accounts for up to 40% of journeys travelled.

There are no similar figures available for Ireland, nor does the Department of Transport have figures regarding the number of cycle ways. All that is known is that cycleways are extremely rare in this country. There are confirmed sightings of about four cycle ways in Dublin. Dublin Corporation regards the bus lanes as cycle ways, which would bring the number up to about 40. But neither the busdrivers nor the cyclists are satisfied about this situation.

Bus

Travelling by bus should be a marvellous experience . . . but waiting for and travelling by bus can be miserable, particularly in Dublin. This is not entirely the fault of the bus service. Time tables and all-round efficiency become a nonsense in a city which is full of traffic jams, which are caused not by the buses but by the cars. The bus fleet has been cut by 1/7 in recent years and the introduction of driver only buses has meant a further decline in the service. All of this results in public transport becoming a less attractive option and to a further build-up in car traffic, and again the bus time tables suffer. It's a vicious circle which we must break if we want an environment friendly transport system.

A cyclist can travel 1,600 miles on the energy equivalent to one gallon of petrol. Cycling uses less energy per passenger mile than any other form of transport, including walking.

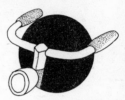

Air travel

Air travel, once a novelty is now taken for granted by many. It is certainly the most convenient and rapid way of travelling long distances. But it does cause environmental problems. Aeroplanes use up a lot of highly refined non-renewable fuel, cause a lot of noise, and damage the ozone layer with high level vapour trails. So, the advice to green minded people is simple: don't travel by air unless you must.

Vehicular Emissions: What we should do

• The Government should consider the possiblity of converting the bus fleet to natural gas.
• Maintenance of bus engines, particularly the fuel injectors, ought to be a priority.
• We need far more State investment in public transport to make it more efficient.
• We need more cycle ways.
• There should be a toll on cars entering the city. Cars with just a driver ought to pay the highest toll.
• Increase the price differential for lead-free petrol to encourage its sale.

213

- The Road Traffic Act, which deals with vehicular emissions, needs to be stringently enforced.
- There needs to be more monitoring of vehicular emissions such as nitrogen oxides, carbon monoxide etc.

What can you do?

- Use your car less. Cycle and walk more.
- If you're buying a new car make sure it is fitted with a catalytic converter.
- Use lead-free petrol and ensure that the engine of your car is well maintained.

Books & Publications

Conservation at Home (Unwin Hyman, 1988) Michael Allaby; *Cutting Car Pollution: The Role of Catalytic Converters* (Johnson Matthey)—free leaflet; *How to Be Green* (Century, 1989) John Button; *New Cyclist*—magazine; *Richard's Bicycle Book* (Pan, 1986); *Taming Traffic* (Deutsch, 1980) Stephen Plowde; *Traffic Calming in Residential Areas* (Friends of the Earth)

Organisations

An Taisce (See Directory)
Cyclefolk, Temple Lane South, Dame St, Dublin 2, 01-771507.

XII
EDUCATION

Education about our environmental responsibilities begins in the home. It is only through the positive example of parents that children learn about the importance of living in harmony with the planet. Recycling paper, bottles and cans, using only environment friendly products and, above all, explaining why it is necessary to do these things ensures that children are instilled from an early age with green values, values which enhance rather than degrade the environment.

Our formal education system is not really environment friendly. Too often education is seen and treated as a form of social and material investment, rather than a fundamental expression of creativity. Young people learn in order to get a good job, and the destructive consumerist line of 'you are what you have' is pushed at them from an early age. A competitive rather than a co-operative spirit is encouraged. Every year our Leaving Cert students engage in a absurd and stressful points race to attain places in university. All this means that subjects such as arts and humanities which do not lead directly to material advancement are relegated and devalued. In short we are taught to remain docile participants in a very destructive system.

Green education policy is both radical and positive in response to the criticisms made by Ivan Illich of schools and other institutions. A green education policy is for people: thinking independently; working co-operatively; contributing positively and creatively to the community.

The Green curriculum emphasises: 1. basic skills of literacy and numeracy; 2. practical life and manual skills; 3. personal responsibility; 4. spiritual, physical and mental development; 5. environmental education; 6. real understanding of the global; 7. out of school activities and community involvement.

Environmental Education in Ireland

The 1990 Young Scientists Exhibition showed very clearly tht young people see the environment as a very important subject. Most of the exhibits had an environmental theme. There are encouraging signs that the curriculum is beginning to reflect the growing interest in environmental issues. An Environmental Awareness Committee has been established in the Department of Education, consisting of representatives from the Department of Education, Department of the Environment, the Environmental Research Unit and Board Failte.

Primary Schools

In particular, the primary school curriculum, with its new emphasis on Social and Environmental Studies, is beginning to make a very positive contribution to children's understanding of the im portance of their environment. Chapter 9 of the teacher's handbook outlines in detail the approaches of this course.

'As the child is the principal agent in his own education, the emphasis should be on learning, rather than on teaching. The aim should be, not to convey the maximum amount of factual information, but to arouse and stimulate the child's interest in his environment, to enable him to understand the various aspects of his experience and to cultivate in him an enquiring attitude of mind. Factual information must indeed be acquired but it is likely to be of greatest value and significance when it results from the child's own experience, observation and investigation. To this end, pupils should be frequently taken out of doors to observe, for instance, plants and animals in their natural surroundings. First-hand observation is essential if an enquiring attitude of mind is to be cultivated.'

Very enlightened stuff. But the writers of the report (Department of Education) should note that the pupils in this country are not exclusively male. Green education also means non-sexist education.

Secondary Schools

Environmental matters are also dealt with in other subjects of the Junior Cert Syllabus. Geography, science and history all have an environmental content and deal with global problems such as the destruction of the rainforests and global warming etc.

The Intermediate Certificate Programme has an integrated course of history and geography, known as Social and Environmental Studies. This has the potential to become an interesting and stimulating course. Unfortunately, it tends not to be taken seriously in many schools and is looked upon in much the same way as the old civics course. At Leaving Cert level there is no Environmental Studies course. In the Points race the environment is a very low priority.

Environmental Education Schools' Network

A unique and significant step in the promotion of environmental education in Ireland was taken at Stranmillis College in Belfast in December 1989. Thirty-two teachers, representing secondary schools of all types equally distributed between northern and southern Ireland, participated in a two day seminar to launch a new environmental network, known as 'European Action for the Environment'.

A total of about eighty teachers were involved. They led about 800 pupils in this first large scale co-operative venture in environmental education to be undertaken in this island.

The project was sponsored by the European Commission's Directorate General for the Environment and followed on from the European Community Environmental Education Network (1978 – 86), which comprised schools from all the then Member states of the Community. The project was operated by the CDVEC Curriculum Development Unit, Trinity College, Dublin in conjunction with the Department of Education, Northern Ireland. If funding is available, this very worthwhile programme will continue into the 1990's.

School Talks and Projects

Most of the environmental organisations here are more than happy to supply speakers for schools. It's simply a matter of ringing up the organisation and arranging for a convenient time.

Every day our environmental organisations are inundated with requests for information by pupils who are doing environmental projects. Again, the organisations will do their best to help, but it's important to remember that most of them are surviving on shoestring budgets – so do at least send a stamped addressed envelope and if possible a small donation.

Adult Education

Education is a lifelong process and shouldn't end when we leave school or university. Adult education is grossly under-funded in this country. The Department of Education's total expenditure for 1987 was £1.6 billion, of which adult education received 0.16%, and this in a country where 400,000 adults read and write with difficulty.

The VECs, FAS and a number of other centres (see the *Wolfhound Guide to Evening Classes for Dublin* information) provide a range of interesting courses for adults at very reasonable rates. Environmental topics are now beginning to figure among these courses. The universities also run extra mural courses on green issues, but the response to date has been poor.

Remember, if there's an environmental subject which interests you, the local VEC will arrange for a course on that subject, providing 13 other people join you.

The FWUI Education Committee will be introducing a section dealing with the Protection of the Environment into the Standard Union course (see Unions).

SONAIRTE, The National Ecology Centre, in Laytown, Co. Meath is presently preparing a software package for use in schools. It will deal with a wide range of environmental issues and can be used by pupils in the school's PC or at home.

A working group of teachers from the Centre are also looking for ways in which all subjects can reflect environmental issues. Traditionally, biology, environmental science and perhaps geography have dealt with environmental concerns, but subjects such as mathematics and languages can and should deal with the environment. For instance, many German teaching texts already discuss the environment, which reflects the Germans concern with problems such as acid rain and nuclear power.

Mathematics and science are vital to an understanding of the complexities of eco systems. For example, pupils could be asked to calculate the effect on the ozone layer from a certain level of CFC emission etc.

Sonairte is also a very good place to bring pupils on a day trip. *For more details Phone 01-412371 or 01-731884.*

ENFO

Under the new Environment Action Programme, the Government is setting up a centre, to be called ENFO, to provide pupils with environmental information. The centre will include an extensive data library and will act as a one-stop shop, providing facilitation for schoolchildren as well as research facilities for more in-depth projects. There are also plans to have a computer link-up with libraries throughout the country. Department of the Environment Tel. 01-793377.

Green Careers and Jobs

There's no doubt that there will be a huge increase in jobs in environmental protection in the coming years. Most of these jobs will be of a specialised nature and will certainly require some form of scientific qualification. Even the various environmental campaign groups are looking for people with a science background, but it's not absolutely necessary.

If you're enthusiastic, dedicated and are willing to work long hours for very little money, then being a professional Green is the career for you. Yes, the financial rewards for being a campaigner are not great, but there's compensation in the knowledge that you're saving the Planet. And forget the glamorous picture you may have of eco-heroes speeding along in their rubber inflatables saving the world from destruction. It's not like that – at least most of the time. A lot of campaign work is done in an office, sifting through report after report, checking facts, compiling data and sitting in front of a PC. But it is rewarding, especially when after months of hard work and careful planning you finally achieve your aim. One Greenpeace action, which maybe takes up two minutes of TV time, could have taken up to six months to plan.

Greenpeace and Earthwatch are expanding their network throughout Ireland and need help and volunteers. If you're over twenty-five and have been on unemployment assistance or benefit for six months, then you're eligible to do a SES scheme with some of the environmental groups. At present An Taisce, Crann, Eco, Earthwatch and the Dublin Food Co-op all run SES schemes.

The waiting list to get on one of the Greenpeace ships gets longer and longer every year. If you are specially qualified in some environmental area or have worked on ships before, your chances of being taken on are better.

Working Abroad

If you're a student, you may be interested in working for an environmental organisation during the summer months. Greenpeace have an extensive fundraising operation in the USA and often need helpers. The work is relatively easy. You go from door to door looking for donations and you work on a commission basis. Greenpeace in Ireland can give you a list of contact names.

Careers

The Careers Office in UCD receive more and more enquiries every year from students who are interested in a career in the Environment. At present their files on this area are inadequate but they are being up-dated to meet the increased demand.

Third Level Environmental Studies

The following institutions have specific courses in Environmental Studies: UCD, TCD, Sligo RTC, DIT, Cathal Brugha Street., Coleraine University.

WHAT SHOULD BE DONE

There should be
• small schools closely connected with their communities facilitating a better exchange of practical learning and skills
• anti-racist and non-sexist curricula
• continuous profiling rather than public examination based assessment
• drastic reduction in pupil teacher ratio
• participation of parents in education wherever possible
• decentralised control of education
• lifelong access to facilities of learning and self discovery
• proper funding of adult education
• in-house training for teachers on environmental matters
• environmental studies should be obligatory on all school courses

WHAT YOU CAN DO

• Lead a green lifestyle and teach your children to do the same
• Take a keen interest in the environmental subjects taught at your child's school
• Get on parent/teacher committee and make sure that the school carries out environmental projects such as can recycling. Also insist that the environment is integrated into as many subjects as possible. (see Sonairte box)

Organisations

Aontas, National Association of Adult Education, 65 Fitzwilliam Sq., Dublin 2, Tel. (01) 610571/612092
Sonairte, the National Ecology Centre (see listings). School trips to the Centre can be arranged. Tel. (01) 412371 or (01) 413226. Sonairte will be setting up a working group of teachers in 1990 to discuss ways of teaching green issues. It should be interesting and stimulating.
ECO (see listings) Tel. (01) 731884
CDVEC (see listings) Tel. (01) 772941 Ext 1715, 1550
Department of Education – Marlboro St., Dublin 1, Tel. (01) 734700
Department of Education – Rathgad House, Balloo Rd., Bangor, Co. Down (080247) 466311

Books and Publications

Anything school can do you can do better, Maire Mullarney (Fontana 1985); *Teach your own*, John Holt (Lighthouse books 1982); *Deschooling Society*, Ivan Illich (Marion Boyars 1970); *Freedom to learn in the Eighties*, Carl Rogers (1983); *The Head's Tale*, Philip Toogood (1984); Green teacher (magazine) available from Sonairte; *Resurgence* (magazine) contains good articles on education.

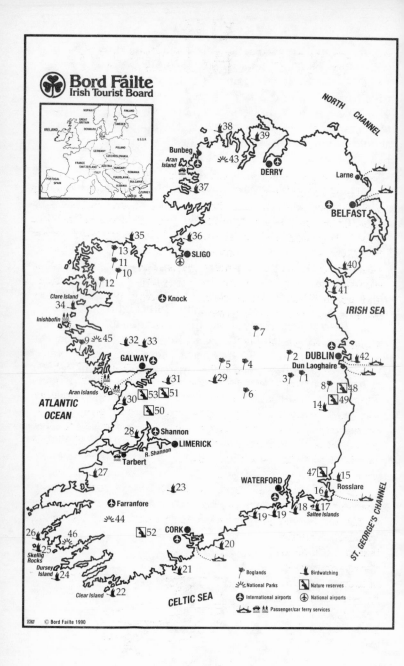

Bord Fáilte
Irish Tourist Board

Boglands

National Parks

International airports

National airports

Birdwatching

Nature reserves

Passenger/car ferry services

© Bord Failte 1990

XIII
GREEN HOLIDAYS

Defining a green holiday is a difficult one. Spending a few weeks in one of the many organic farm guesthouses certainly qualifies as a green holiday. In Italy, for instance, angling and equestrian holidays are regarded as 'green'. Bord Failte have now recognised the great potential in specialised green holidays. Their surveys have revealed that the majority of people who visit this country do so because of the clean environment—or rather the image of this country as clean and green. One thing is certain, in terms of tourism our environment is our greatest asset.

Does Tourism Pollute?

This is an important question, and one which governments, including our own, will have to address in the coming years. There is no doubt that while tourism provides much needed jobs and revenue in many countries, it can also be very damaging to places and people, if uncontrolled. One need only look at the tourist resorts of Spain, with their high rise hotels blotting the landscape, and sewage problems, to know about the ravages of tourism.

Greece, which was once 'unspoilt', now has a similar problem. The Acropolis has been tramped over by more feet in the last twenty years than in the previous two thousand.

Venice is also under threat because of the massive influx of tourists. In 1987, it was estimated that 86,000 visitors a day entered the city.

By the year 2000 tourism will be the biggest industry in the world. With the virtual collapse of the Iron Curtain there will be many more tourists from Eastern Europe. The Far East and Japan are also expected to respond positively to Bord Failte's advertising and an annual 8% increase in the tourist market is forecast. All of this is to be welcomed, but as the experience of other countries has shown caution is required. By building more roads, huge hotels, airports and car parks we are actually ruining our greatest tourist attraction—our environment.

Arranging Your Holiday:

Holidays including visits to boglands and/or birdwatching sites can be arranged through the following:

Arnold's Hotel, Dunfanaghy, Co. Donegal. Tel. 074-36208.
Nick Becker, Knockreagh House, Knockrath, Rathdrum, Co. Wicklow. Tel. 0404-46465.
Corrib Conservation Centre (Dr. Tony Wilde), Ardsillagh, Oughterard, Co. Galway. Tel. 091-82519.
Heritage Rambles (Ray McGrath) c/o Terry Flynn Travel, 47, The Quay, Waterford. Tel. 051-72126/7/3.
Irish Birdwatch Tours, 4, Avondale Park, Killiney, Co. Dublin. Tel. 01-852469. Fax 01-718888
Irish Wilderness Experience, 50, Woodlawn Park, Killarney, Co. Kerry. Tel. 064-32992
Whimbrel Tours (Dave Daly), 29, Carricklawn, Coolcotts, Wexford. Tel. 053-41258

Special Events—Conference, Symposia

CONNEMARA BOG WEEK/WILDLIFE CONFERENCE
A week long celebration of the bog landscape, incorporating a wildlife conference. Held during the second week in May.

CONNEMARA SEA WEEK/WILDLIFE CONFERENCE
Week long study of our marine environment incorporating a wildlife conference. Held during the second week in October.
For further information contact Leo Hallissey, Connemara Environmental Education Centre, Letterfrack National School, Co. Galway. Tel. 095-41054; 095-41006; 095-43443. Fax 095-41005.

CONNEMARA SUMMER SCHOOL

The Connemara Summer School will be held on Inishbofin, an island off the West Coast of Ireland. Using a team of experts—botanists, marine biologists etc—it explores the many aspects of the island.

For further information on the Summer School contact Leo Hallissey, Letterfrack Environmental Education Centre, Letterfrack National School, Co. Galway. Tel. 095-43443. Fax 095-41005.

BURREN WILDLIFE SYMPOSIUM

Each spring and autumn expert lecturers on wildlife subjects join in a weekend Burren Symposium presented by a voluntary organisation. Details from Mr. J.D. McNamara, Burren Wildlife Symposium, Admiral's Rest, Fanore, Co. Clare. Tel. 065-76105.

IOFGA

The Irish Organic Farmers and Growers Association is a member of IFOAM, the International Federation of Organic Agriculture Movements, and is also affiliated to the Soil Association.

It brings together farmers, growers, gardeners and consumers who are concerned about the way in which our food is produced, concerned about the effects of additives and chemical residues upon our health, and concerned that food should be nutritious and taste good, as well as just looking good.

IOFGA is a vigorous and expanding association. If you are interested in becoming a member and receiving the 'Common Ground' newsletter, write to IOFGA, c/o Nicky Kyle, Springmount, Ballyboughill, Co. Dublin Tel 01-433051.

Irish Organic Farm Guesthouses

Irish organic farmers and growers are opening their houses to visitors. Now you can stay in a big house, farmhouse, cottage or hostel and eat fresh organic food wherever you go.

Accommodation can be with the family or self-catering—luxurious or economical.

Each guesthouse owner is a member of IOFGA, The Irish Organic Farmers and Growers Association. Each guesthouse garden is inspected to ensure that organic standards are maintained. Rates given are those for 1989.

Some of the guesthouses are working organic farms, and all of them have an organic garden—large or small. Those which have already passed the IOFGA inspection are entitled to the symbol of organic quality, and their produce is thus guaranteed produced to full organic standards.

Brochure from: Gillies Macbain, Cranagh Castle, Templemore, County Tipperary, Ireland. Telephone 0504-53104.

Lettercollum House, Timoleague, Co. Cork 023-46251
Lettercollum House is a large Victorian house within sight of the sea, set in its own grounds and 12 acre farm, with pigs, goats and poultry. Run workshops and seminars on a wide range of subjects from arts and crafts to vegetarian cooking to yoga. (Send S.A.E. for a brochure.) Accommodation for 30. Dormitories, two family rooms, and a cottage to sleep four. Price guide: £4 to £7 per night. Evening menu £5 to £10. Breakfast from £1. Vegetarians, vegans, macrobiotics catered for. Bicycles for hire. Large organic walled garden. Symbol Holder. Member of Independent Hostel Owners (IHO).

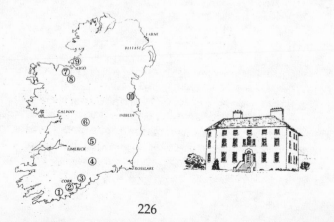

Ann Watson, Ballinrea, Carrigaline, Co. Cork 021-372106
This old fashioned bungalow overlooks its own wooded field. The 15 organically farmed acres carry cattle and poultry. 6 miles from Cork, 12 miles from Kinsale, and convenient to Cork airport and ferry terminal. Access to beaches, riding, tennis and golf. Sailing in our own boat. Accommodation: 2 double rooms with own bathroom. Price guide: bed and breakfast £8.00; evening meal £4.50. Organic garden.

Patricia Madden, Ballynona House, Midleton, Co. Cork 021-667151
Ballynona House is an interesting 19th century country house 4 miles from Midleton overlooking much of East Cork. Convenient to Fota Wildlife Park and Trabolgan Holiday Centre. 5 golf courses within 10 to 30 minutes drive. Fishing can be arranged. Organic farm with poultry, pigs, goats. Accommodation: 5 rooms include 2 large family rooms. Price guide: bed and breakfast £10 (£1.50 extra with private toilet and shower); dinner £11; children half price. Group reductions available. Organic garden. Approved by Irish Tourist Board. Symbol Holder.

Ballybrado House, Cahir, Co. Tipperary 052-66206
Ballybrado House is a 230 acre estate on the river Suir, and the lodge stands in a quiet wooded lane nearby. Wildlife sanctuary. Fishing. Walking. Children welcome. Organic farm with Jacobs sheep, saddleback pigs, poultry and bees. Accommodation: 2 adults, 2/3 children. Price guide: £150 per week. We sell organic flour, eggs and vegetables from our large walled garden. Approved by Irish Tourist Board. Symbol Holder.

Gillies Macbain, Cranagh Castle, Templemore, Co. Tipperary 0504-53104
Cranagh Castle is a large Georgian house and mediaeval tower house. The 25 acre farm has Irish draught horses, cattle, pigs, sheep, geese, ducks and hens. Accommodation: 4 private rooms and a dormitory. Price guide: £4 and £5 per night—self catering. We sell home made bread and garden produce. We run introductory courses in the large walled organic garden. Member of Independent Hostel Owners (HO). Symbol Holder.

John and Rosetta-Anne Paxman, Ballycormac House, Aglish, Near Borrisokane, Co. Tipperary 067-21129

Ballycormac House is a 300 year old farmhouse surrounded by pretty gardens in peaceful countryside. The house is furnished with antiques and curios and has a warm and friendly atmosphere. We specialise in Irish hunting horses. Riding in summer. Shooting arranged in winter. Accommodation: 3 double bedrooms, one single, all with their own bathrooms. Price guide: Bed and breakfast £14; Dinner £12. Wine Licence. Turf fires. French spoken. Cordon bleu food with emphasis on organic vegetables and wholefoods. Approved by Irish Tourist Board.

Cabragh Lodge, Coolaney, Co. Sligo 071-67706

Cabragh Lodge is an old shooting lodge in the Ox Mountains. Set in 7 acres of woodland, coppice, orchard and garden, and surrounded by forest and lakes. Ideal for hill walking. Accommodation: 3 double bedrooms, all with wash basins. Price guide: bed and breakfast £8, dinner £5. All menus are strictly vegetarian, and much is home produced from organic garden. Symbol Holder.

Mrs D Perceval, Temple House, Ballymote, Co. Sligo 071-83329

Temple House is a Georgian Mansion overlooking Temple House Lake, and set in a 1,000 acre wooded estate. The self-catering cottage sleeps 8 and also has a sofa bed, cot, open fire, immersion heater and clothes drier. Price guide: £120/week Jul/Aug; £100/week May/Jun/Sep. Other months negotiable. We sell fruit and vegetables from large organic walled garden. Boats for hire on lake. Approved by Irish Tourist Board. Symbol Holder.

Maggie and Kevin Moran, Moneygold Riding & Horse Driving Centre, Grange, Co. Sligo 071-63337
Moneygold is a traditional stone cottage set between the mountains and the sea. 20 km of beaches. Safe swimming lagoon, islands and sand dunes. Indoor gym and sauna 1km. Organic farm with Connemara ponies. We teach riding, also English for foreign students. Traditional music. Price guide: Bed and breakfast from £8. All hostel beds (8) at £4 per night. Symbol Holder. Organic Garden. Also self-catering cottage, sleeps 6.

Liz Lyons, The Cottages, Seabank, Bettystown, Co. Meath 041-28104
The cottages at Seabank stand in a secluded four acre garden that runs down to a safe sandy beach. There are four thatched cottages and four bungalows. They are equipped with television and duvets, linen if required. Tennis court, home bakery, laundrette. We sell produce from organic flower and vegetable garden. Symbol Holder. Five cottages approved by Irish Tourist Board.

Other Holiday Suggestions for healthy nature-lovers

ADVENTURE

Achill Island Outdoor Education Centre, Co. Mayo. Tel. (098) 45237, canoeing, hill-walking, surfing, field studies etc. *Tiglin Adventure Centre*, Ashford, Co. Wicklow. Tel. (0404) 40169, mountaineering, orienteering, water sports etc. *Cappanalea Outdoor Education Centre*, Oulagh West, Caragh Lake, Killorglin, Co. Kerry. Tel. (066) 69244 or (066) 69205, mountaineering, orienteering, water sports, field studies etc. *Delphi Adventure Sports Centre*, Leenane, Co. Galway. Tel. (095) 42208/42223, archery, water sports, deep-sea fishing, boat trips etc. *Kinsale Outdoor Education Centre*, St. John's Hill, Kinsale, Co. Cork. Tel. (021) 772896, courses in seamanship, rock-climbing, field studies in local history and environmental studies. *Little Killary Adventure Centre Ltd.*, Salruck, Renvyle, Co. Galway. Tel. (095) 43411, multi-activity holidays with canoeing, surfing, mountaineering, orienteering etc. *Malinmore Adventure Centre*, Glencolmcille, Co. Donegal. Tel. (073) 30123, (073) 30016, snorkelling/diving, hill-walking, rock-climbing, boardsailing. *Shannonside Activity Centre*, Killaloe, Co. Clare. Tel. (061) 45396/76622. *Skerdagh Outdoor Recreation Centre*, Glenhest, Newport, Co. Mayo. Tel. (098)

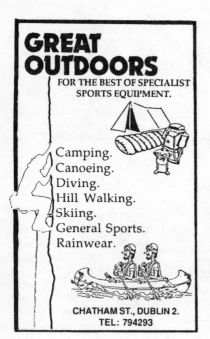

41500, camping, bivouacing, mountaineering, historical tours. *Smarmore Castle Recreation Centre*, Ardee, Co. Louth. Tel. (041) 53474, nature trails, barbecues, art groups.

LEARNING A NEW ART OR CRAFT

An Grianan Adult Education College, Termonfeckin, Co. Louth. Tel. (041) 22199/22478, arts and crafts courses of various types, and local history and archaeology. *Rathmichael Historical Society*: c/o Alison Riseley, 7 Coonoon Ct., Killiney Ave, Killiney, Co. Dublin. Tel. (01) 854425, course in archaeology, with site work on an excavation, tours of sites and lectures.

PAINTING HOLIDAYS

Ballynahow Castle Farm, Thurles, Co. Tipperary, Tel. (0504) 21297. *The Ballynakill Studios*, Moyard, Connemara, Co. Galway. Tel. (095) 41048. *Burren Painting Centre*, Lisdoonvarna, Co. Clare, Tel. (065) 74208. *Kenmare Painting Holidays*, c/o 38 Homefarm Road, Dublin 9. Tel. (01) 374725 or Dunkerron Castle, Kenmare, Co. Kerry. *Pine Forest Art Centre Summer School*, Glencullen, Kilternan, Co. Dublin. Tel. (01) 95598. *Sheephaven Bay School of Landscape Painting*, Arnold's Hotel, Dunfanaghy, via Letterkenny, Co. Donegal. Tel. (074) 36208/36142.

Other Useful Addresses

Cospoir—the National Sports Council, Floor 11, Hawkins House, Dublin 2. Tel. (01) 734700. *Federation of Mountaineering Clubs of Ireland (FMCI)*, 20 Leopardstown Gardens, Blackrock. Tel. (01) 881266. *Association of Adventure Sports (AFAS)*, Tiglin Adventure Centre, Ashford, Co. Wicklow. Tel. (0404) 4169. *An Oige-Irish Youth Hostels Association*, 39 Mountjoy Square, Dublin 1. Tel. (01) 363111. *Bord Failte*, Baggot Street Bridge, Dublin 2. Tel. (01) 765871 for List of 'Live and Learn' Holidays

---

**Hike It
Bike It
Learn Something New
Try Adventure**

**Visit our wonderful National Parks,
Nature Reserves, Bogs, Great Houses and Gardens.**

XIV
CAMPAIGNING

The popular image of environmental campaigners is of people—usually bearded types in anoraks—sitting in front of bulldozers which are about to wreak havoc on nature. In reality, non-violent direct action is always a last resort and most campaigns very rarely get to that stage. Mostly, campaigning is about using the media and other means to inform the public about the issues involved and thus persuade people to give you support. It may also involve using the legal system to prevent any environmentally damaging project from going ahead.

Campaigns may range from local residents objecting to the constant noise from a neighbour's house to a major campaign against a multinational wishing to site a chemical factory in your area.

Running a successful campaign against companies who have power, money, information, expertise and are old hands at dealing with the media, can be a very daunting task for a small group of well-intentioned individuals. But the tide of public opinion is most certainly turning in favour of green groups—so take heart. Those objecting to an environmentally damaging project are often branded 'anti-progress', 'unrealistic', 'emotive', 'cranks' etc. Campaign groups continue to be dismissed in this way, but in the current climate many of these accusations and the tag 'unrepresentative' ring false in the minds of the general public. Large Corporations are seen to be motivated solely by profit and people instinctively mistrust them. In a sense, therefore, you the people have a comparative advantage. You're instantly more believable. The point is to make the most of this advantage. You can do this in a number of ways.

Get the Facts on the Situation

Not always an easy thing to do. Your efforts to obtain information are likely to be thwarted at every level. Information is power and the powers that be don't like giving it out too easily. Be prepared to be fobbed off from one Department to another. People in government departments can be extremely coy about talking to people from campaign groups. But be patient—there's always someone who will eventually talk—if you guarantee confidentiality. And this is something you must do. If you quote your source that person's job could be on the line.

If you're dealing with a multi-national, find out about their record at home and in other bases. The American EPA is a good source of information. Often an employee or former employee of a company will give you information 'off the record'.

Once you're sure that pollution is occurring or that the siting of a factory or project will cause pollution, it may be necessary to have some independent monitoring carried out.

Knowing where to get information can be as difficult as actually getting it. Before starting any campaign get advice from the established environmental groups such as An Taisce, Greenpeace or Earthwatch.

Media Relations and Publicity

If your local issue receives national publicity, then your campaign is succeeding. Extensive media coverage of the issue will result in more and more support for your objectives.

Start your campaign by compiling a comprehensive list—on card file—or if you have a PC—on disc—of local and national media, with the names, addresses, phone and fax numbers of local and national newspapers, radio stations and RTE. Special attention should be given to reporters who are known to be sympathetic. If possible, try to get their home phone numbers.

Don't forget to include free newspapers and student publications or the newsletters and magazines of the environmental organisations.

233

You should also try to get the addresses and telephone numbers of local celebrities, who might be willing to lend the campaign some support. Also have a list of all the local councillors and TD's.

Having a phone, fax, photocopier and PC is a real advantage for any campaign group.

Letters

Campaigning means a lot of letter writing to, among others, TD's, Government bodies and the newspapers. It's important therefore to have an attractive letterhead with the campaign group's logo on top. This should also be used for press releases etc.

All letters should be typed, concise and to the point.

Press Releases

Press releases can include those announcing forthcoming press conferences, public meetings or protests, or those which respond directly to news. The latter can be written as a straightforward statement or in the third person including quotations eg 'The dumping of asbestos in the area should never be allowed,' Ms Murphy said. Using the third person can be more difficult and requires a certain amount of practice.

There are also a number of basic rules which need to be followed when writing press releases:

- Use your headed notepaper.
- Press releases should always be typed, double spaced and on one side of paper only.
- At the top put the date of the press release and the words 'for immediate use' you wish the release to be embargoed, write 'not for use before 10 AM on su and such a day'.
- Put a brief heading on top eg SMOG PROTEST to explain what the press rele is about.
- Basically, journalists are looking for WWWWWH (who, what, why, whe when, how). Put what is most interesting and unusual about your event a activity—usually WHO and WHAT—at the very beginning. Follow it with tw or three sentences, containing the other important details, especially the WHI and WHERE.
- Write the press release in a way that would enable a journalist to use the fi paragraph if stuck for time.
- Keep it clear and concise. That way, it's less likely that it will end up meani something you did not intend.

Normally, a press release should not be more than 1½ pages long, double spaced. Don't forget to put a contact name and telephone number (day and evening) at the end of the press release.

Always keep a copy of all letters and press releases

Photographs

One picture is worth a thousand words in terms of publicity. People are immediately attracted to an interesting photograph in a newspaper.

When staging an event, particularly a protest, try to think of good photo opportunities. And remember, always send a separate press release to the photo desk.

The Broadcast Media

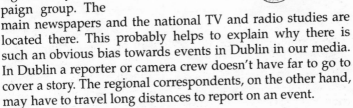

Living in Dublin is a great advantage for any campaign group. The main newspapers and the national TV and radio studies are located there. This probably helps to explain why there is such an obvious bias towards events in Dublin in our media. In Dublin a reporter or camera crew doesn't have far to go to cover a story. The regional correspondents, on the other hand, may have to travel long distances to report on an event.

TV

TV is by far the most powerful and influential of the media and it's essential that a major campaign receives TV coverage. Here are some points to remember:

- Notify RTE (TV newsdesk) about your event or protest a few days in advance.
- Ring up the day before and remind them of the event. Ask if it has been put down as an event to be covered. They may tell you that the schedule is not decided till the next morning. In that case find out who is the editor on newsdesk that day.
- Ring early on the day in question and ask for the editor by name. Use all your charm and imagination to persuade him/her that the event is worth covering.
- TV is 55% appearance, 38% voice and language and 7% what you say. The lesson is obvious—try to look neat and presentable.
- Most TV interviews for news bulletins only last two or three sentences—so make sure to put your main points across very clearly.

Leaflets

The layout and presentation of your leaflet are all important—so get a good layout artist or graphic artist, who is sympathetic to the cause, to help you.

- Make your points as brief and as clear as possible. This is especially true if the leaflet is advertising a public meeting.
- Avoid hysterical claims. Stick to the facts.
- Always make sure the contact address and phone number are printed clearly.
- If possible, print all your material on recycled paper.

Public Meetings

- Advertise your meeting as widely as possible through leaflet drops, posters, an on national and local radio.
- It's better if the venue is centrally located near the main public transport routes
- It looks far better to have a small hall packed to capacity, with only standi room, than to have a big hall half empty. The attendance is one of the first thin that journalists will comment on, and if the TV cameras are there, pictures empty seats can be damaging to the campaign.
- At the very most have four speakers (from both sexes) to talk about differe aspects of the campaign. This avoids boring repetition.
- Speakers should if possible talk for not more than twenty minutes.
- Make sure that all technical facilities such as microphones and slide ar overhead projectors are available and working.
- When the best speaker has finished and the crowd is suitably motivated and we disposed pass around the 'hat'. The chairperson should explain that running campaign is costly and urge people to give as generously as possible.
- If you have a big-name speaker you can charge at the door.
- At the end of the meeting questions and suggestions should be taken from t floor. If one of the 'opposition' avails of the opportunity to disrupt the meetin the chairperson should shut him/her up quickly and courteously.

Public Speaking/Debates

Surveys carried out on what causes the most fear in people show that speaking in public comes out on top. Most people simply dread it, and even those experienced public speakers feel a tingling of the nerves before stepping out on the podium. It's quite natural to feel nervous, and if you're sufficiently prepared the flow of adrenalin will actually enhance your performance rather than impair it. The key really is preparation, knowing your facts and, of course, practice. Impromptu speeches don't really work and those that do are only as good as the paper they're written on, as they say.

You may never become a mighty orator, but you will be able to persuade people about the truth of your cause.

Know your subject. Anticipate the tricky questions that might be asked and prepare suitable answers.

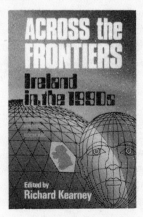

XV
LAW

Legal Action, Environmental
Impact Assessment
and
Irish Environmental Legislation
Legal Action

Most campaigns begin with individuals asserting their legal rights, but knowing just what those rights are can be difficult. The EC has brought with it a tremendous amount of progressive environmental legislation, which the individual can avail of. Irish environmental law is generally recognised to be fairly thorough. But there are problems with enforcement. These problems often arise because of a lack of resources for the relevant authorities or because—up until recently—the environment was not seen as a priority.

The rule is to badger and pester until these people give in. Below are some examples of situations you may encounter.

Air

- *Someone has set up a small garage in your area, doing respray jobs on old cars, —the fumes are having a bad effect on your health:*
- *Someone is burning the plastic coating off old electric cable to retrieve the copper metal beneath, —the emissions are toxic and having serious health consequences in the area:*
- *A neighbour is constantly burning rubbish in the back garden. The smoke from the fire is annoying you:*

If you are being adversely affected by air pollution, you have a number of options under the current laws. Under the Public Health (Ireland) Act 1878, any person aggrieved by a statutory nuisance (which may include air pollution) may complain to the sanitary authority. If the sanitary authority is satisfied that a nuisance does exist, it is obliged to serve a notice to those responsible, requiring the immediate abatement of emissions. If this does not have the desired effect, the sanitary authority is then obliged to prosecute those responsible for the nuisance. A local authority can prosecute the owner or occupier of any premises (except a private dwelling) who causes or permits an emission in such manner or quantity as to cause a nuisance. (Sec. 24, Air Pollution Act 1987). Emissions from a private dwelling must be dealt with at common law.

As an individual you also are entitled to prosecute for statutory nuisance.

- *A nearby factory is emitting smoke or fumes which you feel are injurious to health:*

Get on to the Local Authority immediately and find out about the provision in the licence issued to the factory. Under the Air Pollution Act 1987 a factory from which aerial emissions of pollutants will occur must apply to the Local Authority for a licence. This is granted only when the Local Authority is satisfied that there is no threat to the environment or to health.

The Local Authority does not monitor emissions—that's left to the factory itself. This means that you or your group will have to keep a very watchful eye on the factory, recording accurately the time, duration and type of emissions. Again your task is made all the more difficult by the fact that most illegal emissions occur in the early hours of the morning. Some noxious emissions are also invisible and difficult to detect without specialised equipment.

But even if, after a lot of hard work on your part, it can be proved that the licence conditions have been breached, the factory chiefs can use the 'best practicable means' (bpm) clause to get themselves off the hook. They simply claim that they did their best to contain harmful emissions and used the best available technology.

If you wish to pursue the matter further, you may have to prove that the emissions have damaged people's health—a virtual non-starter legally.

As you can see, it's very much an uphill struggle. Campaign groups such as RICH (Responsible Industry for Cork Harbour) will testify to the difficulties involved. However, John Hanrahan's victory over Merck Sharp and Dohme is a source of hope for all individual campaigners.

- *Urban smog is causing you severe respiratory problems:*

By pursuing the matter through EC channels, it is possible to have this country brought to the European Court of Justice for its failure to comply with its EC agreements. The first step is to write a letter of complaint to the Commission. One letter to the Commission on this subject is worth hundreds of letters to our Minister for the Environment.

- *You're a cyclist, and the black fumes being belched out by buses is making cycling in the city an unenjoyable and unhealthy pursuit:*

If you see a vehicle spewing out black fumes, take the registration number and report it immediately to the Guards. It is an offence under the Road Traffic (Construction, Equipment and Use of Vehicles) Regulations 1963, as amended.

1. To use a vehicle in a public place so that there is emitted therefrom any smoke, visible vapour, grit, sparks, ashes, cinders or oily substances, the emission of which could be prevented by reasonable care.
2. To use, cause or permit the use of a device designed to facilitate starting so as to cause it to supply the engine with excess fuel while the vehicle is in motion.

Enforcement of the Road Traffic Acts 1961 and 1968 and the associated regulations, is the responsibility of the Garda Siochana. But as can be seen every day in our cities, these regulations are very rarely enforced. It's important that more and more people complain to the Guards about this matter. Only then will they begin to take it seriously.

The penalty for breach of the regulations is a fine not exceeding £20 for the first offence and £50 for a second or subsequent offence.

- *Someone is smoking in the no-smoking zone of the bus. You object to breathing polluted air:*

Under the 1961 Road Traffic Act CIE can prohibit smoking in any part of a bus or train. Those who refuse to obey these regulations may be physically removed by the Gardai and prosecuted for a legal offence.

Tell the smoker politely that smoking is forbidden. If that has no effect tell the driver or conductor to take immediate action. If they refuse to do this, which often happens, you should note down the bus registration number and threaten to report the incident to the district manager. At this stage most bus crews will be sufficiently motivated to tell the person to stop smoking.

Water

• *You know of a farm which is causing pollution.*

Contact the local authority and Regional Fisheries Board immediately, giving them all the relevant details. Local authorities, the Minister for Fisheries, Fisheries Boards and any private individual may prosecute if there have been breaches of Section 3(1) of the Water Pollution Act, Section 3 of the Act provides that 'a person shall not cause or permit any polluting matter to enter waters'. The run-off of effluents such as slurry, fertilizers or biocides from land are controlled under this section.

Under Section 12 of the Act the local authority may direct the farmer in question to take specific measures to prevent further pollution of the river within a certain time period. If the farmer fails to comply within the time specified, the local authority may take any steps it considers necessary to prevent further pollution occurring—at the expense of the farmer. He is also liable to a fine not exceeding £250 together with a fine not exceeding £100 for every day the offence is continued and/or 6 months' imprisonment.

The penalty on conviction or indictment is £5000 together with £500 for every day on which the offence is continued and /or 2 years' imprisonment.

NB These fines are set to increase with the introduction of the new Water Pollution Act.

• *Waste milk and whey from a nearby creamery is causing severe damage to the local salmon river*

Contact the local authority and the Regional Fisheries Board, giving them all the relevant details.

Section 4 of the Water Pollution Act 1977 deals with 'trade effluent' (effluent from factories) and 'sewage effluent', which may not be discharged to any waters 'except under and in accordance with a licence under this section'. The difficulty is proving that the amount discharged exceeds that allowable under the provisions of the licence.

There are a number of problems associated with current licencing laws. First of all, the licencing of sewers is exempt from the licencing requirements of Section 4. Secondly, the monitoring of discharges is left to the factory itself—a highly unsatisfactory situation and one which perhaps the new EPA could look at.

If the pollution from this point source (see river pollution, Water Chapter) continues, you or your group should seek to have the factory's licence reviewed. Section 7 of the Act provides that the licence be reviewed at least every three years. You may then submit objections to the issuing of a new licence. You may also prosecute the licence holder, or get a High Court injunction to stop a discharge which does not comply with the licence requirements.

- *You're afraid that a new chemical company proposed for the area will pollute the river.*

An applicant for a licence under section 4 of the Water Pollution Act 1977 must publish notice of the intention to apply for a licence in a local newspaper.

When the application has been received the local authority is obliged to make it and the accompanying documentation available at its office for public inspection during normal office hours—until such time as permission is granted or an appeal heard. Some of this documentation will be extremely technical, so it's better if you bring along someone with experience in these matters to advise you. If, having read the relevant documentation, you are still unhappy, you may submit written objections to the local authority. This facility is recognised in article 11(1) (c) of the Regulations. The local authority must then give you notice of any decision made on the matter. It can do this directly or through a local newspaper. Any such notice should also inform you of your right to appeal against the decision under section 8 of the Act.

You may appeal to the Planning Appeals Board against a decision on a licence. The appeal must be made within one month from the date of the grant. Part 4 of the Water Pollution Regulations 1978 prescribes the procedures to be followed on appeal.

- *You are worried that your water supply is contaminated with nitrates or toxins; your mains supply is discoloured. The water smells and tastes badly.*

Contact the local Environmental Health Officer and have a

sample of the water tested in a laboratory. Contact the local authority (sanitary authority), giving them details. They will then establish the cause of the problem and, if necessary, close down the water supply until it is fit for human consumption.

Under the Public Health (Ireland) Act 1878, the sanitary authorities have a statutory responsibility for ensuring the provision of water which is 'pure and wholesome'. They may take proceedings to prevent pollution of waterworks within the jurisdiction from sewage, they may also seek a court order to eliminate any danger, if there is any reason to believe that the drinking water is injurious to human health.

Section 61 of the Waterworks Clause Act 1847 prohibits the contamination of any stream or reservoir used as a public water supply, or any aqueduct or any other part of the supply system. The penalty is a mere £1 for each day that the offence continues.

Section 17 of the Waterworks Clauses Act 1863 provides that it is an offence for any person wilfully or negligently to cause or to suffer 'any pipe, valve, cock, cistern, bath, soil-pan, water closet, or other apparatus or receptacle to be out of repair, or to be so used or contrived' as to cause the water supplied by the sanitary authority to be wasted, misused, unduly consumed or contaminated or so as 'to occasion or allow the return of foul air, or other noisome or impure matter' into any pipe belonging to the sanitary authority. For any of these offences there is a fine not exceeding £5.

The quality of drinking water is also covered by the Local Government (Water Pollution) Act 1977. Of particular relevance are sections 3,12,13,15,22 and 23.

There have been many EC directives on drinking water quality which have been carried out by the local authorities. The European Community's (Quality of water intended for human consumption) Regulations, 1988, also set out quality standards for all water suppliers.

It should be added that if the water is tested by the environmental officer he or she is not obliged to give you exact details on the results. If you continue to be uneasy about the water supply it may be necessary to have it independently tested.

Litter

• *Someone continues to dump domestic rubbish in a nearby field*
Take all the relevant details: where, when, (if possible get the car registration) then get on to the local authority. If they have

a litter warden talk to him directly. Under the Litter Act 1982, the local authority has considerable powers to deal with the problems of litter, flyposting, graffiti and abandoned vehicles.

The maximum fine for an offence is £800, and a £5 on-the-spot fine is also provided for.

Trees

- *The trees in a small wood nearby are being felled, you need to find out the following*:

1. is the area in question controlled by an Urban District Council or County Council;
2. Who is responsible for the felling (some organisation may have hired a contractor);
3. Who owns the land on which the trees stand;
4. The age, condition and species of tree involved

In County Council areas a felling licence is required from the Forestry Service. There are exceptions to the rule: dangerous roadside trees and trees less than a hundred feet from a building which are being cut down as part of road widening.

If you think the tree felling is illegal, you should get on to the Gardai. Also contact the planning office of the County Council and request a tree preservation order. As a last resort you should consider a High Court Order.

In urban areas a tree felling licence is not required. Felling is only illegal if the protection of the trees has been written into the planning consent. Therefore contact the Local Planning Office to see if the felling is illegal or legal. If it's illegal get on to the Gardai and the Local Authority Planning Department.

Physical Planning

- Someone is seeking planning permission for a hideous hacienda on a nearby hilltop in your area.
- A builder seeks planning permission to turn a nearby field into a housing estate.
- A company intends to open a quarry nearby, which you feel could spoil an amenity area and create noise and dust.

All of the above developments require planning permission under Section 24 of the 1963 Act. The Regulations require that, before an application is submitted, notice of intention to make such an application must be published in either a newspaper or by the erection of a sign on the site.

Invariably those who wish to keep opposition to their application to a minimum will choose the first option. This often means that the notice will appear in say the Irish Times when it's known that the only person in the town who reads the paper is the local vicar. Another trick often used is to put the notice in Irish.

A planning application must be accompanied by prescribed documents and particulars. This allows the general public to inspect the documents and be fully informed on the nature of the development. If you're not happy with the development, then you must submit your objection in writing to the planning authority. Simply writing that you object is not enough. You must give adequate reasons. If you have difficulty dealing with this, the local association of An Taisce will help you. In fact, organisations like An Taisce are sent a list of application for planning permission at regular intervals. So it's quite likely that they will have objected as well.

If planning permission is granted, despite your objection, you may appeal the decision. This will set you back £50. Bord Pleanala have produced a booklet on how to go about appealing a decision. Phone them at 728011.

Environmental Impact Assessment
What it is and How we can use it to protect and improve our environment

by
Jack O'Sullivan, Chairman, Environment Executive Committee

Most Local Associations of An Taisce will by now have encountered the concept of Environmental Impact Assessment (EIA), especially since the implementation in July 1988 of the EC Directive 85/337. Unfortunately, in Ireland at least, there has been little guidance available on the types of projects which should be the subject of an EIA, the content of an EIA, or on how it should be carried out. For Local Associations this has meant:

I) uncertainty on whether or not to demand from the Planning Authority that an EIA should be carried out by the developer, and

II) difficulties in evaluating the documents produced by developers or Local Authorities who claim to have carried out an EIA in accordance with the EC Directive.

The judgement of the High Court in the recent case taken against An Bord Pleanala by four farmers objecting to the proposed Merrell Dow pharmaceutical plant at Killeagh has added further to the difficulty of establishing guidelines for the conduct of environmental impact assessments. Mr. Justice Barron concluded that the circular letter issued by the Department of the Environment in July 1988 not only failed to incorporate the Directive into Irish Law, but it also left all relevant matters to the discretion of the planning authority.

It could be argued that the High Court judgement has deprived Irish citizens of some environmental rights enjoyed by people living in other European Community Member States, especially the right to full and complete information about a proposed project and to a systematic assessment of its impact on their environment, heritage, quality of life and culture.

The appellants in the High Court case had already decided to appeal to the Supreme Court when Merrell Dow announced its intention to abandon the proposal for the plant at Killeagh. In some respects it is unfortunate that the appeal will not take place, since the Supreme Court has the reputation of generally taking a broader and less legalistic view of issues before it and it is possible that it might (as in the case of John Hanrahan v Merck Sharp & Dohme) have overturned the High Court Ruling.

The situation is complex and evolving, and this article can therefore offer only some very broad and preliminary suggestions about how we can make the best use of EIA in order to protect and improve our environment.

Background—The development of Impact Assessment

Over the past twenty years our increasing awareness of the environment has led to a focussing of attention on the environmental consequences and impacts of a wide range of activities and projects. Procedures for appraising or assessing the consequences of large-scale engineering or public projects have been in existence for many years, but they tended to be seriously deficient in predicting or considering long-term, indirect or unplanned (and occasionally disastrous) environmental, public health and social effects.

The most widespread of these techniques, that of Cost/Benefit analysis, attempted to express positive and negative impacts in terms of market valuations and discounted cash flows, and it generally ignored unquantifiable values or attributes of the environment which may be changed or damaged. Cost/Benefit analysis may be very good at telling us which is the most profitable choice among alternative projects or proposals, but it cannot tell us to what extent the alternative development proposals will affect people's quality of life or environment. Unfortunately, but not surprisingly in view of our money-oriented administration system, techniques of this type are still used in Ireland where they have become incorporated into regional planning.

Environmental Impact Assessment (EIA) evolved in the 1960s in the United States as a result of the growing environmental awareness noted above and the observed deficiencies of Cost/Benefit Analysis.

Interest in EIA spread in the 1970s to Europe, where Germany, France and Ireland introduced laws requiring 'Environmental Studies' prior to the authorisation of projects likely to have a significant impact on the environment. There were major differences between the countries however; under Irish planning law for example, public projects were excluded, yet these activities had the most extensive and significant effects on the environment!

The advantages of the EIA procedure were noted by the European Commission, and the contribution of EIA towards proper environmental management and the prevention of pollution was included in the Second Action Programme on the Environment in 1977. A draft directive on EIA was circulated in 1980, and after many modifications, a final draft was agreed in 1985 for implementation in all Member States by 3 July 1988. In Ireland, the Department of the Environment 'implemented' the EC Directive on 1 July 1988 by means of a circular letter which, as we have seen, has no force in law according to the recent High Court judgement.

What is an Envrionmental Impact Assessment?

An Environmental Impact Assessment may seem complex, but it is really a straightforward procedure. When defining it however, the words we choose are important, and it is worthwhile reading carefully the definition and explanation given here. While doing this, it is useful to keep in mind some recent project or development proposal with which you may have been involved as objector.

Environmental Impact Assessment (EIA) may be defined as a systematic integrated evaluation of both positive and negative impacts of projects, programmes or policies on the natural environment, on beneficial uses of the environment, on man-made structures, amenities and facilities, and on the socio-cultural environment. The aim of the approach is to identify and predict any impacts of consequence, to interpret and communicate information about the impacts, and to provide an input to the decision-making and planning processes.

Its value lies not only in the facts gathered but also in the structured way in which these facts and predictions must be analysed and communicated to local people and to the public decision-making authority. Its application has frequently saved time and money for the developer who is made aware of potential problems at an early stage, and can therefore avoid expensive project modifications later.

EIA is therefore a process which by general international agreement is composed of the following steps:
i) identification of whether or not an EIA is required for the project or programme in question;
ii) scoping the EIA;
iii) allocation of responsibility for implementing or carrying out the Environmental Impact Study (EIS) which forms an important component part of the EIA;
iv) review and assessment of the completed EIS (it is this review and assessment which, together with the impact study, now comprises the EIA);
v) public participation and comment; and
vi) decision making.

We will look at each of these steps in turn, but before doing so it might be useful to indicate what an Environmental Impact Study should contain.

The Contents of an Environmental Impact Study

The Environmental Impact Study, or EIS, is a key component of the impact assessment procedure.

A significant number of Environmental Impact Studies produced in Ireland have been deficient in that they have met neither the criteria generally accepted in international practice nor have they contained the information specified in the EC Directive. As a minimum, any EIS should include:

i) a detailed description of the project including land or water use, production processes, wastes generated, transport requirements, additional road traffic, atmospheric emissions, liquid effluent, noise, vibration, heat, light, etc. during all phases including construction, commissioning and operation and probable malfunctions or accidents;

ii) an adequate consideration of alternative means by which the developer's aims may be realised, taking into account the environmental effects and indicating the reasons for the developer's choice, e.g. what alternative site or sites are examined, and why this particular site or process chosen;

iii) a description of the aspects or features of the natural, built, socio-economic and cultural environment likely to be effected by the project, e.g. vulnerable habitats, particular species of living organisms, exploitable living resources, scenic views, traditional communities and life-styles, cultural practices, architectural and archaeological heritage, etc.;

iv) a description of the likely significant effects of the proposed project on the environment features identified as being at risk, e.g. pollution of water or air, visual intrusion in the landscape, impact on agriculture, fisheries, amenities or recreation, changes in life-styles or culture caused by the project, etc.;

v) a description of the measures envisaged or proposed to prevent or reduce the impacts of the project, or to offset any significant adverse effects or losses, e.g. effluent treatment, visual screening, prohibition of certain activities, safety measures, creation of alternative wetland sites, etc.;

vi) a non-technical summary of the information listed above; and

vii) an indication of any gaps in the existing data or of any difficulties (technical deficiencies or lack of knowledge) encountered by the developer in compiling the required information.

Which Kind of Projects require an EIA?

In order to harmonise the application of EIA among member-states, the EC Directive 85/337 has two lists annexed to it:

Annex I   Projects for which an EIA is essential or mandatory;

Annex II Projects not requiring mandatory EIA, it being left open to each member state to decide which projects listed in Annex II should be subject to an EIA

Clearly, any application for planning permission for a development listed in Annex I must be accompanied by an Environmental Impact Study. The list is quite short and includes:

- crude oil refineries,
- fossil fuel and nuclear power stations,
- sites for the storage or disposal of radioactive waste,
- iron and steel smelters,
- large installations extracting or processing asbestos,
- integrated chemical plants,
- motorways, express roads, railway lines and airports,
- inland waterways (canals) and ports for sea and inland waterway traffic, and
- installations for the incineration, chemical treatment or land-fill of toxic and dangerous wastes.

This list (and the much longer in Annex II of the Directive) includes developments formerly exempted under the Planning Acts by reason of their being undertaken by State or Semi-State agencies.

In the case of projects listed in Annex II, for which no guidelines, criteria or thresholds have been set in Ireland by the Department of the Environment, the decision as to whether or not an EIS is required has already given rise to anomalies in that some planning authorities have demanded Environmental Impact Studies on small projects, while others have given permission for major projects without any impact assessment. Yet there are no plans to establish a commission or agency staffed by independent experts (as in the Netherlands) who have the task of advising whether or not an EIA is required, and who can also advise on the scope of each EIA.

It can only be suggested that if a project is likely to have a significant impact, or is to be located in an environmentally sensitive or vulnerable area it should be made subject to the EIA procedure. Another equally valid criterion is the degree of environmental concern expressed locally—if the local community is convinced that there will be adverse environmental effects, the project should be subjected to an EIA.

Scoping

Scoping is an important part of the EIA process. It is designed to:
i) establish the terms of reference for a particular Environmental Impact Study
ii) facilitate the identification and selection of alternatives,
iii) ensure the involvement of interest groups, and
iv) identify the impacts to be studied and provide guidance on how these are to be measured, evaluated and presented in the Environmental Impact Study.

Scoping may be considered as laying the foundation for the Environmental Impact Study, and it should achieve the following aims:
i) to enable the planning authority to properly brief the developer and his consultants on the alternatives and impacts to be examined and how they should be examined.
ii) to provide an opportunity for other interested parties to have their interests and concerns taken into account in the Impact Study and Assessment;
iii) to maintain public confidence in the EIA procedure, and
iv) to focus the Environmental Study on relevant issues and to ensure that the reports and documents produced are relevant to the decision—making requirements and understandable by the public.

Implementation—Who carries out the Impact Study

The Directive and the circular letters issued by the Department of the Environment on 1 July 1988 to local authorities, other Government Departments and semi-state agencies make it clear that the EIS must be carried out by the developer or proponent of the project. In most cases this work will be done by specialist consultants commissioned by the developer. The developer may be a private company, an individual, a co-operative, a state agency (such as ESB) or a local authority (as in the case of a major road or effluent treatment plant).

Review, Assessment and Public Participation

The Environmental Impact Study carried out by the developer should be reviewed or assessed by the 'competent authority' which in most cases will be the planning authority. This formal assessment is a very important part of the EIA process and in most cases the local authority will need to retain experienced consultants in order to perform the assessment effectively.

For example, Limerick Corporation requested Cremer and Warner Ltd., a London-based firm of chemical engineers to carry out a 'technical review' of the proposal by Hydrochlor Manufacturing Ltd. to construct and operate a hydrochloric acid manufacturing plant at Dock Road in Limerick City. The proposal included a 32-page 'Environmental Impact Report' carried out by Eolas on behalf of Hydrochlor Manufacturing.

The procedure fell short of a true EIA however, since the report by Eolas did not meet the criteria for an environmental impact study, the technical review by Cremer and Warner was not an environmental assessment (though it addressed the potential impact of atmospheric emissions and liquid effluent discharges), and the technical documents were not freely available for public comment.

For effective public participation in the environmental review process, it is vital that local communities and environmental groups also carry out their own independent assessments. This need became particularly evident during the appeal by local people against the decision by Cork County Council to grant planning permission to Merrell Dow—experts commissioned by local groups opposed to the development were able to point to major defects in the EIS undertaken on behalf of the developer.

Given the increasing complexity and technical nature of planning applications (e.g. for fish farms, airports, mining operations, chemical processing plants, intensive agriculture and forestry, major roads and other projects) the task of assessing and responding effectively to environmental impact studies could become a real burden for local associations of An Taisce. In many cases, expert help will be needed.

Freedom of Information

Adequate public dissemination and discussion of the EIS and assessment documents is an essential component of the EIA process. The EC Directive and the circulars issued by the Department of the Environment state clearly that copies of Environmental Impact Studies should be made available to members of the public or interested bodies on request. If a planning authority decides to charge a fee for a copy of a study, the fee should not exceed the reasonable cost of making a copy; there should be no attempt by the planning authority to offset its own costs by charging excessively for such studies.

Local groups should also ensure that they are given unimpeded access to, or copies of, feasibility studies or other documents referred to or quoted in the Environmental Impact Study. If any difficulty is encountered, it may be necessary to point out to the planning authority that the public participation is a right guaranteed by Article 6 of the Directive.

Decision Making

In most cases the application of the EIA Directive will not change the process of decision making in Ireland, and planning appeals will continue to be determined by An Bord Pleanala, taking into account the EIS, the review and assessment of it by the planning authority, together with any further assessments and comments by members of the public and environmental interest groups.

What Local Associations Can Do

The Environmental Impact Assessment process is still at an early stage of application in Ireland, it will continue to evolve, and the Department of the Environment appears to have taken little notice of experience gained by other countries in its practice. The Department has tended towards a minimalist approach sufficient only to meet the stated requirements of the EC Directive. The spirit of the Directive, and the broader purposes of EIA have so far been ignored or down played.

Furthermore, the Department of the Environment has chosen the method of sending a letter (which is not normally a public document) to local authorities and other agencies in order to make them aware of the Directive. This method has been judged to be unacceptable as a means of implementing the Directive and, unless the Supreme Court decides otherwise, the Government will have to introduce appropriate legislation or face the possibility of being taken to the European Court by the EC. In such a situation, local associations of An Taisce have a difficult but vital task. It will be important to ensure that:

i) an EIA is demanded and carried out on any project likely to cause an appreciable environmental impact or which gives cause for concern;

ii) the EIS is subjected to detailed analysis and criticism, with particular attention to issues or information excluded or omitted from it (the contents of an EIS listed above will be helpful here);

iii) the planning authority makes available all relevant information, and affords adequate opportunity for public discussion and comment; and

iv) public concerns (including those of local associations of An Taisce) are seen to be taken into account in the decision making process.

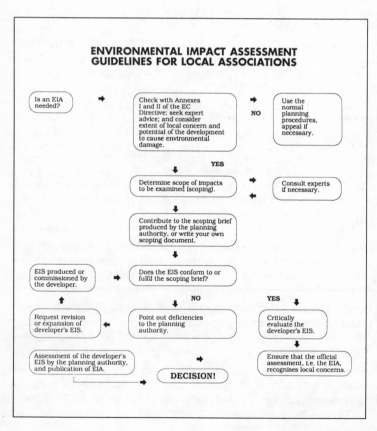

ENVIRONMENTAL IMPACT ASSESSMENT GUIDELINES FOR LOCAL ASSOCIATIONS

Water	Commercial Forestry
Water Resources	Physical Planning
Nuisances	Urban Renewal/Dereliction
Noise	Radiation
Trees, Amenities and Landscape	Air Pollution
	Waste Management and Disposal

Water Supplies and Sewage Treatment

The legal framework which relates to the supply of water and the disposal and treatment of sewage by local authorities is contained in the Local Government (Sanitary Services) Act, 1878 to 1964. Included in this are the following:

The Waterworks Clauses Act, 1847 specifically prohibits the contamination of any public water supply, such as a stream, reservoir, aqueduct or any part of the supply system.

The Waterworks Clauses Act, 1878 makes it an offence for any person negligently to allow pipes, etc., to fall into disrepair so that water is wasted, becomes contaminated or impurities are allowed to get into the water supply system.

Public Health (Ireland) Act, 1878. Under Sections 61, 65 and 74 sanitary authorities are empowered to provide their districts with a supply of water which is proper and sufficient for both private and public purposes and must provide and keep in their waterworks a supply of pure and wholesome water. Section 12 vests existing and future sewers, with some exceptions, in the relevant sanitary authority. Section 17 imposes on sanitary authorities the duty of maintaining sewers. It also requires the sanitary authority to 'cause to be made such sewers as may be necessary for draining their district for the purpose of this Act'.

Public Health Acts Amendment Act, 1907. Under Section 35 any cistern used for the supply of water for domestic purposes which is so kept as to render the water liable to contamination and a possible danger to health is regarded as a statutory nuisance.

Local Government (Sanitary Services) Act, 1948 (No. 3 of 1948). Under Section 27 a sanitary authority may take a sample of water from any supply, either public or private, serving any inhabitants of their sanitary districts for the purpose of analysis.

Local Government (Sanitary Services) Act, 1962 whereby, under Section 8, a sanitary authority can, in certain circumstances require the owner of a premises within their district to connect the premises to the public sewerage or public water system.

OTHER RELEVANT LEGISLATION INCLUDES:

REGULATIONS

Health (Fluoridation of Water Supplies) Regulations, 1971 (S.I. 119 of 1971) in which the sanitary authority will continue to be responsible for the operation of fluoridation on an agency basis.

European Communities (Quality of Water Intended for Human Consumption) Regulations, 1988 (S.I. 81 of 1988) set quality standards which must be met by all water supplies either intended for consumption or for use in food production where the wholesomeness of the food is affected by the quality of the water used.

Health (Fluoridation of Water Supplies) Act, 1960 (No. 46 of 1960) which provides for the fluoridation of water supplies by sanitary authorities. The responsibility of fluoridation of water supplies was transferred to Health Boards under the 1970 Health Act.

Merchant Shipping Acts 1894 to 1906 authorise inspection of provisions and water for the crew of Irish ships.

Water Resources

The principal legal framework for the prevention and control of water pollution is contained in the **Local Government (Water Pollution) Act, 1977 (No. 1 of 1977)** which includes a general prohibition against water pollution as well as provisions on licensing direct and indirect discharges, water quality standards and management plans. All sections except 25 and 34 have been brought into force.

OTHER RELEVANT LEGISLATION INCLUDES:

ACTS

Fisheries (Consolidation) Act, 1959 (No. 14 of 1959) as amended by the Fisheries (Amendment) Act, 1962 (No. 31 of 1962) and by the Fisheries Act, 1980 (No. 1 of 1980). Under sections 171 and 172 of the 1959 Act it is an offence to deposit deleterious matter, as defined, in waters. The 1980 Act raised the levels of fines for breaches of sections 171 and 172.

Harbours Acts, 1946 to 1976, Harbours Act 1946 (No. 9 of 1946). Section 48 provides for the disposal by a harbour authority of material dredged from the harbour. Section 88 prohibits the putting of ballast, earth, ashes, etc., into harbour waters unless authorised by the harbour authority.

Fishery Harbour Centres Acts, 1968 and 1980, empower the Minister for the Marine to make orders regarding the management of fishery harbours, including the control of dumping.

Oil Pollution of the Sea Acts, 1956 to 1988. Oil Pollution of the Sea Act, 1956 (No. 25 of 1956). This Act gives effect to the International Convention for the Prevention of Pollution of the Sea by Oil, 1954, and other measures including a prohibition on the discharge of oil into territorial waters and specified zones.

Oil Pollution of the Sea (Amendment) Act, 1965 (No. 1 of 1965) gives effect to certain amendments of the 1954 Convention including prohibition on the discharge of oil anywhere at sea, subject to specified exceptions.

Oil Pollution of the Sea (Amendment) Act, 1977 (No. 15 of 1977) gives the Minister for the Marine powers to prevent or mitigate oil pollution at sea. The Act gave effect to the International Convention relating to Intervention on the High Seas in cases of Oil Pollution Casualties, 1969 and certain amendments of the 1954 Convention.

Oil Pollution of the Sea (Civil Liability and Compensation) Act, 1988 (No. 11 of 1988) gives effect to the 'Civil Liability' Convention, 1969 and the 'Fund' Convention, 1971 and 1976 Protocols thereto. The main objective of the Act is to ensure that oil tankers entering or leaving Irish ports have adequate insurance to cover their liability for oil pollution damage and to provide supplemental cover where insurance liability is exceeded. The Act also provides a legal framework for the recovery of costs connected with oil pollution incidents.

Local Government (Planning and Development) Acts, 1963 to 1983—details on this Act in the Planning section.

Continental Shelf Act, 1968 (No. 14 of 1968): under section 7 it is an offence if oil is discharged or escapes into the sea during the exploration or exploitation of the continental shelf.

Dumping at Sea Act, 1981 (No. 8 of 1981)—details under the section on Waste.

Under applicable documents:

Local Government (Water Pollution) Act, 1977 (Commencement) Order, 1977 (S.I. No. 117 of 1977) brought sections 1, 2, 3, 10, 11, 12, 13 and 14 and subsections (7), (8), (9), (13), (14) and (15) of section 16 and sections 22, 23, 24, 26, 27, 28, 29, 30, 31, 32, 33, 35 and 36 of the 1977 Act into operation on lst. May of that year.

Local Government (Water Pollution) Act, 1977 (Commencement) (No. 2) Order, 1977 (S.I. No. 296 of 1977) brought sections 4, 5, 6, 7, 8, 9, 15 and subsections (1), (2), (3), (4), (5), (6), (10), (11) and (12) of section 16 and sections 17, 18, 19, 20 and 21 of the 1977 Act into operation on 1st. April 1978.

Local Government (Water Pollution) Act, 1977 (Fixing of Dates) Order, 1978 (S.I. No. 16 of 1978) fixed 1st. October, 1978 and 1st.

January, 1979, as the dates for the purposes of sections 4(1) and 16 respectively of the 1977 Act, which relate to the licensing of certain discharges to waters and sewers.

Local Government (Water Pollution) Regulations, 1978 (S.I. No. 108 of 1978) concern procedural matters regarding licensing of discharges to waters and to sewers, appeals to An Bord Pleanala, registers of licences, etc.

Local Government (Water Pollution) Regulations, 1983 (S.I. No. 36 of 1983) provide for a scale of fees in relation to appeals to An Bord Pleanala but this was revoked by Local Government (Water Pollution) (Fees) Regulations, 1985 (S.I. No. 115 of 1985) which revised the fees payable in respect of such appeals.

Local Government (Water Pollution) Act, 1977 (Transfer of Appeals) Order, 1978, (Amendment) Order, 1983 (S.I. No. 37 of 1983) applies certain provisions of the Local Government (Planning and Development) Act, 1982, to water pollution appeals to An Bord Pleanala.

Local Government (Water Pollution) (Control of Cadmium Discharges) Regulations, 1985 (S.I. No. 194 of 1985) prescription of water quality standards to be applied by local authorities when licensing discharges of effluents containing cadmium to waters, excluding aquifers and to sewers. The regulations give effect to Directive 83/513/EEC of 26th. September, 1983, on limit values and quality objectives for cadmium discharges.

Local Government (Water Pollution) Act, 1977 (Control of Hexachlorocyclohexane and Mercury Discharges) Regulations, 1986 (S.I. No. 55 of 1986) prescribe limits on the content of mercury and hexachlorocyclohexane in effluent discharges. The regulations give effect to Directives 84/419/EEC of 9th. October, 1984, on hexachlorocyclohexane discharges and 84/156/EEC of 8th. March, 1984, on mercury discharges by sectors other than the chloralkali electrolysis industry.

European Communities (Quality of Bathing Water) Regulations, 1988 and 1989 (S.I. No. 84 of 1988 and S.I. No. 99 of 1989) set national quality standards for bathing waters, identified 64 areas to which they apply and require local authorities to conduct monitoring programmes. The regulations give effect to Directive 76/160/EEC of 8th. December, 1975 (O.J. No. L31/1, 5 February, 1976) concerning the quality of bathing water.

European Communities (Quality of Salmonid Waters) Regulations, 1988 (S.I. No. 293 of 1988) prescribe quality standards for salmonid waters and designate the waters to which they apply together with the sampling programmes and the methods of analysis and inspection to be used by local authorities to determine compliance with the standards. The regulations give effect to Directive 78/659/EEC of 18th. July, 1978 (O.J. No. L222/1, 14th August, 1978) on the quality of fresh waters needing protection or improvement in order to support fish life.

Nuisances

Public Health (Ireland) Act, 1878, Sections 107 to 127 as amended contain the principal provisions dealing with a wide variety of nuisances which can arise on public health and other grounds. Examples of typical nuisances are offending pools, ditches, watercourses, drains, accumulations and deposits. Provision is made by the serving of notices by sanitary authorities requiring the abatement of nuisances and for access to the Courts for non-compliance with any notice served.

Public Health Acts Amendment Act, 1907. Section 35 extended the range of nuisances.

Local Government (Sanitary Services) Act, 1948 (No. 3 of 1948). Section 32 further extended the range of nuisances to include temporary dwellings which might be so regarded in certain circumstances.

Noise

ACTS

Local Government (Planning and Development) Act, 1963 (No. 28 of 1963). Under Section 51 the making of any noise or vibration which is so loud, so continuous or repeated or of such duration or pitch or at such times as to give reasonable cause for annoyance to neighbours, etc. is an offence, and provides for procedures for securing the abatement of the noise. Conditions may be attached to planning permission for development in relation to emissions from and/or intrusions into structures of noise. Matters such as noise levels or duration may be encompassed. Section 40 of the Local Government (Planning and Development) Act, 1976 increased the penalties for breaches of Section 51.

REGULATIONS

Road Traffic (Construction, Equipment and Use of Vehicles) Regulations, 1963 (S.I. No. 190 of 1963) Articles 29 and 85 provide for controls on vehicles so as not to cause excessive noise when in use.

European Communities (Construction Plant, and Equipment) (Permissible Noise Levels) Regulations, 1988 (S.I. No. 320 of 1988). These regulations were made by the Minister for Industry and Commerce to give legal effect to EC Directives on the approximation of the laws of the Member States relating to the permissible noise levels of construction plant and equipment, i.e. compressors, tower cranes, welding generators, power generators, powered hand-held concrete breakers and picks, hydraulic excavators, rope-operated excavators, dozers, loaders and excavator-loaders, designed for use in or about civil engineering or building sites.

European Communities (Lawnmowers) (Permissible Noise Levels) Regulations, 1989 (S.I. No. 102 of 1989). These regulations were also made by the Minister for Industry and Commerce to give legal effect to EC Directives on the approximation of the laws of the Members States relating to permissible noise levels of motorised lawn mowers.

Trees, Amenity and Landscape

Local Government Act, 1925 (No. 5 of 1925) Section 34 as amended by section 97 of the Local Government Act, 1946 (No. 24 of 1946) enables a local authority to request that hedges or trees which are 'prejudicial to a road' be trimmed or cut down. Section 34 also contains a prohibition on the cutting or trimming by local authorities of trees during the growth season unless failure to do so would involve serious risk of accident.

The Forestry Act, 1946 (No. 13 of 1946) in which Section 37 contains restrictions on the cutting down and injuring of trees in county council areas, including the giving to the Gardai of notice of intention to cut down a tree. Certain categories of trees are exempted. The Minister for Energy may decide to prohibit the felling of all or any trees within 21 days of lodgement of the tree felling notice with the Gardai.

The Local Government (Planning and Development) Act, 1963–1983 and regulations made thereunder contain specific provision in relation to the planting and protection of trees as follows:

• *Section 19 and Part IV of the 3rd Schedule of the 1963 Act* which allows a planning authority to include in the development plan for its area objectives for the preservation and protection of woods, trees and shrubs;

• *Section 45 of the 1963 Act as amended by Section 14 of the 1976 Act and Section 8 of the 1982 Act.* This section enables a planning authority in the interest of amenity to make tree preservation orders which may prohibit the cutting of specified trees without the consent of the authority;

• *Section 26 of the 1963 Act* enables a planning authority to grant assistance to an organisation or individual concerned in the preservation or development of amenities which could include the planting and preservation of trees;

• *Section 38 of the 1963 Act* enables a planning authority to enter into an agreement with any person for the purpose of restricting or regulating the development or use of the land. Such agreements could relate to the preservation of trees;

• *Section 50 of the 1963 Act* under which planning authorities may plant or assist any persons planting trees or shrubs for the purpose of preserving or enhancing the amenities or natural beauty of land. Assistance by grant of money is a function reserved to the elected members of the authority;

• *Section 26 of the 1976 Act* enables a planning authority to issue a warning notice requiring that a tree or trees shall not be removed or damaged and that reasonable steps are taken for their protection where development works are undertaken beside them.

Commercial Forestry

The Forestry Acts, 1946-1988, deal with commercial forestry, including the establishment of 'Coillte', the State forestry agency, the control of tree felling and the grant schemes for private forestry.

Physical Planning

ACTS

Local Government (Planning and Development) Acts, 1963 to 1983:

Local Government (Planning and Development) Act, 1963 (No. 28 of 1963) provides the framework for the proper planning and development of cities, towns and other areas, including the making of development plans, the control of development and such matters of particular relevance to the environment as special amenity area orders, tree preservation orders, conservation orders, planting of trees and shrubs by planning authorities and neighbourhood noise.

Local Government (Planning and Development) Act, 1976 (No. 20 of 1976) provides for the establishment of An Bord Pleanala and miscellaneous amendments to the 1963 Act.

Local Government (Planning and Development) Act, 1982 (No. 21 of 1982) provides for limits on the durations of planning permissions, increases in penalties for offences under the Acts and power to introduce fees for applications, appeals, etc.

Local Government (Planning and Development) Act, 1983 (No. 28 of 1983) provides for the reconstitution of An Bord Pleanala.

REGULATIONS, COMMENCEMENT AND OTHER ORDERS AND POLICY DIRECTIVES

Local Government (Planning and Development) Act, 1963 (Appointed Day) Order, 1964 (S.I. No. 211 of 1964) brought the 1963 Act into operation on 1st. October, 1964, except Sections 1 (which was in operation since the passing of the Act), 86, 87, 88 and 92 (5).

Local Government (Planning and Development) Act, 1976 (Commencement) Order, 1976 (S.I. No. 166 of 1976) brought into operation, on 1st. August, 1976, certain provisions of the 1976 Act, which amend the 1963 Act in relation to draft development plans, special amenity area orders and other matters.

Local Government (Planning and Development) Act, 1976 (Commencement) (No. 2) Order, 1976 (S.I. No. 227 of 1976) brought sections 22, 25, 26, 27, 28, 29, 30, 36 and 45 (for the purposes of repealing section 24(4)(b) of the 1963 Act), of the 1976 Act into operation on 1st. November, 1976. These provisions mainly related to the enforcement of planning control, including warning notices and High Court Orders.

Local Government (Planning and Development) Act, 1976 (Establishment of An Bord Pleanala) Order 1976 (S.I. No. 307 of 1976) appointed 1st. January, 1977 as the day on which An Bord Pleanala was established and fixed the quorum for meetings of the Board at three.

Local Government (Planning and Development) Act, 1976 (Commencement) Order, 1977 (S.I. No. 56 of 1977) brought into operation on 15th. March, 1977, the provisions of the 1976 Act not already in operation, being mainly those provisions relating to the transfer of appellate functions from the Minister to An Bord Pleanala.

Local Government (Planning and Development) Regulations, 1977 (S.I. No. 65 of 1977) consolidated previous regulations concerning development plans, exempted development, permission for development, appeals, references, etc.

Local Government (Planning and Development) (Amendment) Regulations 1980 (S.I. No. 231 of 1980) amended the 1977 Regulations and provided that licence fees collected by planning authorities in respect of petrol or other pumps should be paid into the County Fund or Municipal Fund, as appropriate.

Local Government (Planning and Development) (Amendment) Regulations, 1981 (S.I. No. 154 of 1981) amend the 1977 regulations to provide for an increase in the maximum floor area of extensions to dwellings which are exempted development. The regulations also provide for the exemption of certain porches.

Local Government (Planning and Development (Amendment) Regulations, 1982 (S.I. No. 342 of 1982) set down the procedure for application for extensions of the duration of planning permissions under the 1982 Planning Act and make miscellaneous amendments to the 1977 Regulations.

Local Government (Planning and Development) Act, 1982 (Commencement) Order, 1983 (S.I. No. 34 of 1983) brought into operation on 11th. April, 1983, section 15 of the 1982 Act for the purposes of repealing section 15 (1) of the 1976 Act relating to the lodgement of a £10 deposit with an appeal to An Bord Pleanala.

Local Government (Planning and Development) Act, 1983 (Commencement) Order, 1983 (S.I. No. 284 of 1983) brought into operation on 7th. October and 25th. October, 1983, certain provisions of the 1983 Act and also the repeal of certain provisions of the 1976 Act on these days.

Local Government (Planning and Development) (An Bord Pleanala) Regulations, 1983 (S.I. No. 285 of 1983) set out procedures for the selection of the chairman and ordinary members of An Bord Pleanala.

Local Government (Planning and Development) (Postal and Telecommunications) (Exempted Development) Regulations, 1983 (S.I. No. 403 of 1983) provide that certain developments carried out by An Post and An Bord Telecom shall be exempted development.

Local Government (Planning and Development) Act, 1983 (Commencement) Order, 1984 (S.I. No. 45 of 1984) brought into operation on 20th. March, 1984, the provisions of the 1983 Act not already in operation.

Local Government (Planning and Development) (Exempted Development and Amendment) Regulations, 1984 (S.I. No. 348 of 1984) amend the 1977 regulations and revise the definition of exempted development in relation to agricultural buildings and structures.

Local Government (Planning and Development) (Fees) Regulations, 1984 (S.I. No. 358 of 1984) introduced a new scale of fees for planning applications, appeals, etc., and revoked earlier regulations on that subject.

Local Government (Planning and Development) (Exempted Development) Regulations, 1987 (S.I. No. 287 of 1987) amend the 1977 regulations by restating categories of exempted development to take account of the assumption by Bord Gais Eireann of the functions of the Dublin Gas Company.

Local Government (Planning and Development) General Policy Directive, 1988 (S.I. No. 317 of 1988). This Directive, which issued to all planning authorities and to An Bord Pleanala relates to the use of smokeless heating systems in new or reconstructed premises (Domestic or otherwise) in built up areas where the air quality standard for suspended particulates (including smoke) is being, or is likely to be, exceeded—see S.I. No. 244 of 1987 in Air Pollution Section.

Urban Renewal/Dereliction

ACTS

Derelict Sites Act, 1961 (No. 3 of 1961) empowered local authorities to take action in relation to privately owned land or buildings (not being used as dwellings) if they are likely to become injurious to health or to the amenities of the neighbourhood or are in a dilapidated or ruinous condition. The Act includes power to acquire such land either by agreement or compulsorily and to require the clearance and improvement of derelict sites.

Urban Renewal Act, 1986 (No. 19 of 1986) provided for the establishment of the Customs House Docks Development Authority to secure the redevelopment of the Customs House Docks area. It designated the Customs House Docks area and empowered the Minister to designate further areas to secure their renewal. It also empowered the Minister to make schemes providing for the remission of rates in designated areas.

Finance Act, 1986 (No. 13 of 1986)—Chapter V provided for a range of financial incentives to promote development and reconstruction in designated areas. These incentives include a capital allowance for commercial buildings, a double rent allowance and an owner-occupier allowance and are available in addition to rates reliefs provided under the Urban Renewal Act 1986.

Urban Renewal (Amendment) Act, 1987 (No. 16 of 1987) amended the Urban Renewal Act, 1986, in its application to the Customs House Docks area.

Finance Act, 1989 (No. 10 of 1989)—Section 4 makes provisions for the granting of income tax relief to encourage individuals to come and live in designated inner city areas and renovate houses there that are determined by the Office of Public Works to be historically or architecturally significant.

REGULATIONS, ORDERS, ETC.

Urban Renewal Act, 1986 (Remission of Rates) Scheme, 1986 (S.I. No. 276 of 1986) provided for remissions of rates leviable in respect of certain premises which are erected, enlarged or improved in areas (other than the Custom House Docks area) which are designated for the purposes of the Urban Renewal Act, 1986.

Urban Renewal Act, 1986 (Designated Areas) Order, 1988 (S.I. No. 92 of 1988) provided for the designation of areas under the Urban Renewal Act, 1986. These areas are located in Athlone, Castlebar, Dublin, Dundalk, Kilkenny, Letterkenny, Limerick, Tralee, Tullamore, Sligo and Wexford.

Urban Renewal Act, 1986 (Remission of Rates) Scheme, 1986 (S.I. No. 93 of 1988) provided for the remission in whole or in part of rates leviable in respect of certain premises which are erected, enlarged or improved in areas designated under S.I. No. 92 of 1988.

Urban Renewal Act, 1986 (Designated Areas) (No. 2) Order, 1988 (S.I. No. 287 of 1988) provided for the designation of an area in Tallaght, Co. Dublin, under the Urban Renewal Act, 1986.

Urban Renewal Act, 1986 (Remission of Rates) (No. 2) Scheme, 1988 (S.I. No. 311 of 1988) provided for the remission in whole or in part of rates leviable in respect of certain premises which are erected, enlarged or improved in the area designated under S.I. No. 287 of 1988 for urban renewal purposes.

Finance Act, 1987 (Designation of Urban Renewal Area) Order, 1988 (S.I. No. 124 of 1988) declared certain areas to be designated areas for the purposes of incentive tax reliefs for urban renewal. The order relates to areas designated under S.I. No. 92 of 1988.

Finance Act, 1987 (Designation of Urban Renewal Areas) (No. 2) Order, 1988 (S.I. No. 313 of 1988) declared an area in Tallaght (as described in S.I. No. 287 of 1988) to be a designated area for the purposes of the incentive tax reliefs for urban renewal.

REGULATIONS, ORDERS, ETC., IN RELATION TO CUSTOMS HOUSE DOCKS DEVELOPMENT AUTHORITY

Urban Renewal Act, 1986 (Establishment of Customs House Docks Development Authority) Order, 1986 (S.I. No. 330 of 1986) appointed 17th. November, 1986, to be the day on which the Customs House Docks Development Authority is to be established.

Urban Renewal Act, 1986 (Remission of Rates) (Customs House Docks Area) Scheme, 1986 (S.I. No. 341 of 1986) provided for remission of rates in respect of certain premises which are erected, enlarged or improved in the Customs House Docks area.

Urban Renewal Act, 1986 (Transfer of Land) Order, 1987 (S.I. No. 26 of 1987) transferred ownership of the Customs House Docks from the Dublin Port and Docks Board to the Customs House Docks Development Authority.

Urban Renewal (Amendment) Act, 1987 (Extension of Customs House Docks Area) Order, 1987 (S.I. No. 206 of 1987) extended the Customs House Docks area in a southerly direction to the centre of the River Liffey.

Urban Renewal (Amendment) Act, 1987 (Extension of Customs House Docks Area) Order, 1988 (S.I. No. 105 of 1988) extended the Customs House Docks area in an easterly direction.

Urban Renewal (Amendment) Act, 1987 (Transfer of Land) Order, 1988 (S.I. No. 308 of 1988) transferred ownership of land in the Customs House Docks area from the B and I Line plc to the Customs House Docks Development Authority.

Finance Act, 1986 (Customs House Docks Area) (Specified Day) Order, 1988 (S.I. No. 314 of 1988) appointed 25th. January, 1988 as the date from which certain incentive tax reliefs for urban renewal were to apply in the Customs House Docks area.

Radiation

ACTS

Nuclear Energy (An Bord Fuinnimh Nuicleigh) Act, 1971 (No. 12 of 1971) provided for the establishment of the Nuclear Energy Board, setting out its functions and providing for the making of orders to control all activities (including import, export and disposal) involving radioactive substances, devices and irradiating apparatus.

REGULATIONS, ETC.

Nuclear Energy (General Control of Fissile Fuels, Radioactive Substances and Irradiating Apparatus) Order, 1977 (S.I. No. 166 of 1977) made under the 1971 Act; all activities involving radioactive substances, devices and irradiating apparatus are prohibited except under licence issued by the Nuclear Energy Board.

Council Regulation (Euratom) No. 3954/87 of 22nd. December, 1987 lays down maximum permitted levels of radioactive contamination of foodstuffs and of feeding stuffs following a nuclear accident or any other case of radiological emergency—O.J. No. L 371 of 30/12/1987.

Council Regulation (EEC) No. 3955/87 of 22nd. December, 1987 sets out the conditions governing imports of agricultural products originating in third countries following the accident at the Chernobyl nuclear power station—O.J. No. L 371 of 30/12/1987 (expired 22nd. December, 1989).

European Communities (Medical Ionizing Radiation) Regulations, 1988 (S.I. No. 189 of 1988) provide that all those engaged in the use of ionising radiation for medical (including dental) purposes must be competent in radiation protection measures and have appropriate training. The exposure of a patient to ionising radiation must be medically justified and the dose to the patient must be as low as is reasonably achievable. The regulations implement the provisions of EC Directive 84/466 Euratom of 3rd. September, 1984 laying down basic measures for the radiation protection of persons undergoing medical examination or treatment.

Air Pollution

The principal legal framework for the prevention and control of air pollution is contained in the **Air Pollution Act, 1987 (No. 6 of 1987)** which provides a comprehensive statutory framework for the control of air quality.

Other relevant legislation includes:

ACTS

Local Government (Sanitary Services) Act, 1962 (No. 26 of 1962) in which Section 10 enables the Minister for the Environment to make regulations to control atmospheric pollution.

REGULATIONS, COMMENCEMENT AND OTHER ORDERS, ETC.

Road Traffic (Construction, Equipment and Use of Vehicles) Regulations, 1963 (S.I. No. 190 of 1963) in which Articles 30 and 90 provide for the construction and use of vehicles to prevent emissions.

Control of Atmospheric Pollution Regulations, 1970 (S.I. No. 156 of 1970) limit the length of time during which smoke of varying degrees of darkness may be emitted from premises other than private dwelling houses.

European Communities (Vehicle Testing) Regulations, 1981–1986 require roadworthiness tests on heavy goods vehicles, buses and ambulances including pollution/smoke tests.

European Communities (Lead Content of Petrol) Regulations, 1985 (S.I. No. 378 of 1985) reduced the lead content of petrol to 0.15g/l with effect from 1st. April, 1986.

European Communities (Lead Content of Petrol) Regulations, 1986 (S.I. No. 374 of 1986) lay down the permitted benzene content, octane ratings and lead contamination of unleaded petrol.

Air Pollution Act, 1987 (Commencement) Order, 1987 (S.I. No. 201 of 1987) brought sections 50 and 52 relating to air quality standards into operation on 1st. October, 1987.

Air Pollution Act, 1987 (Air Quality Standards) Regulations, 1987 (S.I. No. 244 of 1987) specify air quality standards for sulphur dioxide, suspended particulates, lead and nitrogen dioxide.

European Communities (Benzene Content of Leaded Petrol) Regulations, 1988 (S.I. No. 212 of 1988) limit the benzene content of leaded petrol to 5% by volume. There is a similar limit for the benzene content of unleaded petrol under S.I. No. 374 of 1986.

Air Pollution Act, 1987 (Commencement Order), 1988 (S.I. No. 265 of 1988) brought into operation on 1st. November, 1988, sections 6, 7, 30 to 38, 57 and 58 and section 9 for the purpose of repealing the Alkali etc. Works Regulation Act, 1906.

Air Pollution Act, 1987 (Licensing of Industrial Plant) Regulations, 1988 (S.I. No. 66 of 1988) prescribe the procedures for the licensing system for industrial plant under Part 111 of the Act.

Special Control Area (Ballyfermot) Order, 1988 (Confirmation) Order, 1988 (S.I. No. 282 of 1988) confirms with modifications the special control area order made by Dublin Corporation in respect of part of Ballyfermot. The confirmation order also enabled a scheme of grants for converting existing heating systems to smokeless to be brought into operation.

Air Pollution Act, 1987 (Authorised Fireplace) Regulations, 1988 (S.I. No. 297 of 1988) declared a fireplace of the class known as the Full Burning Open Fire Boiler to be an authorised fireplace for the purposes of the Special Control Area (Ballyfermot) Order, 1988.

Air Pollution Act, 1987 (Authorised Fuel) Regulations, 1988 (S.I. No. 298 of 1988) declared Bord na Mona Peat Briquettes to be an authorised fuel for the purposes of the Special Control Area (Ballyfermot) Order, 1988.

Local Government (Planning and Development) General Policy Directive, 1988 (S.I. No. 317 of 1988) which was issued to the planning authorities and An Bord Pleanala, relates to the use of smokeless heating systems in new or reconstructed premises (domestic or otherwise) in built up areas where the air quality standard for suspended particulates (including smoke)—see S.I. No. 244 of 1987—is being, or is likely to be, exceeded.

Air Pollution Act, 1987 (Commencement) Order, 1989 (S.I. No. 167 of 1989) brought into operation from 1st. July, 1989, section 53 of, and the Third Schedule to, the Air Pollution Act, 1987.

Air Pollution Act, 1987 (Sulphur Content of Gas Oil) Regulations, 1989 (S.I. No. 168 of 1989) prohibits the marketing of gas oil, the sulphur content of which expressed as sulphur, exceeds 0.3% by weight.

Council Regulation (EEC) No. 3322/88 of 14th. October, 1988 on certain chlorofluorocarbons and halons which deplete the ozone layer (O.J. No. L 297/1 of 31st. October, 1988). This regulation implements in the EC the requirements of the Montreal Protocol on Substances that Deplete the Ozone Layer.

Waste

The legal framework for the management and safe disposal of waste is contained in a number of Regulations made under the **European Communities Act, 1972.** These are:

European Communities (Waste) Regulations, 1979 (S.I. No. 390 of 1979). Under these regulations local authorities are responsible for the planning, organisation, authorisation and supervision of waste operations in their areas and are required to prepare waste management plans. The regulations also provide for permits to treat, store and tip waste.

European Communities (Toxic and Dangerous Waste) Regulations, 1982 (S.I. No. 33 of 1982). Under these regulations local authorities are responsible for the planning, organisation and supervision of operations for the disposal of toxic and dangerous waste in their areas and for the authorisation of the storage, treatment and depositing of such waste. Local authorities are required to prepare special waste management plans. The regulations also provide for permits to store, treat or deposit toxic and dangerous waste.

European Communities (Waste Oils) Regulations, 1984 (S.I. No. 107 of 1984) which make local authorities responsible for the planning, organisation and supervision of operations for the disposal of waste oils and the authorisation of disposal arrangements. The regulations also provide for permits in relation to the disposal of waste oils.

European Communities (Waste) Regulations, 1984 (S.I. No. 108 of 1984) provide for the safe disposal of and the transformation operations necessary for regenerating polychlorinated biphenyls, polychlorinated terphenyls and mixtures containing one or both such substances.

European Communities (Transfrontier Shipment of Hazardous Waste) Regulations, 1988 (S.I. No. 248 of 1988). These regulations provide for an efficient and coherent system of supervision and control of the transfrontier shipment of hazardous waste. The regulations apply both to exports and imports of hazardous waste. They prohibit holders of waste in the State from commencing a transfrontier shipment until a notification has been sent to the appropriate authorities and duly acknowledged. A consignee in the State is prohibited from accepting hazardous waste from outside the State for disposal in the State unless it is accompanied by the appropriate acknowledgement. Carriers are prohibited from handling such waste unless the waste is accompanied by the appropriate documentation.

SOME OTHER RELEVANT ACTS AND STATUTORY INSTRUMENTS INCLUDE:

ACTS

Foreshore Act, 1933 (No. 12 of 1933)—Sections 3, 13 and 14 of this Act prohibit the erection of structures on the foreshore and the reclamation of the foreshore without a lease or licence granted by the Minister for the Marine.

Local Government (Water Pollution) Act, 1977 (No. 1 of 1977) and the regulations made thereunder.

Dumping at Sea Act, 1981 (No. 8 of 1981) gives effect to the Convention for the Prevention of Marine Pollution by Dumping from Ships and Aircraft, 1972 (the Oslo Convention) and the **Con-**

vention for the Prevention of Marine Pollution by Dumping of Wastes and Other Matter, 1972 (the London Dumping Convention). The Act prohibits the dumping of substances and materials at sea from all vessels, aircraft and marine structures anywhere at sea unless such dumping is carried out under and in accordance with a permit issued by the Minister for the Marine. Dumping at sea outside the territorial seas of the State from an Irish vessel, aircraft or marine structure is also permitted if such dumping takes place under and in accordance with a permit granted by another State that is party to the London Dumping Convention or the Oslo Convention. A register containing particulars of all permits granted is kept for public inspection.

Litter Act, 1982 (No. 11 of 1982) provides for the prevention and control of litter (including litter wardens and on-the-spot fines), prohibition of certain advertisements and the prohibition and removal of abandoned vehicles from land other than public roads and car parks.

REGULATIONS, ORDERS, ETC.

Road Traffic (Removal, Storage and Disposal of Vehicles) Regulations, 1983 (S.I. No. 91 of 1983). These regulations, made under Section 63 of the Road Traffic Act, 1968, provides, inter alia, for the removal, storage and disposal of vehicles which have been abandoned on public roads and in public car parks.

The Litter Act, 1982 (Section 5 Payment) Regulations, 1986 (S.I. No. 176 of 1986) increased from £5 to £25 the on-the-spot fine for litter offences.

Environmental Impact Assessment (EIA)

REGULATIONS, ORDERS, ETC.

Local Government (Planning and Development) Regulations 1977 (S.I. No. 65 of 1977)—Article 28 requires the submission, with applications for planning permission for certain development likely to cost more than £5 million, of a statement of the likely environment effects of the development. The Department of the Environment's circular letter PD 111/8/20 of 1st. July, 1988 set out arrangements for bringing the provisions of the EC EIA Directive (85/337/EEC) into operation from 3rd. July, 1988. The directive applies to certain public and private projects and requires that those which are likely to have significant effects on the environment be subjected to assessment of such effects before development consent is given for them. Measures to give statutory effect to the provisions of this directive (other than for motorways, for which provision has already been made) are being prepared.

European Communities (Environment Impact Assessment) (Motorways) Regulations, 1988 (S.I. No. 221 of 1988) incorporate the requirements of the EC EIA Directive (85/337/EEC) into the motorway scheme procedure in the Local Government (Roads and Motorways) Act, 1974. A road authority is now required to prepare an environmental impact study of a proposed motorway and to send it to the Minister when submitting the motorway scheme for approval.

Books and Publications

The Law and Practice Relating to Pollution Control in Ireland (2nd edition) 1982. Yvonne Scannell. Graham Trotman, Sterling House, London.

EEC Environmental Legislation —a Handbook for Irish Local Authorities (1987). Environmental Research Unit, Dublin.

The Law of Local Government in the Republic of Ireland (1982). Ronan Keane. Incorporated Law Society of Ireland.

Planning and Development Law. Walsh. 2nd edition Ronan Keane (1984). Incorporated Law Society of Ireland.

Planning: The Irish Experience. Edited by Michael J. Bannon. Wolfhound Press, Dublin.

A Guide to Planning Legislation in the Republic of Ireland (1988). Kevin I. Nowlan. Incorporated Law Society of Ireland.

A Sourcebook on Planning Law in Ireland (1984). P. O'Sullivan and K. Shepherd. Professional Books Ltd. 1987 Supplement.

Trees and the Law. H.M. Fitzpatrick. Incorporated Law Society of Ireland, 1985.

Tree Preservation—Advice and Guidelines for Planning Authorities. Department of the Environment, 1986.

The Single European Act. An explanatory guide to the provisions amending the Treaties which established the European Communities. Stationery Office, Dublin.

Wildlife and the Law. A guide to the Wildlife Act, 1976. Wildlife Service. Government Publications, Dublin.

XVI
ON GOING
CAMPAIGNS

Gold-Mining—Naval Nuclear Arms Race—Radiation (NIEMR)

Gold-Mining in the West
(Written by Mining Awareness)

The Situation

The incomparable mountain landscapes of Connemara and Mayo are now the scene of intensive gold prospecting. The gold finds at Croagh Patrick and Doolough, Co. Mayo and Cornamona, Co. Galway have brought an influx of 19 prospecting companies to the wider region. Serious concerns are being expressed by communities throughout this region about the impacts of prospecting and mining. Public meetings in many areas since last July have endorsed the demand for an independent environmental impact assessment. This EIA is now being commissioned by a coalition of groups called GOLD EIA, which needs to raise £70,000.

The Issues

Environment: Gold-mining around the world is generally undertaken in arid areas with little population. How the technology would translate to an area of watery landscape and high rainfall is not clear. Local populations being dependent on surface water for their supplies compounds the problem. Of great concern is the risk of cyanide spillage and overflow, and long-term pollution from heavy metals released during mining/milling. Other problems include noise and dust and of course the destructive impact of mining on the landscape. Would it ever be the same again? Experts are doubtful: restoration of blanket bog would be impossible.

MINING AWARENESS

Mining Awareness has been in existence in Connemara and Mayo for almost a year. Its aims, in relation to mining, are: an informed public; changes in legislation; mandatory independent EIAs; public input into development planning.

Further information from *Barbara Callan, Secretary, Cloon, Cleggan, Co. Galway*. Donations to *Marianne Lavelle, Treasurer, Main Street, Clifden, Co. Galway*, or (anonymously) to *Acc. no. 89976068, Bank of Ireland, Clifden*.

DONATIONS TO *GOLD EIA go to GOLD EIA, Bank of Ireland, Clifden, Co. Galway. Acc. no. is 89981473, Bank Code no. 903779.*

Economy: Gold-mining is a highly profitable venture—for mining companies. Of what profit it would be to the nation, or to local communities, has not been made clear. Communities fear a loss of jobs and future prospects in the existing industries of farming, fishing, aquaculture and tourism as a result of mining pollution. The impact of a short-term boom needs to be studied. Also to be considered are the hidden costs of mining, e.g. maintenance of roads, monitoring of mine sites, long-term maintenance of waste dumps, and reclamation—elsewhere costing taxpayers millions of pounds.

The Law: Ireland's mining and environmental laws are not adequate to provide proper protection for people, land and water. Firstly, the Minerals Development Acts make no allowance for the views of the public. The Minister for Energy has sole authority to decide what is 'in the public interest' in terms of prospecting and mining development. All environmental considerations are referred by the Minister to the planning process: however, some aspects of prospecting and mining are exempt from planning permission! The EC Directive on environmental impact assessments (operative from 3rd July 1988) *should* play an important role. However, the directive hasn't yet passed properly into law at all in Ireland, and much will depend on how (or indeed whether) the enabling legislation will interpret the requirements. Indications are that EIAs will be required for mining, but only *in so far as* planning permission is needed, and will not be

273

required, for instance, for trenching and drilling at the prospecting stage. There is no indication as to whether public involvement in defining the scope of studies, such as is common practice in the US, Canada and Holland, will be required. Since the public may have very little time to react to planning applications, the very least they have a right to expect is that EIAs will cover the issues which they consider relevant. Other legal problems include the lack of statutory protection for environmentally sensitive areas, and the fact that though provision exists in law for the monitoring and regulation of hazardous industries, in practice this is almost non-existent.

HOW YOU CAN HELP

Financial support, particularly for GOLD EIA, is critical. Lobbying is also essential. You can lobby for:
• A halt to the issuing of prospecting licences and mining leases until the independent EIA is made publicly available
• Planning permission to be required for all mining operations and for the advanced stages of prospecting
• The EC Directive on EIAs to be incorporated in adequate legislation, making EIAs mandatory for mining and advanced prospecting, and requiring independent scooping with public input
• An independent agency (e.g. an Environmental Protection Agency) to be responsible for regulating hazardous industries, and for monitoring and effective enforcement of planning and other conditions imposed
• The designation of environmentally sensitive areas, with guidelines as to what developments would be permissible in those areas
• An integrated approach to development planning, recognising the importance of environmental and human resources as well as economic resources to effective development.

The Naval Nuclear Arms Race
By Greenpeace

There are up to 15,000 nuclear weapons and 550 nuclear reactors based on sea-going vessels. These weapons are brought to every part of the globe and can be launched without the consent of a head of state. There are two categories of weapons, strategic and tactical. Strategic weapons are long range missiles designed to destroy an adversary's homeland, most of which are launched from submarines. Tactical weapons are designed for short and medium range ocean combat and land warfare. The newest type of naval nuclear weapon is the sea launched cruise missile, a high-tec low flying deadly accurate weapon that can be used for medium range tactical and long range strategic attacks. The oceans which cover three quarters of the earth's surface provides the world's population with food, trade, transportation and recreation. Our oceans have now become the most dangerous of arenas for the nuclear arms race. Yet, the current negotiations on limiting conventional forces in Europe exclude imposing limits on naval forces. Recently there have been some hopeful developments and renewed interest in naval arms control and disarmament which may well lay the ground work for new initiatives.

The results of a two year study of peacetime naval accidents by Greenpeace and the Institute for Policy Studies in Washington found that since 1945 the major navies of the world have averaged one severe accident a week. The accidents vary from sinkings, groundings and collisions to fires. The increases in the number of nuclear powered and nuclear capable ships and submarines since the 1950's means that many of these accidents happened with the added risk of nuclear explosion or reactor meltdown. Almost one third of the documented accidents occurred in port, raising questions about the safety of bringing nuclear armed and nuclear propelled vessels into civilian harbours. Putting nuclear weapons and reactors at sea has led and will lead to maritime nuclear disasters and also the possibility of an accidental start to a nuclear war.

Since 1967 Ireland's policy has been that 'permission for foreign vessels to visit Irish ports on courtesy calls . . . is normally granted on condition that the vessel does not form part of a naval exercise and that the vessel is not carrying nuclear weapons.' However it has been left to the discretion of the visiting nuclear ships to respect this directive and not violate our nuclear free policy. The nuclear navies adhere to a Neither Confirm Nor Deny (NCND) policy whereby they say nothing as to the vessel's nuclear capability. Research has shown that nuclear capable vessels carry nuclear weapons at all times, also that they visit countries with nuclear free policies similar to Ireland's. Ireland has had visits throughout the years from nuclear capable ships for rest and recreation purposes. It cannot be presumed that exceptions have been made to facilitate Ireland's policy. Ships capable of destruction equal to over twenty Hiroshimas have visited Irish ports since 1982.

The Irish Sea is very busy with submarine activity, which is both a threat to the lives and livelihood of those who operate there. The Firth of Clyde in Scotland has two submarine bases, Faslane and Holy Loch. British Polaris strategic nuclear missile submarines and hunter killer submarines are based at Faslane while one seventh of the United States nuclear arsenal is based at Holy Loch, the only strategic missile base held on foreign land in the world. The new Trident 11 strategic nuclear missile submarine will also operate out of Faslane. There is an area in the Irish Sea designated as a submarine exercise area at all times. Patrol submarines often accompany the nuclear submarines acting as decoys to evade Soviet surveillance. The Soviets have spy ships permanently sited off the Antrim coast. Royal Navy patrol subs are also busy monitoring Soviet naval activity in the Irish Sea. So between the various navies there is an enormous amount of acitivity in the sea which has been attributed to the deaths of over thirty fishermen, the loss of trawlers, fishing gear and numerous towing of unsuspecting civilian vessels. To add to this appalling tragedy is the real possibility of an accident to these nuclear submarines or their weapons. Such an accident is the enclosed and shallow waters of the Irish Sea with its heavily populated coastal areas would have catastrophic effects.

The goals of the Greenpeace Nuclear Free Seas Campaign are
1. The ultimate abolition of nuclear weapons at sea:
2. The inclusion of naval nuclear weapons in disarmament negotiations as a stepping stone to their elimination.
3. To inform the public and the media of the magnitude and danger of these nuclear navies and their provocative naval strategies.
4. To encourage and assist non-nuclear nations such as Ireland to establish and enforce laws banning ships that are nuclear propelled or carry nuclear weapons.

5. To maintain the freedom of the seas for non-military vessels and seafarers.

For further information contact Orla Ni Eili, Greenpeace, 44, Upper Mount Street, Dublin 2, phone 01-619836

SOME IRISH SEA INCIDENTS

April 1982: Clogherhead-based trawler *Sharelga* towed backwards and sunk in the Irish Sea by Royal Navy submarine, *HMS Porpoise*.

July 1982: *Flyfield Number Five*, a yacht owned by retired Royal Navy officer Ken Roberts, towed under by a submarine off the Welsh coast. Roberts is rescued by a Swedish cargo ship.

February 1983: French trawler *Jeanne de Lorraine* loses nets and cables twenty two miles east of Rosslare after being towed backwards by a submarine.

March 1984: Clogherhead-based trawler *The Oriel* forced to cut its nets off County Louth coast after they were snagged by a submarine.

May 1984: Two County Down trawlers, *Willing Hand* and *Family Friend*, towed backwards for several miles off the south coast of the Isle of Man by a US Navy Poseidon submarine.

March 1984: US Navy Poseidon submarine surfaces in the middle of a Kilmore-based fishing fleet off the Waterford coast, narrowly avoiding a collision with the vessels.

February 1985: Scottish trawler *Mhari L* and its crew of five sink in calm weather off the south east coast of the Isle of Man. Fishermen blame a submarine for dragging it under.

April 1986: US Navy Poseidon submarine *USS Nathaniel Greene* damaged on the sea floor off Wicklow.

February 1987: County Down-based trawler *Summer Morn* dragged backwards for twenty miles by a US Navy Poseidon submarine off the west coast of the Isle of Man. The vessel is forced to cut its nets to stay afloat.

May 1988: Unidentified submarine comes to periscope depth within thirty feet of County Down-based trawler *Alliance* on the Ballinahinch Bank, off Ardglass.

Source CND

SOME US NAVY COURTESY CALLERS

June 1983: The destroyer, *USS Scott*, equipped with Harpoon missiles, visits Cobh. *The USS Scott* returned to Cobh in July of 1984.

July 1983: The destroyer *USS Truett*, carrying nuclear-capable ASROC missiles, visits Cork.

April 1984: The tank landing ship *USS Spartenburg County* and the cargo vessel *USS Charlestown* visit Cobh. Both vessels are known to transport US Marine Corps nuclear weapons.

September 1985: The frigate *USS Pharris*, carrying nuclear-capable ASROC missiles, visits Cork.

In the same month, another frigate *USS Aylwin* visits Dublin. The ship's captain, Commander John St Clair Craighill, attended a Nuclear Prospective Commanding Officer Course in 1981. The *USS Aylwin* is also armed with nuclear-capable ASROC missiles.

October 1986: The ammunition ship *USS Nitro* visits Dublin. Based in New Jersey, the *USS Nitro* is configured for storing, transporting and replenishing all non-strategic naval missiles, including nuclear ones.

June 1987: Two weeks after she had been barred from the Faroe Islands because her Commander would not confirm or deny that she had nuclear weapons aboard, the US Navy destroyer *USS McCloy* arrives in Dublin on what the Irish Department of Defence describes as a 'routine visit'. The *USS McCloy* carries nuclear-capable ASROC missiles.

July 1988: US Navy destroyer *USS Conyngham*, equipped with nuclear-capable ASROC missiles, visits Cobh and returns to Virginia with a sixteen year-old Irish girl stowed away. Four crew members punished following an official US Navy enquiry.

September 1988: The assault ship *USS Inchon* visits Cobh. Based in Virginia, the vessel is known to transport Marine Corps nuclear weapons.

March 1989: The US Navy destroyer *USS Yorktown*, equipped with nuclear-capable ASROC missiles, visits Cobh.   Source CND

ABOVE THE HOMES OF IRELAND
Brendan Munelly (CND) makes the case for a nuclear free Ireland

Some 20 times a day, 600 times a month, 7,000 times a year, military aircraft operated by the United States and other foreign governments pass above the homes of Ireland; above our cities, towns and countryside.

More than most of us ever supposed, we in Ireland live in close contact with the weaponry of the nuclear arms race; it touches our lives more frequently than we ever thought; and the consequent risk of a nuclear disaster within our country is more frighteningly real than we ever imagined.

Across the territory of Ireland stretches a transatlantic highway in the sky; an aviation highway which connects the two continents of Europe and North America, and along which thousands of foreign aircraft—both civil and military—travel each year.

The quickest, most direct route for many transatlantic flights is through Ireland's airspace; and, with few exceptions, overflying aircraft which pass above our country are en route between Europe and North America. The tern 'overflying aircraft' describes aircraft which travel over Ireland, without landing, as they journey from one foreign location to another; 'airspace' is simply another word for the skies above us.

The 600 or so foreign air force planes which overfly Ireland each month are not at liberty to pass above this country as they choose; according to Irish and international law, they may do so only with the permission of our government, specifically, with the permission of the Minister for Foreign Affairs.

For more than three decades, such overflying permission has been granted routinely to the United States Department of Defence and to the military authorities of other foreign powers; granted without interruption, virtually without restriction, and effectively without public knowledge, debate or consent.

According to official figures, some 7,000 foreign military aircraft are granted overflying permission each year. Two-thirds are US Air Force aircraft; of the remainder, half are British and half are from various other countries, with Canada and West Germany predominating. In addition, 65,000 foreign civil aircraft pass above our country annually.

On clear days, you may see overflying aircraft as tiny points in the sky, trailed by long, white clouds of water vapour. Known as 'contrails', their visibility depends greatly on the weather: on some days, even cloudless ones, they are barely noticeable; on others, overflight contrails stretch spectacularly from one horizon to the other.

Successive Irish Ministers for Foreign Affairs have stated that foreign military aircraft to which overflying permission is granted are notified that they may not carry 'arms, explosives or dangerous goods'. Permission is then granted as a matter of routine and compliance is expected, in the words of one Irish Department of Defence official, 'as a matter of honour'.

No explicit assurance is sought that any individual aircraft is not transporting nuclear weapons; nor, if sought, would such an assurance be given. The nuclear-armed air forces of the United States, Britain and France all share a common policy of never confirming or denying the presence of nuclear weapons aboard their aircraft.

SOME IRISH INCIDENTS

30 October 1978: USAF MAC C-5 Galaxy transport aircraft returning to United States from Europe declares an emergency over County Dublin as a result of a fuel leak. The aircraft, based at Delaware, returns to Mildenhall USAF base in Britain.

278

1 November 1978: Another USAF MAC C-5 Galaxy transport aircraft suffers a fuel leak over Dublin. The aircraft, based in California, was en route to the United States. It returns to Mildenhall from which it had set out.

12 January 1979: For the third time in just over a year, a USAF MAC C-5 Galaxy transport aircraft overflying Ireland en route to the United States suffers a fuel leak. The incident happened over County Mayo and the aircraft, based in New Jersey, returned to Mildenhall.

May 1979: USAF MAC C-130 Hercules transport aircraft diverts to Shannon Airport after running low on fuel. The aircraft was en route to Mildenhall from the United States.

29 May 1979: A USAF MAC C-5 Galaxy flying from Mildenhall to the United States involved in a near-collision with a Laker Airways DC-10 passenger jet over County Donegal. Subsequent official inquiry by UK National Air Traffic Services blames Scottish air traffic controllers, who manage the airspace above Donegal, for placing two aircraft on same route, at same height and speed—but in opposite directions.

29 February 1980: French Air Force Neptune aircraft makes emergency diversion to Dublin. Aircraft orbits Rush for over an hour to burn off fuel before approaching the airport.

3 February 1981: Royal Saudi Air Force C-130 Hercules transport aircraft suffers tailplane damage over the Atlantic and is forced to make an emergency landing at Shannon Airport. The aircraft was en route from the United States to Saudi Arabia.

YOUR LOCAL AIRWAY

Both civil and military aircraft which pass over Ireland travel along fixed flightpaths known as 'airways'. These airways stretch from the western edge of Britain, across Ireland, and out over the north Atlantic. Each airway is twelve miles wide and has a name composed of a colour and a number. Five main airways cross the Republic of Ireland.

Blue 10 goes from Youghal in County Cork to Valentia Island in County Kerry, over Cork city, Macroom and Cahirciveen.

Blue 2 goes from County Dublin to Cork city, where it joins Blue 10. It passes above the towns of Carlow, Kilkenny, Clonmel and Fermoy.

Green 1 goes from Wexford town to Miltown Malbay in County Clare, over New Ross, Cashel, Limerick city and Ennis.

Amber 38 goes from Cahore Point in County Wexford to Achill in County Mayo, over Tullow, Portlaoise, Athlone and Castlebar.

Blue 1 goes from north County Dublin to Achill in Mayo, over Trim, Longford, Boyle and Ballina.

In addition, airway **Red 3**, which passes over the Six Counties (through British airspace), also passes above County Donegal.

Although they form part of the Republic of Ireland's territorial airspace, the skies above County Donegal are under the operational management of Prestwick Upper Airspace Control Centre in Scotland.

Most of the population of Ireland live directly beneath an airway travelled every day by the USAF and other foreign air forces; what's yours called?

Non-Ionizing Electromagnetic Radiation
Written by John Royds of Sparks

Energy can be transferred by electromagnetic waves consisting of combined alternating electric and magnetic fields. Scottish physicist James Clerk Maxwell (1831-1879) appreciated that light was but a small part of the vast electromagnetic spectrum and he defined the nature of radiation with his famous equations. As can be seen from the diagram, light forms the boundary between ionizing radiation and non-ionizing electromagnetic radiation (NIEMR).

Frequency	Cycles/second		
10^{18}	X-rays	10^8	
10^{17}		10^7	TV
10^{16}	Ultraviolets	10^6	AM & FM radio
10^{15}	Sunlight	10^5	
10^{14}	Infrared	10^4	VDUs
10^{13}		10^3	
10^{12}	Millimetre waves	10^2	Submarine communication
10^{11}	} Radar		
10^{10}		10^1	AC electricity
10^9	} Microwave ovens		

Part of the Electromagnetic Spectrum

There has always been background ionizing radiation in the biosphere but NIEMR has been almost totally absent. Exceptions were sunlight, bursts at about 10 kHz from lightning and the Earth's magnetic field which changes in synchrony with the day/night cycle together with micropulsations between less than 1 Hz to about 100 Hz with the major activity around 10 Hz. Since the turn of the century, a drastic change has taken place in our electromagnetic environment—the Earth is now buzzing with NIEMR which never existed during the evolution of life on our planet.

Early attempts to address the question of the hazards posed by NIEMR exposure resulted in the thermal model—if NIEMR did not cook you or did not electrocute you, it was considered safe. However, it is now accepted that weak or athermal NIEMR may have biological effects with the areas of concern focussing on cancer promotion, foetal abnormalities and effects on the central nervous system.

Clues about the action of athermal effects already exist in the scientific literature. Deep within our brains is the pineal gland which secretes important neurohormones which govern our bio-cycles. Exposure to abnormal NIEMR seems to upset the pineal which could result in stress, weight loss, diminished capacity of the immune system and changes in brain function. NIEMR may disrupt communication between the cells in our bodies and thus allow the unregulated growth of abnormal cells as well as affecting the efficacy of our lymphocytes. Finally, abnormal NIEMR may be able to penetrate the actual interior of our cells by being amplified by the 'forest' of highly charged proteins which protrude from the cell surface. Inside the cell, this may change important enzymes which control the cell's metabolism and which are essential for the synthesis of DNA.

The part of the NIEMR spectrum between 0 and 100 Hz has been called the 'bio-band' because biological effects have been reported here as well as when a higher carrier frequency is amplitude modulated or pulsed in the 'bio-band'. However, athermal effects are complex and occur in 'windows' of frequency, amplitude and time together with interactions with the Earth's magnetic field. Bioelectro-magnetics is indeed a complex new science requiring detailed knowledge in many disciplines.

Electricity

The most ubiquitous source of exposure to athermal NIEMR is from the generation, transmission, distribution and use of electricity which is the 'bio-band' (50 Hz, 60 Hz North America). As it has been claimed by experts that power-frequency magnetic fields may be responsible for up to 15% of childhood cancers, it is important to consider ways of reducing exposure.

Electrical appliances do give off high electromagnetic fields (EMFs) but these fall off rapidly. Health worries focus on when prolonged exposure occurs close to the device. Examples are the computer VDU and the all-night electric blanket (not to be confused with the electric underblanket which is unplugged before going to bed). Manufacturers have succeeded in reducing EMFs from VDUs but redesigning the all-night electric blanket may prove more difficult.

The wires that bring electricity into the home are not a source of excessive EMF exposure provided the cables are bundled close together and no return currents flow through the ground. The ESB are presently replacing the old system of four or five separated wires on poles with one thick insulated multi-cable which should reduce EMFs significantly. Substations are not a cause for concern as the magnetic field falls to background levels within a few metres of the perimeter fence.

Pylons carrying high-voltage powerlines are the big EMF polluters. The magnetic field can spread hundreds of metres and easily penetrates houses. The ESB have bought property when the occupiers were concerned about the health risks and this enlightened approach has also been adopted by a Canadian utility.

EMF polluted pylon corridors can be eliminated by siting generating stations close to the centres of population which require the electricity. This also has the added bonus of allowing the waste heat to be sold giving efficient use of finite energy sources.

The future

A lot more research into athermal NIEMR is needed and an important requirement is that funding should be clearly independent of partisan influence particularly the military and the electric utilities. In the meantime, prudence dictates that exposure to NIEMR from all sources should be kept to the lowest levels achievable.

John Royds (Timmore House, Newcastle, Greystones, Co Wicklow, phone Dublin 819283) is a science graduate who is the researcher for the anti-pylon group SPARKS (Stop Powerlines Across Residences Kindergartens and Schools). SPARKS opposed the erection of pylons by the ESB beside two schools and numerous houses in Co Wicklow.

XVII
UNIONS

The old conflict of jobs versus the environment raises its head when the unions make any attempt to turn green. While the annual conferences of the various unions pass motions on the importance of the environment, many union officials have publicly backed unacceptable industries on the grounds that they provide much needed employment. The **ICTU** were in favour of the proposed Merrell Dow plant in Cork, although some of its unions disagreed with this. Because of the local opposition in Cork, the district secretary of the **ATGWU** Waterford hoped that the plant would locate in that County. This despite some very positive motions on the environment put at their annual conference (see below).

The Sandoz plant brings with it the immediate prospect of 1,000 construction jobs and has been backed by the district secretary of the ITGWU Cork.

Only the FWUI have produced an environmental policy document (see below). Another union which would appear to take the environment seriously is IDATU which organised a series of lectures on the environment in 1988/89 for its members.

Following on the heels of its Political Party survey, Earthwatch intend to conduct a survey of the unions to establish how green they are.

Extracts from ATGWU Policy Statement, November 1989

'This Conference believes that there is an urgent need for the Labour Movement to give high priority to environmental issues, and to demonstrate its very real concern for the possibly irreversible damage being done to the planet, with the ensuing serious consequences for both this and future generation . . .

Conference believes that, further, the T.G.W.U.'s sincerity of support for these policies should be demonstrated by the Union itself adopting conservation-conscious practices . . .

This Conference adopts a policy opposed to the continuing destruction of our planet from wholesale plundering of natural resources, and the creation of pollution of our food, land, sea, rivers, and air we breathe by man's selfish activities . . .

This Conference states that the General Executive Council should become publically more active on environmental and conservation issues. In the furtherance of these aims the Union could apply pressure on those industries with whom it has some influence. The Union should exert particular efforts in an attempt to reduce—

(a) Carbon dioxide and sulphur dioxide emissions from Power Stations, and

(b) Chemical pollution of the North Sea.

In order that it might be more effective in these areas, we suggest that the Union should try to co-ordinate some of its efforts with other environmental pressure groups, such as Greenpeace.'

Extracts from Environmental Policy of F.W.U.I.

The F.W.U.I. recognises that both Development and Conservation are equally necessary, they make up a vital partnership . . .

All Shop Stewards, Committees and Union Members should be encouraged to become aware of the vital importance of environmental consciousness, both within and without the work-place.

To assist in this matter, the F.W.U.I.'s Education Committee is actively considering the introduction into the standard Union Course of a section dealing with the Protection of the Environment . . .

The F.W.U.I. would also like to see Job Creation Schemes directly connected with the protection and improvement of the Environment. Similar European projects have developed many such jobs. These jobs are created in industries which provide environmental equipment and services such as the construction and operation of pollution abatement systems, waste collection, disposal and recycling, sewage and water treatment and environmental research. . . .

The Union recognises that certain areas of western and mountain bogs are of particular conservational value for their benefits to the natural habitat not to mention plant and animal life . . .

The development of our national tree resources must not be left to private industry. An increasing proportion of trees grown in state forests should be hardwood or native trees. Coillte Teo should also be developed to the stage where this country becomes a net exporter of young trees rather than a net importer. The F.W.U.I. feels that Coillte Teo should become involved in the commercial development of sawmills and other wood processing projects.

The F.W.U.I. would also seek the full implementation of the new E.E.C. Directives on the Environmental Impact Studies on Safety and the Environment.

XVIII
POLITICS

Okay, as a member of the Green Party, I must be biased on this subject, but the greenest party is without doubt the Green Party. Now that the green bandwagon is moving at quite a pace the other political parties have not been slow to hop on it. If there's a few votes in it—why not? Their environment policy documents get longer and more detailed, but the gap between actions and words gets bigger. It's very easy to say you're for a clean environment and against pollution, but doing something about it means treading on the toes of vested interests—the very people who often finance the main stream political parties. Whoever pays the piper calls the tune and it's high time that political parties declared the source of all corporate donations, in order to dispel any fears in the minds of environmentalists about a possible conflict of interest.

The real problem with our main political parties is that they still don't see the environment as fundamental to all policies. When drafting an energy policy, the environmental considerations and effects—acid rain, greenhouse effect—are often ignored. Similarly, agricultural policies, which encourage intensive farming and the use of pesticides, and fertilizers containing nitrates, will eventually wreak environmental havoc. In fact, when examined closely, all government policies have a bearing on the environment and this has to be recognised by the mainstream parties. There is a real need for co-ordination between the various departments on environmental matters. In response to public pressure, some of the political parties are now becoming more progressive on environmental issues. The Government's new environment active programme is a very welcome move, but it still does not go far enough and the pressure has to be maintained.

Until as recently as 1978 there wasn't even an official Department of the Environment in this country, which gives some indication of our evaluation of environmental matters. This shortsighted approach continued with the abolition of An Foras Forbartha, which was a disgrace. The body which replaced it, the Environmental Research Unit (ERU), is bound by the Official Secrets Act and the standing joke among environmentalists is that its Irish name is Ciúnas (Silence). The Foras was not as independent as it ought to have been, but the staff were always friendly and helpful and the library and resources were offered to the public free of charge. It is to be hoped that some of this openness can be regained when the ERU is incorporated into the new EPA.

The Environmental Protection Agency

It's generally agreed that the new Environmental Protection Agency is being set up to head the Greens off at the pass. That's fine. But the EPA has to live up to expectations. It can only do so by being totally independent and free to give out information to the public. And that means all information and not just that selected by the Government of the day.

Below are the recommendations of An Taisce for the new EPA. If this new body is going to work then it is essential that this country have a Freedom of Information Act. It's also vital that the main environmental groups are represented at the highest level in this body. This will ensure the independence of the EPA. It will also ensure that environmental and not industrial considerations come first. The EPA is certainly a start in the right direction, but the American EPA—on which our legislation is modelled—has shown that pollution reduction does not work in the long term. The elimination of pollution should be our goal.

Political Parties

The Earthwatch survey on the 'greenness' of the various political parties revealed that the further away a political party is from power, the easier it is to have green tendencies. Filling in a questionnaire is one thing, acting upon it is quite another. Since the election there have been the usual U-turns, the most notable coming from the PDs. Before the election they claimed that if elected they would bring a legal case against Britain to ensure the closure of Sellafield. They now say this is not possible. They also said they would retro fit scrubbers at the Moneypoint power plant. Again, this is not to happen. Earthwatch will soon be carrying out a follow-up survey. That should be interesting.

It's also interesting to note how the mainstream political parties attempt to accommodate environmentalism into their own political ideologies. For Fine Gael, green issues are 'consumer' issues. The Workers' Party, on the other hand, claims that the environment is a 'class issue'. But surely it is rampant consumerism which is the root cause of most environmental problems? And surely bad air and polluted water affect us all regardless of class? Both the parties of the left and right will have to realize that it is the materialistic philosophy, espoused wholeheartedly by them, which is causing so much pollution worldwide. However, there are some mainstream politicians who are sincere in their concern for the

HOW GREEN IS YOUR PARTY?
These are the results of the Earth-watch Survey on the 'greenness' of the different Political Parties, based on a detailed Questionnaire covering all aspects of Environmental Policy:

Green Party	98%	Progressive	
Workers'Party	96%	Democrats	81%
Sinn Fein	92%	Fine Gael	54%
Labour Pary	85%	Fianna Fail	31%

environment. One such politician, who has long since won the admiration of environmental groups, is Mary Bannotti of Fine Gael.

The formation of the Northern Ireland Green Party in 1990 should have a healthy influence on politics in that part of the country. But the mainstream parties there are preoccupied with the national question and their environmental policies don't differ radically from one another.

Extract from: Green Party/ Comhaontas Glas Manifesto

The Green approach is an ecological one—it goes back to the root causes.

All of the Green Party's policies acknowledge the vital importance of Ecology, that is, our whole environment.

Our whole future is vitally dependent on that environment. We depend upon a network of links with the rest of creation. Green politics acknowledges the reality and importance of that web of life.

Over the years human beings have set themselves up to dominate and exploit the planet. Many of the problems which the Greens have long predicted (they were called 'alarmist' for doing so) are now coming to pass. It is clear that if our warnings are ignored much longer humankind will destroy the planet.

The potential catastrophes which we face are finally beginning to convince people that the existing power structures cannot be trusted. The policies of traditional Left, Right and Centre have been abject failures. Their promises of unlimited growth, a technological 'fix' for all our problems and universal affluence are false. The unbridled consumerism of the developed countries is the root cause of the poverty of two thirds of the world's human family. Conventional politics cannot supply an adequate answer to our dilemma. If planet Earth is to have a future, a totally new, radical, spiritual approach will have to be adopted—an approach which holds that the fundamental problem is our materialistic society. We can no longer ignore the spiritual dimension of our lives in the interests of selfish consumerism.

Labour Party:

All Things are Connected

Humanity's relationship to the environment, the one world which we inhabit, must be based on the recognition of our total dependence upon that environment and of our responsibility to maintain and renew its riches and resources for future generations. In exploiting the vast riches of our environment to satisfy the needs of this generation we have an obligation and a duty to leave intact and/or to replenish those riches for future generations. This generation of humanity must not prosper at the expense of our children or our children's children.

In particular, economic activity must respect the real balance that the environment needs and that common sense demands. All forms of economic activity must now recognise our total dependence upon the environment for our very own survival. The full cost of extracting, processing and distributing the natural riches of our world must include the components necessary to replenish them, if possible, so as to maintain a balanced environment. These components must be made an integral part of the cost benefit analysis of any commercial project.

Poverty cannot be eliminated by impoverishing our world. Equality cannot be established by destroying the delicate balance of our environment.

Fine Gael:

The Environment as a Consumer Issue
All of us as consumers are entitled to a clean, healthy and pleasant environment. As citizens we are trustees of our environment and we all have a contribution to make in protecting the environment for both this and future generations. As a political party FINE GAEL IS COMMITTED TO A DYNAMIC ENVIRONMENTAL POLICY. We recognise the importance of our environmental heritage. We know that if we do not treat our domestic environment with respect we will not be taken seriously when we speak out on important international environmental issues in which we have a legitimate interest. We also recognise that one of the crucial factors on which our tourist industry depends is an attractive and clean environment. THE NEED FOR A NEW DYNAMIC COMMITMENT BY GOVERNMENT TO A HEALTHY ENVIRONMENT IS CLEAR. FINE GAEL HAS THAT COMMITMENT.

The Progressive Democrats (PDs)

The PDs have published a very lengthy document of Policy Proposals entitled 'A Green Clean Environment', too lengthy to itemise here. The Introduction sums up its focus:

'The Progressive Democrats believe that there is an urgent need for a major international campaign to halt . . . ecological damage before the recuperative and regenerative potential of our fragile ecosystem is exhausted. Ireland should be seen to be encouraging and, where possible, initiating such actions internationally. Above all, we should set the highest possible standards with regard to environmental protection in our own country. This we have failed to do so far.'

The document then goes on to deal in detail with such issues as Air Quality, Water Quality, Waste Management, Noise Pollution, Nature Conservation, Wildlife Conservation, Environmental Education, Environmental Information and Finance.

Fianna Fáil

Protecting the Natural Environment (Extract)

Fianna Fáil will continue to give top priority to the protection of our natural environment, making environmental issues central to national policy-making and giving Ireland a strong international voice on these matters. We will complete the comprehensive protective framework for our environment that we have been rapidly building over the past two years.

The Taoiseach has for well over a decade been directing attention to the need to protect the natural environment and give it top priority. Care for the environment will remain central in every aspect of national policy-making and Ireland will support enlightened policies in all international fora.

The present Government put Ireland's natural environment centre stage and more protective legislation and regulations have been brought into force in the past two years than in any previous Dáil session.

Extract from The Workers Party Manifesto:

The environment cannot be considered in isolation from its social and economic context.

The environment is a class issue. We may all live on the island of Ireland, or in the city of Limerick or Dublin, but the quality of environment experienced by rich and poor are radically different. On a global level, this is shown by the contrast between the vulgar consumerism of the wealthy in capitalist society, and the degrading poverty and struggle for survival by the millions in the Third World. At home, it is reflected in the contrasts in standards and size of housing, in the maintenance of housing estates and in the costs and opportunities for leisure and recreation.

The relentless pursuit of profit, by shifting costs to society, has resulted in Bhopal, Seveso, industrial wastelands, decaying inner cities, ghettoisation and even the depletion of the ozone layer.

POLITICAL PARTIES

Communist Party of Ireland, James Connolly House, 43 East Essex Street, Dublin 2. Tel: 711943 General Secretary—James Stewart.

Fianna Fail, Arus de Valera, 13 Upper Mount Street, Dublin 2 Tel: 761551 or 613415 Fax: 785690 General Secretary: Frank Wall

Fine Gael, 51 Upper Mount Street, Dublin 2. Tel: 761573/4 Fax: 609168 General Secretary: Edward O'Reilly

The Green Party, 5A Upper Fownes Street, Dublin 2. Tel: 771436 Fax: 771436

Progressive Democrats, 25 South Frederick Street, Dublin 2. Tel: 794399 Fax: 794757 General Secretary: David O'Keefe

The Labour Party, 16 Gardiner Place, Dublin 1. Tel: 788411 Telex: 90570 General Secretary: Ray Kavanagh

The Workers Party, 30 Gardiner Place, Dublin 1. Tel: 740716/741045 Fax: 789119 General Secretary: Sean Garland

Sinn Fein, 44 Parnell Square, Dublin 1 Tel: 726932/726100 Fax: 733074 General Secretary: Joe Reilly

Democratic Socialist Party, P O Box 806 Dublin 8, Secretary: Michael Conaghan

Northern Ireland

The Workers Party, 6 Springfield Road, Belfast 12. Tel: 084-326852 Fax: 084-333475 Contact: John Lowry

The Alliance Party, 88 University Street, Belfast BT7 1SZ Tel: 084-324274 Fax: 084-333147 General Secretary: David Forde

Democratic Unionist Party, 296 Albert Bridge Road, Belfast Tel: 084-456418 Fax: 084-732010 General Secretary: Alan Kane

Ulster Unionist Council, 3 Glengal Street, Belfast BT12 5AE Tel: 084-324601 Fax: 084-246738 General Secretary: Jim Wilson

Social, Democratic and Labour Party, 38 University Street, Belfast BT7 1SZ Tel: 084-323428 Fax: 084-323428 General Secretary: Patsy McGlone.

Sinn Fein, 51/55 Falls Road, Belfast Tel: 084-246841 Fax: 084-231723

XIX
ANIMAL WELFARE
by Nuala Donlon

The Irish Council Against Blood 'Sports'

I.C.A.B.S. (founded in 1966) is a non-political, non-denomina-
tional, voluntary organisation. Originally founded to discourage
prospective tourists to Spain from attending bullfights, but is
now almost exclusively campaigning against the legal abuse
of Irish wildlife.

Prior to the setting up of the Council, many Irish people were
blissfully unaware of some activities which enjoyed legal
status, but it involved appalling cruelty to animals. The
campaign is directed at three particular activities: hare
coursing, fox hunting and other hunting. In terms of cruelty,
priority is given where one animal is set against another, and
which results in the maiming, harassment or death of that
animal. Although hares and otters are both listed as protected
species in the Wildlife Act (1976), loopholes do exist to enable
our 'sportsmen' to organise the pursuit and killing of these
animals.

HARE COURSING: Although law changes would be required to render
hare coursing illegal, it may be of interest to readers to know that Ireland has
the dubious honour of being the sole host in Europe to both enclosed hare
coursing and otter hunting.

FOX HUNTING: The fox, unfortunately is classified as vermin, and
enjoys even less protection than either the otter or the hare. Depicted as wily
and cunning, the fox is probably one of the most wronged animals in
creation. Its plight is not confined to Ireland alone . . . these animals are
persecuted the world over. Recent neutral studies in England showed that
over 70% of farmers do NOT consider the fox as a pest.

The Council's primary aim is the abolition of barbaric blood 'sports'
through legislation, and vigorously pursues this by all legal means. Although
blood 'sports' remain legal, ICABS is not discouraged. Recently there has
been a tremendous upsurge in support of their aims, membership has
increased ten-fold and in the Dail more T.D.'s are won over. For more
information contact—ICABS, POB 147, Cork.

BADGER BAITING is illegal in Ireland, though its practice is believed to be
widespread. The baiting involves setting dogs against badgers in artificially
constructed trenches— extreme cruelty to both animals.

In recent years badgers have also been the innocent victims of a vast
slaughter carried out mostly by farmers to eradicate bovine T.B. Despite

mounting evidence from England and Northern Ireland that the badger is not responsible for the spread of the disease, the killing continues. The I.W.F., the Green Party and Badgerwatch are running campaigns to stop this practice.

Animal Rights

HARE COURSING. This is officially known as a blood sport. To describe it as a sport of any type is a misuse of language. Ireland has a special position in the world when it comes to blood sports. Closed hare coursing is banned in all other countries except in this one, it seems.

Coursing officials only ever refer to the number of hares killed at public meetings which take place from November to March every year. No reference is ever made to the killing of 'substandard' hares at trials held prior to meetings. Neither is mention made of hares, cats, rabbits and other live animals used to blood the dogs. This is a particularly horrendous practice, still legal in fox hunting, where cubs are used, but is actually illegal in coursing.

The public often receive assurances from the various coursing bodies that 'coursing is not all about killing hares'. However, the Irish Coursing Club Book of Rules states (Rule 1.13): 'The Judge shall decide all courses upon the uniform principle that the greyhound which does most towards the killing of the hare . . . is to be declared the winner.'

71% of the Irish public favour abolishing live hare coursing, according to a 1988 Today Tonight/Irish Marketing Survey. In spite of this, live hare coursing is supported by tax payers money through grants from Bord na gCon, a State organisation.

The Meat Industry

In our mind's eye, the farm is a peaceful place where calves play in the fields, pigs loaf in the mudhole and chickens scratch in the barn-yard. Such idyllic scenes abound in books and advertisements. BUT in the West, the reality of modern animal production is starkly different. Now, virtually all of our poultry and most of our red meat comes from animals produced in huge factory-like systems, where there are no pastures, no streams, no seasons and not even day and night. This industrial approach to agriculture has led to the widespread abuse of animals, for whom every day is at best a day of slavery and at worst a massacre, where cages, stalls, crates, markets and slaughterhouses make up the nightmare of their existence.

The fate of the battery hen is the most publicised. In this system, hens are crowded five to a cage measuring just 18" x 20". With only 450 sq. cms of space the hen cannot spread her wings or turn around freely. She cannot fulfil her natural instincts to scratch the ground, perch, rest or dustbathe. Instead she stands all day and night on a sloping wire mesh floor, strains her neck through the cage to reach her conveyor belt feed, and may be victimised by her frustrated cage mates. To prevent cannibalism, (rampant in such conditions) her beak is cut off with a red hot metal guillotine. Fortunately her life is short. After a year of high production, her egg-laying tails off so she is slaughtered. Too old and tough for roasting, she ends up as soup, paste or dog food.

The fate of table chickens is no better. Packed in thousands in reeking sheds, they live a brief 7 week life, many suffering breast and leg burns by having to rest on ammonia ridden floors. Turkeys are reared similarly, but for longer, 12-24 weeks. Recently, here in Ireland, the poultry industry has become highly specialised and intensive. In 1988, we consumed 585.6 million eggs from hens living in battery conditions, and 37 million table chickens and 3.2 million turkeys were slaughtered.

Likewise, our pig industry is also now highly intensive. In 1988, 2.3 million pigs were slaughtered and a further 51,000 exported live; of whom 95% were reared under factory farm conditions. Like battery hens, 'factory' pigs spend their lives in confined spaces. Breeding sows are often kept in individual metal-barred stalls with concrete or slatted floors, unable to move backwards or forwards, with some permanently chained to the floor. When the sow is ready to give birth, she is put in another metal stall, being forced to give birth lying on a concrete floor. She remains here for 3 weeks, unable to exercise, simply standing or lying on her side, suckling her piglets. When weaned, the piglets are moved to tiered, wire mesh and darkened cages for the next few weeks, whilst the sow is back in season and the cycle is repeated. When the piglets are strong enough, they're moved to fattening pens, often just boxes with concrete walls and floor, with a slatted area for drainage. Crowded together they are kept in darkness, without bedding, with tails docked to prevent cannibalism, until they gain sufficient weight for slaughtering.

Unlike pigs, most beef cattle reared in Ireland still spend much of their lives grazing in fields, a relatively cruelty-free existence until slaughter. However, there is an increasing trend to bring them indoors for quicker fattening, and some are now in pens without bedding and kept permanently on concrete floors. The veal calf, of all animals reared in intensive farming conditions, suffers the harshest. New born calves are immediately placed in narrow stalls, lined up row on row in confinement. Each calf, for 14-16 weeks, is confined to a space scarcely larger than its body, often tied at the neck to restrain movement. To induce anaemia—a necessity to have their flesh white enough to fetch the market price for 'prime' veal—they are fed only with iron-deficient milk-replacer. They never taste hay, roughage or any solid food which might darken the flesh. All movement is restricted to prevent them from licking their own excretions to satisfy the craving for iron. Anaemic, and often neurotic, the short pathetic life of the calf ends in the slaighter house, where its carcass is processed to meet the demands of the 'gourmet' food industry.

Slaughter

Whatever the conditions in which they are reared, all animals end up in the slaughter house, to be killed and processed. Slaughterhouse legislation is designed to ensure animals are humanely stunned before slaughter to prevent pain. The notion of humane slaughter is a myth. It is recognised that in many cases, pre-stunning doesn't work, resulting in animals being fully conscious when shackled by the back legs and hoisted on the slaughter-line to have their throats cut. The most humane method of stunning for example is the 'captive bolt pistol', used to shoot adult cattle. Yet a U.K. report (1986) revealed that about 1/3rd of all cattle shot are not stunned, but stand greviously wounded and fully conscious while the pistol is reloaded. In some cases no attempt is made to stun animals before slaughter. Ritual slaughter as practised by Muslims and Jews is exempt from the legislation. Thus the animal's throat is cut while it is fully conscious and in pain bleeds to death.

WHAT CAN YOU DO?

The most effective step you can take to help is to become a vegetarian. It is estimated that for every person who becomes vegetarian, 40 to 90 creatures are saved each year, depending on usual consumption. As well as helping to reduce animal suffering, a vegetarian lifestyle also contributes towards fighting world hunger, and reduces the incidence of disease in the developed world. In the West, 90% of our agricultural land is used to grow feed for farm animals instead of food for humans. 60% of the cereals imported to Europe for animal feed comes from the Third World—thereby diverting potential famine relief to feed animals. To turn vegetarian, therefore, seems a particularly significant step to take in opposition to all suffering inflicted on animals, since no other action embraces the concept of compassion for all creatures, rational use of resources and a healthy diet for all.

For more information: The Vegetarian Society, 31, Pembroke Road, Ballsbridge, Dublin 4. If you would like to find out more about factory farming, contact the U.K. based Compassion in World Farming, 20, Lavant Street, Petersfield, Hampshire GU32 3EW, England.

The Fur Trade

Each year, to meet the demands of the fur trade, over 20 million of the world's most beautiful fur-bearing animals are systematically trapped and hunted in the wild for their skins. Species taken by the fur industry include beaver, mink, coyote, muskrat, wolf, lynx, fox, racoon, badger and squirrel. But behind the carefully constructed glamour image of the fur industry, lies the shocking reality of animal suffering.

Trapping animals for their fur involves a great deal of cruelty. The steel-jawed trap, though banned in Ireland and 63 other countries, is still used widely throughout the U.S.A., U.S.S.R. and Canada. With powerful steel jaws, the trap is designed to snap shut on the paw of the wild animal, who may be left in pain and terror for several days until the trapper comes to collect his catch. Snares, coinbear traps and the infamous leghold traps are also used widely, although they have been condemned by scientists and neurologists as primitive, uncivilised and inflicting maximum pain. Some measure of the extreme agony suffered by an animal in such a device can be gauged from the fact that it will often attempt to chew off the trapped limb in order to free itself.

Methods used to kill the trapped animal are equally barbaric. Bullets are not used as these could damage the fur. The trapped animal is killed either by repeated bludgeoning on the head, or suffocation whereby the trapper stands on the animal, trampling its vital organs, usually for 14-15 minutes.

As well as their intended victims, traps are also responsible for killing millions of other wild animals and birds each year. Conservationists have become alarmed at the widespread destruction of wildlife including swans, eagle and deer, who are indiscriminately caught in traps each year and discarded by the hunters as 'trash'. But they are even more worried about the decline of many species for which the trade in wild animal furs has been responsible for the past two centuries. The sea mink has been hunted to extinction for example, while big cats such as the leopard, tiger and jaguar almost suffered the same fate until an international appeal succeeded in protecting them from the fur trade. With the large cat protected, small cats such as the ocelet are trapped on a massive scale.

Ireland also imports fur. In 1988 we imported almost £1 million worth though this had decreased from almost £4 million in 1980. Our exports of fur—ranging from rabbit skin to musk and fox—amounted to £4 million in 1988, also a slight decrease on our 1980 figures.

WHAT CAN YOU DO?

Recently a strong anti-fur lobby has developed, especially in the U.K. Increasingly, fur coats are being seen as an obscene and vulgar anachronism. As a result, more and more department stores in Ireland and the U.K. are denying retail outlets to the fur trade. As a consumer the most obvious way you can protest is to boycott products. You can also become actively involved in anti-fur protests. *For more information contact LYNX, P.O.B. 509, Great Dunmow, Essex CM6 1UH, England.*

The Cosmetic Industry

Every year the cosmetics industry is responsible for the suffering and death of thousands of animals, which serve two main functions:—they are used as raw ingredients for the formulations and perfumes, and they are submitted to laboratory testing in the names of innovation and human safety. The list of animal ingredients used by the industry is long.

A substance used in most protein shampoos is gelatine, made from various slaughter-house by-products such as skin, tendons, ligaments and bones. Oleic acid, made up of animal fats, is used in nail polish, lipsticks, soaps, vanishing creams, perm solutions, cold creams and shaving cream. Hormones such as oestrogen and progesterone, obtained from the urine of pregnant mares, is used in hormone creams, while crushed snails are often used to add a sheen to various face creams.

The perfume industry, too, is for the most part still based upon the use of traditional animal based fixatives. Substances commonly used include ambergris (from the stomachs of sperm whales), musk (from the male musk deer), castoreum (from the glands in the groins of Canadian or Siberian beavers) and civet (from a gland under the tail of the African civet after keeping it caged for several years).

In addition to the ingredients used in production, the mainstream toiletries and cosmetics industry also employs extremely cruel testing methods for the products they manufacture. Three tests commonly used are for toxity, eye and skin irritation. The toxicity test (LD 50 Procedure), entails taking small animals (e.g. mice or rats) and feeding them large doses of lipstick or perm lotion until 50% of them die. This routine test is used despite the fact that its usefulness has been challenged by scientists. For skin irritation an animal is shaved and deodorants or face cream are taped onto it. Animals often suffer inflammation and swelling.

The notorious Draize Eye Test for irritation, uses albino rabbits for three reasons. Their clear eyes make it easier to observe and chart the progressive destruction of eye tissue; secondly, since the thin corneas of their sensitive eyes are extremely susceptible to injury, the damage being caused by the chemicals is far greater than the damage that would be caused in human eyes; and thirdly, since albino rabbits' eyes do not shed tears effectively, chemicals placed in their eyes do not drain out easily, thereby magnifying the damage caused. During the test, rabbits are held in restraining devices, while products such as hair spray, perm lotion, or shampoo are sprayed or dripped into their eyes while they are fully conscious. In addition their eyes may be held permanently open by the use of metal clips which keep the eyelids apart. This can continue for up to seven days to measure the amount of damage to the eyes.

WHAT CAN YOU DO

In 1986 in the U.K. alone, almost 16,000 animals were used in such tests, though the numbers have been falling, as more companies, under increasing pressures from consumers switch to cruelty-free methods of production. If you wish to join the growing lobby demanding an end to these cruel and unnecessary tests then you should boycott the products produced by companies still using them. Write to the companies whose products you now use, enquiring about their policy and practices in this regard. Remember your right to choose.

Vivisection

Of all the cruelties inflicted on animals by humankind, the worst is undoubtedly vivisection. It is estimated that every hour 20,000 animals die in laboratories throughout the world. Dogs, cats, rabbits, rats, mice, monkeys and birds. They die to test cosmetics, household products, weapons, drugs, pesticides or tobacco. They are blinded, scalded, poisoned and infected with diseases. They are driven insane, shocked, irradiated and gassed. In most cases no pain relief is given. Behind the locked doors of the world's laboratories, they suffer in silence. Death is the only release for the billions of animals who endure these unspeakable tortures in the name of scientific progress.

Many of the most painful experiments are performed in the field of psychology. Some involve experiments on the brains of living animals, including cutting, coagulating and removing brain tissue, and stimulating the brain by electrical and chemical means. Other psychological experiments are designed to find out how animals react to various forms of punishment, usually delivered in the form of electric shock, terminal deprivation of food and water or maternal deprivation.

Another major field of experimentation involves the poisoning of millions of animals annually, using the tests already described in the section on cosmetics. As well as cosmetics, drugs and inessential foodstuffs such as colouring agents and sweeteners are tested using the same methods. All kinds of industrial and household goods—insecticides, anti-freeze, brake fluids, oven cleaners, fire extinguishers, bleaches and many more—are force fed to animals and tested in their eyes as a matter of routine.

The induction of shock in laboratory animals for research purposes is also a standard occurrence. Methods used include crushing of the skull, compression, muscle trauma by contusion with light hammer blows, Noble-Collip Drum (the animals are placed in a rotating drum where they repeatedly tumble to the bottom and injure themselves), gunshot wounds, strangulation of the intestinal loops, freezing, burning, induction of hemorrhage and so on.

Radiation experiments, in which animals are exposed to or injected with various radioactive substances, are also common in medical research and warfare research carried out by many national government defence departments. Poisonous gases are also tested in a similar manner. Cats, dogs and primates are primarily used in such tests.

On scientific grounds, since animals react differently to humans, it is both dangerous and misleading to extrapolate the results of tests from one species to another. This was highlighted in the case of Thalidomide. Over the course of three years, thousands of animals were used in toxicity tests for Thalidomide, which without exception was demonstrated to be a uniquely safe compound. Yet after marketing, over 10,000 deformed children were born to mothers who had used it while pregnant.

Books and Publications

Linsey, Andrew. *Animal Rights* (London: 1976). Midgley, Mary. *Animals And Why They Matter* (London: 1983). Ryder, Richard. *Victims Of Science* (London: 1975). Singer, Peter. *Animal Liberation* (New York: 1975). Singer, Peter. *In Defence*

Of Animals (Oxford: 1985). Singer, P. & Regan T. *Animal Rights And Human Obligations* (New York: 1976). Regan, Tom. *The Case For Animal Rights* (London & New York: 1984). Rollin, Bernard. *The Upheeded Cry* (Oxford: 1989). Gold, Mark. *Living Without Cruelty* (London: 1988). Clark, Stephen. *The Moral Status Of Animals* (London: 1977). Wynne-Tyson, Jon. *The Extended Circle* (London: 1986). Ruesch, Hans. *Slaughter Of The Innocent* (London: 1979). Wynne-Tyson, Esme. *The Philosophy Of Compassion* (London: 1970). Turner, E. *All Heaven In A Rage* (London: 1964). Salt, Henry. *Animals' Rights* (London: 1922). Salt, Henry. *Seventy Years Among Savages—An Account Of A Life Lived Entirely In England* (London: 1921).

Animal Rights Groups

CO. ANTRIM: ANTRIM TOWN: Ulster Society for the Prevention of Cruelty to Animals, Hutlefoot, 08494-63993.
BALLYCLARE: Royal Society for the Protection of Birds, 26, Ballymena Road, Doagh, BT39 0DR. Contact George Acheson.
BELFAST: Animal Rights Movement, 3, Donegal Street, BT21 2FF. Contact Michael Hewitt. Aims to defend the rights of animals to live out their natural lives without the threat of abuse or exploitation by man. Campaigns peacefully against the many forms of animal abuse and seeks to alleviate animal suffering wherever it occurs.
Cats Protection League, 147, Cliftonpark Avenue, 0232-748663.
The Northern Ireland Bat Group, Ulster Museum, Botanical Gardens, BT9 5AB, 0232-681606.
The Royal Society for the Protection of Birds, 3 Cranmore Gardens, BT9 6JL, 0232-669286. Contact Mrs D. Blamire. Ulster Society for the Prevention of Cruelty to Animals, Bank Road, 0232-238372.
LARNE: The Royal Society for the Protection of Birds, 24, Wyncairn Road, BT40 2DY, 0574-4823.
LISBURN: The Royal Society for the Protection of Birds, 16, North Circular Road, BT28 3AH, 08462-3301.
Ulster Society for the Prevention of Cruelty to Animals, Knockeen, Drumview Road, 0232-813126.
NEWTONABBEY: Irish Deer Society, 'Cranfield', 20, Twinburn Road.
CO. CARLOW: CARLOW: The Irish Society for the Prevention of Cruelty to Animals Hon. Secretary—0503-42742, Inspector—0503-31116, Shelter—05626332.
CO. CLARE: Irish Society for the Prevention of Cruelty to Animals. Inspector—065-24669.
CO. CORK: CORK CITY: Cork Society for the Prevention of Cruelty to Animals, Clontarf Street, 021-270079 (day) 021-9612440 (night).
Irish Council Against Blood Sports, 31, Endsleigh, Douglas Road. Contacts Rosemary McCarthy 021-292197 and Pat Felam 025-31298.
LISCARROLL: Irish Society for the Prevention of Cruelty to Animals, The Restfields, 022-28398.
MALLOW: Animal Health Co-op, River View, 022-21718
CO. DERRY: COLERAINE: Ulster Society for the Prevention of Cruelty to Animals, The Old Cotts, Semicock Road, Ballindreen, 0265-2677.

LIMAVADY: The Royal Society for the Protection of Birds, 27, Ballyquinn Road, Deerpark, BT49 9EY, 05047-4941.

CO. DONEGAL: DONEGAL: Irish Society for the Prevention of Cruelty to Animals. Hon. Secretary—074-51037, Inspector— 074-51115.

CO. DOWN: BALLYNAHINCH: Rare Breeds Survival Trust, Laurelbank Road, Saintfield, BT24 7LT.

BANBRIDGE: The Royal Society for the Protection of Birds, 'Rathard', Tullyear Avenue, BT32 3PR, 08206-23668. Contact Robert Bell.

BANGOR: The Royal Society for the Protection of Birds, 45, Beverley Gardens, BT20 4ND, 0247-472909. Contact Bertie Lyttle.

Ulster Society for the Prevention of Cruelty to Animals, 1, Old Bangor Road, 0247-812622.

World Wildlife Fund, 4, Lowry's Lane, BT19 1HU.

CO. DUBLIN: BLESSINGTON: Irish Horse Protection League, Aldave Manor, Killbride, 01-582460.

CABRA: see under Dublin 7.

CHAPELIZODO: see under Dublin 20.

DRUMCONDRA: see under Dublin 9.

DUBLIN CITY: D1: Pets Advisory Bureau and Humane Society, 220, Parnell Street, 01-725559.

D2: Captive Animals Protection Society, 40, Charlemont Street, 01-714303. Campaigns against the use of animals in circus acts.

Dogs and Cats Home, 1, Grand Canal Street, 01-772567. Dublin Society for the Prevention of Cruelty to Animals, 1, Grand Canal Street, 01-772779.

Green Party Animal Rights Group, c/o The Green Office, 5a, Upper Fownes Street. Contact Gerry Boland, 01-797168 Fax. 771436.

Irish Society for the Prevention of Cruelty to Animals, 1, Grand Canal Street, 01-775922.

Irish Wildlife Federation, c/o 112, Grafton Street, 01-608346. National Action Committee for Dog Control, 1, Grand Canal Street, 01-772567.

The Wildlife Service, Leeson Lane.

D3: The Cats Protection League, 3, Victoria Villas, 01-333468. The Irish Wildlife Federation, 132A, East Wall Road.

D6W: The Cats Protection League, 22, Springfield Avenue, 01-533019.

D7: Blue Cross (Our Dumb Friends League), Annamoe Road, Cabra, 01-385085.

D8: Cats Protection League, 32, Synge Street, 01-772567. Pet Watch, 384, South Circular Road, Dolphin's Barn, 01-534787. Stop Animal Experiments, P.O.B. 1620. Contact Paraic Kenny on 01-792388/792647 (office hours). Dedicated to the legal abolition of all experiments on animals.

D9: Irish Council Against Blood Sports, 01-378364. North Dublin Society for the Prevention of Cruelty to Animals, 45, Millmount Avenue. Contact is Marie O'Byrne (W), 01-6122085.

D13: The Catholic Organisation for the Defence of Animals, c/o Father Padraig O'Sarai, The Presbytery, 1, Elton Park, 01-476152.

D20: Badgerwatch, 3, Drummond House, Chapelizod, 01-268479. Contact Angela Tinney.

FINGAL: Irish Society for the Prevention of Cruelty to Animals, 01-375630.

MONKSTOWN: Irish Wildbird Conservancy, Rutledge House, Longford Place. Contact Richard Nairn 804322.

SANDYFORD: International League for the Protection of Horses, Burrow Road, 01-954198.

CO. FERMANAGH: FERMANAGH TOWN: The Ulster Society for the Prevention of Cruelty to Animals, Monalla, 036581-549.

LEGGS: The Royal Society for the Protection of Birds, Castlecaldwell, Leggs Post Office, 036 565 328.

CO. KERRY: TRALEE: Kerry Animal Shelter, 066-22250/21779.

CO. KILDARE: KILDARE: Kildare Society for the Prevention of Cruelty to Animals. Hon. Secretary—01-288347.

CO. KILKENNY: KILKENNY: The Kilkenny Dog Shelter, 056-26332.

CO. LIMERICK: LIMERICK TOWN: Irish Society for the Prevention of Cruelty to Animals, Arthur's Quay, Office 061-45618.

CO. LONGFORD: LONGFORD: The Irish Society for the Prevention of Cruelty to Animals. Hon. Secretary—043-71094.

CO. LOUTH: LOUTH: Louth Dog Shelter, 042-35457.

The Irish Society for the Prevention of Cruelty to Animals. Inspector—042-35045.

CO. MEATH: The Irish Society for the Prevention of Cruelty to Animals. Hon. Secretary—046-24131.

CO. OFFALY: ATHLONE: Irish Society for the Prevention of Cruelty to Animals. Hon. Secretary—0905-86612. Inspector— 0902-74181.

Society for the Prevention of Cruelty to Animals, Station House, Kiltoon, 0902-89165.

CO. TIPPERARY: NORTHERN AREA: I.S.P.C.A. Hon. Secretary 067-31376. Inspector—067-31361.

SOUTHERN AREA: I.S.P.C.A. Hon. Secretary—052-31227. Inspector— 051-40414. South Tipperary Dog Shelter, 052-33322.

CO. WATERFORD: WATERFORD: The Irish Society for the Prevention of Cruelty to animals. Hon. Secretary—051-74955.

The Waterford Dog Shelter, 051-72247.

CO. WESTMEATH: Irish Society for the Prevention of Cruelty to Animals. Hon. Secretary—044-42205. Inspector— 044-48886.

CO. WEXFORD: GOREY: The Irish Society for the Prevention of Cruelty to Animals. Hon. Secretary—054-83189.

CO. WICKLOW: BLESSINGTON: The Horse Protection League, Aldave Manor, Kilbride, 01-582460.

WICKLOW: Wicklow Society for the Prevention of Cruelty to Animals. Hon. Secretary—01-874184. Inspector—01-862279. Dog Control—01-819865.

XX
DIRECTORY
(a) Ireland: Non-Government
(b) Ireland: State and State-Sponsored
(c) Northern Ireland: Government
(e): Northern Ireland: Non-Government

(a) Ireland: Non-Government

AONTACHT CUMANN RIARTHA AITREABHTHOIRI A.C.R.A.
(The Central Body for Residents' Associations)
30 Newtown Drive, Ayrfield, Dublin 13 Tel: 01-470224
Membership: All Householders nationally by affiliation. **Activities:** Involvement in all aspects of householders' problems. Sponsorship of Research; Community Games Perpetual Cup and support for National Organisations. i.e. An Taisce and those considered appropriate by our members. **Objectives:** To foster the development of Residents' Associations so as to promote civic spirit, to encourage local initiative and self-reliance and to advance the ideal of community service for the common good. To serve the needs of the Residents' Associations movement by fulfilling the functions of a central body in establishing liaison and securing co-operation between Residents' Associations in matters of common concern. To promote and protect the interests of its affiliated Associations in every practical way, including negotiations on their behalf with Government and other Bodies with this end in view. **Status:** Voluntary Organisation by Member Subscriptions. **Publications:** Newsletter—Monthly. **Contact:** Fergus Martin, Hon. General Secretary.

AN OIGE
39 Mountjoy Square, Dublin 1
Tel: 01-363111/364750. Fax 365807 Telex 329888
Membership: Ordinary: 30,000. **Objectives:** To help all, but especially young people, to a love and appreciation of the countryside. To foster an appreciation of the Irish cultural and historic heritage. To co-operate with other organisations for the purpose of: a) preservation of the beauties of the countryside; b) securing and marking rights-of-way and other footpaths. To co-operate with kindred associations in other countries. **Activities:** Education and training. **Status:** International Youth Hostel Federation Winner of UDT Endeavour Award for Tourism in 1979. **Publications:** *An Oige Handbook*; Retail sale. Circulation 11,000. *Fifty Years Young*. Terry Trench 1981 £3.30. 1,000 sold. **Contact:** Administrator, Simon Evans.

AN TAISCE—THE NATIONAL TRUST FOR IRELAND
Tailor's Hall, Back Lane, Dublin 8 Tel: 01-541786. Fax 533255
Membership: 6,000. **Objectives:** Conservation of the natural and man-made environments. **Activities:** Research. Education. Advisory services. Professional representation. Environmental Research. Education, Heritage gardens, and Munster Pollution Projects. **Status:** Prescribed Body under the Planning Acts, 1963 and 1976. Representation on: European Environmental Bureau. Environment Council. Wildlife Advisory Council. Water Pollution Advisory Council.

Dangerous Substances Advisory Council. Europa Nostra. International Union for the Conservation of Nature and Natural Resources. Sponsorships through the Heritage Trust. **Publications:** Books, booklets, reports, policy documents. **Contact:** Dr. Emer Colleran, Chairman. Founded in 1947, An Taisce is the oldest and, in many ways, still the most active environmental group in the country. If you look at the range of issues that An Taisce tackles from conifirization to bungalow blitz to bogs and Cork Harbour, it gives you some idea of its importance. In recent years An Taisce has suffered unfairly because of its 'tweedy' image and the membership numbers have been decreasing. But with the more radical approach which they are now adopting and the talent and expertise, which they have in depth, An Taisce look set to become a more dominant force on the Irish green scene.

COMMITTEES AND WORKING GROUPS: **Environment Executive Committee:** Mrs Margaret Sweeney (Chairwoman), Dr Kevin Bradley, Dr. Emer Colleran, Professor Frank Convery, Dr Paul Dowding, Mr. Philip Geoghegan, Dr Frank Hegarty, Dr. David Jeffrey, Dr. Daphne Levinge, Dr. Charles Nelson, Mr. Derry O'Connell, Mr Jack O'Sullivan, Mr. Russell Poole, Dr. Julian Reynolds, Mr. David Rowe, Miss Geraldine Walsh, Mr. Richard Webb. **National Planning Group:** Chairman, Mr David Rowe. **Heritage Gardens Committee:** Chairman, Dr. Charles Nelson. **Organisation Executive Committee:** Miss Geraldine Walsh (Chairwoman), Mr. Gordon Ackland, Mrs. Rosalie Andrews, Mrs. Eileen Collins, Mrs Maura Fennell, Miss Carmel Kelly, Mr. John O'Loughlin Kennedy, Dr TJ O'Driscoll, Mr David Willis. **Properties Committee:** Chairwoman: Miss Geraldine Walsh. **Corporate Membership:** Mr Liam Roche. **Governors of Tailors'Hall:** Professor Kevin B. Nowlan, Dr. Frank Hegarty, Mr Gordon Ackland, Dr. TJ O'Driscoll, Mrs Consuelo O'Connor. **Tailors'Hall Committee:** Mrs Consuelo O'Connor Chairwoman, Mr Bernard Ryan, Mrs Stella Dunphy, Mr David Rowe, Mrs Patricia Oliver, Mr John O'Loughlin Kennedy, Fr Michael Mernagh, Mr Noel Boland. **Living Heritage:** **Editor:** Mrs Patricia Oliver. **Editorial Assistant:** Mrs Margaret Boyd. **Editorial Board:** Professor Frank Convery, Dr David Jeffrey, Mr John O'Loughlin Kennedy, Mr Jim Rowe.

STAFF: **Secretary:** Miss Valerie Bond. **Membership Secretary:** Miss Bernadette Smith. **Assistant:** Mrs Mary O'Loughlin (part-time) **Environment Officer:** Mr David Hickie. **Representatives on National and International Bodies: Tree Council of Ireland:** Mr. Richard Webb, **Irish Historic Properties Committee:** Miss Geraldine Walsh, Mr. J O'L Kennedy, **Wicklow Mountains Environment Group:** Mr David Rowe, Mr Michael Beagon, Dr Kevin Bradley, Mr David Hickie, **Heritage Trust:** Mr G Ackland, Dr E Colleran, Dr Frank Hegarty, Mrs C O'Connor, **Alfred Beit Foundation:** Mrs C O'Connor, **Craggaunowen Project:** Mrs Grania Weir, **European Environmental Bureau:** Dr Kevin Bradley, **Europa Nostra:** Dr TJ O'Driscoll. **IUCN:** National nongovernment organisation membership. **An Taisce Associations exist in the Following Areas:** Carlow, Cavan, Clare, Cork, Donegal NW, Donegal SW, Dublin City, South County Dublin, North West Co. Dublin, South West Co. Dublin, Dun Loaghaire, Fingal, Galway, Howth & District, Kerry, Kildare, Kilkenny, Limerick, Longford, Louth, Meath, Sligo, Tipperary NR, Tipperary SR, Waterford, Wexford, Wicklow North, Wicklow South.

THE ASSOCIATION FOR ADVENTURE SPORTS
The Director, Tiglin Adventure Centre, Ashford, Co. Wicklow. Tel: 0404-40169. **Membership:** The total of 45 members include Individual and Associate members with substantial membership in their own right. Total representation is approximately 60,000 individuals. **Objectives:** To create interest in adventure sport among young people. To promote proficiency and safety in all adventure sports. To promote the beauty and amenities of the Irish countryside. **Activities:** Education and training. Advisory services.

Status: Representation on the Management Boards of Outdoor Pursuits Centres set up by Vocational Education Committees. **Publications:** Occasional periodicals, to members only and non-members on request.**Contact:** P. O'Leary, Director, Bill Hallowes, Secretary, 18 Greenville Road, Blackrock, Co. Dublin, Tel: 01-809974.

BOTANICAL SOCIETY OF THE BRITISH ISLES, IRISH REGIONAL BRANCH
c/o The Wildlife Service, Sidmonton Place, Bray, Co. Wicklow. Tel: 867751
Membership: 90. **Objectives:** To become familiar with the vegetation of Ireland. To know the location and distribution of rare plants. To monitor changes in distribution and point up the causes. To encourage members to write individual floras for each county. **Activities:** Research, education and training, advisory services, professional representation, pressure group. **Status:** National plant association in Ireland. Assists research and publications done by members. Occasionally funds leaders on field trips of specialist interest. **Publications:** List on request, including *Flora of Carlow* and *Flora of Burren and Connemara*. **Contact:** Dr. Tom Curtis.

THE BURREN WILDLIFE FOUNDATION (BWF)
Fanore, Co. Clare
Objectives: To ensure the conservation of the Burren area. **Activities**: Immediate priority is the construction of a Wildlife Centre at Fanore which will have displays of Archaeology, Marine Biology, Flora, Fauna, Environment and Cave Systems. There will be seminars, teach-ins and ongoing courses in conservation. **Status**: Non-profit Conservation Organisation. **Publications**: News Magazine once yearly. **Membership**: 720 and increasing, from many parts of the world. Open to anybody interested in the objectives. Individual Membership £15 pa. Subscriptions acceptable from individuals, societies and firms. **Contact**: John MacNamara, The Burren Wildlife Foundation, Fanore, Co. Clare. Tel. 065-76105.

CATHOLIC BOY SCOUTS OF IRELAND
19 Herbert Place, Dublin 2. Tel: 01-761598
Membership: 38,000. **Objectives:** To develop all young scouts spiritually, mentally and physically, so they can take their place in society as mature adults. **Activities:** Scouting. **Publications:** *Scout Leader* (monthly), *Scout Handbook*. **Contact:** Director of Relationships, Joseph Lawlor.

CND see IRISH CND

COOPERATION NORTH
37 Upper Fitzwilliam Street, Dublin 2. Tel: 01-610582/3/4/8. Fax 618456
Objectives: Non-profit making, non-political and non-sectarian organisation founded in 1979 to encourage cooperation in school and youth links, business and trading links and social and cultural links between Northern Ireland and the Republic of Ireland. **Activities:** Research; Education and training, Advisory service. **Status:** Cooperation North is funded by the EC and the British and Irish Governments and by business interests. **Publications:** Include *Co-operation North News*, a quarterly newsletter. **Contact:** Brian O'Neill, Chief Executive.

CRANN
Carrigallen, via Cavan, Co. Leitrim, Tel: 049-39820
Membership: 2,000—open to all. **Objectives:** To re-tree Ireland with broadleaved trees—through education, educational material, demonstration workshops, seasonal newsletters, local action amongst branches, awareness campaigns, lobbying government bodies and politicians. **Contact:** Jan Alexander.

DUBLIN BAY ENVIRONMENT GROUP (DBEG)
8 Belgrave Square, Monkstown, Co Dublin, Tel. 802501.
Membership: open. **Objectives**: The DBEG was founded in 1983 by Karen

Dubsky and a small group of marine and environmental scientists. The initial objective of the Group was to focus attention on the outstanding resources of Dublin Bay and to highlight the increasing threats to the bay. The Group broadened its aims in 1985 to marine and coastal environmental management and agreed to strive for more public awareness and involvement in such environmental issues. **Activities**: The organisation of Coastwatch Europe and follow up events that centre on habitat protection and waste management. The Group also gives advice on a range of coastal pollution issues. Since 1988 the Group has also been involved in air pollution issues. **Publications**: The group has also produced a series of posters on areas of scientific interest (ASI) in the country as well as the Coastwatch survey.

EARTHWATCH LTD
Harbour View, Bantry, Co. Cork. Tel: 027-50968
Membership: 1,200—open to all. **Objectives**: Environmental protection. Promotion of environmental issues. Environmental education. Produces quarterly environmental magazine. **Contact**: Angie Constable.
Earthwatch, the Irish representative of Friends of the Earth, was founded by Jeremy Wates in 1986, it emerged from the earlier West Cork based group, HOPE, and has become one of the most credible watchdogs of the Irish environment. Focusing initially on nuclear issues and acid rain, it has developed into multi issue organisation, providing accurate information and effective action on environmental issues. An important dimension of Earthwatch's work involves working with people in their own communities. Earthwatch also works closely with young people and a school's information pack is available. The Earthwatch quarterly magazine is recognised as being the best environmental publication in the country. Members receive this plus other informational material. How Earthwatch manage to maintain such high standards on such a low budget is amazing. They need your support to continue the good work. **Earthwatch Cavan**, **Contact**: Helen Cherry, **Tel**. Work 049-31544, **Address**: Kinaghamore, Belturbet, Co. Cavan. **Earthwatch Clonmel**, **Contact**: Bobby Walsh, **Tel**. 052-25305, **Address**: 93 Willow Park, Clonmel, Co. Tipperary. **Earthwatch Dublin**, Contact: Marcus McCabe, Tel. 6799672; Address: 7 Anglesea Street, Dublin 2. **Earthwatch Clondalkin**, **Contact**: Christy Sinclair, **Tel**. home 01-572383, **Address**: 41 Cherrywood Grove, Clondalkin, Dublin 14. **Earthwatch Fingal**, **Contact**: Bill O'Neill, **Tel**. home 01-492273, **Address**: 36 Sherwick Road, Skerries, Co. Dublin. **Earthwatch Tallaght**, **Contact**: Miriam O'Brien, **Tel**. home 01-526080, **Address**: 8 Kiltalawn, Jobstown, Tallaght, Dublin. **Earthwatch UCD**, **Contact**: David O'Gorman, **Tel**. 01-860257, **Address**: 8 Old Court Park, Bray, Co. Wicklow. **Earthwatch Galway**: **Contact**: Jack Eising, **Tel**. home 091-37382, **Address**: Caherawoneen, Kinvara, Co. Galway. **Earthwatch Limerick**, **Contact**: Gus Quinn, (mornings), **Tel**. 061-44195, **Address**: Earthwatch c/o Co-Op Resource Centre, 5 Broad St, Limerick. **Earthwatch UCC**, **Contact**: Clodagh O'Mara, **Tel**. 027-50968, **Address**: Earthwatch Harbour View, Bantry, Co. Cork. **Board of Directors**: Bill Chase, Harry Dixon, Jacqi Hodgson, Marcus McCabe, Maeve O'Sullivan, Jeremy Wates, Jim Woolridge. **Staff**. **Co-ordinator**: Jeremy Wates, **Development Officer**: Bridin Ashe, **Media Relations Officer**: Marcus McCabe, **Ozone Campaigner**: Clare Heardman, **Marine Pollution Campaigner**: Dominic O'Brien, **Energy & Greenhouse Campaigner**: Jim Woolridge, **Nuclear Campaigner**: Brian Wall, **Toxics Campaigner**: Tom Whitty, **Fundraising Co-ordinator**: Dave Walden, **Merchandise Manager**: Clodah O'Mara, **Information Officer**: Jacqi Hodgson, **Schools Officer**: Eddie Murphy, **Local Groups Co-ordinator**: Clodah O'Mara.

ECO—THE IRISH ENVIRONMENTAL CONSERVATION ORGANISATION FOR YOUTH, 37 North Great Georges Street, Dublin 1. Tel: 731884
Membership: Under 26 years of age. **Objectives**: To implement the objectives of An Taisce in environmental conservation relevant to youth through

education and participation. **Activities:** Voluntary youth work in community; field studies and work; provision of environmental education resources; advice on job opportunities, education, environmental problems, publication of newsletter and manuals; fundraising; evaluation and supervision of economically sustainable youth employment projects as Community Co-operatives, co-operation with An Taisce at Local, Regional, and National levels through all relevant Committees; co-operation with all Local, National and International Bodies in Youth Work and the Environment; consultation with Government and State Agencies. **Status:** Local Association Committees, Regional Councils, National Council, Organisation Executive and specialist Committees of An Taisce; applicant to National Youth Council of Ireland; International Youth Federation for Environmental Studies and Conservation. Co-operation with: European Environmental Bureau, Council of Europe Centre for Nature, International Union for Conservation of Nature/World Wildlife Fund, United Nations Educational, Scientific and Cultural Organisation, United Nations International Children's Fund, United Nations Environmental Programme, International Commission on Monuments and Sites. **Contact:** Peter Byrne.

ECONOMIC AND SOCIAL RESEARCH INSTITUTE
4 Burlington Road, Dublin 4. Tel: 01-760115 Fax 686231
Membership: Corporate 260. Individual 200. **Objectives:** The Institute's primary purpose is to bring to bear on the problems of Irish society and the Irish economy, economic, sociological and psychological research at recognised professional standards. The Institute has also evolved a training role to increase the stock of qualified economic and social research workers in Ireland. **Activities:** Economic and social research undertaken by the Research staff of the Institute and published in the Institute's various publication series. It also undertakes research on a commissioned basis for other organisations, both public and private. **Status:** Private Limited Company. **Sponsorships:** The Institute provides study fellowships for post-graduate studies overseas, preferably courses of study leading to a Ph.D. degree or equivalent. **Publications:** Periodicals and books. **Contact:** Director.

THE ENERGY CONSERVATION ASSOCIATION OF IRELAND
c/o 22 Clyde Road, Ballsbridge, Dublin 4. Tel:01-684341
Membership: 30—open to all. **Objectives:** To promote and develop group, district heating and combined heat and power schemes. The association keeps up a continuous dialogue with the relevant government departments to push through appropriate legislation in the areas of interest. **Contact:** Peter J. Byrne, Public Relations Officer.

ENVIRONMENT POLICY COMMITTEE
Confederation of Irish Industry, Kildare Street, Dublin 2
Tel: 01-779801 Fax 777823
Membership: Industry representation to Government, State Agencies, EEC, International Organisations, and the General Public. **Objectives:** To ensure as far as practicable that environment policy matters reflect industry's views. To inform industry of environmental developments at national, international and EEC levels. **Activities:** Essentially a forum for policy making and information dissemination. **Status:** The Environment Policy Committee is an advisory committee to the National Executive Committee of the Confederation. **Contact:** Aidan O'Boyle, Secretary to the Committee.

FEDERATION OF LOCAL HISTORY SOCIETIES
Laurel Lodge, Carlow
Membership: 34 Societies. 2 Associate Members: Royal Society of Antiquaries of Ireland. Federation for Ulster Local Studies. **Objectives:** To encourage research into and the recording of local history, archaeology, folklife and folklore.To preserve and protect local heritage. To seek legislation on matters of mutual concern and to influence the decisions of Ministers and

Local Authorities. To exchange information via a newsletter and directory of members. To give mutual support by bringing together societies to co-operate on studies and publications, and by co-operating with An Taisce and similar bodies. To encourage and undertake the publication of books and periodical reviews and the collection and copying of archives. To provide any other services to affiliated societies as shall be considered appropriate from time to time. **Activities:** Two annual meetings which include workshops. Activities of individual societies include restoration, research, lectures, guided tours, and publications. **Contact:** Mrs. S.A. Fitzmaurice, Honorary Secretary.

FEDERATION OF MOUNTAINEERING CLUBS OF IRELAND
Ashford, Co. Wicklow. Tel: 0404-5195
Membership: 2,400. **Objectives:** To represent, co-ordinate and encourage mountaineering Clubs in Ireland. **Representation/Status:** Irish Mountaineering Training Board, N.I. Mountain Training Board, Union International des Associations Alpinism, Commission des Expedition de l'UIAA, Irish Mountain Rescue Association, Ulster Way Committee, Mournes Advisory Council. 32 country recognised mountaineering representative body, by both Governments of Ireland and abroad. **Publications:** List available on request. **Contact:** Dermot Sommers, Secretary.

FOROIGE, NATIONAL YOUTH DEVELOPMENT ORGANISATION
Irish Farm Centre, Bluebell, Dublin 12. Tel: 01-501166
Membership: 18,000. **Objectives:** The personal development of its members, leaders and others through involvement in its programmes, activities and events. **Activities:** Environmental Workshops. Eight out-of school education programmes: Citizenship; Leadership; Culture; Health; Science; Agriculture/Horticulture; Family and Life Skills; Youth Co-operation Education. **Status:** Voluntary organisation. **Publications:** Leaflets and booklets. Monthly newssheet.**Contact:** Michael B. Cleary, Director.

GEOGRAPHICAL SOCIETY OF IRELAND
c/o The Dept. of Geography, U.C.G. Tel: 091-24411
Membership: 200. **Objectives:** To promote the study of geography of Ireland in all its aspects. **Activities:** Research, education, public lectures, fieldtrips. **Representation/Status:** National Committee for Geography of the RIA. **Publications:** Newsletter. **Contact:** Hon. Secretary, Mary Cawley.

GOLD-EIA
c/o Microbiology Dept., University College, Galway. Tel: 091-24411
Objectives: This was set up by a dozen organisations concerned with the preservation of the countryside to consider what topics should be covered in an environmental impact statement submitted as part of a planning application to open a gold mine. **Contact:** Dr. Emer Colleran.

GREENPEACE
44 Upper Mount Street, Dublin 2. Tel: 01-619836
Membership: 2,000—open to all. **Objectives:** Through scientific research, public education, lobbying of national and international fora and where necessary, non-violent direct action, Greenpeace campaigns to protect the natural environment. **Contact:** John Bowler. The stormtroopers of the Green Movement, Greenpeace have captured the imagination and hearts of the general public through their feats of daring on the seas throughout the world. A recent poll in Ireland showed that a massive 40% of the people questioned saw Greenpeace as the group doing most for the environment. This makes them by far the most popular environmental group in the country. Founded in the US in the early 1970s, Greenpeace today manages to combine idealism with high tech professionalism. What you see on TV when they carry out an action is only a small part of their operation. Their annual

budget of over £100m is also used to pay for lawyers and scientists and for the preparation of detailed reports. Although the Greenpeace ships have been visiting Ireland for many years, a Dublin office was not established until 1987, John Bowler, who was an activist with both the Sea Shepard and SAVE, was the first staff member and since then additional campaigners have been brought in. In recent years Greenpeace have become more involved in the whole question of toxic waste in Ireland and their toxics campaigner, Bob Edwards, has made it quite clear that Greenpeace will be opposing the proposed national incinerator. **Campaigners:** John Bowler, **Campaign Director**; Helen Kingham, **Sellafield**; Bob Edwards, **Toxics**; Orla Ni Eili, **Naval vessels**.

THE HERITAGE TRUST
Shell House, 20 Lower Hatch Street, Dublin 2. Tel: 01-613611
Membership: Board of Trustees: 21. **Objectives:** To reconcile economic progress and protection of the physical heritage by funding conservation projects and environmental research in Ireland appropriate to these aims. **Activities:** Research. Education and training. Community environmental projects. **Sponsorships:** All applications for funding must be received by 31 July each year. Funds generally provided from following 1 January. **Publications:** *Heritage Inventory Series: Carlow, Bray, Tullamore, Ennis.* William Garner et al. Various dates. An Foras Forbartha. *Irish Local Architecture* Patrick Shaffrey; An Taisce; N.Y.P. *Urban Report Survey of Dublin Buildings for Listing* An Taisce; O'Brien Press. **Contact:** Nicholas Robinson, Executive Director.

H.I.T.H.A.
Historic Irish Tourist Houses & Gardens Association, 3a Castle Street, Dalkey, Co. Dublin. Tel: 01-801185/859323.
Membership: 51. **Objectives:** To increase the number of visitors to member properties. To educate members towards greater participation in tourism. To preserve parts of the Irish heritage. **Status:** The required body under the auspices of Bord Failte representing Houses and Castles open to Public. Founder member of European Historic Houses Association. **Publications:** Annual Report. **Contact:** Secretary.

HOLIDAY FELLOWSHIP
3 Southwood Park, Blackrock, Co. Dublin. Tel: 888189
Membership: 100. **Objectives:** Holiday Fellowship aims to encourage the love of the open air and thereby to promote social and international friendship. **Activities:** Weekend walks in Co. Wicklow. **Publications:** Quarterly programmes for walks. **Contact:** Mrs. Gilligan, Secretary.

INLAND WATERWAYS ASSOCIATION OF IRELAND
c/o Stone Cottage, Claremont Road, Killiney, Co. Dublin. Tel: 01-852258
Membership: Circa 1400-1500 **Objectives:** To promote the development, use and maintenance of Ireland's navigable rivers and canals. To ensure the preservation of navigable waterways. **Activities:** Lobbying and advising national and local government and other bodies on all matters including pollution and future developments. Organising work-parties, rallies and events to promote the objectives and encourage good standards of boatmanship and seaworthiness. **Sponsorship of Research/Publications/Scholarships:** Guide-books to Grand Canal, Barrow Navigation, Shannon. **Publications:** *Inland Waterways News. Grand Canal Guide* including Barrow Line to Athy, reprinted 1983. Addis and Delany. **Contact:** President.

INSTITUTE OF BIOLOGY OF IRELAND
c/o Dublin Institute of Technology, Kevin Street, Dublin 8. Tel: 757541 ext. 231
Membership: 400 professional biologists. **Objectives:** Environment, education research, biotechnology and standards in relation to all branches of biology. **Activities:** Organises Biology Today, lectures and symposia, weekend and

day trips. Facilitates the exchange of information among biologists in Ireland and abroad, presents prizes for Leaving Certificate Biology and Young Scientists Biology Section. Runs Undergraduate Biology Conference. **Publications:** *Beatha.* **Contact:** Dr. C. Mothersill, Hon. Secretary.

INSTITUTE OF FISHERIES MANAGEMENT

c/o Thomas Prior House, Ballsbridge, Dublin 4. Tel: 01-210111
Membership: 100 approx. Regional organisation through number of branches. **Objectives:** Promoting the efficiency of persons engaged in fisheries management. **Activities:** Education and Training. Certificate Course—recognised qualification for Fishery staff. Diploma Course—2 years Exchange of information about a fast-changing industry. Symposia, lectures, training courses. **Publications:** List on request. **Contact:** Secretary, Dr. Edward Fahy.

INSTITUTE OF LANDSCAPE HORTICULTURE OF IRELAND

c/o Science Section, RDS, Ballsbridge, Dublin 4. Tel: 331941
Membership: 70—graduates of degree course in landscape horticulture. **Objectives:** To advance knowledge, appreciation, conservation and enhancement of the Irish landscape. **Activities:** Defining and implementing standards of landscape and professional practice; organising conferences, seminars, lectures and demonstrations, etc. **Contact:** G. Cousins, Secretary.

INSTITUTE OF WATER POLLUTION CONTROL

Republic of Ireland branch,
c/o Regional Technical College, Sligo. Tel: 071-43261
Membership: Corporate: 10 Technician: 3 Affiliates: 16.
Objectives: To promote the advancement of the science and practice of water pollution control; the various interests of persons engaged in the profession of sewage purification and to encourage and direct the training of such persons. **Publications:** Water Pollution Control (6 per year); Newsletter. **Contact:** Mr. Tom Higgins, Honorary Secretary.

INSTITUTE OF WOOD SCIENCE

Irish Branch, Eolas, Glasnevin, Dublin 9. Tel: 379620 Fax 379620
Membership: 1,500 (worldwide)—open to all. **Objectives:** To advance the scientific, technical, practical and general knowledge of persons interested in the study of wood and allied subjects. **Activities:** Holding meetings, lectures, symposia and visits to relevant scientific and industrial concerns. The institute is the examining body in timber technology for both the certificate and associateship examinations. **Publications:** Journal. **Contact:** Dr. J.A. Evertsen.

IRISH ARCHITECTS' SOCIETY

35 Fitzwilliam Place, Dublin 2. Tel: 01-793690/715901
Membership: 102. **Objectives:** To promote the appreciation and study of the art and science of architecture. To further the study of the principles and practice of economic building construction and allied subjects. To supervise and protect professional interests of members. To promote and supervise a code for professional practice and conduct. **Activities:** Advisory services. **Status:** Nominating body for Senate elections. **Contact:** Mr. O'Grady, Honorary Secretary—307241.

THE IRISH ARCHITECTURAL ARCHIVE

63 Merrion Square, Dublin 2, Tel: 01-763430
Membership: (Company): 75. **Objectives:** To collect records, mainly photographic (but also drawings, manuscripts, books, pamphlets and press cuttings), of all aspects of Irish architecture, and to make these available for consultation by the public. **Activities:** Public reading room. Cataloguing of accessions. Photographic survey work, particularly of buildings threatened by decay or demolition. **Status:** Limited company, registered as a charity. **Contact:** Mr. David Griffin, Archive Director.

IRISH ASSOCIATION FOR QUATERNARY STUDIES
Department of Environment Studies, University of Ulster, Coleraine, Co. Derry
Tel: 080265-44141
Membership: Open to all—approx. 53 members. **Objectives:** The advancement of education and research in the discipline of quaternary studies in Ireland. **Activities:** Organises field meetings/excursions, on research and thematic seminar per year, occasional lectures. **Publications:** Include a field guide and extended abstracts of papers delivered at seminars. **Contact:** Dr. Peter Wilson, Hon. Secretary.

IRISH ASTRONOMICAL SOCIETY
PO Box 2547, Dublin 15, Tel: 202135 and 344869 (after 6 p.m.)
Membership: 328—open to all. **Objectives:** To promote interest in astronomy and allied subjects. **Activities:** Meetings twice a month in Dublin which include lectures for beginners and the more advanced. Officers for help and advice. Telescope making classes. Trips to places of astronomical interest including several astronomy week-ends each year. Weekly observing with large telescope. **Publications:** Bi-Monthly magazine *Orbit*. **Contact:** James Lynch, Secretary.

IRISH BIOGEOGRAPHICAL SOCIETY
Department of Zoology, Trinity College, Dublin 2, Tel: 772941 ext. 1882
Membership: 120—open to all.
Objectives: To record and study the distribution of the Irish flora and fauna; to issue and publish information on flora and fauna and to promote interest. **Activities:** Field trips, lectures, courses, etc. Joint committee with the Irish Wildlife Federation; Areas of Scientific Interest Committee, Survey of Pollardstown (Newbridge), Fen (Biological). **Publications:** Newsletter; Field meetings programme. **Contact:** Dr. Paddy Ashe.

IRISH CAMPAIGN FOR NUCLEAR DISARMAMENT
Box 2599, Dublin 1, Tel: 808247
Membership: 700—open to all. **Objectives:** The abolition of all weapons of mass destruction, for the dissolution of military alliances; the strengthening of the United Nations, the promotion of Irish neutrality as a force for peace and disarmament and the transfer of funds from military spending to the relief of world poverty. Promotes alternatives to nuclear power. **Activities:** Meetings, demonstrations, lobbying politicians, etc. **Contact:** Carol Fox.

IRISH CO-OPERATIVE ORGANISATION SOCIETY
Plunkett House, 84 Merrion Square, Dublin 2
Tel: 01-764783 Telex 30379 Fax 681784
Membership: 230 co-ops with 200,000 members. **Objectives:** Co-ordination, promotion and development of the Co-operative Movement in Ireland. **Activities:** Management and Technical consultancy. Education and Training. Professional Representation. Financial Services. **Status:** Represented on NESC, NCEA, AFT, ACOT, COGECA, CEA, various Departmental committees, Advisory Council on Pollution. **Sponsorships:** Co-sponsors of Bank of Ireland Centre for Co-operative Studies, U.C.C. Sponsors of Irish Foundation for Co-operative Development. **Publications:** *Co-op Ireland*. Annual Report. **Contact:** James C. Moloney, Director General.

IRISH COUNTRYWOMEN'S ASSOCIATION
58 Merrion Road, Dublin 4. Tel: 01-680453
Membership: 26,500. **Objectives:** To develop and improve the conditions of rural life in Ireland. **Activities:** Education and training. Advisory services. **Publications:** *Irish Woman*, Newsletter, quarterly; non-members on request. **Contact:** Miss Maureen Holden, General Secretary.

IRISH FEDERATION OF SEA ANGLERS
Hon. Secretary, 67 Windsor Drive, Monkstown, Co. Dublin. Tel: 01-806901

Membership: 5,000. **Objectives:** The promotion of the sport of sea-angling. Conservation of fish stocks and spawning and nursery grounds around the coast. Monitoring, and where possible, prevention of pollution. **Activities:** Research in connection with fish stocks, conservation, pollution. Education and training. Advisory services. **Status:** National Federation (inc. N. Ireland). Angling Council of Ireland. **Publications:** Gaff. **Contact:** Hugh O'Rorke, Hon. Secretary.

IRISH FISHERMEN'S ORGANISATION LTD.
Cumberland House, Fenian Street, Dublin 2. Tel: 01-612400 Fax 612424
Objectives: To present the interest of Irish Fishermen at national and international level; to provide a forum for discussion on fishery matters; to formulate proposals for fisheries development, and to use whatever means are open to the company to have such proposals put into effect; to concern itself with any development which the company considers to be of interest or benefit to Irish fishermen. **Activities:** Professional representation. **Status:** National Committee: Special Committee on Boat Arrears and Boat Repayments. International Committees: Europeche (EEC Association of Fishing Enterprise); EEC Joint Committee on social problems in sea fishing; EEC Fishing Advisory Committee. **Publications:** I.F.O. News. **Contact:** J.F. Doyle, Secretary General.

IRISH WILDBIRD CONSERVANCY AND WAGBI.
Affiliated members of The Game Conservancy, UK. **Contact:**James Emmet, Honorary Secretary.

IRISH GARDEN PLANT SOCIETY
c/o National Botanic Gardens, Glasnevin, Dublin 9. Tel: 01-377596
Membership: c.550. **Objectives:** To research, locate and cultivate garden plants. To take an interest in the preservation of gardens throughout Ireland. At all times particular attention will be given to Ireland's great heritage of fine gardens and splendid plants. **Activities:** Research by completion of question-naires about plants in their gardens. Lectures, Garden visits, Publications, Conservation. **Representation/Status:** Associated with similar groups in Britain. **Sponsorship of Research/Publications/Scholarships:** Papers from non-members published. **Publications:** Newsletter; Quarterly Members only; non-members on request. An annual journal will be published, *Moorea*. **Contact:** Chairman. Catherine Gorman, Secretary, works at National Botanic Gardens.

IRISH GEOLOGICAL ASSOCIATION
c/o Geology Department, University College, Belfield, Dublin 4.
Tel: 01-693244 ext. 2841 Fax 694409
Membership: Ordinary: 86 Honorary: 1,100. Amateur 52: Professional 74. **Objectives:** To further interest in the geological sciences in Ireland and to provide a meeting ground for professional and amateur geological scientists and other interested persons. **Activities:** Education, social. **Representation/ Status:** Irish National Committee for Geology. **Sponsorship of Research/ Publications/Scholarships:** Travel grant of £150 pounds annually for Irish Postgraduate research students of Geology. **Publications:** *IGA Circular*; non-members on request; IGA Field Guides. **Contact:** Julian Menuge ext. 2841.

IRISH GEORGIAN SOCIETY
Leixlip Castle, Celbridge, Co. Kildare. Tel: 01-244211
Membership: 3,500. **Objectives:** To protect buildings of architectural merit in Ireland, particularly those of the 18th century. To stimulate interest in Irish art and architecture and to encourage research. **Activities:** Lectures, concerts, tours of houses both in Ireland and abroad, volunteer work camp during summer months, and other social activities. **Sponsorship of Research/ Publications/Scholarships:** Sponsors student for University College Dublin Summer School and also West Dean Summer School on Conservation. **Publications:** *Irish Georgian Society Bulletin* Newsletter. **Contact:** Miss Audrey Emerson, Executive Director.

THE IRISH GIRL GUIDES
27, Pembroke Park, Dublin 4. Tel: 01-683898

Membership: 19,000. **Objectives/Activities:** Through Guiding to help and encourage girls to deepen their religious faith. By a system of tests and badges to challenge each other to reach the highest development of which she is capable. Senior members represent their country abroad at conferences and through exchanges. **Status:** Members of the World Association of Girl Guides and Girl Scouts. **Publications:** Trefoil News (monthly), Brownie Branch Book of Tests, Guide Branch Book of Tests, Training Notes for Brownie Guiders, Training Notes for Guide Guiders, Hints for Patrol Leaders. Why Guiding for the Handicapped. **Contact:** Miss Kitty Richardson, Secretary General.

IRISH GRASSLAND AND ANIMAL PRODUCTION ASSOCIATION
c/o Agricultural Institute, Belclare, Tuam, Co. Galway. Tel: 093-55455

Membership: 750: Progressive farmers, research, advisory and agri-business personnel. **Objectives:** To promote the knowledge of grassland and animal production. To procide opportunities for those interested in modern grassland farming to meet and exchange views and ideas. To foster and encourage research into the production and utilisation of grassland. To co-operate with other organisations which have in common the improvement of grassland farming. **Activities:** Summer meeting. Autumn Tour—Overseas Farm Study. Winter Conference—2 days. Spring Conference—2days. AGM and Spring Show Dinner. **Regional Activities:** Local Seminars and Farm Walks organised by Regional groups of the Association in Cork, Donegal and Galway areas. **Publications:** *Irish Grassland and Animal Production.* Journal. Annual. **Contact:** Dr. S. Flanagan.

IRISH MARINE SCIENCE ASSOCIATION
Aquaculture Unit, Zoology Department, University College, Cork. Tel: 021-276871 ext. 2745

Membership: 150. **Objectives:** To strive for a national policy for the development of our marine resources. **Activities:** Two meetings per year in different locations which have a theme and are jointly organised with a specialist professional marine group—Irish Aquaculture Association, Geological Survey. Open to all. **Contact:** Gavin Burnell.

IRISH METEOROLOGICAL SOCIETY
c/o Meteorological Service, Glasnevin Hill, Dublin 9

Membership: 200—open to all. **Objectives:** The promotion of an interest in meteorology. The dissemination of meteorological knowledge pure and applied. **Activities:** Field trips, outings, seminars and regular lectures. **Publications:** Newsletter. **Contact:** The Secretary.

IRISH ORGANIC FARMERS & GROWERS ASSOCIATION (THE)
representing farmers, growers, consumers, dieticians etc. have adopted an internationally recognised set of production standards. A producer will be awarded the symbol and can display it on the produce, if and only if:

The producer is operating according to those strict standards under a legally binding contract.
The land has been farmed organically for at least two years.

An independent review body of inspectors, members of the Consumers Association of Ireland, Department of Agriculture and IOFGA awards the symbol on the basis of the result of inspections and spot checks.

IOFGA: A Portrait: The Irish Organic Farmers & Growers Association was founded in 1981. It's membership of 400 (1988) contains not only farmers and growers, but also consumers who want to promote Organic food production and protect our countryside. IOFGA is a voluntary organisation which is involved in Organic research projects which encourages the government to introduce and enforce strict regulations on pollution, which seeks to increase awareness of the potential of Organic production, be it field or garden, through a network of local groups, conferences, farm and garden trips and workshops. IOFGA also produces a bimonthly magazine: **Common Ground.** To be an effective protector of the environment and qualify food much work has to be done, if you agree with our objectives, please ask for a membership form—we need your support. **The Irish Organic Farmers & Growers Association,** Clare Mooney (Hon. Secretary), Killegland Farm, Ashbourne, Co Meath, Tel: 01-350225.

IRISH PEATLAND CONSERVATION COUNCIL
3 Lower Mount Street, Dublin 2. Tel: 01-616645

Membership: 400—open to all. **Objectives:** To identify and monitor peatland sites of conservation value, to make the public aware of the need for peatland conservation through education and publicity; to lobby agencies responsible for peatland conservation and exploitation; fund raise to purchase threatened bogs and for education and publicity programmes. **Activities:** Purchased Scragh Bog in Co. Westmeath, organised a national poster competition and are actively involved in developing a Peatland Education Pack for schools and an Irish-Dutch peatland exhibition. **Publications:** Booklets on peatland conservation, contact: Dr. Catherine O'Connell.

IRISH PLANNING INSTITUTE
8 Merrion Square, Dublin 2

Membership: Ordinary: 138 Student: 56 Affiliates: 7. **Objectives:** The Institute is a professional body and a learned society concerned with the advancement of the art and science of urban, rural and regional planning in Ireland for the benefit of the Community. **Activities:** Education and training; professional representation. **Sponsorship of Research/Publications/Scholarships:** The Institute publishes the proceedings of its Annual Conference (ie. authors'papers) and distributes them free to its members. Publishes occasional research papers by individual members and distributes them to members. **Publications:** *Pleanail*; Proceedings of Annual Conference. Occasional series of research papers. **Contact:** Honorary Secretary.

THE IRISH RAMBLERS CLUB
13, La Vista Avenue, Sutton, Dublin 13. Tel: 01-322358

Membership: 350. **Activities:** Hiking Activities all over Ireland, including weekly walks in the Dublin/Wicklow area, and occasional Weekends in Ireland, and Trips abroad. Conservation Interest. **Publications:** The Rambler published Monthly. Access Routes in Wicklow. Ireland East Walk Guide, Gill and Macmillan. **Contact:** Margaret Herman, President.

IRISH SOCIETY OF TOXICOLOGY
Membership: 90—open to all. The State Laboratory, Abbotstown, Castleknock, Dublin Objectives: Encouraging and extending interest in toxicology, to studying various aspects of toxicology. **Activities:** Arranging meetings and promoting scientific work connected with any form of toxicology. **Publications:** Periodic bulletins. **Contact:** Dr. Brian Brady.

IRISH WILDBIRD CONSERVANCY
Ruttledge House, 8 Longford Place, Monkstown. Tel: 01-804322

Membership: Total 3,300—open to all. **Objectives:** Conservation (in relation to wild birds). Education and research. Promotion of field ornithology. **Activities:** Research, education and training, advisory services, conservation—site protection, publishing, organisation of local activities through network of branches, junior branches. **Representation/ Status:** International: International Council for Bird Preservation, Working Group of European Bird Societies. National: Wildlife Advisory Council. **Sponsorship of Research/Publications/Scholarships:** Current projects: Survey of Important Areas for Birds. Atlas of Wintering Birds (jointly with BTO). **Publications:** Periodicals: *Irish Wildbird*

Conservancy News; Members Newsletter; Quarterly, Members (and non-members on request). *Irish Birds*; Scientific journal; annual; Retail; £3.50 pounds including postage. *IWC Annual Report and Accounts*; annual; members (and non-members on request).**Books** *Ireland's Wetlands and their Birds*; Clive Hutchinson; 1979; £5.50. *Birds of Galway and Mayo*; Tony Whilde 1980; £2.50. *Birds of North Munster*; Phil Brennan and Ewart Jones; 1982; £2.50. *Project on Birds*; Roger Goodwillie; 1981; £1.30. (All prices include postage and packing.) **Contact:** Director.

IRISH WILDLIFE FEDERATION
132A East Wall Road, Dublin 3. Tel: 01-366821
Membership: 2,460. **Objectives:** Conservation of Ireland Wildlife and its habits; promotion of conservation awareness. **Activities:** Education and training for conservation: 'groundwork' habitat management. **Status:** Registered charity; member of IYP; member of European Environmental Bureau. **Publications:** Quarterly newsletter. Irish Wildlife Book by Fergus O'Gorman. Guide to Birds of Ireland by Gordon D'Arcy. **Contact:** Chairman, Tony Hempenstall 366821. Hon. Secretary, Mary Kelly-Quinn.

IRISH INSTITUTE OF LANDSCAPE CONSULTANTS.
8 Merrion Square, Dublin 2. Tel: 01-789211
Membership: Ordinary + student: 54. **Guest Affiliates**: 17. Honorary: 4 **Objectives:** The advancement of landscape architecture and the promotion of the highest standards of professional service in the arts and sciences of landscape architecture and management. The planning, design, supervision and management of rural and urban landscape for the benefit of the present community and its heirs. **Activities:** Education and training, Professional representation. Promotion of landscape architecture through symposia, lectures etc. **Representation/Status:** International Federation of Landscape Architects, Coastlines Committee; Council of Landscape Institute—UK. Planning Advisory Committee, An Foras Forbartha. **Publications:** Newsletter; Occasional—members only. *Towards an Environment Policy: An Alternative Approach* February 1980; Free, on request. *Landscape at Work*, June 1982; Free on request. **Contact:** Secretary.

MACRA NA FEIRME
Irish Farm Centre, Bluebell, Dublin 12. Tel: 01-501166 Fax 514908
Membership: 12,000. **Objectives:** Personal Development. Leadership Training. Agricultural Development. **Activities:** Competitions. Courses. Projects. Seminars. **Status:** Voluntary. **Sponsorship of Research/Publications/Scholarships:** Farmers, members, Business firms, Government. **Publications:** Annual Diary. Annual Report. Newssheet. Page in Irish Farmers Journal. **Contact:** Tony Garahy, Chief Executive.

MARINE CONSERVATION SOCIETY
Environmental Sciences Unit, Trinity College, Dublin 2. Tel: 01-772941 ext. 1640
Membership: 12—open to all. **Objectives:** The promotion of marine conservation and preservation of the marine environment. **Activities:** Courses and projects and an information service. **Publications:** Quarterly magazine and other publications. **Contact:** Dr. J. Wilson.

MARITIME HISTORY (INTERNATIONAL COMMISSION ON)
Patron: Dr. Hillery.**Sponsorship of Research/Publications/ Scholarships:** As funds are limited, they barely cover running expenses and those of Research Section. This year two trainees were sponsored for a course in sailtraining vessel 'Asgard 2'. **Publications:** *Maritime Journal of Ireland*; quarterly; members only (circulated to all shipping companies in Ireland and to approx. 50 museums and kindred establishments. *The Sea and the Easter Rising* (1966); 2,500 copies. *The Ships of Ireland* (1980); 750 copies. **Contact:** Honorary Secretary, James Wolahan—01-883043.

MARITIME INSTITUTE OF IRELAND (THE)

Haigh Terrace, Dun Laoghaire, Co. Dublin. Tel: 01-800969
Membership: 350—open to all. **Objectives:** To promote greater awareness in the sea, shipping, naval defence, fisheries, ports and off shore resources. **Activities:** Operates the National Maritime Museum which houses a Maritime library of some 3,000 books. **Contact:** Mr. R. Lewis, President.

MUINTIR NA TIRE

Headquarters, Canon Hayes House, Tipperary Town. Tel: 062-51163
Membership: Nó individual membership; Affiliated Community Councils (c.200,000 persons). **Objectives:** To promote the establishment of local representative Community Councils so as to improve the whole life of the people of the Communities—Economic, Social, Cultural and environmental. **Activities:** Various projects in Community Development. **Status:** Voluntary, Community. **Publications:** Periodic Publication of relevant documents. **Contact:** Tom Fitzgerald, Chief Administrative Officer.

MINING INFORMATION RESOURCE GROUP

The Pottery, Moyard, Co. Galway
Tel: 095-41015
Objective: To furnish information on mining; has an extensive library on all types of mining together with slides and a video about gold extraction. **Contact:** Nes Porter.

NATIONAL ASSOCIATION OF REGIONAL GAME COUNCILS

Gortaclera, Bushy Park, Galway. Tel: 091-24266
Membership: 26,000 (approx.) **Objectives:** To promote co-operation between Regional Game Councils and all appropriate interests, sporting, wildlife, conservation, agricultural and rural, for the proper development of Game Wildlife Resources and the conservation of Wildlife, and to represent these interests at National and International level. To actively advise and assist the development of Regional Game Councils within each County. To safeguard the legitimate and traditional rights of nature sportsmen. **Activities:** Co-ordinating efforts of Regional Game Councils. Promoting an interest in Game Wildlife and field sports. Advising and assisting relevant Government Departments in all matters concerning Game propagation, Game Laws, Wildlife Conservation etc. **Sponsorship of Research/Publications/Scholarships:** Presently sponsoring research project on pheasant survival in the wild by University students. Carry out research on Red-legged Partridge, Quail, Woodcock, Canada Geese, Greenland White-Fronted Geese. **Publications:** *Irish Wetlands Survey Parts I and II.* Booklet on Red-legged Partridge. **Contact:** Chairman, Jim Cummins. 12 Laurel Grove, Bishopstown, Co. Cork. Tel: 021-541381. Honorary Secretary, Dr. James Dunne.

NATIONAL YOUTH COUNCIL OF IRELAND

3 Montague Street, Dublin 2. Tel: 01-784122
Membership: Full: 31 Associate: 15. **Objectives:** To bring together the voluntary youth serving organisations and agencies of Ireland in order: to encourage co-operation among all concerned with the development of young people in Ireland. To promote the advancement of learning and education of young people and youth leaders. To promote and to safeguard the common interests of young people. To afford Irish youth organisations a further means of representation. **Activities:** Research, education and training, advisory services, professional representation, lobbying, organising conferences, agency for international activities. **Representation/Status:** National Road Safety Association, Advisory Committee, on Development Cooperation, Association for Personal Service Overseas, National Savings Committee, Youth Employment Agency. **Publications:** *Youth Forum;* 5 per year; *Irish Youth Directory.* **Contact:** Director, Tom Curran.

NATIONAL YOUTH FEDERATION

2 Belvedere Place, Dublin 1. Tel: 01-729933 Fax 364871

Membership: 16 Regional Councils of Youth Clubs (385); 35,000 young people aged 11-21 years.
Objectives: To enable young people in Ireland to develop their physical, mental and spiritual capacities so that they may grow to fulfillment as individuals and as members of whatever groups or communities to which they belong. To promote and develop strong self-managing regional groupings of youth clubs. **Activities:** Leadership Training programmes. Community Project Awards. National Competitions. International opportunities. Staff and Management Training. **Status:** Recognised as a voluntary youth organisation by the Youth Affairs Section of the Department of Labour.
Sponsorship of Research/Publications/Scholarships: No regular scheme of sponsorship but we are prepared to consider any application relating to developmental youth work. **Publications:** *Fedlink*—youth work magazine (monthly).Youth leader handbooks. **Contact:** Charles O'Connor, Communications Officer John Dunn, Chief Executive.

RICH—RESPONSIBLE INDUSTRY FOR CORK HARBOUR.

(Address: See contact names below)
Membership: consists of people (mainly parents) living in the Cork harbour area—RICH welcomes the participation of all persons who share similar concerns for the Cork harbour environment. **Membership and Subscriptions:** Ad Hoc with no subscription charge. **Aims & Activities:** To act as a Pressure Group on environmental matters relating specifically to industry in Cork harbour. (a) to ensure that existing development is properly controlled and does not threaten the health, safety, and welfare of people living in the area; (b) to ensure that industry seeking to locate in the Cork harbour area is both clean and beneficial and does not threaten the health, safety and welfare of people living in the area; (c) to act as a pressure group for monitoring the performance of local and state authorities in discharging their environmental duties; (d) to set up and maintain links with local residents and groups, to liaise with local industry and the developing agencies, to have regular communication lines to local and state authorities, and to operate an information service for local people. **Publications:** None. **Meetings:** Committee Meetings usually held fortnightly pending current situation. RICH also organises Public Meetings on specific relevant issues. **Contacts:** Angela Morrissey, Conti Terrace Crosshaven, Co. Cork, **tel.** 021-831302; Mary Collins, Conti Terrace, Crosshaven, Co. Cork, **tel.** 021-831046; Peter Murray, Ferry House, Currabinny, Co. Cork, **tel.** 021-378193.

ROYAL DUBLIN SOCIETY

R.D.S., Ballsbridge, Dublin 4. Tel: 01-680645 Fax 604014

Membership: 10-11,000. **Objectives:** To promote agriculture, industry, science and arts. **Publications:** Journal of Life Sciences, bi-annually; books and pamphlets. **Contact:** Science Officer, Dr. C. Mollan Tel: 01-680645, Registrar, Kevin Bright.

ROYAL HORTICULTURAL SOCIETY OF IRELAND

c/o Swanbrook House, Bloomfield Avenue, Morehampton Road, Donnybrook, Dublin 4. Tel: 01-684358 am only (Tues,Wed, Thurs 10-1 pm)

Membership: 1,150-1,200. **Objectives:** To encourage and promote the practice of horticulture in Ireland. **Activities:** Schedule of shows, lectures, garden tours, visits in Ireland and abroad, garden courses for beginners. **Sponsorship of Research/Publications/Scholarships:** Perpetual challenge cups awarded. **Publications:** Newsletter; Bi-annual. *Irish Gardening and Horticulture*; A. Brady and E.C. Nelson (1980) **Contact:** Mrs. Monica Nolan, Secretary.

THE ROYAL SOCIETY OF ANTIQUARIES OF IRELAND
63 Merrion Square, Dublin 2. Tel: 01-761749

Membership: 1,050 (approximately). **Objectives:** 'To preserve, examine and illustrate the ancient monuments of the history, language, arts, manners and customs of the past as connected with Ireland'. **Activities:** Publication of *The Journal of the Royal Society of Antiquaries of Ireland*. Maintains its own special Library for members and students engaged in research. Organises 10 formal, professional lectures per annum, together with more informal talks. Has three main excursions during each year, rotating through the four provinces, as the Society embraces the entire island. Afternoon outings are held during the winter months. **Status:** The R.S.A.I. is the premier archaeological society of Ireland. **Publications:** List of the Society's publications may be had on request. **Contact:** Tony Smith, Director.

THE ROYAL TOWN PLANNING INSTITUTE
Irish Branch—Southern Section, 5 Wilton Place, Dublin 2. Tel: 01-602511

Membership: Total: 104. **Objectives:** To advance the science and art of town planning in all its aspects, including local, regional and national planning for the benefit of the public.—extract from Charter of Institute 1914. **Activities:** Research; education and training; advisory services; professional representation. **Representation/Status:** In Ireland the Institute is represented on the advisory committees of An Foras Forbartha. Internationally the RTPI is governed by a council of 44 members, one third of whom are elected by branches. There are 11 branches in the UK and the Republic of Ireland, and two in Central Africa and Hong Kong. In addition the Institute is affiliated in Canada, Australia and New Zealand. **Sponsorship of Research/Publications/Scholarships:** The Institute funds research and scholarship grants to members through various endowments sponsored by members past and present of the RTPI. **Publications:** A. Periodicals. *The Planner*, available to non-members on request. B. Other Publications. Various publications on planning practice, research and education, seminar and conference papers. For details apply to Royal Town Planning Institute, 26 Portland Place, London W1N 4BE. **Contact:** William Murray, Chairman.

SCOUT ASSOCIATION OF IRELAND
National Headquarters—66 Lower Leeson Street, Dublin 2. Tel: 01-610266

Membership: Approximately 15,000. **Objectives:** The aim of the Association is to encourage the physical, mental and spiritual development of young people so that they may take a constructive part in society. **Activities:** The method of achieving this aim is to provide an enjoyable and attractive scheme of progressive training, including outdoor activities based on the Scout Law and Promise and guided by adult leadership. **Status:** Voluntary Youth Organisation. **Publications:** *Irish Scouting News*—magazine for leaders, published monthly except July and August. Also various Handbooks for leaders and scouts. **Contact:** The National Secretary.

SOCIETY FOR THE HISTORY OF NATURAL HISTORY (IRISH SECTION)
c/o National Botanic Gardens, Glasnevin, Dublin 9. Tel: 01-377596

Membership: c.500 (12 in Ireland). **Objectives:** Principal forum for everyone interested in natural history's past and in the books and other sources from which our knowledge of this comes. Brings together book collectors, historians, librarians etc. studying the work of their predecessors. **Activities:** Forum of discussion, publications, evening talks, conference and exhibition—annual. Visits to libraries and archives of interest. **Representation/Status:** No formal representation. Subgroup of International society based in London. **Sponsorship of Research/Publications/Scholarships:** Papers for non-members are published. **Publications:** Archives of Natural History; Bi-annually members + retail. Newsletter quarterly; members only. **Contact:** Irish Representative, Dr. Charles Nelson.

SOCIETY OF IRISH FORESTERS

c/o Royal Dublin Society, Ballsbridge, Dublin 4. Tel: 01-615666
Membership: Technical: 516, Student: 28, Associate: 124. **Objectives:** To advance and spread in Ireland the knowledge of forestry in all aspects. **Activities:** Education and Training. 2/3 field days/year, in N. Ireland and the 26 counties. 2/3 indoor meetings during winter. Annual Symposium for members and invited guests. Annual Study Tour (1 week). Annual Forest Walks at 30 centres around the country, Examinations—certificates. Occasional public meetings; Queries from schools and public. **Representation/Status:** Representation on Central Forestry Examinations Board. **Publications:** *Irish Forestry* (a technical forestry journal); bi-annual; non-members on request. *Why Forests* and *Guided Forest Walks*—Brochures. *The Forests of Ireland* (out of print) New issue due. **Contact:** Honorary Secretary: Kevin Collins, Forestry Officer, Leeson Lane, Dublin 2. Tel: 01-615666.

THE SOCIETY OF IRISH PLANT PATHOLOGISTS

c/o Department of Plant Pathology, Agriculture Building, University College, Dublin, Belfield, Dublin 4. Tel: 01-693244 ext. 7746
Membership: 70—open to all. **Objectives:** To promote an exchange of information and ideas in plant pathology, to promote an interest in plant pathology, to represent Irish plant pathologists internationally and to advise in matters of importance relating to plant pathology. **Activities:** The organisation of scientific meetings (spring and autumn). **Publications:** Annual newsletter. **Contact:** Dr. Una Lee, Hon. Secretary.

SOLAR ENERGY SOCIETY OF IRELAND

Department of Electrical Engineering, University College, Dublin, Belfield, Dublin 4. Tel: 693244
Membership: 50—open to all.**Objectives:** To provide a focus for professional and public interest in the development of renewable sources of energy. **Activities:** Organises lectures, workshops, seminars, site visits, etc., participates as national section of international solar energy society. **Publications:** Co-operates in production of publications, such as Sun at Work in Europe. **Contact:** Mr. R. Watson, Hon. Secretary.

SONAIRTE

The National Ecology Centre, Laytown Co. Meath.
Tel. 01-413226/01-374673 **Contact**: Ms Anna Doran or Tom Simpson.
Sonairte, is a registered educational charity situated along the banks or the river Nanny between Laytown and Julianstown, Co-Meath. The centre is being developed to educate and demonstrate how we can live a sustainable lifestyle and not harm our environment. When finished it will consist of lecture facilities, conference rooms, accommodation, wholefood restaurant, interactive nature trail and a two acre walled organic garden. Sonairte is an old Irish word meaning 'Positive Strength'. A *mnemonic* describes its activities, S—sustainable living, O—organic agriculture, N—nature conservation, A—appropriate technology, I—intercultural exchange, R—reconciliation and inner peace, T—third world partnership, E—educational resource. Sonairte has received support from statutory bodies and private companies which include;—FÁS, Meath Co. Council, Environmental Awareness Bureau, Ireland funds, CRH Wavin. Various courses on practical sustainable alternatives to wasteful living are planned. The centre will also have alternative energy displays.

TREE COUNCIL OF IRELAND

Address: 33 Botanic Road, Glasnevin, Dublin 9, Tel 306996. **Objectives**: The promoting, the propagation, planting, conservation and management of trees in both town and country and the dissemination of knowledge about trees and their care. **Activities**: The organisation of National Tree Week in March of every year. Other activities include tree planting in schools. **Status**: It is a non-governmental organisation comprising representatives of various professional and environmental groups as well as public service bodies. **Publications**: various on all aspects of tree planting. Also literature available on the importance of broadleaf trees. **Contact**: The secretary.

TREES FOR IRELAND

Honorary Secretary, 22 Cabinteely Green, Dublin 18. Tel: 01-857543
Membership: 100. **Objectives:** To promote an interest in trees, tree planting, utilization of timber. **Activities:** Arbor Days, Lectures, Meetings, Distribution of Literature and booklets and publications. **Sponsorship of Research/Publications/Scholarships:** Sponsorship by Forest and Wildlife Service Insurance Co., Irish Forest Products, Irish Creamery Milk Suppliers Association. **Publications:** *Trees of Ireland, Planting for Profit. Ireland's Countryside* (£1.00). *Ash Trees for Hurleys. Forestry. Planning Arbor*, all publications available on request. **Contact:** S. Cahill, Hon. Secretary.

TROCAIRE—THE CATHOLIC AGENCY FOR WORLD DEVELOPMENT

169 Booterstown Avenue, Blackrock, Co. Dublin
Tel: 01-885385 ext. 04 Fax: 883577
Objectives: Trocaire was established in 1973 by the Catholic Bishops of Ireland in response to the poverty and injustice affecting the people of the Third World. In the world campaign entitled 'Action for Justice', Trocaire seeks to provide people with the opportunity of contributing towards the elimination of poverty and injustice in the world. Trocaire seeks to increase awareness and understanding among Irish people of the causes and means of eliminating poverty and injustice. **Activities:** Trocaire provides 70% of its income for development work in the Third World and supports projects in disaster relief, agriculture and rural development, health and community welfare, the promotion of human rights, leadership training and the advancement of women. As part of its education programme, Trocaire also provides wide ranging material and resources on most major areas e.g. aid, trade, environment, history, geography. **Publications:** Trocaire maintains a library in Dublin containing general reference material, statistical sources and teaching aids which are at the disposal of all. In addition, Trocaire publishes educational materials, (posters, information packs, information charts) and a newspaper. Trocaire also publishes a newsletter for trade unionists. Up-to-date briefings on various Third World countries are also published. Films, slide kits and tapes are also available. Trocaire also provides support staff for educational activities in schools, youth clubs, colleges and community groups. Examples: Information Packs a) South Africa (1982) £2.50. b) South America (1981)—Free. School Packs: Three Worlds. Problems of World Hunger 9-12 year olds—Free. School Information Charts: Situate Ireland in World Context—Free. Also Posters—Free. Slide Kits: Arming the World—postage charge only, etc. **Contact:** Dr. Colm Regan, Education Consultant.

Ireland
State & State-Sponsored
Organisations

AN BORD IASCAIGH MHARA (BIM)

Crofton Road, Dun Laoghaire, Co. Dublin. Tel: 01-841544. Fax: 841123. Telex: 93237. **Membership:** Staff: 127 (approx.). **Objectives:** Development of Ireland's Commercial Sea Fishing and Fish Farming Industries. **Activities:** Fishing gear trials, exploratory fishing, shellfish stock surveys, experimental mari-culture projects. Grant aid of fishing boats and fish farms, processing plants, etc. Marketing of fish. Training of fishermen. Advisory services to the industry. **Status:** Semi-State body. **Sponsorship of Research/Publications/ Scholarship:** Resource Record Series. **Publications:** Annual Report. **Contact:** The Secretary.

BORD FAILTE
Baggot Street Bridge, Dublin 2. Tel: 01-765871. Fax: 764764. Telex: 93755
Membership: Staff—262. **Objectives:** To develop and promote tourism in the Republic of Ireland. It also has responsibility for the development of amenities and facilities in Ireland of a touristic nature. One of its primary concerns is with the care and preservation of the physical and cultural heritage of the country and it has a high interest in matters relating to the environment, the prevention of pollution, town planning and encouragement of community involvement in local efforts to enhance the appeal of towns and villages. **Activities:** Abroad: active marketing of the Republic of Ireland as a tourist destination; at home: organising such events as the National Tidy Towns Competition, The National Gardens Competition, The Heritage Awards and various other events designed to raise the level of awareness and involvement in community environmental effort. **Status:** Semi-State. **Sponsorship of Research/ Publications/Scholarships:** Commissions Plans and Studies to contribute to the environmental programmes and development of recreational facilities in Government Departments, local authorities and voluntary bodies. **Publications:** All tourist literature for domestic and foreign use. **Contact:** to come.

BORD NA MONA, IRISH PEAT BOARD
76 Lower Baggot Street, Dublin 2. Tel: 01-688555. Fax: 601800
Objectives: Bord na Mona was set up by the Government of the Republic of Ireland to develop the country's peat resources. The main functions of the Bord are the mechanised production of peat fuel for use in power stations and for the general industrial and domestic consumption and the production of horticultural peat for sale both at home and abroad. **Activities:** Amenity tree planting; cutover bog development for land use; conservation; information on bog survey and drainage; free information service for the public. **Status:** Semi-State. **Publications:** Annual Report. **Contact:** Manager, Amenity planting/cutover bog use; Manager, conservation.

THE CDVEC CURRICULUM DEVELOPMENT UNIT
28 Westland Row, Trinity College, Dublin 2. Tel: 01-772941 exts. 1715, 1550
Objectives: To develop curricula geared to the needs of students based on their own communities. To develop new forms of assessment consonant with the aims of the new curricula. To prepare young people for the transition from school to adult life. To provide a support service for teachers. **Activities:** The City of Dublin Humanities Curriculum, which includes the study of students' local areas, contrasting environments and contemporary issues of environmental significance. Integrated Science Curriculum Innovation Project (ISCIP), which includes the study of different habitats and environmental matters within an activity-based integrated science programme. Outdoor education which includes introduction to adventure sports, courses for teachers and students, and which places an emphasis on environmental field studies. Environmental Education network. **Publications:** List of publications on request. **Contact:** Anton Trant, Director.

CENTRAL FISHERIES BOARD
Balnagowan, Mobhi Boreen, Glasnevin, Dublin 9. Tel: 01-379206
Objectives: Management, development, protection and conservation of freshwater angling waters and sea angling. **Activities:** The Board has primary responsibility for the overall coordination and direction of the activities of the seven regional fisheries boards in the area of protection, conservation, management and development of every aspect of Ireland's

inland fisheries and sea angling resources and provides a wide range of research, scientific, technical, legal, financial, personnel, promotional and planning services to the regional boards. **Status:** State agency. **Contact:** Micheal S. Breathnach, Chief Executive.

CONSERVATION AND RECREATION BRANCH—NATIONAL PARKS AND MONUMENTS DIVISION

51 St. Stephen's Green, Dublin 2. Tel: 01-613111. Telex: 90160. Fax: 610747
Objectives: Identification, preservation, protection, management for the public and fostering of public interest in national monuments, national parks and other heritage properties and sites. **Activities:** Protection, preservation, management and presentation of national monuments, parks and the Grand and Royal Canals; acquisition and management for conservation; interpretation to the public of national parks and other properties; conduct of national archaeological survey; licensing, support and servicing of archaeological investigations. **Status:** Branch of the Office of Public Works. **Sponsorships:** Scientific research in national parks and financing archaeological excavations. **Publications:** Guide booklets and leaflets to National Monuments, Parks, Nature Trails, etc. **Contact:** Ann Grady—Monuments and Dominic McNevin—Parks.

COSPOIR LONG DISTANCE WALKING ROUTES COMMITTEE

Floor 11, Hawkins House, Dublin 2. Tel: 01-734700. Fax: 777342
Objectives: To establish a national network of short and long distance walking routes for the benefit of those who enjoy walking as a recreation. **Activities:** Surveying and recording existing footpaths and rights-of-way; preparing plans for future development and provision of long-distance, medium and short distance walking routes; negotiating way-leaves with owners of property; advising others interested in establishing routes and co-ordinating activities. **Status:** Advisory Body to the Minister for Education. **Publications**: leaflets. **Contact:** Donal O'Driscoll, Secretary.

DEPARTMENT OF AGRICULTURE AND FOOD

Agriculture House, Kildare Street, Dublin 2. Tel: 01-789011. Fax: 616263. Telex: 93607
Objectives: Development of the agricultural and food industry. **Activities:** The Department is concerned with the development of the agricultural industry. Its work embraces the improvement of agricultural production and marketing, veterinary research, cereal breeding and propagation. The Department also administers a large volume of legislation aimed at maintaining high standards of quality in farm products and controlling diseases of crops and livestock. The Department is also responsible for the formulation and operation of land policy. **Publications:** *Guidelines and Recommendations on Control of Pollution and Farm Wastes.* L. Mannion. Farm Development Service, October 1977. **Contact:** The Secretary.

DEPARTMENT OF THE ENVIRONMENT

Custom House, Dublin 1. Tel: 01-793377. Telex: 5800. Fax: 742710
Activities: The Department of the Environment guides and co-ordinates at national level the activities of local authorities in matters of physical planning and has sections dealing with development, housing policy, water and sewage schemes, building and maintaining roads. It administers the Environment Works (Youth Employment) Scheme and an annual Environmental Awareness week/day. The Minister for the Environment has the general responsibility to promote the protection and improvement of the physical environment. **Publications:** Long list available on request. **Contact:** the Secretary.

DEPARTMENT OF HEALTH (PUBLIC HEALTH SECTION)

Hawkins House, Dublin 2. Tel: 01-714711 ext. 2549

Objectives: The protection of public health. **Activities:** the Department maintains liaison with the various government departments and agencies in carrying out their responsibilities relating to environmental matters and gives assistance on medical and related aspects. **Contact:** Noirin O'Sullivan.

DEPARTMENT OF THE MARINE

Leeson Lane, Dublin 2. Tel: 01-615666; 785444. Fax: 618214. Telex: 90253
Activities: Promotes the development of and undertakes planning and coordinating activities in relation to sea and inland fisheries, aquaculture and fish processing. It channels state funds to a number of other bodies concerned with such matters. In addition, the Department has responsibility for shipping policy, ship-building, harbours, marine service industries, dumping at sea, research and development, and aquatic leisure and recreation. **Contact:** the Secretary.

ELECTRICITY SUPPLY BOARD

27 Lr. Fitzwilliam Street, Dublin 2
Tel: 01-765831/771821. Telex: 93727. Fax: (01) 615376
Objectives: Electricity Generation and Supply. To provide adequate low-cost energy to meet the needs of the community and to be ready at all times to supply the full requirements of an expanding economy. **Activities:** Considerable expertise and resources in all environmental aspects of the electricity system including the design, operation and monitoring of the system for minimum impact on the environment and including gaseous liquid, solid, thermal and electrical discharges, noise, handling of dangerous substances and visual aspects. The Board has statutory obligations which require it to manage, conduct and preserve the Shannon Fisheries. The Board carries out extensive commercial operations in salmon, trout and eels on the Rivers Shannon and Lee. The Board has established particular areas as recreational and is responsible for a wild-bird sanctuary. The Board provides free advisory service on matters of energy conservation and organises talks to schools and interested organisations. The Library is available to staff members only. **Status:** Statutory body operating under the Electricity Supply (1927-1980) Acts. **Sponsorship of Research/Publications /Scholarships:** Postdoctoral fellowship to establish and calibrate standard methods for monitoring Sulphur Dioxide, and smoke in relation to reference methods. **Publications:** *Environmental Surveys in the Electricity Supply Industry* (Air and Noise Pollution)—G.A. Lawlor. Paper to IEI and IMechE, 1976. **Contact:** Henry C. Mangan, Technical & Economic Section, Generation Department.

ENVIRONMENTAL RESEARCH UNIT

St. Martin's House, Waterloo Road, Dublin 4. Tel: 01-602511. Fax: 680009. Telex: 30846
Activities: Provides research, analytical, monitoring and advisory services for the Minister for the Environment and the local authorities in relation to environmental and infrastructural matters. **Contact:** Bill McCumiskey, Director.

ENVIRONMENTAL SCIENCES UNIT, TRINITY COLLEGE

188 Pearse Street, Trinity College, Dublin 2. Tel: 01-772941 ext. 1610
Objectives: To facilitate research, education and consultancy in the environmental sciences, concentrating on inter-disciplinarity. **Activities:** Teach on M.Sc. course—3 terms of teaching plus dissertation. Run courses for undergraduate students. Educate and train research students. Facilitate individual and group research. Facilitate environmental consultancy. **Sponsorship of Research/Publications/Scholarships:** Funded by the Higher Education Authority as a development in the Faculty of Sciences. Research funded by various sources: NBST, EEC, Industry. **Publications:** M.Sc. Course Brochure, Individual Publications and research reports by staff. **Contact:** Dr. D.W. Jeffrey, Director. Chris Stilman, Director.

EOLAS, THE IRISH SCIENCE AND TECHNOLOGY AGENCY
Glasnevin, Dublin 9. Tel: 01-370101. Telex: 32501. Fax: 01-379620.
Activities: Responsible for the development, application, coordination and promotion of science and technology in Irish Industry. It develops the role of science and technology by forging links between higher education and industry; initiating participation in national and international programmes and advising government on science and technology policy. The range of technical services offered to industry includes professional advice, industrial research, product development and identification, testing, patents, licencing and industrial education. **Publications:** List available on request. **Contact:** Tom O'Connor.

EUROPEAN FOUNDATION FOR THE IMPROVEMENT OF LIVING AND WORKING CONDITIONS
Loughlinstown House, Shankill, Co. Dublin
Tel: 01-826888. Telex: 30726 EURF. Fax: 01-826456
Objectives: The aim of the Foundation is to contribute to the planning and establishment of better living and working conditions through actions to increase and disseminate knowledge in fields which deal in particular with the following themes: Man at work; Organisation of work and particular job design; Problems peculiar to certain categories of workers; Long-term aspects of improvement of the environment; Distribution of human activities in space and in time. **Contact:** Norman Wood, Head of Information.

FOREST SERVICE
Spruce House, Leeson Lane, Dublin 2. Tel: 01-615666. Telex: 90253. Fax: 01-789527
Activities: Responsible for development of afforestation with a view to providing as far as possible the country's requirements of timber and timber products. Its programme includes the management and development of State Forests and the encouragement of private forestry. Under the Forestry Act any felling of trees in rural situations has to be covered by a permit from this body. State grants are provided under certain conditions for various forms of private planting. The services of the Services technical officers are made freely available to advise on all aspects of planting. A nursery stock list is available on request. **Publications:** List available on request. **Contact:** The Secretary.

GEOLOGICAL SURVEY OF IRELAND
Beggars Bush, Dublin 4. Tel:01-609511. Fax: 773169
Activities: Advisory work on ground water resource protection. Restoration of mining sites—advise the Minister on clauses of lease and monitoring of restoration on conclusion of mining activity. **Contact:** Donal Daly, Principal Geologist.

IRISH NATIONAL COMMISSION FOR UNESCO
Department of Education, Dublin 1. Tel: 01-734700 ext. 2156
Objectives: (1) To involve in UNESCO's activities the various ministerial departments, agencies, institutions, organisations, and individuals working for the advancement of Education, Science, Culture and Information; (2) To contribute to the maintenance of peace and security and the common welfare of mankind by participating in the activities of UNESCO which aim to advance the mutual knowledge and understanding of peoples, give fresh impulse to popular education and to the spread of culture, and preserve, increase and diffuse knowledge; (3) To play an ever increasing role in UNESCO's work, and particularly in the formulation and execution of its programmes; (4) To co-operate with their governments and with services, organisations, institutions and individuals concerned with questions within UNESCO's competence; (5) To encourage participation of national, governmental and non-governmental institutions and various individuals in the formulation and execution of UNESCO's programmes so as to secure for the

organisation all the intellectual, scientific, artistic or administrative assistance, that it may require; (6) To disseminate information on the objectives programme and activities of UNESCO and endeavour to arouse public interest in them. **Activities:** Clearing house for UNESCO queries. **Sponsorship of Research/Publications/Scholarships:** Biennial Participation Programme. **Contact:** Sean Horken.

NATIONAL ARCHIVE
Four Courts, Dublin 7, Tel:01-733833 and The State Paper Office, Tel:01-792777 ext. 2518
Objectives: Preservation of records accessioned from government departments, courts, other organisations and private individuals. Making those records available for use by members of the public.

NATIONAL BOTANIC GARDENS
Glasnevin, Dublin 2. Tel: 01-374388
Objectives: To cultivate a wide selection from all areas of the world of plants subject to limitation of space, soil and climate. To grow these collections in a pleasing environment so that students can be trained and the public can both enjoy and be stimulated by the collections. To maintain the National Herbarium in a collection of dried specimens of all plant genera with an emphasis on Irish material. Training course for students in Horticulture is carried out. **Activities:** Botanical research associated with the collections. Open Days—conducted tours. Any activity concerned with objectives as above. **Status:** State institution. **Publications:** *Glasra* (Contributions from the National Botanic Gardens, Glasnevin, Index Seminum. Occasional Papers. *Illustrated Short Guide to Gardens*. Handbooks: *Trees and Shrubs. Census Catalogue of the Irish Flora.* **Contact:** Aidan Brady, Director.

NATURAL HISTORY MUSEUM
Merrion Street, Dublin 2. Tel: 01-618811
Objectives: Displays of the National Zoological Collection in which every aspect of Irish Fauna is represented. Foreign collections include specimens of all the Orders of Mammals and a large number of bird and reptile species. **Activities:** Provides public information by way of publications, identifying Zoological and Geological Specimens, answering queries and giving occasional lectures. In particular it identifies insects and other pests for Health Board Inspectors, Government Departments and importers. It also provides facilities for research workers. Information Leaflets available for teachers from the Education Officer. Hours of opening: Tuesday—Saturday 10.00am— 5.00pm. Sunday 2.00pm— 5.00pm. **Status:** National Institution. **Publications:** Guides, Catalogues, Slides. List available on request. **Contact:** Director, National Museum of Ireland, Kildare Street, Dublin 2. National History Museum is re-opened now.

NATIONAL MONUMENTS ADVISORY COUNCIL
Ely Place Upper, Dublin 2
Objectives: To advise the Commissioners of Public Works on archaeological matters. To advise local authorities on planning matters which affect national monuments or areas of architectural and historical interest. **Activities:** Advisory services. **Status:** State sponsored. Prescribed body under Planning Acts. **Contact:** Assistant Secretary.

NUCLEAR ENERGY BOARD
3 Clonskeagh Square, Clonskeagh Road, Dublin 14
Tel: 01-697766. Telex: 30610. Fax: 697437
Objectives: To advise the Government and Ministers on nuclear energy and associated matters and to keep itself informed of developments in nuclear technology. To regulate and control the use, transportation and disposal of radioactive materials and to ensure that the public and the environment are

adequately safeguarded. To prepare safety codes and regulations for the safe use of ionising radiation. To regulate activities involving sources of ionising radiation. **Activities:** The monitoring of radiation in the environment and assessing their significance; assessing proposals for the construction, operation and supervision of nuclear power stations; preparing and implementing appropriate safety regulations and codes of practice; promoting knowledge of, proficiency and research in nuclear sciences and technology; provision of a consultancy and library service; operates on a non-fee paying basis. Radiation Protection Services provides a personnel dosimetry service for those who work with radiation, provides check calibrations of radiation monitors and a safety consultancy service for those working with ionising radiation. The Environmental Monitoring Service carries out studies of radioactivity in our marine and terrestrial environments, including analysis of foodstuff samples. **Status:** Statutory State Sponsored body. **Contact:** the Secretary.

OFFICE OF PUBLIC WORKS
51 St. Stephen's Green, Dublin 2. Tel: 01-613111. Telex: 90160. Fax: 01-610747
Objectives: The principal fields of the Office of Public Works are primarily related to and derive from the responsibility of the Commissioners of Public Works for the development and care of State property, including national parks and monuments, engineering and the promotion of certain engineering works. **Activities:** *Environmental Protection*: Coast Protection. Arterial Drainage. State Harbours. National Parks. Pollution. *Architecture:* Archaeology. National Monuments. Maintenance and Restoration Work. New Buildings. Furnishings. *Heritage Houses and Gardens*: Parks. As a secondary activity the OPW issues information on matters which are its concern either through occasional publications or by replying to individual enquiries and it co-operates with other bodies which have parallel interests and functions. But its services are not available in a general way to the Public as a consultancy and it can only take action on projects which are directly related to State property. **Contact:** Secretary.

RESOURCE AND ENVIRONMENTAL POLICY CENTRE
University College, Dublin, 'Richview', Clonskeagh Road, Dublin 14
Tel: 01-612958
Membership: The REPC is in 3 faculties—Arts, Commerce and Engineering. It is interactive and catalytic with the assignment of assisting, stimulating and coordinating existing resources, rather than developing a self-contained academic unit. **Objectives:** To undertake teaching, research and public service in resource and environmental policy. **Activities:** Staff are involved in teaching courses to students in economics, civil engineering, social science and public administration. The Research Programme involves policy studies on air quality, natural gas, renewable energy, demography, housing. The work of the Centre includes consideration of the economy, natural resources and the environment and is particularly concerned with policy analysis. **Status:** To give expression to the aims of the Heritage Trust, which endowed a Professorship of Environmental Studies at the university. **Publications:** *Natural Resource Allocation and State Enterprise*: NET as a Case Study by Blackwell, Convery, Walsh and Walsh, REPC 1983. *Environmental Policies. Promise and Performance: Irish Environmental Policies Analysed,* edited by Blackwell and Convery, 1983. **Contact:** Professor Frank J. Convery.

TEAGASC—AGRICULTURE AND FOOD DEVELOPMENT AUTHORITY
19 Sandymount Avenue, Ballsbridge, Dublin 4
Tel: 01-688188. Fax: 01-688023. Telex: 30459
Objectives: To provide advisory, research, education and training services to the agricultural and food industry. **Activities:** Advisory services are provided through a network of country/district offices. Training for young farmers in all aspects of agriculture is carried out at local centres and in residential

colleges owned by Teagasc, or privately owned and financed by Teagasc. Advisory and training activities are coordinated regionally, through five regional offices. Agricultural research is carried out at seven research centres, dealing with beef, sheep, land use and environment, dairying and pigs, horticulture and forestry, tillage crops and agricultural engineering, economics and rural welfare. It also provides research and consultancy services for the food industry. **Contact:** Dr. Pierce Ryan, Director.

WILDLIFE SERVICE
Spruce House, Leeson Lane, Dublin 2. Tel: 01-615666. Fax: 01-618214. Telex: 90253
Objectives: The conservation of wild flora and fauna and their habitats.
Activities: The Wildlife Service's programme is aimed towards the protection and management of the natural environment and includes the regulating of the level of wildlife exploitation. **Status:** Office of Public Works Branch since 1987 when it was transferred from the Department of Energy. **Contact:** Principal Officer.

Northern Ireland: Government

DEPARTMENT OF AGRICULTURE, WATER DRAINAGE AND CONSER-VATION DIVISION
Hydebank, 4 Hospital Road, Belfast, Co. Antrim BT8 8JP. Tel: 0232-647161
Objectives: Providing specialist advice on all environmental matters relating to farmland. **Status:** Government Department. **Contacts:**
Co. Antrim: Kilpatrick House, 38-54, High Street, Ballymena BT43 6DP 0266-44121
Co. Armagh: 2 Newry Road, Armagh Town BT60 1EN 0861-524979
Co. Derry: Crown Buildings, Artillery Road, Coleraine, Co. Derry BT52 2AJ 0265-2181
Co. Down: Knockbreda Crown Buildings, Upper Knockbreda Road, Belfast, Co. Antrim BT8 4SU 0232-797221
Co. Fermanagh: Crown Buildings, Queen Elizabeth Road, Enniskillen, Co. Fermanagh BT74 7JF 0365-25151
Co. Tyrone: Crown Buildings, Mountjoy Road, Omagh BT79 7BD 0662-3101

DEPARTMENT OF THE ENVIRONMENT (COUNTRYSIDE AND WILDLIFE BRANCH)
Calvert House, 23 Castle Place, Belfast, Co. Antrim BT1 1FY 0232-230560
Objectives: The Countryside and Wildlife Branch is concerned with the identification of the most important places for wildlife as Areas of Special Scientific Interest (A.S.S.I.), and offers help, within a nature conservation management agreement, to the owners and occupiers of these sites to conserve them. It aims to influence the management of the remainder of the countryside in a way that is sympathetic to wildlife. **Activities:** It manages about fifty National Nature Reserves e.g. Quoil pondage, Marble Arch Glen and Brakle Moss. The Branch administers the following country parks and centres:

Castle Archdale, Co. Fermanagh
Crawfordsburn, North Down
Ness Wood, Co. Derry
Peatlands Park, Co. Armagh
Redburn, North Down

Roe Valley, Co. Derry
Scrabbo, North Down
Mournes Centre, Newcastle
Portnadoo Centre, Portrush

Status: Government Department. **Publications:** The Branch publishes booklets to make the public aware of the implications of the Nature Conser-vation and Amenity Lands Order and the Wildlife Order. **Contact:** Mary Moffatt.

Northern Ireland:
Non-Government

THE ARMAGH FIELD NATURALISTS' SOCIETY
Armagh County Museum, The Mall East, Co. Armagh BT61 9BE.
Objectives: The Society exists to encourage an active interest in the natural history of County Armagh and further afield. **Activities:** Summer field meetings and winter indoor lectures are organised. Current projects: Milford Cutting Nature Reserve, butterfly survey, bird census of Gosford Park and botanical survey of County Armagh. **Status:** Voluntary. **Contact:** Mr. D.R.M. Weatherup (Hon. Secretary) 0861-523070

THE ASSOCIATION OF LOUGH NEAGH USERS (A.L.N.U.S.)
3 Oaklands, Waringstown, Craigavon BT66 7QQ. Tel: 0762-881158
Objectives: To identify and where possible resolve problems arising through multiple user demands, having particular regard to water quality and quantity and conservation of the resources. **Status:** Voluntary, Community. **Contact:** Harry Averley (Secretary)

THE BANBRIDGE FIELD CLUB
11, Tullyear Avenue, Banbridge, Co. Down BT32 3PR
Objectives: To study and promote all aspects of natural history in the Banbridge district of Ireland in general. **Status:** Voluntary. **Contact:** Robert Bell 08206-23668.

THE BELFAST CIVIC TRUST
Bryson House, 28 Bedford Street, Belfast, Co. Antrim BT2 7FE
Objectives: To foster a spirit of civic consciousness amongst both the public and those (planners, Government) whose decisions affect all who live in and use the city. To monitor current and impending environmental schemes in the city, and to provide a forum for the public to represent itself on important issues. To make positive proposals for social and environmental improvement in the city. To achieve a greater government awareness of and sensitivity to the issue of urban conservation. To secure a city which is attractive and harmonious from an environmental point of view, and one which can engender pride. **Status:** Civic. **Contact:** Noel Wilson (Secretary) 0232-225835.

THE BELFAST GEOLOGISTS' SOCIETY
6 Gibson Park Avenue, Belfast, Co. Antrim BT6 9GL
Objectives: To further the study and interest in Geology in all sections of the community. **Status:** Voluntary. **Contact:** H.S. Black M.A., 0232-58993.

THE BELFAST NATURALISTS' FIELD CLUB
12 Woodland Avenue, Helen's Bay, Bangor, Co. Down BT19 1TX
Objectives: The practical study of natural sciences and archaeology in Ireland. The observation and study of the works of nature and of man. The preservation and enjoyment of our countryside and heritage. **Activities:** Summer field trips and winter lectures and displays are held, normally in the Ulster Museum. **Status:** Voluntary. **Contact:** Trevor D. Boyd (Hon. Secretary) 0247-852276.

THE BELFAST PARKS DEPARTMENT
Malone House, Barnett Demesne, Belfast, Co. Antrim BT9 5PB
Objectives: To manage the 2,500 acres of parkland and open space owned and maintained by Belfast Parks Department, creating a balance between leisure and amenity use and the needs of wildlife. To conserve and encourage

the varied flora and fauna of Belfast's Parks. To encourage a greater interest in natural history and animal conservation, and to help schools and the public make greater use of resources provided by local parks and the zoological gardens. **Status:** Civic. **Contact:** Doctor Robert Scott 0232-681246.

BETTER BELFAST
(formerly known as The Environment Resource Project)
Bryson House, 28 Bedford Street, Belfast, Co. Antrim BT2 7FE
Objectives: To educate and enliven local communities to become involved in improving their own environment and to cement a positive working relationship between communities and statutory bodies. Advice, support and volunteering facilities are on offer together with tools and equipment on loan. **Status:** Community. **Contact:** Jim Kyle 0232-225835.

THE CAMPAIGN FOR NUCLEAR DISARMAMENT (N.I.)
15a Hopefield Avenue, Portrush, Co. Antrim BT56 8LD
Objectives: The primary aim is the worldwide abolition of nuclear weapons and all weapons of mass destruction. They oppose manufacture, stock-piling, testing, use and threatened use of nuclear, chemical and biological weapons by any country and oppose the policies of any country or group of countries which make war more likely or which hinder progress towards a world without such weapons. **Status:** Voluntary. **Contact:** Liz Breadon 0265-824456.

CAUSEWAY COAST CONSERVATION VOLUNTEERS
c/o Bann Area Training Systems, Old Irish Society School, Beresford Place, Coleraine BT52 1HB
Objectives: see under Community Service Volunteers. **Status:** Voluntary. **Contact:** Anthony McQuillan 0265-55352.

COMMUNITY SERVICE VOLUNTEERS
2nd/3rd Floor, 22 High Street, Belfast, Co. Antrim BT1 2DB
Objectives: To encourage young people to appreciate and take an interest in their environment and identify projects in which volunteers can assist in these aims. It helps teachers, youth workers and others who want to establish community projects in their own areas. **Status:** Voluntary. **Contact:** Dereck Duke 0232-246981.

THE CONNSWATER RIVER CONSERVATION COMMITTEE
'Tudor Lodge', 2 Station Road, Belfast, Co. Antrim BT4 1RE. Tel: 0232-655556
Objectives: To clean the entire length of the Connswater (approx. 3 miles). To landscape and plant the banks and surrounding areas. To provide walkways in parts and natural habitat for wildlife, etc. **Status:** Voluntary. **Contact:** W. Wallace Hunter.

THE CONSERVATION SOCIETY
6 Cyprus Gardens, Belfast, Co. Antrim BT17 1NN
Objectives: To preserve and improve the quality of the environment and to encourage the wise use of natural resources. To control pollution of all kinds and in particular to extend the recycling of paper, bottles and metals, and to improve the appearance of the countryside. Special attention is given to alternative technology, organic growing of garden and farm crops, lignite mining and radioactive pollution. **Status:** Voluntary. **Contacts**: Doctor Michael and Mrs. Mary Beton (Joint Secretaries) 0232-652258.

CONSERVATION VOLUNTEERS (C.V.N.I.)
The Pavilion, Cherryvale Playingfields, Ravenhill Road, Belfast, Co. Antrim BT6 OBZ
Objectives: To get involved in practical conservation work—tackling jobs that would otherwise not get done. People, tools and equipment together with careful organisation and energy provide a unique work-force dedicated to meet the needs of the rural and urban landscape. Trees are planted, wasteland sites are cleared, clogged-up streams and ponds restored, foot-

paths cleared and dry stone walls rebuilt. Advice is also supplied on any aspect of practical conservation for local groups, landowners or anyone else who is concerned for their environment. **Status:** Registered Charity. **Contact:** John McClean (Regional Officer) 0232-645169.

THE COOKSTOWN WILDLIFE TRUST
30 Claggan Lane, Cookstown, Co. Tyrone BT80 8PX
Objectives: To carry out botanical surveys. **Activities:** Lectures and field trips to see migratory birds are offered during the winter months, with further field trips on the subjects of botany, local history and ornithology taking place during the summer. **Status:** Voluntary. **Contact:** Mr. J.M. Rutherford (Hon. Secretary) 06487-63576.

THE DOWN FIELD CLUB
30 Mearne Road, Saul, Downpatrick, Co. Down BT30 6SY
Activities: The club holds talks on subjects covering all aspects of natural history and the countryside and has plans to undertake local survey work and to establish a junior branch for younger members. **Status:** Voluntary. **Contact:** Miss T. McMullen 0396-5400.

DOWNPATRICK AND ARDGLASS RAILWAY SOCIETY
40 Teconnaught Road, Seavaghan, Downpatrick, Co. Down BT30 8QB
Objectives: To restore the line (which was closed in 1950) into operation. As of February 1990 1½ miles of track restored. **Activities:** Provides rides to the public on Saint Patrick's Day, on Easter Monday and Easter Tuesday. £1 a head (50p for children). **Status:** Voluntary. **Contacts:** Gerry Cochrane (Chairperson) 0396-830141 or Mr. Collins 0232-776608.

THE ENVIRONMENTAL RESOURCE PROJECT see under BETTER BELFAST

FARMING AND WILDLIFE ADVISORY GROUP
Hydebank, 4 Hospital Road, Belfast, Co. Antrim BT8 8JP. Tel: 0232-647161
Objectives: To give advice on general environmental matters relating to farmland. **Contact:** Mr. D. Magill.

FARSET CITY FARM
77 Springmartin Road, Belfast BT13 8J
Objectives: Provision of City Farm where children can see and experience traditional farm animals. **Contact:** Lee Livingstone 0232-231181.

FRIENDS OF THE EARTH (NORTHERN IRELAND)
99 Prospect Road, Portstewart, Co. Derry BT55 7LQ
Objectives: To promote awareness of the need for conservation and protection of the environment and to campaign on issues related thereto. Such issues include the destruction of tropical rain forests, the provision of cycle and foot paths, the purchase of wild areas for conservation and recreation, peat bog, marsh, woodland and soil conservation, power lines and health. **Status:** Voluntary. **Contact:** 026583-2301/2348.

FRIENDS OF WILLIS'S LAKE
10 Aberfoyle Gardens, Belfast, Co. Antrim BT10 0DZ
Objectives: see under Conservation Volunteers. **Status:** Voluntary. **Contact:** Adrian Dorman 0232-621400.

FERMANAGH CONSERVATION VOLUNTEERS
Castle Archdale Country Park, Lisnarick, Co. Fermanagh
Objectives: see under Conservation Volunteers. **Status:** Voluntary. **Contact:** Susanna Chance 03656-28184.

FERMANAGH NATURALISTS' FIELD CLUB
The Crannog, Rakeelan Glebe, Enniskillen, Co. Fermanagh
Objectives: The practical study of natural history and archaeology. **Activities:** Lectures and outings are held. **Status:** Voluntary. **Contact:** Walter Brady (Hon. Secretary) 0365-22375.

FORUM FOR COMMUNITY WORK EDUCATION
123-137 York Street, Belfast BT15 1AB
Objectives: To promote community work through education and training. To develop skills and awareness of people involved or interested in local environmental projects. **Activities:** Runs an environmental course—Introduction to Environment Studies. **Contact:** Anne Sloan 0232-232587.

FRIENDS OF THE EARTH (BELFAST)
7 Richill Crescent, Knock, Belfast BT5 6HF
Objectives: see under Friends of the Earth (Northern Ireland). **Status:** Voluntary. **Contact:** Allen Johnston 0232-657829.

GRASS ROOTS CONSERVATION CORPS
37 Malone Hill Park, Belfast, Co. Antrim BT9 6RE
Objectives: see under Conservation Volunteers. **Status:** Voluntary. **Contact:** Mrs. Hilary Brown 0232-668242.

THE GREENMOUNT AGRICULTURAL AND HORTICULTURAL COLLEGE
22 Greenmount Road, Antrim Town, Co. Antrim BT41 4PU
Activities: Schools and organised groups can book to see the nature trail which was started in 1979. This includes lakes and breeding ponds with about 30 species of wildfowl and five species of geese. In the animal house and surrounding fields can be seen different breeds of farm animals. There is a display of farm machinery from times past, and an information centre showing many native birds and animals in their natural habitats. **Status:** Voluntary. **Contact:** 08494-62114

THE INSTITUTE OF IRISH STUDIES
c/o Queen's University, University Road, Belfast, Co. Antrim BT7 1NN
Objectives: To encourage work in any academic subject relating to Ireland. **Activities:** Helping individuals who are working on the conservation theme in both the natural and built environments. **Status:** Voluntary. **Contact:** 0232-245133 ext. 3386

ISLAND MAGEE AND DISTRICT CONSERVATION SOCIETY
1 Causeway Villas, Ballycarry Station, Larne, Co. Antrim.
Objectives: To maintain and enhance the natural beauty of the district and to protect its wildlife. To combat all forms of pollution from whatever source. **Activities:** Provides a non-political forum at which local people may express their views on conservation and related matters. **Status:** Voluntary. **Contact:** Geo. Rutherford 09603-73772

KNOCK RAILWAY CONSERVATION VOLUNTEERS
86 Sandown Road, Belfast BT5 6GU—**Objectives:** see under Conservation Volunteers. **Status:** Voluntary. **Contact:** Tony Waterman 0232-612235

LAGAN VALLEY REGIONAL PARK COMMITTEE
Belvoir Park Forest, Belfast, Co. Antrim BT8 4QT
Objectives: To conserve and enhance the natural beauty of the Lagan Valley and to adapt the waterway, tow-path and adjacent lands to form a major element in the recreational system of Belfast and district. **Activities:** Consults with all interested authorities, organisations and members of the public for the purpose of preparing an overall development plan. Advises government departments and local authorities on the development of the park and co-ordinates and encourages efforts at improvement. **Status:** Civic. **Contact:** Miss J. Mitchell (Park Officer) 0232-643922

THE LISBURN CONSERVATION SOCIETY
73 Benson Street, Lisburn, Co. Antrim BT28 2AD
Objectives: To promote and encourage all aspects of conservation in the Lisburn Borough area. **Status:** Voluntary. **Contact:** Alan Elliott 08462-81237

MARINE CONSERVATION SOCIETY
116 Glenholm Park, Belfast, Co. Antrim BT8 4LR
Activities: Through research the Society is increasing our knowledge of marine life and our ability to live in harmony with it.

MOURNE CONSERVATION VOLUNTEERS
30 Moneynabana Road, Dromara, Co. Down
Objectives: see under Conservation Volunteers. **Status:** Voluntary. **Contact:** Teresa O'Hare 0238-532286.

THE NEWCASTLE FIELD CLUB

NORTH DOWN CONSERVATION VOLUNTEERS
5 Ardkeen Avenue, Carnalea, Bangor, Co. Down BT19 1ER
Objectives: see under Conservation Volunteers. **Status:** Voluntary. **Contact:** the Secretary 0247-466624.

QUEEN'S CONSERVATION VOLUNTEERS
22 Marlborough Park S., Belfast BT9 6HR
Objectives: see under Conservation Volunteers. **Status:** Voluntary. **Contact:** Ms. Helen Gilmour 0232-669155.

VOLUNTARY SERVICES LISBURN CONSERVATION GROUP
50 Railway Street, Lisburn, Co. Antrim BT28 1XP
Objectives: see under Conservation Volunteers. **Status:** Voluntary. **Contact:** 08462-82479

SOURCES

Air (Ozone Layer): *Nuacht Ghlas* Richard Douthwaite, Winter 1989; *Ozone Depletion 1988* Fiona Weir (Friends of the Earth, 1988); *Friends of the Earth: The Montreal Protocol 1989* Fiona Weir; *The Ozone Layer* (UNEP, 1987).

Greenhouse Effect: *The Greenhouse Effect* Steward Boyle and John Ardill (New English Library, 1987); *Green Magazine* November 1989; *The Heat Trap* J. Karas and P. Kelly (Friends of the Earth, 1988).

Acid Rain: *Acid Rain and Power Plant Emissions in Ireland* Jeremy Wates (Earthwatch, 1986).

Smog: *Air Quality in Ireland* Michael Bailey (An Foras Forbartha 1985).

Water: *Inland Waters; The State of the Environment* (An Foras Forbartha, 1985), Ed. David Cabot; *Farm Wastes and Water Pollution* (Environmental Research Unit, 1989); *Fish Kills 1969-1987* Desmond T. McCarthy (Roinn na Mara 1988); *Fish Kills in 1988* Desmond McCarthy, Christopher Moriarty (Roinn na Mara, 1989); *Earthwatch Magazine* November 1989, Dom O'Brien; *The Biographical Survey of River Quality 1988* (ERU Oct. 1989).

Coastal Waters: *Coastwatch Survey 1989* Karen Dubsky (Dublin Bay Environment Group 1990); *Earthwatch Magazine* Autumn 1989, Dom O'Brien; *Dublin Bay* (ERU 1989); *Water Pollution and Sea Dumping Operations in Cork Harbour: A Preliminary Report* Robert Allen and Bob Edwards (Greenpeace 1989); *The State of the Environment* (An Foras Forbartha, 1985); *Clean Irish Sea* (Greenpeace 1989).

Drinking Water: *Environmental Health Officers Association Yearbook 1989*; *Consumer Choice Magazine* Feb. 1990; *The Pollution of Wells and Springs* Donal Daly (Geological Survey).

Fish Farming: *A Cause for Concern* Roderick O'Sullivan (Anglers' Task Force on Pollution and Conservation 1989); *Agscene Magazine* May 1988.

Soil and Food: *Red or Green for Farmers (and the rest of us)* Richard Body (Broad Leys Publishing 1987); *The State of the Environment* Ed. David Cabot (An Foras Forbartha 1985); *Nuacht Ghlas Magazine* Autumn 1989, Mike Curtis; *Green Party Agricultural Policy* (draft), Mike Curtis 1989.

Organic Farming: *Blueprint for a Green Planet* John Seymour and Herbert Giradet (Dorling Kindersley, London 1987); *The Guardian* 9 Sept. 1989; *How Green is Your Garden? The Irish Times* ??? Month, 1989, Fergus Brogan.

Irradiation: *Agscene Magazine* May 1988; *Food Irradiation* Professor Paul McNulty (paper presented at the seminar 'Radiation Protection: The State's Responsibilities' on February 24, 1989).

Pesticides: *This Poisoned Earth* Nigel Dudley (Piatkus 1987).

Health: *The Health of the Irish* series *The Irish Times* Katherine Holmquist, October 1989; *Irish Alternative Health Directory 1989/1990* Irish Institute for Holistic Medicine; *Green Party Health Policy 1989*.

Trees: *Green Party Forestry Policy* Alison Badrian 1989; *Earthwatch Magazine* Summer 1989.

Bogs: *The Irish Peatland Institute: Programme IPPC Action Plan 1989-1992* Ed. Catherine O'Connell (IPCC, 1989).

Waste and Recycling: *Waste, Incinerators and Clean Technology: The Greenpeace Approach to the Waste Crisis* Bob Edwards (Greenpeace, Irl. 1989); *The State of the Environment* Ed. David Cabot (An Foras Forbartha, 1985); *Alternative Energy Options for Ireland* Jim Woolridge (Earthwatch 1990); *Earthwatch Magazine* Winter 1988, Brian Wall; *Face of the Earth Recycling Fact Sheet* (RTE 1988); *Recycling Fact Sheet* (Dept. of the Environment 1988).

Household Consumer: *The Green Consumer Guide* Julia Hailes and John Elkington (Gollancz 1988); *Greenpeace.*

Urban and Rural Landscapes: *The Destruction of Dublin* Frank McDonald (Gill and MacMillan, 1985); *Saving the City* Frank McDonald (Tomar, 1989); *Bungalow Blitz* series *The Irish Times* September, 1987; *Wildlife Service Annual Report 1988.*

Energy: *Energy Policy in Ireland* (draft), Jim Woolridge (Earthwatch 1989); *Alternative Energy Options for Ireland* Jim Woolridge (Earthwatch 1990); *Green Party Energy Policy* Tom Simpson 1988.

Transport: *Green Party Transport Policy* Aidan Meagher 1988; *Mass Madness on Wheels* Frank McDonald *The Irish Times* Nov. 11, 1989; *Alternative Energy Options in Ireland.*

Education: *Education for Freedom* Máire Mullarney (Green Party 1990); *Junior Cert Syllabus* (Dept. of Education); *Inter Cert Syllabus* (Dept. of Education); *Leaving Cert Syllabus* (Dept. of Education).

Campaigning: *Peaceworking: A campaigning handbook for branches of the United Nations Association and other groups (UNA UK 1982).*

The Law: *The Law and Practice Relating to Pollution Control in Ireland* Yvonne Scannell (Environmental Resources Ltd.).

Unions: *Earthwatch Magazine* Autumn 1989, Tom Whitty; *Environmental Policy* FWUI.

Politics: *Green Party Manifesto; Labour Party Environment Policy Document* (Ruairi Quinn); *Fine Gael Environment Policy Document* (Alan Shatter); *Progressive Democrat Environment Policy Document* (Michael Keating); *Fianna Fáil Election Manifesto* (1989); *Workers Party Environment Policy Document* (Eamon Gilmore).

Book News from WOLFHOUND PRESS

THE GREEN GUIDE FOR IRELAND
JOHN GORMLEY

Covers all the 'green' issues: air, water, energy, organic farms, 'green' holidays in Ireland. A comprehensive guide for everybody.
ISBN 0 86327 251 7

POT LUCK: Potato Recipes from Ireland
NEILL DONNELLY

Combines the traditional and the innovative. From quick and easy Potato and Cheese Pie to Frosted Lamb Loaf. Imaginative yet simple recipes for every occasion.
ISBN 0 86327 119 7

THE IRISH COUNTRYSIDE: Landscape, Wildlife, History, People
Edited by Desmond Gillmor

Contributors: David Drew, Frederick Aalen, Anne O'Dowd, Mary Cawley, Roy Alexander

The Irish Countryside describes Ireland's wealth of historical features, the richness of its folk traditions, its natural resources and wildlife, its religious, domestic and agricultural archaeology, its rural society and economics, land development and conservation and its future. A fascinating, indispensable and engrossing study. Over 100 illustrations. ISBN 0 86327 159 6

TOM McCAUGHREN'S WILDLIFE TRILOGY

Winners of the IBA medal in 1987; RAI Award 1985; White Raven selection 1988. A brilliantly achieved wildlife series about a skulk of foxes and their quest for survival. *Run with the Wind* ——— and its sequels *Run to Earth* ——— and *Run Swift, Run Free* ——— have won the hearts of children worldwide. Beautifully illustrated by Jeanette Dunne.

ON FOOT IN DUBLIN & WICKLOW Exploring the Wilderness
Christopher Moriarty

A collection of 46 walks, some long, some short, but none too strenuous. Provides an easy escape route from the city for Dubliners and a lively range of discoveries for all walkers and ramblers. Most of these routes are as attractive to dogs and children as they are discerning adults bent on discovery. Routes, maps, directions, distance.
'A gem of a book.' *Evening Press*
ISBN 0 86327 226 6

Sláinte! is more than just a guide to good health. It is a practical reference tool for all the family. It is the first directory of natural alternative and preventative healing methods. It explains simply and clearly what each discipline is, how it works, and helps you to decide which method is best for you.

With contributions from leading well-known practitioners, this extensive guide also includes a directory of organisations, practitioners and advice centres.

Sláinte! is *the* definitive health guide for the 1990s.

Susanna Hassett is a qualified clinical psychologist. Her working experience includes community work with the caring professions.

WOLFHOUND PRESS

68 Mountjoy Square, Dublin 1.